IN THE DARKEST OF DAYS

EXPLORING HUMAN SACRIFICE AND VALUE
IN SOUTHERN SCANDINAVIAN PREHISTORY

Edited by
Matthew J. Walsh, Sean O'Neill and Lasse Sørensen

with
Editorial Assistant Eva-Johanna Marie Lafuente Nilsson

with contributions by
Pauline Asingh, Klas Wikström af Edholm, Christina Fredengren,
Svein H. Gullbekk, Bo Jensen, Mads Dengsø Jessen, Niels Lynnerup,
Ulla Mannering, Marianne Moen, Poul Otto Nielsen, Jesper Olsen,
Sean O'Neill, Pernille Pantmann, Mads Ravn, Samantha S. Reiter,
Lasse Sørensen, Sidsel Wåhlin, Matthew J. Walsh and Rane Willerslev

Foreword by
Rane Willerslev

OXBOW | books
Oxford & Philadelphia

Published in the United Kingdom in 2024 by
OXBOW BOOKS
The Old Music Hall, 106–108 Cowley Road, Oxford, OX4 1JE

and in the United States by
OXBOW BOOKS
1950 Lawrence Road, Havertown, PA 19083

Paperback Edition: ISBN 978-1-78925-859-2
Digital Edition: ISBN 978-1-78925-860-8 (epub)

A CIP record for this book is available from the British Library

Library of Congress Control Number: 2023948998

Printed in the United Kingdom by Short Run Press
Typeset in India by DiTech Publishing Services

For a complete list of Oxbow titles, please contact:

UNITED KINGDOM
Oxbow Books
Telephone (0)1226 734350
Email: oxbow@oxbowbooks.com
www.oxbowbooks.com

UNITED STATES OF AMERICA
Oxbow Books
Telephone (610) 853-9131, Fax (610) 853-9146
Email: queries@casemateacademic.com
www.casemateacademic.com/oxbow

Oxbow Books is part of the Casemate Group

Front cover: Skidendam (lit. 'shit pond' in Danish) bog in Teglstrup Hegn forest west of Helsingør, north Zealand, Denmark. Skidendam is one of just a handful of untouched raised bogs left in Denmark. Raised bogs like this one have produced some of the best-preserved bog bodies found to date, largely due to their oxygen-deprived and acidic conditions and the composition of sphagnum moss. Having never been subjected to modern peat cutting, it remains a mystery what (if any) sacrificial offerings may lie beneath Skidendam's unassuming, tranquil surface. Photo: Matthew J. Walsh

Contents

List of figures, plates and tables

List of figures

List of plates

List of tables

List of contributors

Pauline Asingh is an archaeologist focusing on prehistory and the lead exhibition developer at Moesgaard Museum, Denmark. She is responsible for innovative exhibition and communication concepts aimed at attracting three generations of visitors at Moesgaard Museum. Among several research and communication projects, she was the initiator and leader of the scientific investigations of the Grauballe Man in 2001–2002. She is the recipient of the Westerbyprisen in 2023 for longstanding pioneering efforts in communication of Danish prehistory.

Klas Wikström af Edholm, Ph.D. in Study of Religions, has published on subjects such as cult sites and ritual practices of the Iron Age, the god Týr in Old Norse mythology and the rite of the 'blood eagle' in Old Norse religion. He wrote his doctoral thesis on human sacrifices in Old Norse religion, entitled 'Människooffer i myt och minne. En studie av offerpraktiker i fornnordisk religion utifrån källtexter och arkeologiskt material' (Åbo Akademi). He is associated to Stockholm University and Åbo Akademi University. ORCID: https://orcid.org/0000-0002-5563-4065

Christina Fredengren, a professor active at both Stockholm and Uppsala Universities, carries out research in archaeology, heritage studies, and environmental humanities. This involves research on topics such as critical animal studies, deep time, personhood of waters, wetland depositions, and sacrifice, with a particular emphasis on the Bronze- and Iron Ages. Fredengren has also contributed to the development of the philosophies of more-than-human intra-generational justice and care as affirmative interventions in sustainability matters and has worked with artistic research practices.

Svein H. Gullbekk is Professor of Numismatics at the Museum of Cultural History, University of Oslo. His areas of research are Viking and Medieval history and numismatics with emphases on the use of money in Viking and Medieval Northern Europe. He was PI of the project 'Religion and Money: Economy of Salvation in

the Middle Ages' (2013–2017), and most recently PI on the project 'Human Sacrifice and Value: The Limits of Sacred Violence' (2018–2022), both funded by the Norwegian Research Council.

Bo Jensen is an archaeologist at Kroppedal Museum, Denmark, working full-time in the Danish commercial excavation sector. His published works include *Viking Age Amulets in Scandinavia and Western Europe* (Archaeopress, 2010) and *Archaeologies of Gender and Violence*, co-authored with Uroš Matić (Oxbow, 2017). Forthcoming work will present excavation results from a Late Bronze Age bronze casting site near Smørum on Zealand.

Mads Dengsø Jessen, Ph.D., is a Senior Researcher at the National Museum of Denmark. He has a background in archaeology, where he has done research into the aristocratic settlement of the Late Iron Age and the Viking Age, as well as the fortifications of those periods.

Niels Lynnerup is Professor and MD at the Dept of Forensic Medicine, University of Copenhagen, Denmark. He has also been Head of the Laboratory of Biological Anthropology and has as such done much research on archaeologically found human remains, including mummies from all over the world and bog bodies.

Ulla Mannering is a textile archaeologist, Research Professor and curator with responsibility for the collections of prehistoric textiles and skin items at the National Museum of Denmark. She has focused her work on the development of Bronze and Iron Age skin and textile production, clothing design and visual appearance, as well as clothing iconography in the Late Iron and Viking Ages. Mannering is one of the three founders of the Centre for Textile Research at University of Copenhagen, Denmark.

Marianne Moen holds a Ph.D. in archaeology from the University of Oslo. Her research has focused largely on gender, mortuary archaeology and the Viking Age, the construction of archaeological knowledge and the ongoing relationship between the past and the present. She has also worked extensively on sacrifice, specifically human sacrifice, and the social implications thereof. She currently holds the post of Head of Department of Archaeology at the Museum of Cultural History, University of Oslo.

Poul Otto Nielsen earned his MA in Prehistoric Archaeology at the University of Copenhagen in 1977. He was employed in 1978 at the National Museum of Denmark as a curator. From 1986 to 2013 he was Head of the Danish prehistoric collections and from 2003 to 2013 he was also Head of the museum's section for Environmental Archaeology. Over five decades, his work has focused on excavations and research concerning Neolithic settlements in Denmark.

Jesper Olsen, Ph.D., is Director for the Aarhus AMS Centre (AARAMS). He is an expert in radiocarbon dating methods and his research is on radiocarbon statistical methods, radiocarbon reservoir marine and freshwater ages and reconstructing prehistoric dietary patterns using stable isotopes.

Sean O'Neill is an ethnologist and archaeologist based in the UK. He has a special interest in cultural transmission studies and intellectual history. Sean obtained a Ph.D. in Archaeology from the University of Aberdeen, has been appointed Member, the University of Cambridge (posting at the Fitzwilliam Museum), served two consecutive postdoctoral fellowships at the University of Aarhus, and most recently as Research Counsel for the Museum of Cultural History in Oslo. He is an academic book series editor for Routledge, Taylor & Francis. He is also the co-founder of the Two Towers Press, a private press based in East Anglia.

Pernille Pantmann holds a Ph.D. in archaeology. Her research focus is wetland living in north-eastern Denmark during the Iron Age. She is mostly preoccupied with the archaeological perception of past human interactions with wetlands and the general balance of the sacred and the profane throughout prehistory. Currently she is working on a post-doc on skeletal bog bodies looking at how we understand them archaeologically – especially in relation to their prehistoric contexts. She is based at the Museum of Northern Zealand, Denmark.

Mads Ravn is Head of Research at Vejle Museums in Denmark. He holds a Ph.D. and M.Phil. in Archaeology from Cambridge University. He specialises in studies of the Iron Age and Viking Age and has worked throughout Scandinavia and around the world in various fieldwork projects. As such, he has worked as an archaeologist and researcher in association with Aarhus University as a lecturer, Australian National University as a visiting

researcher and as an associate professor and Head of Section at University of Stavanger and University of Oslo before coming to Vejle. The study of bog bodies and sacrifice was initiated in Vejle where the Haraldskær Woman is on exhibit in the museum.

Samantha S. Reiter has been working with mobility, identity, culture change and gender studies for over ten years, principally within European prehistory. She has a Ph.D. from Aarhus University, Denmark and has worked throughout Western and Central Europe as well as the USA, Caribbean and the Near East. Reiter has been employed at the National Museum of Denmark since 2017 working for the 'Tales of Bronze Age Women', 'Tales of Bronze Age People' (both with PI Prof. Karin M. Frei) and COREX (PI Prof. K. Kristiansen) projects, respectively.

Lasse Sørensen, Ph.D., is a Senior Researcher and former head of the Department of Ancient Cultures of Denmark and the Mediterranean at the National Museum of Denmark. His main research interest is the social and economic changes within the Mesolithic and Neolithic of Northern Europe and the Eastern Mediterranean regions.

Matthew J. Walsh is an anthropological archaeologist with a Ph.D. from the University of Montana. His work focuses on cultural evolution and cultural transmission studies in diverse contexts. Matt's research has ranged from modelling cultural evolutionary processes in the circumarctic and Western Plains to the evolution of ritual practice and social identities in the Nordic Bronze Age to studies of the emergence and diversity of ritualised violence in cross-cultural perspective. He is a Senior Researcher in Native American Studies at the National Museum of Denmark.

Sidsel Wåhlin is curator of archaeology at Vesthimmerlands Museum (until December 2022 Vendsyssel Historiske Museum [VHM]) and has excavated the Svennum bog. She has also curated the extensive human bone collection at VHM. Currently she is participating in research relating to prehistoric genomics and is doing research into human sacrifice in Danish wetlands.

Rane Willerslev is General Director of the National Museum of Denmark. In 2021, he was appointed Knight of The Order of Dannebrog. Rane is a highly decorated scholar holding a Ph.D. in Anthropology from the University of Cambridge. Between 2008–2017, he held positions as Full Professor of Anthropology at Aarhus University, Head of Department at Moesgaard Museum and Director of the Museum of Cultural History, University of Oslo, respectively. He developed and co-PI'd the 'Human Sacrifice and Value: The Limits of Sacred Violence' project, funded by the Norwegian Research Council (FRIHUMSAM 275947).

Acknowledgements

The present volume was made possible by the Norwegian Research Council's generous funding of the 'Human Sacrifice and Value' project (FRIPROHUMSAM 275947). The editors wish to thank each of the contributors for making this volume a reality. We would also like to thank (in alphabetical order by first name) Anders Klostergaard Petersen, Anne Pedersen, Armin W. Geertz, Eric S. Carlson, Frans-Arne Stylegar, Joanna Brück, Karin Margarita Frei, Karl-Göran Sjögren, Kirsten Green Mink, Leszek Gardeła, Louise Felding, Mads Lou Bendtsen, Marianne Moen, Melanie Giles, Merete Moe Henriksen, Mette Løvschal, Mette-Louise Johannsen, Peter Pentz, Steiner Solheim, Steven Ashby and Svein Harald Gullbekk for various and valuable insights and efforts along the way. We also wish to express our gratitude to the amazing folks at Oxbow Books, particularly Jessica Hawxwell, Julie Gardiner, Felicity Goldsack and Eduard Cojocaru for their professionalism, enthusiasm and above all patience in making this volume come together. We are also deeply indebted to the diligence and hard work of editorial assistant Eva-Johanna Marie Lafuente Nilsson.

Foreword

Rane Willerslev

The present volume has been a long time in the making. It came about as the result of some strange and somewhat difficult circumstances, not least of which has been the ongoing global Covid-19 pandemic. Some of the papers collected in this volume were initially presented at a conference organised by Lasse Sørensen and hosted at the National Museum of Denmark on 16 March back in 2018. At the time, I had recently been appointed as the Director of the National Museum of Denmark. Concurrently, the three-year research project 'Human Sacrifice and Value: The Limits of Sacred Violence', of which I was the PI, had just received funding from the Norwegian Research Council with research to be hosted at the Museum of Cultural History at the University of Oslo. The project was developed while I was still at Aarhus University with Sean O'Neill and Matt Walsh, in close collaboration with Mette Løvschal and Mette-Louise Johansen also at Aarhus University (AU) and Svein Gullbekk at the Museum of Cultural History at University of Oslo (UiO). Years before, I had been Museum Director at the Museum of Cultural History and had remained partially employed there as Professor of Anthropology with UiO while maintaining a full professorship at AU prior to the move to the National Museum. My tenure in Copenhagen was in its infancy when the project was first funded and it seemed the perfect opportunity to gauge, through a small conference, the level of interest in the project's undeniably morbid objective of exploring concepts of value in relation to ritualised human violence. Somewhat surprisingly, and somewhat not, as it turns out lots of people are interested in human sacrifice.

My own interest in the subject of sacrifice, not only that of the human variety, stems from my fieldwork in north-eastern Siberia. There, diverse hunting and reindeer-herding peoples still regularly beseech unseen forces through blood sacrifices. Within this genre of ritual, certain animals, plants and even otherwise mundane objects may be attributed with transcendent agency and import – sometimes even being considered theanthropic themselves. Thus, animistic principles play a large part in determining what and how may be or become proper sacrificial tender. My own work among the Chukchee people struggled to come to terms with how sacrificial identities are negotiated, how animal victims are transformed into 'people' (and sometimes vice versa) and how chains of substitutes can cascade through sacrificial logics turning a pebble or a dried fish, for example, into the ultimate, conceptually 'human', sacrifice.

As such, I have sought to explore a rather different line of inquiry than can often be gleaned from the archaeological and historical record. After all, living informants will often (but not always) tell you more than what has been left in layers of dirt or etched upon a page. Working among the Chukchee, I formed a keen interest into the phenomenology of sacrifice. Human sacrifice in particular poses some very paradoxical problems. It has what I like to call 'slippery logics', all of which are tied to diverse emic meanings and functions within any given society. Even while the phenomenon itself is rife with intercultural dissonances, sacrifices – and particularly human sacrifices – carry inherent, if not exceptional, value. One of the most interesting aspects of sacrifice for me is how sometimes vastly different offerings can serve parallel aims. How is it that a slave or a king, or an enemy or a stone, can make for a proper offering given the right conditions? How does it come to be, as for example famously discussed by E. E. Evans-Pritchard among the Nuer, that an ox conceptually replaces man as a necessary sacrificial offering, but a wild cucumber can then replace the ox? Similarly, among the Chukchee, a reindeer is conceptually a fellow human, but can be offered as a sacrifice either on its own merit or as a replacement for a human life, but a pebble might replace the reindeer if needs must. In either case, why not always just offer the cucumber or the rock? Of course, even this question ignores a vast oversimplification of complex cultural actions and rationales, but it warrants thinking about. Why is it that human victims are deemed necessary at some times, in some places and circumstances while not at others, even when seemingly parallel necessities mark the occasion? It was in the hope of shedding light on these kinds of questions that originally piqued my own curiosity and which ultimately led to the 'Human Sacrifice and Value' project and the conference that spawned this volume five long years ago.

The conference in question was held in the Guldbergsalen, a cosy meeting room in a quiet corner of 'The Princes' Palace', the home of the National Museum of Denmark at Frederiksholms Kanal 12 in Copenhagen. This was pre-coronavirus times and attendees and presenters were packed tightly into the small Baroque meeting hall. Onlookers lined the walls of the room shoulder to shoulder. Indeed, the turnout for such a little conference on such a grisly subject seemed remarkable at the time. Attendees hailed from institutions in and around Copenhagen, but also from Aarhus University and numerous regional museums and cultural institutions from all over Denmark, as well as from the Museum of Cultural History in Oslo. I was delighted to see that I was not alone in my interest in the subject. Human sacrifice has for so long remained an enigma largely relegated to the morbid fascinations of armchair anthropologists, scholars of religion and curious (but dubious) archaeologists. Outside of this limited and very specialist scholarship, the subject of human sacrifice of course looms large in the public imagination as well. It is quite often brought to life in film and fantasy. It gets dusted off during times of war and societal crises to be rekindled as a philosophical trope and re-entered into the rhetoric of the day. But, when the smoke clears, human sacrifice is reconsidered, re-questioned and eventually re-shelved. It gets put out of sight and out of mind until the next calamity calls for new victims to be had. In many ways human sacrifice presents a riddle: it is rarely fore-fronted but it never really goes away. It gets shelved for a darker day.

As I write this, the rhetoric of human sacrifice has once again resurfaced as the world struggles its way into the third year of the Covid-19 pandemic with a global death toll of over six million lives. In many ways, sacrifice has been on everyone's mind. It has been expressed in calls from some politicians, governments and agencies in the early days of the pandemic to come to terms with 'sacrificing' the old, the weak or the infirm as the virus raged through 2020. We were all told that we must make sacrifices in the form of various precautions like social distancing and mask-wearing, and we were ordered to stay home and settle in to cloistered lives for the sake of 'flattening the curve'. Whatever the take, the language of sacrifice has been everywhere of late. Even more recently, the Russian invasion of Ukraine places war at the very doorstep of Europe for the first time in eight decades. Frighteningly, sabre-rattling talk of the use of nuclear weapons has been thrust back onto the negotiating table in an increasingly volatile and stressful time. This has

awakened looming fears in many that have not been felt since the Cold War. Add to this that the inevitable effects of global climate change lap at our feet, with environmental and ecological changes being increasingly felt at every walk of life. It is in such dark days that sacrifice rears its head. Indeed, it has been both fascinating and horrifying to watch how effortlessly the concept of human sacrifice has gone from macabre to mainstream. Perhaps this is why studying it now more than ever may be so important?

Could it be that the use of human victims in broader sacrificial logics is one extreme expression of desperation in a world of constant sacrificial potentialities? While human lives do not necessarily seem to be the most valuable offerings in every case, the use of a human life as sacrificial currency is a decisive act. It fills in nicely when all else fails or all the possible substitutes have been exhausted. Like the young bride Scheherazade recounting a new story every night in *One Thousand and One Nights*, with her own death looming if she should fail, do we make other sacrifices similarly to buy time, with the full knowledge that time cannot actually be bought? Like sacrificial victims, time remains ultimately to be spent. Maybe at a conceptual level it is through sacrifices that we attempt to cunningly borrow beyond our means, only to eventually and inevitably run out of stories with the clock still ticking? Could it be that at times throughout human history, as we hurtle through dark days and troubling times, there come moments when societies simply stop telling stories and start choosing victims?

I do not know the answers to any of the questions posed above. Perhaps there are no definitive answers when it comes to sacrifice, only diminutive insights? What I do know, and what the papers collected here attest and explore for Scandinavian prehistory, is that human sacrifice and related rituals of violence and offering serve many different purposes and reflect diverse value systems and logics. Whether as a desperation measure to appease the agrarian gods or as a means of maintaining social control, for punishing enemies or sending a loved one off to the afterlife properly equipped, sacrifice has been used by those undertaking it in an attempt to give light to the darkest of days. And it has been so used in very different ways and for a very long time.

I should like to conclude by pointing out that the present volume would not be a reality were it not for the hard work, dedication and patience of all involved. Our work has paid off, even though in getting here many sacrifices were made along the way.

Rane Willerslev
May 2022
Copenhagen

Introduction: In the Darkest of Days: Tracing human sacrifice in southern Scandinavian prehistory

Matthew J. Walsh, Marianne Moen, Sean O'Neill, Svein H. Gullbekk and Rane Willerslev

The present volume brings together novel explorations into the diverse phenomena of human sacrificial violence evident in prehistoric southern Scandinavia, from the earliest examples in the Meso- and Neolithic up through to the Viking Era. In this regional review, we approach sacrifice (and human sacrifice in particular) in broad strokes. Using Bruce Lincoln's (1991, 204) definition that sacrifice is

> most fundamentally a logic, language, and practice of transformative negation, in which one entity – a plant or animal, a bodily part, some portion of a person's life, energy, property, or even the life itself – is given up for the benefit of some other species, group, god, or principle that is understood to be 'higher' or more deserving in one fashion or another.

With this in mind, the following introduction and subsequent contributions seek to highlight and explore cases suggestive of the offering of human lives in ritual fashion as indicated in the archaeological record of prehistoric Nordic world, mainly southern Scandinavia. We seek to frame the following chapters with a high-level overview of sacrificial practices within this region. Whilst we cannot claim that any of the cases explored herein provide concrete or indisputable evidence for human sacrifice, we instead posit that they represent forms of violence that can feasibly be interpreted as (ritual) offerings of human lives. Furthermore, we do not claim to present a full overview of viable case studies, but instead present a selection of material that we consider representative of a broader picture. The subsequent chapters in the volume continue to explore sacrificial interpretations of a variety of archaeological contexts.

Reviewing selected archaeological material

Emergence of human sacrificial traditions may have to do with the advent of increased population and population pressures (as in a Malthusian model), and the emergence of subsequent social complexity (*cf.*, Watts *et al.* 2016), with the ritual sublimation of violence, *e.g.*, arising as a way to subvert subsistence crises resulting from reliance on less flexible food ways (domestic crop failures), or as a by-product of developing social hierarchies amid increasingly institutionalised wealth and social inequality (*i.e*, such as power displays through ritualised executions), from superstitions or from any combination of related pathways (Hubert & Mauss 1964; see contemporary reviews in Winkelman 1998; 2014; Acevedo & Thompson 2013; Swenson 2014; Murray 2016). Suffice it to say, in the late prehistory of Northern Europe, evidence begins to emerge for the ritual taking of human life. Such traces are from then on found throughout the subsequent millennia. We note that if human sacrifice took place during earlier periods, these left no trace that we currently recognise in the material record.

Danish Neolithic

The earliest material remains that indicate ritual violence in Northern Europe come from a bog at Sigersdal in north-east Zealand, Denmark.[1] This assemblage adds a human element to an existing tradition of object and animal offerings going back millennia (Sørensen and Nielsen, this volume). Here the remains of two individuals were recovered during peat extraction in April of 1949. The pair were ^{14}C dated to the Early Neolithic in Denmark, *c.* 3500 BC. Bennike & Ebbesen (1987) estimated that both individuals were female. Examinations by Bennike established that one was between 18–20 years old, whilst the other was around 16 years when they were placed in the bog. The former had a cord around her neck (Bennike & Ebbesen 1985, 36; Bennike *et al.* 1986a, 92). Numerous animal bones were also recovered at the site, principally those of domesticated animals (Bennike *et al.* 1986a, 86). According to the peat diggers who initially discovered the bones, they lay at the base layer between dark and lighter strata, indicating that the remains had been placed in an exposed area of bog. Bennike's skeletal analysis of the remains noted both typical male and female characteristics in both, though with the overall conclusion that they were most likely both female (Bennike *et al.* 1986a, 81; however, they make this determination with considerable trepidation) as the relatively young age of the individuals further complicated an accurate determination of sex from the skeletal remains. Similar facial features indicate that the individuals may have shared a similar appearance, leading to the suggestion that they could have been related. Based on femur length, the older was over average height at 167 cm, whilst the other was within the average at 154 cm (Bennike 1985, 51). Despite the inconclusive nature of these observations, the bodies have often been interpreted as a human sacrifice.

Elsewhere, in south-east Denmark on the island of Als, the remains of a pair of individuals were found – this time both probably male – who had also met their ends in a bog at around this same period, *c.* 3370–3490 BC (Bennike *et al.* 1986b, 199). According to the report of the peat diggers who uncovered the skeletons, both had lain on their backs, parallel to one another, at about 2.5 m below the surface of the bog. Bennike *et al.* (1986b) determined that one individual – skeleton I – was a relatively slender, probably male individual of *c.* 16 years old at the time of death. The other – skeleton II – was also male and significantly older, at around 35–40 years of age, and evinced considerable skeletal abnormalities. In addition to some deterioration of the alveolar cavities of the jaw, he suffered from various points of arthritis and a crippling injury of his left hip, which must have caused chronic pain and considerably hindered movement. As with the Sigersdal pair, the elder was in this case also found to have had a cord around their neck.

Other finds of pairs from bogs from the Danish Neolithic include two male individuals found in close proximity in a bog in Døjringe in south-western central Zealand. One of these individuals was *c.* 21–35 years of age and the other between 18–21 years old (Bennike 1985). Interestingly, the skulls of both individuals show signs of healed trepanations, though they show no indications of terminal violence. Another pair – this time of two children aged *c.* 8 to 10 years old – found at Tysmosen, west-north-west of Copenhagen attest to the variability in age of those that may have fallen victim to ritual violence and bog deposition during the Neolithic (Bennike *et al.* 1986a, 93). These (like the Sigersdal finds) were accompanied in the bog with numerous parts of animals.

Another well-preserved example from the Danish Neolithic in which a preserved cord remained around the victim's neck comes from Stenstrup, south-south-east of Næstved on Zealand (Bennike & Ebbesen 1985). In this case, the rope that was secured around the neck was tied at the other end

around two large stones (Bennike & Ebbesen 1985, 28). This find was ^{14}C dated to the later phase of the Danish Neolithic, *c.* 1795–1890 BC. Robust cranial features suggested that the individual was male with muscular facial features, and probably around 40 to 60 years old at the time of his death. The skeleton showed no signs of deficiency or malnutrition, and the individual would have been of average height for the period. Damage to the left side of the skull suggests that he may have suffered an unhealed injury close to the time of death, though taphonomic processes cannot be ruled out.

Other material that can be argued to represent possible human sacrifice and subsequent bog deposition during the Danish Neolithic have also been documented. As Sørensen and Nielsen (this volume) lay out, these finds are often in votive settings and are frequently accompanied by animal bones and other objects. These remains usually represent only parts of human bodies, principally skulls and long bones and fragments thereof (see *e.g.*, Becker 1947, 275; 1952; Albrectsen 1954; Struve 1967, 54, 76; Skaarup 1985, 64, 72, 76–77; Wåhlin, this volume).

From the above evidence, a case can be made for human sacrifices as early as the Neolithic in Denmark. As enumerated here, cases of what appear to have been double sacrifices are also not uncommon. Many of the human remains uncovered appear in contexts with offerings of a domestic nature, *e.g.*, ceramics, wooden implements and slaughtered livestock. These observations have led many scholars to speculate that such sacrifices may have been related to fertility rites connected to these early agrarian societies. It is especially within the Neolithic, where humans organise themselves into more hierarchical societies, that a progression towards increased inequality and social control emerges in congruence with ritualised human violence.

Swedish Neolithic and Bronze Age

A wide range of material from prehistoric Sweden lends itself to sacrificial interpretations (see footnote above on the Motala Kanaljorden site). In Falbygden, western Sweden, two young women known respectively as the 'Raspberry' Girl and the 'Härlingstorp' Girl, were found deposited in bogs, both between the ages of 15 and 20 years (Sjögren *et al.* 2017). Both individuals' remains dated to the Early Neolithic (*c.* 3900 cal BC). At least one of the individuals, the Raspberry Girl (so-called because raspberry seeds were recovered from the area of her stomach, suggesting that she died in late summer), appears to have been bound and possibly drowned. She had been positioned face down on her stomach, oriented north to south with her head to the north. While no remnants of rope or cord were recovered, the position of the body suggests that her ankles may have been bound together and hyper-flexed to the backs of her knees, perhaps connected to her wrists, as her arms were extended in the front, down towards the pelvis in what would have been an exceptionally awkward position for her body to remain in during deposition were she not bound. Strontium isotope (Sr^{87}/Sr^{86}) analysis indicates that she was not originally from the local area, having likely been from farther south in Scania, a distance of around 100 km or more from where she was found.

The remains of a five- to six-year-old child were uncovered from a Late Neolithic well in the Lindängelund district of southern Malmö in Scania (Carlie *et al.* 2014). Evidence suggests that the child likely died by drowning, and the well and surrounding area had been used for ritual depositions at the time. The 'doubled-up' position of the body suggests a non-accidental death, as does placement of a large stone and a series of branches apparently set over the body, which may have served to cover up or hold down the corpse.

Sjögren *et al.* (2017, 112) refer to one bog find of the partial remains of two individuals, along with a variety of animal bones, from Sandåkra, south-west of Malmö. They also note a previous find of ten flint axes from the same site, suggesting expanded ritual use of the locality. The finds were dated to between 3712–3122 cal BC. At least one of the individuals was a woman in her mid- to late 20s. During her life she had suffered and healed from fracturing injuries to her lower arm and collarbone. She too had raspberry seeds between her teeth. The skeletal remains from a second individual, also likely a woman, were represented by only the bones of the left forearm. Other animal finds at the site include remains of wolf, pig, capercaillie (wood grouse) and marsh turtle (Karsten 1994, 304). Other fragmentary human remains from Östra Vemmerlöv show a similar dating (see Sjögren *et al.* 2017, 112–114 for an overview).

Fredengren (2011, 122; see also this volume) describes what seems to be particularly charged wetland deposit from the Högtorpsmossen bog in Närke. There, the skull of an adult female was found with a canine mandible, cattle scapulae, species-indeterminate rib bones, the leg bones of a sub-adult horse and the leg of a pig, all dated to the Late Bronze Age. Over the last decade, Fredengren (2011; pers. comm., 23 January 2020[2]; and this volume) has collated data on diverse wetland deposits throughout mid- and south Sweden, documenting the depositions of no less than 514 animals and 239 humans, although many of these finds remain scantily published to date. Overall, the Neolithic, Bronze Age and Early Iron Age finds in Sweden evince a similar pattern. That is, wetland depositions of individuals (in some cases in generally poor health and malnutrition), many with evidence of pre-mortem physical trauma with apparent decapitations being common. Fredengren has referred to this trend as 'the slow violence of the poor'.

Like their Danish counterparts, the bog finds from the Swedish Neolithic are often interpreted as sacrificial in nature. Sacrificial context is often implied from the unnatural placement of the remains in a wetland, often in context with other votive materials, and in rare circumstances where a

violent death can be attested. At least two cases correspond to late summer events involving young female victims. Thus, the pattern suggests sacrificial practices associated with wetlands, sometimes consisting of pairs of individuals, with a particular focus on sub-adults. All of this is in addition to other sacrificial deposits of objects such as ceramics and flint tools, as well as animals in both whole and part (see *e.g.*, Becker 1947; Degerbøl & Fredskild 1970), and suggests extensive, long-standing and diverse ritual use of sites.

Nordic Bronze Age

There is little to indicate human sacrifice during the Bronze Age in southern Scandinavia, *c.* 1700–500 BC (although there are some from the Late Nordic Bronze Age; see Ravn 2010; Van Beek *et al.* 2023). Despite this general scarcity, there is a proliferation of votive offerings of material wealth in wetlands across the Nordic Bronze Age.

Walsh and Reiter (this volume) offer that for the Early Nordic Bronze Age, the most convincing evidence for human sacrifice comes from 'elite' oak-tree coffin burials in which an adult inhumation was accompanied by the cremated remains of another (usually a sub-adult) individual, with the individuals' remains treated in conspicuously disparate ways. The inhumed body is often accompanied by high-status material goods, whilst the cremated body is usually found at the feet of the other body. Although rare, the contexts of these burials are strikingly similar between cases.

Examples include the well-known oak-tree coffin grave of the so-called Egtved Girl. Others include a mature woman's stone cist grave from Erslev in Thy, north-west Jutland (Aner & Kersten 2001, 142–143) and similar stone cist burials also from Thy with cremations apparently placed at or in the area of the deceased individual's feet observed at Højsager (Aner *et al.* 2001, 138–139) and Nørhågaard (Aner *et al.* 2001, 106–108). The differential treatment of remains in *e.g.*, the Egtved coffin (Thomsen 1929) and others can be argued to indicate a difference in the social status of the inhumed individual and the accompanying cremation.

Elsewhere, there is possible evidence for ritualised violence in connection to funerary rites at *e.g.*, Stubberup, Nebel, Ubby, Over-Vindinge and Klampenborg. Each of these graves contains inhumations of individuals who were interred with the partial remains of others. In some cases (as at Stubberup and Ubby), the evidence also points to the burning (but not cremation) and splitting of human bones potentially as part of what has been interpreted as a cannibalistic feast in association with the funerary rite. For example, at Stubberup, a single human femur was also placed in the lap of one individual of a pair of occupants in a tree coffin double burial (Lomborg 1964). Scattered atop the coffin prior to the grave being covered were the burnt and fragmentary remains of at least three individuals, including those of a sub-adult. In a multiple burial at Ubby in Holbæk

(Ke 645, Grave B), the remains of a single adult individual were inhumed, accompanied with the non-cremated remains of a young child, along with the heads of two other individuals, which were placed to the left of the adult's legs (Boye 1884). At Nebel (Aner & Kersten 1979, 30), the bones of at least three individuals were uncovered amid concentrations of mussel shells, along with the crushed skull of an eight- to ten-year-old child, leading the investigators to posit the possibility of human sacrifice and an accompanying funerary feast (Olshausen 1920).

For Scania, Thomsen (1929, 34) mentions finds by Hans Hildebrandt in Fjelkestad which the latter interpreted as human sacrifices in burials, similar to that at Egtved. First, from a site called 'Presta-bakken' was a stone cist containing the inhumations of two individuals, each with a bronze knife. Near the legs was a small pile of burnt bones and at the foot of the grave lay, in four places, piles of unburnt bones which appeared to be the remains of an individual set in a sitting position. Hildebrandt submitted that these could be the remains of an attendant sacrificed and placed in the grave in such a way as to watch over the deceased. Second, from Osterslof was a grave with an adult inhumation which also contained, at the right shoulder of the deceased, a small, concentrated pile of burnt human bones. At the foot of the grave lay a child's skeleton lying in a flexed position on its side at the feet of the deceased. Third, from a site called 'Bastubakken' at Torseke, was a stone cist containing an adult inhumation wearing an elaborate spiral arm ring and a 'breastplate'. At the feet of the deceased lay the leg of a child.

Early Iron Age in southern Scandinavia

The literature listing and describing sacrificial evidence in Early Iron Age Scandinavia is vast and need not be reiterated here (see *e.g.,* Glob 1969; Turner & Scaife 1995; van der Sanden 1996; Green 2001, among others). This evidence suggests that victims were selected for any number of criteria, but it appears that both men and women were eligible, as were individuals seemingly from all age categories. Adults in the range of 20–30 are common. In some cases, only a severed head has been deposited, often conspicuously wrapped up in a textile or skins. For example, the skull and hair of Osterby Man were deposited in a bog at a depth of around 65–70 cm. The head had been wrapped in a sewn deerskin cape or bag. A similar find is the head of the so-called Roum Man, found in Jutland north-east of Viborg, whose severed head had been wrapped in sheepskin. Thus, as Wåhlin (this volume) illustrates with the additional case of detached heads recovered from the wetland site at Svennum, it may be safe to assume that observance of the so-called 'Cult of the Head' as seen elsewhere in Iron Age (*i.e.,* Celtic) North-west Europe may have been a significant ritual practice in southern Scandinavia as well.

P. V. Glob (1969) provides a detailed treatise on the bog bodies of Denmark. In this, he describes a number of examples of bodies from the Early Iron Age that evince clear indications of individuals having met violent and, in some cases, ritually charged ends. This includes Grauballe Man, placed naked in the bog, after having his throat cut. His death occurred *c.* 265±40 cal BC. However, as Lynnerup and Asingh (this volume) point out, the interpretation of hyper-violence must be considered carefully. Other bodies are the famous Tollund Man, found lying on his right side, naked but for a skin cap secured to his head and a smooth leather belt around his waist, and with a rope tightly cinched around his neck (Glob 1969, 18). Another body uncovered not far from Tollund Man had been wrapped in an animal hide and presumably strangled by way of a leather strap and buckle which were found with the body (Glob 1969, 25). Like Tollund Man, Borremose Man (Borremose I) also had a thick rope around his neck, as well as the back of his skull crushed (Bennike 1985, 121). Elling Woman was found nearby to Tollund Man. She also showed signs of strangulation, and a cord was found around her neck. She was approximately 25 years old when she died, around the same time as Tollund Man. She was laid to rest wrapped in a sheepskin cape and leather belt and another section of cloak and a blanket of cow skin were wrapped around her feet. Her hair was braided, plaited and tied in an elaborate manner. Her plaited braids were tied into a bun at the nape of the neck, possibly in preparation for her hanging (Fischer 1999, 96). This at least supports a structured and solemn undertaking at the time of death (Lynnerup and Asingh, this volume), and not simply a deviant burial involving the summary execution of a criminal; this is also inferred from the apparent careful positioning of Tollund Man in his sleeping position. Haraldskær Woman, recovered from a bog in Vejle, dates to the pre-Roman Iron Age, *c.* 1st–2nd century BC (Frei *et al.* 2015). She was naked, but covered by a skin cape and had woollen textiles which were placed on top of her in the bog. She also wore a sprang hairnet. Re-examination of the body in 2000 revealed that her stomach contained unhusked millet and blackberries (placing her death in late summer). Due to a slight groove observed along the neck, examination at that time suggested that she may have been hanged/strangled like many of her contemporaries, but the findings remain inconclusive. According to some of the results generated by Frei *et al.*'s (2015) analysis of strontium in her hair, she was likely born in the area in which she died (*i.e.,* present-day Denmark, excluding Bornholm), but she had also travelled an exceptional distance to and fro[3] from her homeland in the months prior to her death.

Conspicuously, the vast majority of bog bodies which evince potential violence were naked or at least barely outfitted when deposited in their final resting place (Glob 1969; van der Sanden 1996, 93). If this was indeed an aspect of the ritual practice of sacrifice it could also illuminate the non-ritual contexts of individuals like the woman from Hul-dremose, who was well clothed (Mannering, this volume). Many of the bodies were set in the bogs at locations of ancient peat cuttings, which presumably would have been exposed and provided a convenient location at which to stage the body. Relatedly, many such locations appear to have been at the base of the peat layer, just above the sandy sub-soil, effectively where the peat had been exhausted by the harvesting of turfs. Thus, it is possible that such offer-ings were made in the hopes of rejuvenating a landscape exhausted from peat cutting. Both Grauballe Man and Tollund Man had eaten a gruel or porridge containing wild grains and seeds immediately prior to their deaths (Glob 1969, 57), perhaps similar to the last meals of other bog sacrifices such as Lindow Man (II) from Lindow Moss in Cheshire, UK, who also died a rather violent death. These last meals can be contrasted with the finely ground wheat flour and buttermilk consumed by Old Croghan Man prior to his violent mutilation and deposition in a bog in County Offaly, Ireland (Mulhall & Briggs 2007). Also in Ireland, Cloneycavan Man may similarly have been mutilated prior to his deposition in a bog in County Meath.

Iron Age war-booty and post-conflict offerings/depositions (in ritual/sacrificial contexts)

The Early Iron Age in southern Scandinavia was a time of considerably widespread and seemingly frequent use of sacrifices and the making of a variety of votive offerings, particularly in wetland contexts (*e.g.*, Fabech 1991; 1997, 149; 1998; Ilkjær 2002; 2003). Løvschal and Holst (2018) present that for the few centuries on either side of the 1st millennium, post-conflict sacrifices and ritual depositions of all manner of things in wetlands occurred. Notably, depositions of everyday objects such as 'ceramics, white stones, agricultural tools, vertically hammered stakes, teth-ering poles, and the (disarticulated) remains of animals' were also made in and out of martial contexts at many sites (Løvschal & Holst 2018, 32). Ritualised war-booty sacrifices involved a number of key common features, including specific treatments of offerings such as: inten-tional damage, dismantling or destruction, submergence and display (Løvschal & Holst 2018, 32). This argument is taken up in the present volume by Ravn, who argues that the Haraldskær Woman may reflect an insightful non-martial parallel to the phenomenon of ritual governance in relation to Iron Age bog sacrifices. Indeed, these intentional acts persist in post-conflict contexts across a wide swathe of Northern Europe. Weapons (often intentionally destroyed or 'killed'), accessories, animals and, in some cases, human remains appear to be common in the depositions. As Walsh, Pantmann and Moen (this volume) also discuss, white and white(ish) stones, which do not accumulate naturally in wetlands, are yet another little-understood aspect of many wetland deposits, suggesting that a diversity of objects and assemblages likely served an equally diverse suite of ritual importance and functions in relation to sacrifices.

Martins (2011) provides an overview of pre-Roman Iron Age deposits from Zealand and Scania, as well as a discussion focused on weapon depositions. Animals involved in conflict appear to have been ritually killed and submerged in wetlands as well, as horses from Illerup Ådal attest (Dobat *et al.* 2014). Similarly, as Holst *et al.* (2018) discuss from analyses of skeletal remains at Alken Enge, human corpses were subject to ritual treatments, including the intentional crushing of skulls and arranging of body parts, as well as including the treatments listed above as described by Løvschal and Holst (2018). Evidence suggests that the human remains in these cases had been exposed for some length of time prior to wetland deposition. While the deaths of individuals in these cases – presumably in combat – do not fall within any sort of rigid definition of human sacrifice (even the highly ritualised combat-related sacrifices as among *e.g.*, the Aztecs), the treatment of their remains exhibits evidence of a ritually charged and system-atic undertaking which could be interpreted as one form of sacral offering.

Elsewhere in the valley of Illerup Ådal, other forms of wetland offerings can also be attested. For example, the depositional finds from Forlev Nybølle suggest that fertility-related sacrificial offerings continued as a theme well into the late Roman Iron Age. At this site, numerous concentrations of stones, wood and ceramics, along with depositions of flax and a wooden female idol, suggest ritual use of the area for more than just conflict-related sacrifices (Lund 2002).

Norwegian prehistory

There is scant evidence for bog deposits of humans in Norway when compared to those further south in Scan-dinavia (see reviews in Henriksen 2014; Bukkemoen & Skare 2018; Moen & Walsh 2022). Depletion of the peat landscape has been extensively regulated in Norway since the 1940s, limiting the contemporary finds of bog deposi-tions. This lack of finds may of course indicate a genuine lack of depositions, but may also have to do with features of the rugged and isolated landscape as well as issues of climate. Wetland finds have been made in areas around the coastal regions in particular, and of course different cultural propensities in this region. Unlike in Denmark, the UK and elsewhere, no finds have been made that preserve soft tissue, so comparison to well-preserved bog bodies is not possible (see Moen & Walsh 2022), nor is comparison of soft tissue injury as illuminated by Lynnerup and Asingh (this volume).

Bukkemoen and Skare (2018) provide an account of human and animal remains recovered from a wetland depo-sition at Starene in Stange, Hedmark, in south-east Norway.

Lillehammer (2011) describes a find of skull fragments of at least four infants from a bog in Bø, in Rogaland. While fragmentary, it appears that the individuals' heads were put into the wetland together and intact (*cf.*, Wåhlin, this volume). The cranial remains were found together in close proximity at a depth of 1 metre at the intersection layer of the peat and underlying clay. They have been dated to the late 1st century and early 5th century AD.

The so-called 'women of Leinsmyra' represent the skulls of two females who died around the ages of 15 and 30, respectively. They too date to the Iron Age, between the 3rd and 5th centuries AD. They too were found at the bottom of the bog at the transition layer between peat and clay, suggesting that they had been interred in a section exhausted from peat cutting (Henriksen & Sylvester 2007).

Classical literature from the Early Iron Age

Early literary sources also quite commonly attest to sacrifice, as presented in the present volume by Jensen and Edholm, respectively. For example, elsewhere in Northern Europe, Caesar suggests that the Celts (but interestingly not the Germans) made war-booty sacrifices of captured animals and spoils to their god of war. He also notes in general that:

> The nation of all the Gauls is extremely devoted to superstitious rites; and on that account they who are troubled with **unusually severe diseases**, and they who are **engaged in battles and dangers**, either **sacrifice men as victims,** or vow that they will sacrifice them, and **employ the Druids as the performers of those sacrifices**; because they think that **unless the life of a man be offered for the life of a man**, the mind of the immortal **gods** can not be rendered propitious, and they have sacrifices of that kind ordained for **national purposes**. Others have figures of vast size, the limbs of which formed of osiers they fill with living men, which being **set on fire**, the men perish enveloped in the flames. **They consider that the oblation of such as have been taken in theft, or in robbery, or any other offense, is more acceptable to the immortal gods**; but when a supply of that class is wanting, they have **recourse to the oblation of even the innocent**. (bold emphases ours; Caesar, VI: xvi; trans. McDevitte & Bohn 1869)

Strabo, writing in the later 1st century BC and early AD, makes a number of points about sacrifice among Northern Europeans in his *Geography*. In Book IV, chapter IV he observes that among the Gauls, the Vates were in charge of sacrifices, echoing Caesar's mention of burning wicker figures, and further elaborating on the practice of using victims for prophecy. In Book VII, chapter II Strabo claims that the Cimbri would slash the throats of prisoners taken in war, and from the flow of blood into a vessel, soothsayers would make divinations.

Diodorus Siculus (V: XXXI) describes a druidic sacrifice made for the purpose of divination in which they used living victims, sometimes humans, to divine the future.

Tacitus, meanwhile, provides his oft-cited reference to ritual execution practices among the Germanic tribes in his *Germania* (Peterson 1920, 281), noting that the manner of death was determined by the offence, with punishments ranging from hanging to strangulation and deposition in a bog. But Ström (citing Mogk 1909) suggests that Tacitus may have been misinterpreting sacrificial practice as penal execution, suggesting that the division between execution and sacrifice need not necessarily be made in that, for the Germanic tribes at least, the death penalty could function as a sacrifice (Ström 1942, 36–42). Elsewhere in the *Germania* (ch. 39), Tacitus again refers to human sacrifices, this time relating to the Semnones.

A final source of note, is Orosius (V. 16), writing in the 5th century AD, describes a celebration by the Cimbri of their success in battle against the Romans in southern Gaul, that paints a picture reminiscent of other war-booty finds (Løvschal & Holst 2018). In it, he writes of how, after a victory, they celebrated by throwing the spoils into the river, and hanging their prisoners so that the conqueror kept no booty and the conquered knew no mercy. Indeed, this deposition of war-booty does seem to echo in the archaeological record, as discussed in Jørgensen *et al.* (2003).

Thus, we have persuasive narratives of sacrificial practices in the Early Iron Age in Northern Europe that seem to correlate with archaeological material in many ways. The human sacrifice among the Germanic tribes in the Early Iron Age and into the Roman Iron Age is presented by classical writers as highly organised, timed and repeated, principally apotropaic, but also variously ancestor- and warfare-related, and celebratory depending on the contexts. A note of caution ought to be made, however, in that these accounts are all written by outsiders: they were written by those who sought to conquer these areas and the people in them. We may perhaps consider that they wrote with a certain agenda in this regard, seeking to paint the practices they described as strange and barbaric in order to justify eventual colonisation. We may here add the thought that the sanctioned violence of any society may be made to look barbaric from the outside. And yet, all societies accept their own such practices as right and necessary. Though we ought to read their descriptions of motivations and methods with some caution, we can nevertheless accept that these sources build upon real and observed practices as backed up by the archaeological record. We can discern two separate types of offerings, although both are probably based on a singular sacrificial logic: single human victims and large-scale depositions of war-booty, including the purposeful destruction and deposition in wetland areas of valuable commodities.

Viking period literature

Edholm (this volume) provides numerous examples of sacrificial motifs presented in an array of Norse skaldic poetry, highlighting the value of contemporary literature in weeding out the vicissitudes of pre- and proto-historic sacrificial traditions. In addition to the skaldic materials, other written sources treat various aspects and cases of sacrificial human killings in the Viking world. Written around AD 1075, Adam of Bremen's oft-cited account of human sacrifice at Old Uppsala, in his *History of the Bishops of Hamburg* (Book 4, Ch. 26) dictates that

> Near this temple stands a very large tree with wide-spreading branches, always green winter and summer. What kind it is nobody knows. There is also a well at which the pagans are accustomed to make their sacrifices, and to plunge a live man into it. If he is not found, the people's wish will be granted.

In Book 4, Ch. 27 he records his famous account of the *blót* at Uppsala in Sweden, where he asserts that every nine years a feast at which nine specimens of every living thing that is male is sacrificed, their bodies hung in a sacred grove near the temple. The same festival is echoed by Saxo Grammaticus, who notes that these festivities originated at Uppsala with human offerings of 'dusky victims to the god Frey' (Elton 1894, 36, 90). A strikingly similar account is offered by Thietmar of Merseburg, describing sacrifices at Lejre in Denmark (Jensen, this volume; Jessen and Olsen, this volume). These accounts are so similar that there is reason to speculate that one may have inspired the other (Thietmar's account pre-dating Adam of Bremen's by around 50 years). However, though their accuracy and veracity may certainly be doubted, there are also striking similarities in some of the motifs that can be corroborated by other sources. The remains of a tree, interpreted as a sacred votive site, surrounded by fragments of animal and human bone has been found at Frösö in Sweden (Näsström 2001, 78), whilst the hanging motif recurs in the Oseberg tapestries as well as in mythological motifs.

So-called '*blót*' sacrifices in the literature were held at various times (and proscribed seasonally) and do not seem to have usually consisted of human sacrifices but rather those of animals and libations in the form of a ritual feast as a means to appease the gods and build and strengthen social relations. Though most sources refer to animal sacrifices, the term '*mann-blót*' appears a few times in the literature.

Throughout Snorri Sturluson's works are many examples of Norse sacrifices and sacrificial practices. In *Heimskringla* there are several references specifically to human sacrifice. For example, during the battle with the Jomsvikings, when the outcome looks bleak, Jarl Håkon considers making an anonymous human sacrifice to the divinity Þorgerðr Hölgabrúðr. She pre-emptively rejects this offer, but accepts his subsequent offer to sacrifice his own son, Erlinger, a boy of just seven. Håkon immediately has his thrall dispatch of the child. When the battle is rejoined, Þorgerðr Hölgabrúðr intervenes, winning the day for Håkon (Blake 1962, 36). Elsewhere, we are told that during a midsummer *Thing* at

Ladir, King Olav Tryggvason addressed a promise that he had made under duress to let himself to be goaded by his apostate followers into making blood offerings in the old ways. In response, he tells the assembled gathering that if he shall make sacrifices, he will make the greatest sacrifice that can be made: *i.e.*, that of men. But, instead of the usual victims of thralls and criminals, the king then names as victims a number of noble men in attendance and from among the community. Rather than accomplish the deaths of the best among them, the assembly agree to be baptised, swear loyalty to the king and give up altogether the making of sacrifices. Other stories occur in the Saga corpus, including the casual mention of places named for their role in human sacrifice (*Eyrbyggja Saga*; Morris & Magnússon 1892, 18), and the sacrifice of a king to ensure a much-needed good harvest (in *Ynglingasaga*, chapter XVIII). Returning to the hanging motif, *Hávamál* from the Poetic Edda (*i.e.*, 'Elder' or 'Sæmund's' Edda; Bray 1908, 103), Oðinn sacrifices himself to himself on the world tree Yggdrasil in order to attain wisdom. He hangs for nine days and nights and is pierced by a spear during the ordeal, but comes away with knowledge of runes and words and untold deeds.

Ibn Fadlan's famous description of a thrall sacrifice amongst a group of Rūs on the Volga *c.* AD 921 stands as one of the few direct observations of a human sacrifice in historical contexts which is largely accepted as a more or less genuine account (Lunde & Stone 2012; Montgomery 2000). In this instance, a chieftain's death is marked by the burning of his body and numerous valuables, including a slave girl who voluntarily goes to her death to attend him. Both were burnt on a ship which had been pulled onto land, and a mound was built over the ashes. In the course of the rituals, several animals were slaughtered and added to the ship, before the slave girl was drugged, raped and ritually killed. The girl's death is violent and clearly of deep symbolic importance. We may imagine that her death meant more than met Ibn Fadlan's etic eye (see Moen & Walsh 2021). Interestingly, overkill – spectacular, extravagant and ultra-violent means of killing – seems to be the norm in many human sacrificial acts, and this first-hand example is no different. Notably, Ibn Fadlan is not the only Arabic writer who mentions the Rūs fondness for killing slaves in connection with funerals (see Upham 2019; Moen & Walsh 2021).

Multiple burials involving ritual killing also appear in myth and folktale, as a well-understood theme. Pertinently, Major (1924, 140) relates mythological evidence of suttee- and attendant-sacrifice reflected in the Norse story of Balder's death in which Balder's wife Nanna dies of grief and is placed on the pyre next to him (Edholm, this volume). Sacrifice is also alluded to in the same story as Thor, in his rage, kicks the dwarf Litr onto Balder's funeral pyre (Balder was placed aboard his own ship and other offerings were placed on his pyre: the magical arm-ring called Draupnir and his horse) (Turville-Petre 1964, 107; Olsen 2007, 69). In the *Volsunga Saga*, overtaken by both anger and grief at Sigurd's death, Brynhild takes her own life and joins him on his funeral pyre along with his three-year-old son, whom she had killed, in addition to five bondswomen and eight servants (Finch 1965, 61). Interestingly, Finch (1965, 60) also notes that in the *Poetic Edda* version of events, it is implied that Brynhild entreats her free-born attendants to accompany her in death, but none take her up on the invitation. It is interesting to note that, in order to be understood by listeners at all, all of these narratives imply sacrificial logics that would have made sense within their communal contexts.

Sacrifice reflected in double graves at Flakstad, Kaupang and elsewhere?

North of the region under discussion here, Naumann *et al.* (2014) investigated a number of Viking Era double graves from the cemetery at Flakstad in north-west Norway. They approached the double graves as possible evidence for the sacrifice by decapitation of slaves (*i.e.*, thralls) upon the death of high-status elites (*cf.*, Walsh and Reiter, this volume). Here, the evidence in some cases does indicate different diets between individuals placed in the same grave, suggesting social inequality. Also, genetic evidence between those buried in the double graves shows that individuals were probably not related. But the evidence does not support that the apparently decapitated individuals had distinctly poorer diets than the overall population (based on analyses of single burials). If we assume that the decapitated or headless individuals were indeed attendant sacrifices, they do not appear to have come from a particularly marginal population, at least not as far as diet was concerned.

Elsewhere in Norway, other double graves in boats are at times interpreted as reflecting attendant sacrifices. For example, the cemetery at Kaupang contains the greatest frequency of Viking Era double/multiple graves in Scandinavia. Roughly one in five graves at the site are believed to contain multiple individuals. Six burials contained multiple individuals placed in boats, including four double graves and two triple graves. Stylegar (2007) provides descriptions of these, as well as a discussion of the possibility that some other graves (*e.g.*, those without coffins, with decapitations and with prone inhumations) may suggest the burial of thralls. Davidson (1992) describes a number of similar burials in Anglo-Saxon England, including the famous cases from Sutton Hoo. Elsewhere, the nature of such 'deviant' burials has been disputed (*e.g.*, Reynolds 2009; but see also Walsh *et al.* 2020).

Jessen and Olsen (this volume) explore cases of 'extreme' differential treatment of the deceased in Viking Era graves containing decapitations. At Stengade in Langeland, Denmark, the double grave FII contained an intact clothed individual laying extended and supine, along with a decapitated (seemingly bound) and prone unclothed individual (Skaarup 1976). This grave has often been interpreted as evidence of a thrall attendant sacrifice. A somewhat similar burial at Lejre, Grave 55, also contained an inhumed supine individual with grave offerings, and over this person's grave lay a bound and prone individual who had been decapitated (Bennike 1985, 108–109). Vedel (1897, 57) describes two graves at Lousgaard on Bornholm (Graves 47 and 48) in which richly adorned individuals – a male and female, respectively – were buried with what appear to have been a male thrall along with a horse, and a female thrall, respectively. Here, the status of 'thrall' is speculated from the conspicuous inequality in grave offerings between the deceased and the individuals accompanying them.

Schetelig (1910, 185) reviewed other examples from archaeology, focused on double graves of men and women as possible examples of suttee, including a catalogue of relevant Norwegian graves that could fall under this phenomenon. However, a review of his chosen material – and indeed that of other known multiple burials from the Viking Age, easily shows there is little evidence to support such an interpretation. A key argument that suttee was not habitually practised in the Viking Age can further be found in that although many multiple burials contain male and female bodies, almost as many contain same-sex constellations, and again many contain an adult and child. Some contain more than two bodies, further demonstrating the inadequacies of suttee as an interpretation (Ratican 2020).

Sacrificial wells at the Viking fortress at Trelleborg

There is archaeological evidence for possible human sacrifices having occurred at Harald Bluetooth's fortress at Trelleborg, west Zealand. These included the deposition of humans, animals and objects in three ritual wells, around the 9th–10th century AD. According to Gotfredsen *et al.* (2014, 150, table 1) well 47 at Trelleborg, for instance, contained objects including textile working tools and an arrowhead, as well as the skeletal remains of two children. Well 50, meanwhile, contained a variety of tools as well as fragmented skeletal remains from a human adult, whilst well 121 contained various objects along with the skeletal remains of two children and an adult. The wells also contained numerous animal remains from a variety of domesticated (and a few wild) species, including a whole large-breed dog and a horse leg that entered the well with the flesh still intact. Gotfredsen *et al.* (2014, 159) suggest that some depositional contexts could indicate ritual use of the wells, including possible 'propitiatory sacrifices'. These cases reflect earlier traditions described above which revolve around the deposition of pairs of young individuals in water.

Here, humans – particularly young children in pairs – animals (mostly domestic and some whole) and a variety of everyday objects were apparently ritually deposited in man-made wells. If any distinction was understood between natural water features and man-made ones for sacrificial purposes, it remains unclear – although it should be noted that even in cases of bog deposition the places where offerings were made were well-established features of a largely anthropogenic landscape and not the far-off wild fens often conjured in the popular imagination.

Discussion: how did forms of sacrifice develop over time and space?

Considering the cases presented above (and throughout this volume) as a regionally constrained sample of possible sacrificial traditions through time, is there any pattern in the current data to suggest if/how human sacrificial practices evolved from the Early Neolithic through to the Viking period in this region of northernmost Europe (*cf.*, Van Beek *et al.* 2023)? While certainly individuals and cultural groups moved about at various times, following the large-scale and temporally rapid Yamnaya expansion out of the Eurasian Steppe into Europe *c.* 3000 BC, the overall populations within the Nordic region have been relatively static (Allentoft *et al.* 2015; Haak *et al.* 2015). This is certainly not to say that in-migrations and cultural movements at varying scales did not occur, but that the general nature of such movements was in and between relatively adjacent or closely related groups and not reflective of the wholesale cultural replacement scenarios hypothesised for the advent of Yamnaya/Corded Ware Culture throughout much of Europe at the end of the Neolithic (Kristiansen *et al.* 2017). In the Nordic region, it appears that slower local processes of acculturation occurred between interacting peoples, *e.g.*, between Funnel Beaker groups and incoming Corded Ware groups during the Neolithic. While we acknowledge that the two often go hand in hand, here we are not concerned with the question of genetic admixture between populations so much as we are with the cultural transmission of the core ritual and penal practices of ritualised human killing, *i.e.*, human sacrifice. In any case, it appears that diverse but congruent sacrificial practices – including the use of humans as sacrificial tender – continued throughout the Nordic area prior to any major demographic transition in the Late Neolithic (at whatever scale and tempo it may have occurred) as well as after. That such practices persisted unabated suggests that some form of cultural transmission of ideas surrounding the necessity or utility of ritualised human violence may have driven congruent, and possibly even coherent, sacrificial traditions or practices across time.

A notable shift in sacrificial traditions can be observed between the Neolithic, the Nordic Bronze Age and the Early Iron Age. In the Neolithic, human sacrifices appear to have been relatively rare, but where there is existing evidence, we see victims of either sex and of various ages (but often youthful), sometimes in pairs, with victims deposited in wetlands that were already commonly used and continued to be used for other forms of offerings such as those of animals and domestic objects. For the Nordic Bronze Age there emerges the possibility that attendant sacrifice came into vogue. This practice was still rare (but it is safe to surmise that human sacrifices have always been at least relatively uncommon and exceptional events). Victims appear to often have been children who were killed and their bodies cremated and the remains placed in the grave of a deceased individual of high status, presumably under the notion that the victim would accompany the dead into the next life and serve them there; similar notions can be observed much later during the Viking period. As the Iron Age comes into full swing, there was a resurgence of human sacrifices placed in wetlands and there appears to be a possible increase as time goes on for increased violence levelled at victims.

Pivotally in each case, regardless of temporal or cultural context, we can see the use of humans as somehow 'proper' sacrificial offerings (at least in some circumstances) yet in diverse forms. This may have been key to the seeming persistence of ritualised human violence, given that we see different offerings made in different contexts suggesting a flexibility in sacrificial logics. And yet, human victims continued to be used, despite seemingly very different functions, purposes or goals. This begs the question of whether the use of humans as sacrificial offerings was conceptually any different from many other forms of offerings undertaken in Northern European prehistory (see Pantmann, this volume) – *why humans*? It seems quite clear that distinctions between *human* sacrifice and any other form of sacrificial offering may not have (always or explicitly) existed in the past.

When attempting to better understand trends over long periods of time evolutionary approaches are appropriate. Evolutionary methods of analysis allow us to systematically identify patterns (or lack thereof) in cultural data. To date, even among studies of the evolution of religion, few studies have actually levelled systematic evolutionary analyses at investigating changes in rituo-religious practices over time. One of the goals of the 'Human Sacrifice and Value' project has been to better understand the trajectory of human sacrificial practices over time. Thus, for this regional study presented in this volume focusing principally on Nordic Europe, we query from the examples in the following chapters whether there are any patterns of congruence between traditions, and/or any pattern of coherence within or between traditions over time. To do this, we collated data drawn from the following contributions into a data matrix comprising 63 cases (*i.e.*, 'taxa'; here these represent various sites or examples of possible human sacrifice as described in the following chapters). These cases span from the Early Neolithic through to the Late Viking Era. For these taxonomic units, 55 traits were identified and coded for presence/absence across the sample. Traits include contexts relating to the number of possible victims (single, pairs, multiple), demographics (sex and age groups), physical characteristics of the find (*e.g.*, physical abnormalities evident for victims, evidence for decapitation, strangulation/asphyxiation, blunt force trauma, or slashing, etc.), other deposition contexts (*e.g.*, remains pinned in place or deliberate destruction of the remains [beyond the means of dispatch], depth and position of the find), other objects/offerings associated with the find (*e.g.*, ceramics, flint tools, domestic/agrarian-associated objects, jewellery or other valuable objects, etc.), animal remains (by *genus* or *family*), other find contexts (*e.g.*, completeness or composite nature of the remains, position or situation of the victim such as laying extended, flexed, supine or prone, in a 'hocker' position, etc., and inhumation vs. cremation), and finally whether the find was in a martial context (such as associated with weapons or war-gear, or at an established site of conflict such as near a battlefield, like at Alken Enge in Illerup Ådal in east Jutland). We collated data on deposition type (*e.g.*, in a bog or wetland, in a burial mound, or *e.g.*, associated with a 'ship'). Ultimately, we left this data out of our analyses as it was determined to too-specifically delimit certain periods/traditions and thus unduly bias outcomes into culture-specific groups. That

our results basically do this anyway without the inclusion of tradition-specific data merely strengthens the argument that particular temporal cultural norms are indeed reflected in different sacrificial practices across time.

We subjected this original dataset to a series of phylogenetic analyses with the aim of identifying any pattern of evolutionary change over time. A suite of Bayesian phylogenetic analyses (Lewis 2001; Drummond *et al.* 2005; 2006; Bouckaert *et al.* 2019) following methods outlined in Gjesfjeld and Jordan (2019) and Prentiss *et al.* (2022; 2023) produced trees with relatively weak support for a phylogenetic branching pattern across time at the higher scale, meaning that descent with modification from an early ancestral form or forms of sacrificial practice is not evident from the data (Plate 1). However, a weak-phylogenetic evolution pattern in a seemingly foundational ritual tradition observed across millennia at a relatively small regional scale is also informative (*e.g.*, Cochrane 2015). Simply put, for a ritual practice like sacrifice that is so ubiquitous and seemingly persistent over time, we may expect greater continuity and fidelity, especially at a regional scale. These results fit a 'diffusion' or 'ethnogenesis' evolutionary pattern (Moore 1994; Collard & Shennan 2000) in which a cultural unit emerges independently (or practically so). And here there does seem to be considerable coherence within temporal cultural traditions and 'suites'

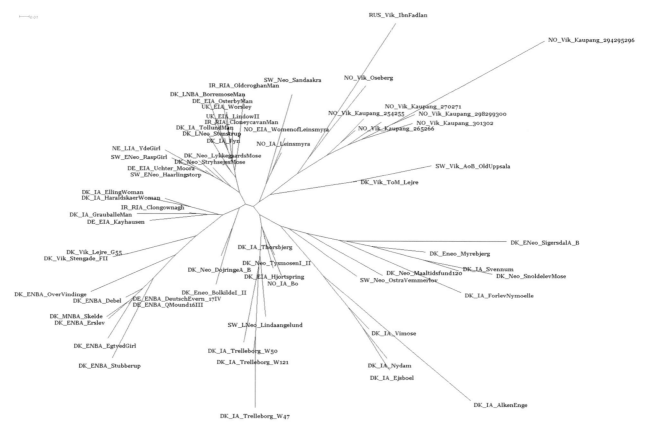

Figure 1. Neighbour-joining dendrogram of cases described in the text.

of practice at the lower scales: generally speaking, many of the Neolithic cases group in a clade, the Bronze Age cases form a clade, the Iron Age bog bodies and skeletons make up a clade, ship-related cases and war-booty depositions form clades, and so on. Neighbour-joining (Figure 1) and NeighborNet analyses (Figure 2) generated using Splitstree4 (Huson & Bryant 2006) also prove insightful in this regard, offering similar interpretive results. The NeighborNet split graph shows greater reticulation within clades such as that of the more violent of the bog body cases, the Early Nordic Bronze Age attendant sacrifices, the multi-person boat graves from Kaupang and most of the Iron Age war-booty offerings, for example. The pattern, however, is again not one strongly suggestive of an evolutionary branching trajectory, but rather indicative of polytomies (cases where a branching pattern is not fully resolved) within specific temporal-cultural traditions. What

resolution can be found is evident within clades largely grouped by specific types of victims (*e.g.*, male, female, children, pairs), forms of ritual violence (*e.g.*, hanging or strangulation, slashing, beheading or other conspicuous or asymmetrical treatment of victims), other ritual contexts such as offerings of objects and/or animals, and within coherent temporal and cultural traditions. Likewise, clusters of culture-complex specific groupings can also be seen in the correspondence analysis scatter plot (Plate 2). In the correspondence analysis, for example, the loose grouping at the top of the diagram shows cases in which diverse animal and domestic-sphere object offerings appear along with those of humans – and conspicuously – with parts of humans, including young adults and sub-adults, with many of the Neolithic cases falling into this group. At the bottom right can be found the Iron Age bog bodies and Viking warrior graves with mostly adult and mature males (but also

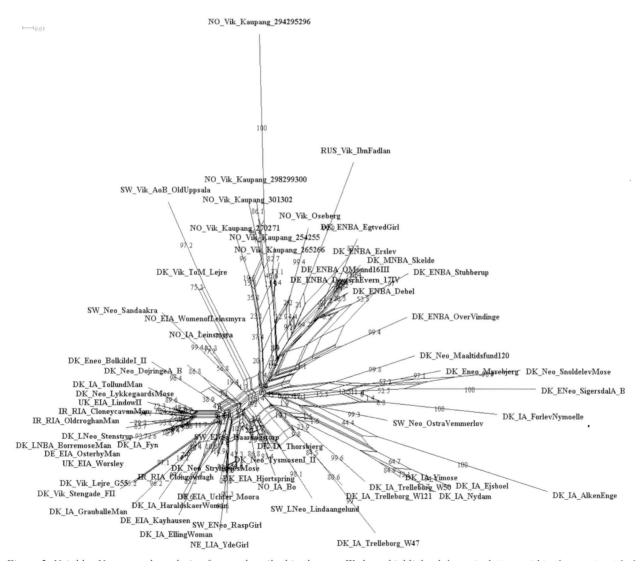

Figure 2. NeighborNet network analysis of cases described in the text. We have highlighted the reticulations within the matrix with the highest bootstrap support.

females) with evidence corresponding to violent death. At the bottom left can be seen many examples of women and children and multiple interments, with also an abundance of related high-status objects such as weapons and jewellery as well as expensive burial contexts such as ships and burial mounds and possible attendant sacrifices – all the funerary trappings of the elite. This pattern may lend credence to the potential of a tripartite structure to the logic of sacrificial practices in Nordic prehistory based on sovereign, martial and domestic ritual schema (see discussion in Walsh, Pantmann and Moen, this volume). Together, these results suggest that there is little congruence (*i.e.*, no strong pattern of descent with modification) *between* temporal traditions, but that there is strong coherence *within* specific temporal traditions. In other words, there appear to be similarities within the different temporal cultural traditions: the Vikings did what the Vikings did; Early Iron Age sacrificers did what other Early Iron Age sacrificers did, and so on. Hence, we may say that to some degree, each sacrificial tradition reflects the cultural norms or values of its time, whatever those may have been.

While the different sacrificial practices presented in the following volume do not appear to have evolved from an identifiable Ur-type ancestral form of sacrifice, they do appear to have emerged and persisted as coherent suites of historical or circumstantial 'norms' in their own right. Human sacrifice does not appear so much to evolve as it seems to be transformed to fit the morays and necessities of the times and the societies undertaking it within their own culturally relative contexts. In other words, ritualised human violence may be said to have emerged and been institutionalised at various points in Northern European prehistory to fit the particular social, political, economic and/or religious needs (or whims) of the societies in question. In this way, we suggest that human sacrifice – in a number of different permutations – was a core feature of different societies at different times and its expression also varied with the times, even within this relatively limited regional context. Thus, rather than suggesting that human sacrifice played a direct role in social stratification (*cf.*, Watts *et al.* 2016) – which we acknowledge it very probably did – we suggest from our analysis that ritualised human violence was and is more complicated and much more multi-functional in the societies that undertook it. Given the variability seen in its expression and practice here, it would seem that violence was likely ritualised in order to sublimate its perceived necessity, whether that was to please gods or spirits, make it rain, provide a deceased person with attendants in the afterlife, punish deviants, signal or maintain wealth and/or social status, or what have you. As such, we ought to carefully consider statements regarding the presence of human sacrificial violence in too over-reaching terms, applying the concept *ad hoc* or ahistorically wherever or however we may see it arise.

Concluding thoughts

Written sources such as Saxo, Snorri and the sagas, as well as the skaldic literature (Edholm, this volume; Jensen, this volume) suggest that human sacrifice was generally a desperation measure, at least in the Late Medieval and Viking periods. It was an undertaking reserved for the darkest of days, when the crops continued to fail, when battle ensued or defeat was imminent. Humans as currency in sacrifice was reserved for times when calamity was on the horizon or seemed inevitable. But sacrifice is also, and always has been, a powerful symbolic gesture. It could establish or reinforce social or political hierarchies. It could please gods. And it could even invest the very landscape with the spirits of ancestors or guardian spirits. It could renew the earth. It could also neatly eliminate pariahs from society. With the strike of a sword, a deceased individual's brethren could honour his or her life, provide a fitting bookend to their legacy and/or secure the deceased a servant for the afterlife (Jessen and Olsen, this volume; Walsh and Reiter, this volume). But thralls or attendants were not the only thing of value to enter into sacrificial exchange. The choice of what kinds of offerings to make or whether to make any at all must have been considered against diverse social, religious and economic considerations (*e.g.*, Mannering, this volume). Additionally, the inclusion of some over other or none over any lives or objects as offerings likely also served to reify and regulate social norms (Fredengren, this volume), perhaps even doing so in a symbolic/semiotic sense by defining them through occasional acts of difference or even deviance (Ravn, this volume).

Clearly, the values of human and associated object offerings were carefully weighed. The treatment of sacrificial tender (victims as well as objects) is also telling in this regard. For example, violent means of dispatching victims seem to have become increasingly popular over time (Walsh *et al.* forthcoming), and this also appears to have been tied to the very deliberate and individualised nature of ritualised violent acts (Lynnerup and Asingh, this volume). Was this increase in, or at least predilection towards, violence the result of individual or social biases? Were some victims treated to more violent ends because they were seen to deserve it, whether by merit, malice or meaning? Likewise, were some individuals simply viewed as more killable than others (Fredengren, this volume)? Or could the increase in violence evident in some cases reflect shifts in the social and political landscape? For example, could ritualised expressions of violence be a response to emerging desperation among indigenous populations, *e.g.*, towards the Roman Iron Age, brought on by incursion, crisis or conflict? Add to this that sacrifices and their logics may have been negotiated through victim transformation, substitution or even ritual chicanery (Pantmann, this volume; Walsh, Pantmann and Moen, this volume; Wåhlin, this volume). Indeed, a picture of what human sacrifice was or was meant to be becomes blurry at best from any angle on the past. This is perhaps no better illustrated than in the earliest examples given in the present volume, where regular offerings of animals and domestic objects appear to have long-sufficed for whatever ritual necessity was perceived (Sørensen and Nielsen, this volume), and yet human sacrifice emerges on the scene nonetheless, even among what appear to be (at least for the time being) relatively egalitarian and tight-knit communities who should have had little need to regulate deviancy, enforce social control or negotiate non-interpersonal conflict through ritualised killings. Thus, the picture of human sacrifice and its attributable values is complex, even at a relatively small regional scale.

This, we posit here, is why there is no strong phylogenetic signal in our collated data; human sacrifice has emerged and re-emerged in places and contexts when, where and how it served diverse purposes or functions under very different circumstances, sometimes as genuine acts of communion, other times and places as a regulatory measure for signalling and maintaining social order or control, and others as a means of sublimating (or alternatively even celebrating) the necessity for violence, or as a means of mitigating calamity. Importantly, none of these circumstances, conditions or functions are mutually exclusive, rather they are often complementary. In point of suggestion, the more concerns or crises that could be addressed or alleviated by a single sacrificial event, probably the better.

Notes

1   Here we should note that the human crania placed on display by Mesolithic hunter-gatherers at the Motala Kanaljorden site in Sweden, *c.* 8000–7500 BP are arguably the earliest in the region to evince human remains subjected to trauma in relation to some form of ritual activity (Hallgren & Fornander 2016; Gummesson *et al.* 2018; Hallgren *et al.* 2021; Sørensen and Nielsen, this volume). The evidence there suggests that the skulls of individuals were put on display with other ritual offerings, including the remains of animals and tools of bone and antler. But there is no evidence that the individuals were killed on the spot for ritual purposes. Rather, the remains appear to have been put on display (mounted on stakes) sometime after having been buried and there is currently no evidence that the physical traumas suffered by them in life were the cause of death. Rather, the blunt force traumas suffered by the individuals at Motala appear to have been the result of interpersonal violence that occurred during their lifetimes (Gummesson *et al.* 2018; Hallgren *et al.* 2021). Likewise, a bog body of a female found in Viksø Mose (Rolandsgårdens Mose, Zealand; just about 1.5 km from the Sigersdal individuals), also dates to the Danish Neolithic (*c.* 5050 BP) and is associated with other votive offerings of animals, ceramics and stone tools. But here again there is no observable evidence of violence on the remains. Thus, placement in the wetland may certainly indicate a ritual aspect to the deposition, but we should approach an interpretation of sacrifice with caution.

2.   Personal communication. Conversation with the author and the presentation 'Sacrifice and the nature of the (in-) humane – depositions of human and animal bodies in Swedish Wetlands'. Presented at the workshop '*Transitions in Sacrifice*', organised by M. Løvschal. Moesgaard Museum, 23 January 2020.

3   The nearest location with a strontium Sr86/Sr87 ratio to fit the values present in Haraldskær Woman's hair closest to her scalp is to the south, roughly 600 km away from her place of deposition. Strontium values in the wool of one of her garments also indicate far-off access.

References

Acevedo, G.A. & Thompson, M. 2013. Blood, war, and ritual: Religious ecology, 'strong' culture, and human sacrifice in the premodern world. *Anthropological Forum* 23(3): 266–288.

Albrectsen, E. 1954. Et offerfund i Sludegårds mose. *Fynske Minder* 1954: 4–14.

Allentoft, M.E., Sikora, M., Sjögren, K.-G., Rasmussen, S., Rasmussen, M., Stenderup, J., Damgaard, P.B., Schroeder, H., Ahlström, T., Vinner, L., Malaspinas, A.-S., Margaryan, A., Higham, T., Chivall, D., Lynnerup, N., Harvig, L., Baron, J., Della Casa, P., Dąbrowski, P., Duffy, P.R., Ebel, A.V., Epimakhov, A., Frei, K., Furmanek, M., Gralak, T., Gromov, A., Gronkiewicz, S., Grupe, G., Hajdu, T., Jarysz, R., Khartanovich, V., Khokhlov, A., Kiss, V., Kolář, J., Kriiska, A., Lasak, I., Longhi, C., McGlynn, G., Merkevicius, A., Merkyte, I., Metspalu, M., Mkrtchyan, R., Moiseyev, V., Paja, L., Pálfi, G., Pokutta, D., Pospieszny, Ł., Price, T.D., Saag, L., Sablin, M., Shishlina, N., Smrčka, V., Soenov, V.I., Szeverényi, V., Tóth, G., Trifanova, S.V., Varul, L., Vicze, M., Yepiskoposyan, L., Zhitenev, V., Orlando, L., Sicheritz-Pontén, T., Brunak, S., Nielsen, R., Kristiansen, K. & Willerslev, E. 2015. Population genomics of Bronze Age Eurasia. *Nature* 522(7555): 167–172. doi:10.1038/ nature14507. www.nature.com/nature/journal/ v522/n7555/abs/nature14507.html#supplementaryinformation. PMID: 26062507 2.

Andersen, H. 1960. Hovedstaden i riget. *Nationalmuseets Arbejdsmark* 1960: 13–35.

Andersen, S.R. & Geertinger, P. 1984. Bog bodies in the light of forensic medicine. *Journal of Danish Archaeology* 3: 111–119.

Aner, E. & Kersten, K. 1979. *Die Funde der älteren Bronzezeit des nordischen Kreises in Dänemark, Schleswig-Holstein und Niedersachsen*, Vol. 5. Copenhagen: Verlag Nationalmuseum.

Aner, E., Kersten, K. & Willroth, K.-H. 2001. *Die Funde der älteren Bronzezeit des nordischen Kreises in Dänemark, Schleswig-Holstein und Niedersachsen*, Vol. 11. Copenhagen: Verlag Nationalmuseum.

Becker, C.J. 1952. Skeletfundet fra Porsmose ved Næstved. *Fra Nationalmuseets Arbejdsmark* 1952: 25–32.

Bennike, P. 1985. *Palaeopathology of Danish Skeletons*. Copenhagen: Akademisk Forlag.

Bennike, P. 1999. The Early Neolithic Danish bog finds: A strange group of people! In *Bog Bodies, Sacred Sites and Wetland Archaeology*, edited by B. Coles, J. Coles and M. Jørgensen, 27–32. Exeter: Short Run Press.

Bennike, P. & Ebbesen, K. 1985. Stenstrupmanden. *Fra Holbæk Amt*, 28–39.

Bennike, P., Ebbesen, K. & Bender Jørgensen, L. 1986a. The bog find from Sigersdal: Human sacrifice in the Early Neolithic. *Journal of Danish Archaeology* 5: 85–115.

Bennike, P., Ebbesen, K. & Bender Jørgensen, L. 1986b. Early Neolithic skeletons from Bolkilde bog, Denmark. *Antiquity* 230: 199–209.

Bouckaert, R., Vaughan, T.G., Barido-Sottani, J., Duchêne, S., Fourment, M., Gavryushkina, A., Heled, J., Jones, G., Kühnert, D., De Maio, N., Matschiner, M., Mendes, F.K., Müller, N.F., Ogilvie, H.A., du Plessis, L., Popinga, A., Rambaut, A., Rasmussen, D., Siveroni, I., Suchard, M.A., Wu, C.-H., Xie, D., Zhang, C., Stadler, T. & Drummond, A.J. 2019. BEAST 2.5: An advanced software platform for Bayesian evolutionary analysis. *PLoS Computational Biology* 15(4): e1006650.

Boye, V. 1884. *Fundberetning 4058, 'Thinghøj' Udby (sic).* Archive National Museum of Denmark, Copenhagen.

Bray, O. 1908. *The Elder or Poetic Edda: Commonly Known as Sæmund's Edda, Part I.* London: Viking Club.

Bukkemoen, G.B. & Skare, K. 2018. Humans, animals and water: The deposition of human and animal remains in Norwegian wetlands. *Journal of Wetland Archaeology* 18(1): 35–55.

Caesar, C.J. 1869. *Caesar's Gallic War.* Translated by W.A. McDevitte and W.S. Bohn. New York: Harper & Brothers, Harper's New Classical Library.

Cochrane, E. 2015. Phylogenetic analysis of Polynesian ritual architecture suggests extensive cultural sharing and innovation. *The Journal of the Polynesian Society. Polynesian Society (N.Z.)* 124(1): 7–46. doi:10.15286//jps.124.1.7-46.

Collard, M. & Shennan, S.J. 2000. Ethnogenesis versus phylogenesis in prehistoric culture change: A case study using European Neolithic pottery and biological phylogenetic techniques. In *Archaeogenetics: DNA and the Population Prehistory of Europe*, edited by C. Renfrew and K. Boyle, 89–97. Cambridge: McDonald Institute for Archaeological Research.

Davidson, H.R.E. 1992. Human Sacrifices in the Late Pagan Period in North Western Europe. In *The Age of Sutton Hoo: The Seventh Century in North-Western Europe*, edited by M.O.H. Carver, 331–340.

Degerbøl, M. & Fredskild, B. 1970. *The Urus (*Bos primigenius bojanus*) and Neolithic domesticated cattle (*Bos taurus domesticus Linné*) in Denmark.* Copenhagen: Munksgaard.

Dobat, A.S., Price, T.D., Kveiborg, J., Ilkjær, J. & Rowley-Conwy, P. 2015. The four horses of an Iron Age apocalypse: Warhorses from the third-century weapon sacrifice at Illerup Aadal (Denmark). *Antiquity* 88: 191–204.

Drummond, A.J., Rambaut, A., Shapiro, B. & Pybus, O.G. 2005. Bayesian coalescent inference of past population dynamics from molecular sequences. *Molecular Bbiology and Evolution* 22(5): 1185–1192.

Drummond, A.J., Ho, S.Y.W., Phillips, M.J. & Rambaut, A. 2006. Relaxed phylogenetics and dating with confidence. *PLoS Biol* 4(5): e88.

Dumézil, G. 1973. *From Myth to Fiction: The Saga of Hadingus.* Chicago: University of Chicago Press.

Dutton, D. 2016. *An Encapsulation of Óðinn: Religious Belief and Ritual Practice Among the Viking Age Elite with Particular Focus Upon the Practice of Ritual Hanging* (Ph.D. thesis, the University of Aberdeen).

Ebbesen, K. 1993. Sacrifices to the powers of nature. In *Digging into the Past: 25 Years of Archaeology in Denmark*, edited by S. Hvass and B. Storgaard, 122–125. Aarhus: Aarhus University Press.

Engdahl, K. 1990. *Människooffer i gravar i Skandinavien under yngre järnålder.* C-Uppsats in Archaeology. Stockholm: University of Stockholm.

Ethelberg, P. 2000. En fronem kvinde af højfolket. In *Vor skjulte kulturarv: Arkæologien under overfladen*, edited by S. Hvass and Det Arkæologiske Nævn, 74–75. Esbjerg: Rosendahls Bogtrykkeri.

Fabech, C. 1991. Samfundsorganisation, religiøse ceremonier og regional variation. In *Samfundsorganisation og Regional Variation. Norden i romersk jernalder og folkevandringstid*, edited by C. Fabech and J. Ringtved, 283–303. Aarhus: Aarhus University Press.

Fabech, C. 1996. Booty sacrifices in southern Scandinavia – a history of warfare and ideology. In *Roman Reflections in Scandinavia*, edited by L. Franchi dell'Oro, 135–138. Rome: L'Erma di Bretschneider.

Fabech, C. 1997. Slöinge i perspektiv. In Johan Callmer and Erik Rosengren: '… gick Grendel att söka det höga huset …'. Arkeologiska källor till aristokratiska miljöer i Skandinavien under yngre järnålder, 145–160. Halmstad: Hallands Länsmuseums Skriftserie No. 9.

Fabech, C. 1998. Kult og samfund i yngre jernalder – Ravlunda som eksempel. In *Centrala platser – Centrala frågor. Uppåkrastudier, vol. 1*, edited by L. Larsson and B. Hårdh, 147–163. Lund: Almqvist & Wiksell International.

Finch, R.G. 1965. *Volsunga Saga.* London: Thomas Nelson and Sons.

Fischer, C. 1999. The Tollund Man and the Elling Woman and other bog bodies from central Jutland. In *Bog Bodies, Sacred Sites and Wetland Archaeology*, edited by B. Coles, J. Coles and M.S. Jørgensen, 93–97. Exeter: Short Run Press.

Fredengren, C. 2011. Where wandering water gushes – the depositional landscape of the Mälaren Valley in the Late Bronze Age and Earliest Iron Age of Scandinavia. *Journal of Wetland Archaeology* 10(1): 109–135.

Fredengren, C. 2018. Becoming bog bodies. Sacrifice and politics of exclusion, as evidenced in the deposition of skeletal remains in wetlands near Uppåkra. *Journal of Wetland Archaeology* 18(1): 1–19.

Fredengren, C. & Löfqvist, C. 2015. Food for Thor: The deposition of human and animal remains in a Swedish wetland. *Journal of Wetland Archaeology* 15(1): 122–148.

Gibson, A. 1992. The timber circle at Sarn-y-Bryn-Caled, Welshpool, Powys: Ritual and sacrifice in Bronze Age mid-Wales. *Antiquity* 66: 84–92.

Gjesfjeld, E. & Jordan, P. 2019. Contributions of Bayesian phylogenetics to exploring patterns of macroevolution in archaeological data. In *Handbook of Evolutionary Research in Archaeology*, edited by A.M. Prentiss, 161–182. Cham: Springer International Publishing. doi:10.1007/978-3-030-11117-5_9.

Glob, P.V. 1969. *The Bog People. Iron-Age Man Preserved.* London: Faber & Faber.

Green, M.A. 2001. *Dying for the Gods.* Stroud: Tempus Publishing.

Gummesson, S., Hallgren, F. & Kjellström, A. 2018. Keep your head high: Skulls on stakes and cranial trauma in Mesolithic Sweden. *Antiquity* 92(361): 74–90. doi:10.15184/aqy.2017.210.

Haak, W., Lazaridis, I., Patterson, N., Rohland, N., Mallick, S., Llamas, B., Brandt, G., Nordenfelt, S., Harney, E., Stewardson, K., Fu, Q., Mittnik, A., Bánffy, E., Economou, C., Francken, M., Friederich, S., Pena, R.G., Hallgren, F., Khartanovich, V., Khokhlov, A., Kunst, M., Kuznetsov, P., Meller, H., Mochalov, O., Moiseyev, V., Nicklisch, N., Pichler, S.L., Risch, R., Rojo Guerra, M.A., Roth, C., Szécsényi-Nagy, A., Wahl, J., Meyer, M., Krause, J., Brown, D., Anthony, D., Cooper, A., Alt, K.W. & Reich, D. 2015. Massive migration from the steppe was a source for Indo-European languages in Europe. *Nature* 522(7555): 207–211. doi:10.1038/nature14317; WOS:000356016700037. PMID: 25731166 3.

Hallgren, F. & Fornander, E. 2016. Skulls on stakes and skulls in water. Mesolithic mortuary rituals at Kanaljorden, Motala, Sweden 7000 BP. In *Mesolithic Burials – Rites, Symbols and Social Organisation of Early Postglacial Communities. International Conference Halle (Saale), Germany, 18th–21st September 2013*, edited by J. Grünberg, B. Gramsch, L. Larsson, J. Orschiedt and H. Meller, Band 13/I, 161–174. Tagungen des Landesmuseums für Vorgeschichte Halle.

Hallgren, F., Berggren, K., Arnberg, A., Hartzell, L. & Larsson, B. 2021. *Kanaljorden, Motala. Rituella våtmarksdepositioner och boplatslämningar från äldre stenålder, tngre stenålder och järnalder*. Stiftelsen Kulturmiljövård. Rapport 2021: 12. Västerås.

Henriksson, G. 2003. The pagan Great Midwinter Sacrifice and the 'royal' mounds at Old Uppsala. In *Calendars, Symbols, and Orientations: Legacies of Astronomy in Culture; Proceedings of the 9th annual meeting of the European Society for Astronomy in Culture (SEAC), held at the Old Observatory in Stockholm, 27–30 August 2001*, edited by M. Blomberg, P.E. Blomberg and G. Henriksson, 15. Uppsala Astronomical Observatory Report No. 59. Uppsala: Uppsala University.

Hubert, H. & Mauss, M. 1964. *Sacrifice: Its Nature and Function*. Translated by W.D. Halls. Chicago: University of Chicago Press.

Huson, D.H. & Bryant, D. 2006. Application of phylogenetic networks in evolutionary studies. *Molecular Biology and Evolution* 23(2): 254–267.

Ilkjær, J. 2000. *Illerup Ådal – et arkæologisk tryllespejl*. Aarhus: Moesgård.

Ilkjær, J. 2002. Den bevidste ødelæggelse i krigsbytteofringerne. In *Plats och praxis. Studier av nordisk förkristen ritual.Vägar til Midgård, vol. 2*, edited by K. Jennbert, C. Raudvere and A. Andrén, 203–214. Lund: Lund University Press.

Ilkjær, J. 2003. *Danske krigsbytteofringer*. In *Sejrens triumf – Norden i skyggen af det romerske imperium*, edited by L. Jørgensen, B. Storgaard and L.G. Thomsen, 44–64. Copenhagen: Nationalmuseet.

Jørgensen, L., Stotgaard, B. & Gebauer Thomsen, L. 2003. *The Spoils of Victory: The North in the Shadow of the Roman Empire*. Copenhagen: Nationalmuseet.

Karsten, P. 1994. *Att kasta yxan I sjön: En studie över rituell tradition och förändring utifrån skånska neolitiska offerfynd*. Stockholm: Almqvist & Wiksell International.

Kristiansen, K., Allentoft, M.E., Frei, K.M., Iversen, R., Johannsen, N.N., Kroonen, G., Pospieszny, Ł., Price, T.D., Rasmussen, S., Sjögren, K.-G., Sikora, M. & Willerslev, E. 2017. Re-theorising mobility and the formation of culture and language among the Corded Ware Culture in Europe. *Antiquity* 91(356): 334–347. Epub 2017/04/04; doi:10.15184/aqy.2017.17.

Lewis, P.O. 2001. A likelihood approach to estimating phylogeny from discrete morphological character data. *Systematic Biology* 50(6): 913–925.

Lillehammer, G. 2011. The Children in the Bog. In *(Re)Thinking the Little Ancestors: New Perspectives on the Archaeology of Infancy and Childhood*, edited by M. Lally and A. Moore, 47–62. Oxford: British Archaeological Reports.

Lincoln, B. 1991. *Death, War, and Sacrifice: Studies in Ideology and Practice*. Chicago: University of Chicago Press.

Lomborg, E. 1964. Gravfund fra Stubberup, Lolland. Menneskeofringer og kannibalisme i bronzealderen. *KUML* 1964: 14–32.

Løvschal, M. & Holst, M.K. 2018. Governing martial traditions: Post-conflict ritual sites in Iron Age Northern Europe (200 BC–AD 200). *Journal of Anthropological Archaeology* 50: 27–39.

Lund, J. 2002. Forlev Nymølle. En offerplads fra yngre førromersk jernalder. *KUML* 2002: 143–195.

Mierow, C.C. 1915. *The Gothic History of Jordanes*. Princeton: Princeton University Press.

Moore, J.H. 1994. Putting anthropology back together again: The ethnogenetic critique of cladistic theory. *American Anthropologist* 96: 370–396.

Morris, W. & Magnússon, E. 1892. *The Story of the Ere-Dwellers (Eyrbyggja Saga)*. London: Chiswick Press.

Morris, W. & Magnússon, E. 1893. *The Stories of the Kings of Norway (Heimskringla), Vol. 1*. London: Chiswick Press.

Mulhall, I. & Briggs, E.K. 2007. Presenting a past society to a present day audience. Bog bodies in Iron Age Ireland. *Museum Ireland* 17: 71–81.

Murray, C.A. 2016. The value and power of sacrifice. In *Diversity of Sacrifice*, edited by C.A. Murray, 1–12. Albany: State University of New York Press.

Näsström, B.-M. 2001. *Blot: tro og offer I det førkristne Norden*. Oslo: Pax.

Olshausen, O. 1920. *Amrum. Bericht über Hügelgräber auf der Insel nebst einem Anhange über die Dünen*. Berlin: Kommissionsverlag der Prähistorischen Zeitschrift.

Prentiss, A.M., Laue, C., Gjesfjeld, E., Walsh, M.J., Denis, M. & Foor, T.A. 2023. Evolution of the Okvik/Old Bering Sea Culture of the Bering Strait as a major transition. *Philosophical Transactions of the Royal Society B* 378: 20210415. doi:10.1098/rstb.2021.0415.

Prentiss, A.M., Walsh, M.J., Gjesfjeld, E., Denis, M. & Foor, T.A. 2022. Cultural macroevolution in the middle to late Holocene Arctic of East Siberia and North America. *Journal of Anthropological Archaeology* 65: 101388.

Ravn, M. 2010. Burials in bogs: Bronze and Early Iron Age bog bodies from Denmark. *Acta Archaeologica* 81: 112–123.

Skaarup, J. 1985. *Yngre Stenalder på øerne syd for Fyn*. Rudkøbing: Langelands Museum.

Struve, K.W. 1967. Die Moorleiche von Dätgen: Ein Diskussionsbeitrag zur Strafopferthese. *OFFA* 24: 33–83.

Swensen, E. 2014. Dramas of the dialectic: Sacrifice and power in ancient polities. In *Violence and Civilization: Studies of Social Violence in History and Prehistory*, edited by R.B. Campbell, 28–60. Oxford: Oxbow Books.

Tacitus, C. 1894. *The Agricola and Germania*. Translated by R.B. Townsend. London: Methuen & Co.

Tacitus, C. 1904. *The Annals of Tacitus*, Books I–VI. Translated by G.G. Ramsay. London: John Murray.

Thomsen, T. 1929. Egekistefundet fra Egtved, fra den ældre Bronzealder. *Nordiske Fortidsminder* II(4): 165–214.

Turville-Petre, E.O.G. 1964. *Myth and Religion of the North.* Connecticut: Greenwood Press.

Van Beek, R., Quik, C., Bergerbrant, S., Huisman, F. & Kama, P. 2023. Bogs, bones and bodies: The deposition of human remains in Northern European mires (9000 BC–AD 1900). *Antiquity* 97(391): 120–140. doi:10.15184/aqy.2022.163.

Walsh, M.J., Moen, M., O'Neill, S., Gullbekk, S.H. & Willerslev, R. Forthcoming. From obligation and oblation to sublimated violence? Transformation of human sacrifice in the prehistory of northernmost Europe. In *Archaeologies of Pre-Christian Religion*, edited by P. Szczepanik. Turnhout: Brepols Publishers.

Ward, D. J. 1970. The threefold death: An Indo-European trifunctional sacrifice? In *Myth and Law Among the Indo-Europeans*, edited by J. Puhvel, 123–142. Berkeley/Los Angeles/London: University of California Press.

Watts, J., Sheehan, O., Atkinson, Q.D., Bulbulia, J. & Gray, R.D. 2016. Ritual human sacrifice promoted and sustained the evolution of stratified societies. *Nature* 532: 228–234. doi:10.1038/nature17159.

Winkelman, M. 1998. Aztec human sacrifice: Cross-cultural assessments of the ecological hypothesis. *Ethnology* 37(3): 285–298.

Winkelman, M. 2014. Political and demographic-ecological determinants of institutionalised human sacrifice. *Anthropological Forum* 24(1): 47–70.

Noble hunter-gatherers and 'cruel' farmers – a discussion of the evidence of human sacrifices during the Mesolithic and Neolithic in South Scandinavia

Lasse Sørensen and Poul Otto Nielsen

Abstract

Clear evidence of human sacrifice from the Mesolithic and Neolithic in South Scandinavia is difficult to identify. This is because there may be many alternative explanations as to why and how people actually died. If the interpretations are examined, natural causes of death are often preferred for the Mesolithic burials, compared to the assumption that more violent behaviour characterised the Neolithic involving human sacrifice. This fits in with the narrative of the increased emergence of social hierarchies within agrarian societies during the Neolithic. However, when empirical patterns emerge, we should be open to human sacrifice as a relevant interpretation for some of the double burials in the Mesolithic, which may contain examples of infanticide and the 'merciful' killings of specific individuals. More significant, and not documented from the Mesolithic, are the apparent violent deaths of many younger individuals found in bogs and wetland areas dating to the Early and Middle Neolithic in South Scandinavia, amongst which the strangled bog bodies from the Neolithic stand out as some of the most convincing evidence that human sacrifice took place during the Stone Age in South Scandinavia.

Keywords: human sacrifice, violence, Mesolithic, Neolithic, South Scandinavia

Introduction

Studies of human sacrifice have often focused on a number of general explanations for this act. The first argues that some communities offered human individuals, who were either willing or unwilling, as offerings to a deity. This was undertaken in order to make amends for wrongdoings, gain advantages or to create some sort of balance for the benefit of the society as a whole. The second explanation involves victims of human sacrifice as subordinates, individuals who were ritually killed with the intent that they should follow individuals of higher status into the afterlife. An alternative to both explanations is the offering of human substitutes in the form of animals, specific objects or foodstuffs, although this too is difficult to prove within prehistoric societies. This noted, here we will only focus upon human sacrifice. This can include individuals whose skeletal remains do not show any indications of violence, such as strangulation. In other cases, there can be signs of violence, but how can we know whether such acts of violence were hostile acts inflicted by an enemy or were intentional acts associated with human sacrifice? In this article, evidence of human sacrifice from the Mesolithic and Neolithic in South Scandinavia is discussed, along with alternative reasons for the deaths of individuals, therefore adding nuances to the stereotypical view of 'noble' hunter-gatherers and 'cruel' farmers.

Mesolithic burials

The practice of human sacrifice is most often encountered among so-called 'complex', food-producing and non-egalitarian societies. Social differentiation and complex organisation are seldom seen among hunter-gatherers.

However, historical sources reveal examples of so-called complex hunter-gatherers, who lived in ranked and stratified societies with high population densities, sedentism, warfare and slavery, as on the north-west coast of North America (Fitzhugh 2003). Slaves owned by the local leaders could here be killed in connection with rituals, or they were sacrificed at their master's funeral, presumably in order to serve him in the afterlife. For example, at potlatch feasts among various north-west coast groups, where extensive material goods were exchanged or destroyed, slaves could be sacrificed for the sake of giving prestige to their masters (Donald 1997, 235–236). Does archaeology reveal any such ranked societies in South Scandinavia during the Mesolithic? Some have stressed the complexity of the grave rituals at Skateholm and Henriksholm-Bøgebakken from the Early Ertebølle Culture, *c.* 5400–4700 cal BC. These reflect communities of several people divided in separate groups that were at least semi-sedentary, maybe claiming their own territorial rights, and where there were apparently social differences (Larsson 2016). These cemeteries were not the only ones that could indicate the existence of growing hunter-gatherer populations with some signs of institutionalised social ranking, as similar grave complexes such as Téviec and Hoëdic existed along the Atlantic coast of Western Europe at the same time (Newell & Constandse-Westermann 1988). Evidence of human sacrifice among these and other Mesolithic groups cannot easily be found, as our primary sources are limited to the graves themselves.

Mesolithic graves were mostly created for one person, but some burials also contain several individuals. In burials containing multiple individuals, it appears that all were placed simultaneously, and these have often been interpreted as specific events that were associated with drowning accidents (*e.g.*, Strøby Egede) (Brinch Petersen 1990), death during childbirth (*e.g.*, Henriksholm-Bøgebakken 8 and 15) and conflicts (*e.g.*, Henriksholm-Bøgebakken 19) (Albrethsen & Brinch Petersen 1977). Other double burials from this period containing adults and children or two adults can be attributed to infectious diseases or famine (Kannegaard Nielsen & Brinch Petersen 1993). All these South Scandinavian burial sites are dated from the Late Kongemose to the Early Ertebølle Cultures (approximately 6000–4700 cal BC). Very few articles have so far been published focusing on whether some of the double burials may represent human sacrifice, and especially on the question of whether one of the two individuals in the double burials (adult, child or infant) were forced or obliged to accompany the other individual into the grave (*ibid.*, 80). It has recently been suggested that it was perhaps culturally determined for one person to follow another in death in some of the burials at Nivå 10 in north Zealand, indicating that human sacrifice may have been an integrated practice within some Mesolithic hunter-gatherer societies (Lass Jensen 2016, 105). In general, there seems to be a typical view of these hunter-gatherer societies, one

in which they only rarely utilised the ritualised practices associated with intentional human sacrifices. However, this is mainly because it is simply difficult to observe such evidence in the burials.

Another reason is associated with the argument that human sacrifice is more common in stratified societies in which people have many different and competing interests, in contrast to egalitarian societies and intentions (Ember & Ember 1994, 217). Researchers nevertheless acknowledge that there is a relatively high proportion of especially double burials dating to the Mesolithic, which may extend beyond the natural interpretations of accidents, childbirth and ailments (Grünberg 2016, 16). In South Scandinavia, the percentage of documented double burials varies between 5% and 20% at burial places such as Skateholm I and II, Henriksholm-Bøgebakken, Tågerup and Nivå 10 (Albrethsen & Brinch Petersen 1977; Larsson 1988; Karsten & Knarrström 2003; Lass Jensen 2016). As mentioned, in European Mesolithic graves containing several individuals, the deceased were typically buried simultaneously (Grünberg 2016, 16). Several individuals may have died shortly after one another, for example, in cases of childbirth, accidents or disease. But there could also have been other causes, such as the practice of self-sacrifice or committing suicide to follow the deceased into the afterlife. These acts may have involved drowning or strangulation and would not therefore have been visible on the remains of the individuals in question. This is observed when survivors, typically women losing a male partner, experience a loss of status or shame, or material deprivation within their societies (Miller 2007, 138). Could such practices of self-sacrifice by suicide (*e.g.*, suttee) have been utilised by members of these hunter-gatherer societies? Is this why some older men who died first were covered by the body of a young female? This applies to burial 14 at Skateholm (Larsson 1988, 102), whilst in burial A137 at Nivå 10, a juvenile woman probably died first, as the grave was too short for the adult male found next to her, and his legs had to be bent to fit into the burial (Plate 3). In burial A137 at Nivå 10, the man may instead have depended upon the woman, as he had a healed thighbone fracture, which had grown back together at an angle, no doubt causing the man to have had a severe limp (Lass Jensen 2016, 105).

Infanticide in hunter-gatherer societies

Another phenomenon that could have occurred in hunter-gatherer societies and been reflected in the burial of multiple individuals together is the practice of infanticide (Miller 2007, 134). Infanticide is the deliberate killing of very young offspring, either directly by strangulation, poisoning or drowning, or indirectly by more prolonged practices, such as food deprivation. Such killings may have been undertaken due to deformations or disabilities of the child, or simply as the result of a lack of resources to take care of an additional family member, especially if the primary provider of the family had died (Vang Petersen 2016, 109). In these cases, the child may have been the subject of a 'mercy killing' and was then respectfully placed in the grave, following the adult provider into the afterlife. This was a relatively common custom, and in small, highly mobile Arctic societies, it was not always possible to save an infant whose mother had died. Instead of allowing the child to gradually die of hunger, because no other woman could be found to feed it, the father would immediately put the child to death. It was often suffocated and buried with its mother, so they could make journey to the land of the dead together, or in other cases, the infant child was simply buried alive (Freeman 1971; Chapman 1980). Could the 'mercy killing' of children explain burial 41 at Skateholm (Plate 4), where an older man was buried holding a child in the hocker position, with the child between his arms and facing his face (Larsson 1988, 131)? Another example is burial A129 at Nivå 10, where the adult male was in a bent position and there was only limited space for the child, thus indicating that the adult died first and the child followed shortly afterwards. The adult's arm lies across the child and may have been lifted when the child was placed in the grave (Lass Jensen 2016, 105). A similar later placement of a child is also observed in the double burial at Gøngehusvej, in which an adult woman has apparently been pushed aside to make space for a child (Brinch Petersen *et al.* 1993; Lass Jensen 2016, 105). Some single child burials were associated with natural death, but other burials containing remains of children aged three to six, apparently boys, contain numerous grave goods, and have been interpreted as possibly reflecting an inheritance system within these hunter-gatherer societies (Kannegaard Nielsen & Brinch Petersen 1993, 80). But most of the burials from this period are characterised by an absence of grave goods. An alternative interpretation might be that the special care expressed with which some children were given many objects to accompany them into the afterlife was due to the fact that they were sacrificed for the benefit of the whole community. We would generally expect many more burials containing children than the current evidence suggests, especially given that younger children have a much higher mortality rate in hunter-gatherer societies. However, there are perhaps also taphonomic reasons for the lack of buried children that are associated with shallower burial pits, which would have resulted in faster decomposition and exposure to scavenging animals.

The living dead

The clustering of some Mesolithic double burials at Skateholm I (Fahlander 2008, 36) and Nivå 10 (Lass Jensen 2016, 104) indicates that these burials in particular were marked or acknowledged in group memory. Markers in the form of stones overlying the burials or larger postholes have been recorded in graves at Skateholm, Bloksbjerg, Vedbæk Boldbaner and Gøngehusvej (Kannegaard & Brinch Petersen 1993, 77; Larsson 2016, 179). Awareness of the position of the burials is also indicated by the possible deliberate reopening of graves, during which the body parts of ancestors were removed and presumably used in ritual practices by their living descendants, as is reflected in the many loose human bones at numerous sites and within huts (Brinch Petersen 2001, 49; Lass Jensen 2006; 2009; Sørensen 2009). Many burials from the Mesolithic have been found near habitation sites, thus indicating an integration and lack of boundaries between the areas of the living and the dead. This was probably associated with a complex set of symbolic practices concerning loose bones, as many of these remains also have cut marks (Sørensen 2016, 69). Bones with cut marks, fresh fractures and marrow breakages could either represent ritualised practices involving the removal of body parts from the corpse after death or acts of cannibalism (Degerbøl 1942; Brinch Petersen 2001, 50; 2016, 55; Nilsson 2003, 81). The removed body parts from the corpse and circulation of these amongst the living may have functioned as material mediators and memories of the dead (Nilsson 2003, 362). Human flesh could, however, also have been part of the diet, because of famine or for its role in ritualised practice, although cannibalism (especially of the human brain) can have serious side effects and spread neurological diseases (Miller 2007, 99). Such loose human remains, including teeth or finger bones, may also have been used as amulets representing the protective powers of the ancestors, while other bones, such as skulls, could be evidence of headhunting and the taking of trophies from neighbouring enemies (Brinch Petersen 2016, 55). Others have argued that the loose bones seen in many Mesolithic contexts are evidence of violent enemy attacks (Brinch Petersen 2015, 107).

Killing enemies or intentional sacrifice?

Evidence of scalping has been identified on skulls from Dyrholmen (Degerbøl 1942) and Ålekisterbro (Brinch Petersen 2016, 55), found as loose bones together with faunal remains, that may represent trophies taken from enemies. Another scalped individual was buried at Skateholm I:33 and is perhaps either evidence of punishment or an act of sacrifice (Ahlström 2008, 59). A skull cult clearly existed during the Mesolithic, as this is evident from the groups of skulls at Grosse Ofnet, Hohlenstein-Stadel and Kaufertsberg in southern Germany (Grünberg 2000). Recent finds of skulls on stakes and in water have been documented at Motala in Sweden (Hallgren & Fornander 2016, 173; Hallgren *et al.* 2021). Strontium analysis has identified local and the non-local individuals at that location, and two of the disarticulated skulls are those of non-local people, which are therefore interpreted as the trophy heads of enemies (*ibid.*, 173). Interpersonal violence was common during the Mesolithic, as is apparent in the triple grave at Henriksholm-Bøgebakken 19 (Albrethsen & Brinch Petersen 1977, 14), containing an individual that was initially believed to have been an adult male (19A), but which should, however, probably be reinterpreted as a female (Meiklejohn *et al.* 2000), another woman (19C), based on the grave goods, as well as a one-year-old child (19B) (Plate 5). The latter woman (19A) was of 25–40 years of age and the child did not show any signs of violence.

However, a flint blade just below her chin could be evidence of a violent death (Brinch Petersen 2015, 143). The adult woman aged 25–30 (19A) had, however, definitely been killed by a bone lance- or spearhead, which was lodged between her second and third thoracic vertebrae (Albrethsen & Brinch Petersen 1977, 14). The precise impact position of the bone point indicates that this woman had been intentionally executed at close range, resulting in instant death (Brinch Petersen 2006). Was this execution a merciful act for the benefit of the local community as a whole or a hostile action against enemies or territorial intruders? The stable isotopic values ($\delta^{13}C$ and $\delta^{15}N$) of the woman (19A) and infant child (19B) do not reflect a different diet compared to the other individuals buried at Henriksholm-Bøgebakken, which thus indicates that these individuals could all have been local inhabitants of the Øresund region (Brinch Petersen 2015, 143). From the beginning of the Atlantic period (7000 cal BC) some animals became extinct on Zealand, such as the aurochs (*Bos primigenius*), elk (*Alces alces*) and brown bear (*Ursus arctos*), along with the polecat (*Mustela putorius*), badger (*Meles meles*) and lynx (*Lynx lynx*) (Aaris-Sørensen 2009), as Zealand became an island during this period. These changes were caused by the continuous melting of the North American ice sheet (Christensen 1993, 21), and these ecological shifts may have caused tensions within and between local communities and/or driven migrations between neighbouring territories, instigating increasing levels of conflict.

Many pendants made from the teeth of these extinct species have been found in burials on Zealand, suggesting that there were exchanges and travel across the Øresund between Zealand and Scania, where these animals were present (Vang Petersen 1990). The two regions were inhabited by several groups of hunter-gatherers, who may have come into conflict over the territorial rights to the best hunting or fishing grounds. Could such conflicts have resulted in the execution that was observed in burial 19 at Henriksholm-Bøgebakken? Evidence of violence in the form of cranial injuries has often been recorded on individuals within the Øresund region during the Late Mesolithic (Bennike 1985). Today, around 100 to 120 skeletons of a Mesolithic date are known from South Scandinavia, with around one in ten of these showing signs of serious injuries (Andersen 2015). Most skull injuries are observed in adult males, although some women also have serious injuries that were caused by violence. Most of the head injuries have healed, however, and only in three or four examples, involving the individuals buried at Henriksholm-Bøgebakken, Vængesø II, Skateholm and Tågerup, has this evidence of violence been fatal.

Mesolithic violence and mercy killings

Mesolithic violence has been interpreted as resulting from a higher population density within the region (Meiklejohn & Zvelebil 1991). However, new studies suggest that the skull injuries often only involved one blow rather than several, as is the norm in most actual conflict. The single skull injuries were previously interpreted as evidence of territorial conflicts between hunter-gatherer groups living in the Øresund region from around 6000 to 5400 cal BC, but the groups were very small in size and were therefore likely dependent on one another, with ties possibly established through intermarriage (Lass Jensen 2016, 104). In such an environment, violence would have been limited, with conflicts resulting more likely in injury rather than death. The execution in burial 19 at Henriksholm-Bøgebakken may therefore be the result of a different practice, one that was perhaps associated with ritualised killing, in which the bone lancehead was deliberately left in the victim's neck. The act of killing was followed by the carrying of the three individuals and then their placement next to one another in the same grave. This may be the most convincing evidence of the existence of human sacrifice within the hunter-gatherer societies of the southern Scandinavian Mesolithic and constitutes an alternative interpretation of the fate of these enigmatic individuals.

We should reiterate that human sacrifice is difficult to identify from most archaeological material. Based on evolutionary narratives that such practices are associated with societies with an increased amount of social hierarchy and wealth and status inequality, they are regarded as unlikely within egalitarian societies. But we should be open to the possibility of human sacrifice in hunter-gatherer societies, as it may have occurred in the form of mercy killings, in which children, and disabled or older family members followed the deceased into the grave as a regulated cultural practice. Double burials may be the empirical indicator of such behaviour. Detailed information about how the individuals have been placed in the grave, the order in which they were positioned and location of specific objects, provide crucial data, along with their sex and age, for the interpretation of various possible scenarios, including human sacrifice.

The Neolithic narratives about human sacrifice

In Neolithic societies, the appearance of human sacrifice is closely related to arguments concerning competition and the emergence of surplus production, population growth and increased social stratification, along with violence and conflicts over agrarian land (Sørensen 2014; Price & Gebauer 2017; Nielsen & Sørensen 2018; Nielsen & Nielsen 2020). The competitive aspect of Neolithic societies is apparent when one looks at the time that was spent on monumental constructions, which may have helped affirm the role of leaders and create social cohesion amongst greater numbers of individuals, as well as marking the territorial rights of those leaders in the landscape (Nielsen & Sørensen 2018, 16–19). Monuments created a visual link between the past, present and future, functioning as markers of the genealogical origins of those responsible for their construction. Meanwhile, they also signal the ability of the group to produce a significant surplus and mobilise a substantial workforce (Earle 2011, 35). Monument construction may therefore also have been a competitive measure of the capabilities of a social group and its leaders to create a surplus not only of supplies but also of status and authority. Differences in production surpluses would have enabled some groups to flourish, thus creating the foundation for a permanent degree of social stratification, in which chiefdoms or more archaic forms of chiefdoms could emerge (Kosse 1990, 284; Ember & Ember 1994, 236; Miller 2007, 263; Earle 2011). Chiefdom societies are characterised by a degree of redistribution which leads to increased inequality in the consumption and access to goods. The degree of social stratification is dependent upon the chief's success and ability to plan, organise and deploy labour, thus creating a constant surplus, in which some of the goods are exchanged in ceremonial and religious practices as offerings of objects, food products, animals and humans, in order to remain on good terms with nature and the powers that be.

The material culture and flint mining activities going on during the southern Scandinavian Neolithic suggest that the first farmers migrating to southern Scandinavia around 4000 cal BC originated from, or had close social relations with, the central European Michelsberg Culture (Biel *et al.* 1998; Klassen 2004; Sørensen 2014). Human skeletons from the Michelsberg Culture have been found in silo-shaped pits, in which the body interred last is sometimes carelessly placed and lacks any grave goods. This suggests that subordinate people were buried along with their masters, perhaps indicating the existence of slavery (Gronenborn 2001, 23–27; Jeunesse 2010a, 95; 2010b, 62). The Michelsberg Culture is also associated with mass graves containing the skeletons of men, women and children, which have been interpreted as evidence of raids and massacres (Wahl 2010; Gronenborn *et al.* 2017). The instability within the Michelsberg Culture could also explain the construction of causewayed enclosures. The causewayed enclosures are circular, oval or more irregularly shaped earthworks covering one or more hectares, which are enclosed by one or several palisades, fences and ditches, and are often located on elevated ground next to a stream (Andersen 1997). Some ditches are filled with finds and remains of human skeletons, which have been interpreted as cult sites: locations for death ceremonies and initial burials accompanied by feasting (Bertemes 1991; Andersen 1997; 1999). The enclosures may also have functioned as protective structures for goods and cattle, as well as defensive, political, social and ritual gathering places (Andersen 1997, 307; Christensen 2004, 142–151; Klassen 2014, 239; Nielsen & Nielsen 2020, 164). The varying size of such large-scale causewayed enclosures within the Michelsberg Culture indicates that, like the monumental burial structures, they were symbols of wealth and power for each individual society and their elites (Bertemes 1991, 456).

The planning of the causewayed enclosures was probably initiated by the elite within Michelsberg Culture societies, who competed with one another for land and territories. During times of continuous conflict and stress, some of these communities would have undertaken pioneering migrations towards different locations in Northern Europe that were populated by resourceful hunter-gatherers (Sheridan 2010; Sørensen 2014, 267–268). It was these Central European pioneering farmers who brought agriculture to southern Scandinavia through immigration. The pioneering farmers cleared the forest and learnt how to implement productive agrarian practices on the sandy soils of the moraine landscape of this new region (Sørensen 2014, 266). The cult practices of these first farmers from 4000 to 3800 cal BC were initially associated with wetlands, involving offerings of bog pots containing food products and depositions of stone axes (Nielsen 1977; Koch 1998). But interestingly, during the first centuries after the introduction of agriculture, these societies did not engage in the construction of large, monumental structures whilst clearing the landscape for cultivation. The pioneering learning behaviour, combined with a lack of any pre-existing large-scale organisation in the region, may partly explain why monumental structures and also human sacrifices only appeared a few centuries after farming was introduced into southern Scandinavia (Nielsen & Sørensen 2018, 19).

Monuments, feasts and sacrifices

In southern Scandinavia, the earliest long barrows and causewayed enclosures are dated to *c.* 3800/3750 BC (Beck 2013; Eriksen & Andersen 2014, 113–115; Sørensen 2014, 213–221; Klassen 2014). The founding burials in these monumental grave complexes are often associated with the individuals who occupied a high-ranking position in these early agrarian societies, but skeletal remains are unfortunately only rarely preserved, as the barrows are located on non-calcareous soils (Madsen 1993, 98; Nielsen & Sørensen 2018). Nevertheless, in a few cases, skeletal remains have been recorded. Surprisingly, these have been identified as being from very young individuals: a six-year-old child at Stengade (Skaarup 1975) and a juvenile in grave A at Bygholm Nørremark (Rønne 1979). It seems unlikely that these children and youngsters would have held a high-ranking position in their respective societies, so the burials instead probably indicate something other than rank. We suggest that these deceased young individuals may have belonged to wealthy families, who organised the construction of the earthen long barrows according to the traditions of the time, which would have included holding feasts for the dead. The economic wealth and social status of the monument builders is demonstrated by their ability to mobilise a surplus of resources and command a large workforce that extended beyond immediate kinship, both for the construction work itself, but possibly also for the feasts that would likely have been required to motivate and placate those involved (Hayden 2014). The slaughtering of domestic animals, which is recorded in pits near megaliths and causewayed enclosures, could be evidence of just such special occasions, when larger groups of people gathered (Strömberg 1968; 1971; Andersen 1997; 2000; Holten 2000; 2009; Persson & Sjögren 2001). The 'competitive feast model' is based on the ability to create a production surplus, thus stimulating increased rivalry between families. Theoretically, this competition creates hierarchies within individual families, as well as between different family groups, ultimately resulting in the construction of monumental structures (Tilley 1996, 113). Monument construction and its associated feasting therefore created a political arena for powerful individuals to display their legitimising power, and to create narratives and myths for the future, in which human sacrifices could play an important role (Holten 2000; Jeunesse *et al.* 2016; Adams 2019; Sørensen 2020).

For example, human sacrifice interpretation has also been applied to grave D in the long barrow at Bygholm Nørremark near Horsens. The grave contained four adult individuals, identified as one male and three females, with at least one of the females having been killed by force, possibly as a human sacrifice associated with the construction of the long barrow (Rønne 1979).[1] Another mass grave was also recorded at Skibshøj near Salling in northern Jutland, which contained five individuals ranging from a newborn to adults of 20–30 years of age. This suggests that the long barrows were not always constructed for high-ranking individuals, but could also contain graves with several individuals, who appear to have died and were buried at the same time (Jørgensen 1977). Could these graves containing several individuals be interpreted as human sacrifices or are we dealing with more natural explanations, such as accidents or diseases? It is clear that from around 3800 cal BC there is an increase in depositions of material culture and animals, as well as obvious evidence of human sacrifice, in southern Scandinavia (Nielsen 1977; Bennike & Ebbesen 1987; Karsten 1994; Koch 1998; Sjögren *et al.* 2017; Van Beek

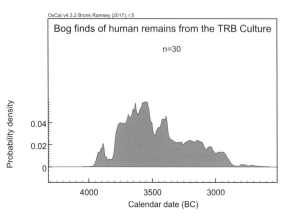

Figure 1.1. Radiocarbon dates of individuals found in wetland areas during the Early Neolithic (after Nielsen & Sørensen 2018).

et al. 2023) (Figure 1.1 and Table 1.1). Intensification of peat extraction during the Second World War resulted in the recovery of numerous bog finds, especially large numbers of human remains dating to the Neolithic, as a result of which a more detailed picture emerged (Ebbesen 1993) (Plate 6).

Human sacrifices in wetland areas

The construction of monumental structures is also contemporary with the first clear evidence of human sacrifice in southern Scandinavia. This is documented in wetland areas, where objects and animals were sacrificed. Economic growth may have resulted in a community being able to take specific objects out of use and undertake ceremonial sacrificial offerings (Ebbesen 1993; Karsten 1994; Koch 1998; Sjögren *et al.* 2017; Van Beek *et al.* 2023). Given the considerable investment in ritual activities during the Funnel Beaker Culture period (*c.* 4100–2800 BC), it is likely that ideology and its physical manifestations were a particularly important organisational factor in this phase of large-scale societal consolidation. The use of ideology and ritual practices may have evolved around prominent individuals, as described in Sahlins' (1963) 'big man' system, or possibly around important families and lineages, as in the formation of clan systems. It was also these highly competitive communities that were able to organise the communal building of up to 25,000 large megalithic monuments, including long and round dolmens and passage graves, during the later parts of the Early Neolithic and beginning of the Middle Neolithic (Skaarup 1993; Ebbesen 2011).

Human remains found in the bogs all over southern Scandinavia are of particular importance, as many of these date to the Early Neolithic and earlier part of the Middle Neolithic. These include young people probably aged 15–20 who have been subjected to violence; both sexes are represented almost equally and the age of the individuals varies from infants to adults (Bennike *et al.* 1986). These individuals fit the narrative of competing agrarian societies that are

Table 1.1. Radiocarbon dates of individuals found in wetland areas during the Early Neolithic (after Nielsen & Sørensen 2018).

Site nr.	Site	δC^{13}	Lab.nr	BP		Cal BC (2 sigma)	Ref.
0	Viksø Mose	−20.9	UCIA-232706	5050	15	3946–3791	Allentoft *et al.* 2022
1	Bodal Mose	−20.7	AAR-5360	5025	40	3945–3711	Heinemeier & Rud 2000
2	Saxtorp ind. 3		Ua-9808	4975	75	3946–3647	Sjögren *et al.* 2017
3	Hallonflickan		UBA-30518	4964	42	3928–3651	Sjögren *et al.* 2017
4	Veksø Mose	−20.5	Poz-17006	4985	27	3915–3696	Fischer *et al.* 2007
5	Ferle Enge	−22.6	K-6299	4940	95	3961–3527	Fischer *et al.* 2007
6	Tagmosegård	−22.4	K-6297	4873	45	3941–3377	Fischer *et al.* 2007
7	Näbbe Mosse		Lu-1828	4920	60	3934–3538	Sjögren *et al.* 2017
8	Trudstrupgård	−20.7	AAR-6881	4870	45	3765–3532	Fischer *et al.* 2007
9	Andemosen	−19.6	K-3579	4800	90	3764–3370	Bennike & Ebbesen 1987
10	Salpetermosen	−20.2	AAR-21343	4789	25	3641–3523	Jørgensen & Hagedorn 2015
11	Hesselbjerggårds Mose	−20.5	AAR-7310	4778	32	3643–3386	Fischer *et al.* 2007
12	Vængegårds Tørvefabrik		K-6300	4760	95	3760–3348	Sørensen 2014
13	Saxtorp ind. 1		Ua-9810	4760	75	3660–3369	Sjögren *et al.* 2017
14	Sandåkra		St-3771	4730	100	3712–3122	Sjögren *et al.* 2017
15	Härlingstorp		OxA-33832	4730	33	3635–3377	Sjögren *et al.* 2017
16	Hallebygård	−21.1	Poz-17025	4711	40	3633–3372	Fischer *et al.* 2007
17	Saxtorp ind. 2		Ua-9809	4690	75	3646–3196	Sjögren *et al.* 2017
18	Døjringe II	−20.5	K-3624	4670	90	3646–3109	Bennike & Ebbesen 1987
19	Porsmose	−20.4	K-3748	4664	90	3642–3106	Bennike & Ebbesen 1987
20	Døjringe I	−19.8	K-3623	4640	90	3636–3104	Bennike & Ebbesen 1987
21	Myrebjerg Mose		K-3702	4640	320	4218–2485	Bennike & Ebbesen 1987
22	Ulvemosen	−20.1	K-6306	4580	90	3630–3022	Fischer *et al.* 2007
23	Sigersdal B	−19.2	K-3745	4564	75	3519–3026	Bennike & Ebbesen 1987
24	Sigersdal A	−20.4	K-3744	4554	140	3631–2916	Bennike & Ebbesen 1987
25	Øgårde 13 Boat III	−20.5	K-3746	4509	60	3484–3015	Fischer *et al.* 2007
26	Boelkilde I/II	−22.6	K-4593	4487	65	3364–2937	Fischer *et al.* 2007
27	Østrup Mose 2 (II)		K-5741	4434	90	3552–2907	Sørensen 2014
28	Østrup Mose 2 Leda I		K-5742	4419	90	3348–2902	Sørensen 2014
29	Jordløse Mose XXXVI	−20.3	K-6302	4301	90	3328–2629	Fischer *et al.* 2007
30	Rolfsåker		Ua-7836	4430	70	3329–2916	Sjögren *et al.* 2017

in conflict with one another, resulting in either the capture or sacrifice of enemies, or the execution of individuals in these societies. The most well-known examples are two men from Boelkilde on Als, southern Jutland (*ibid.*, 1986), two young women from Sigersdal Mose on Zealand (Bennike & Ebbesen 1987) (Figure 1.2), an individual with a head injury from Stenstrup Mose and a skull with a fracture made with an axe from Salpetermosen (Jørgensen & Hagedorn 2015).

Important to the interpretation is the fact that some of the presumed sacrificed human bodies were found in the same bog environments as other sacrificed items. A 'bog pot' in the form of an intact, Early Neolithic lugged vessel was found between the two young women from Sigersdal

Mose and animal bones, consisting of ten goat skulls, were recovered from a neighbouring peat-digging hole. A hoard containing 13 polished, thin-butted flint axes was also deposited in the bog roughly 300 metres from the two young women (Bennike & Ebbesen 1987). This is one of the largest flint axe hoards known from Denmark and must have been regarded as highly valuable by the individual(s) making this offering.

The remains of a number of people have been found in bogs on the island of Langeland, most of which date to the Early-Middle Neolithic transition, *c.* 3300 BC. Skeletal remains of at least five individuals were found in Myrebjerg Mose: one adult woman, two young people aged

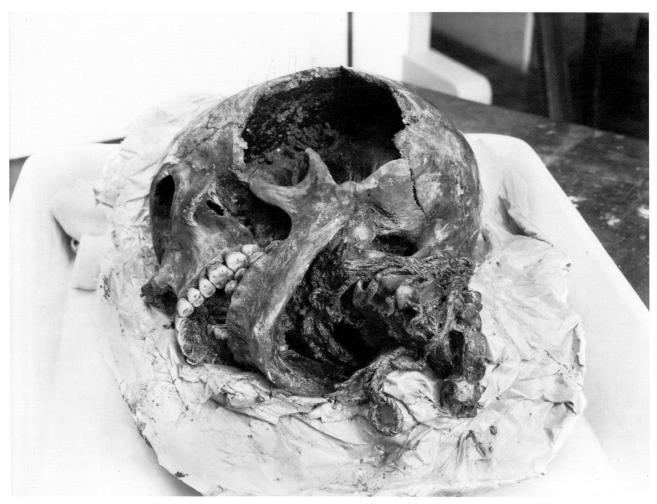

Figure 1.2. The skull of individual A from Sigersdal with the cord around the neck (photo: National Museum of Denmark).

respectively 15–18 and 18–20 years, and two children of respectively three and four years of age. These remains were found in a mixed pile of human and animal bones that was nearly 2 metres in diameter, in which some of the human skull fragments were concentrated (Skaarup 1985, 76–77). In the bog Gammellung, near Troldebjerg on Langeland, skeletal remains of two children, two women and another adult person were found together with numerous animal bones, including skulls of oxen killed with an axe blow to the forehead. One of the women, of 35–50 years of age, seems to have been killed with a blow to the top of her head (*ibid.*, 71–72). None of the human bones had been split like the animal bones or showed any other traces of cannibalism. They may therefore indicate that the human individuals were sacrificed during feasts, at which the flesh of wild and domestic animals was consumed, or at locations where these feasts took place.

Individuals from Boelkilde, Sigersdal and Stenstrup had a rope fixed around their neck, indicating that they did not voluntarily choose their death, but had to be strangled, and are therefore perhaps the most convincing examples of

human sacrifice in southern Scandinavia (Jørgensen 1987, 105; Nielsen & Sørensen 2018, 23). There is also the famous Porsmose individual from southern Zealand with a bone arrowhead lodged in the sternum, which could represent an execution of an enemy, punishment or a sacrifice (Becker 1952) (Plate 7). But how can we be sure that all these finds represent intentional sacrifices and not just the punishments of individuals who had committed crimes or otherwise done something wrong, such as violating some taboo? One important aspect, especially of the Boelkilde and Sigersdal examples, is that these individuals were found in pairs and were deposited shortly after one another. Other skeletons lying close to each other in bog contexts from the Early Neolithic have been documented at Døjringe near Sorø, with two males showing signs of trepanations, and in the Tysmosen bog, near Copenhagen, where two children of eight and ten years of age can also be interpreted as possible human sacrifices (Bennike & Ebbesen 1987, 93; Bennike 2006, 108). The bog bodies most likely reflect increasing violence amongst groups competing over territorial rights, which resulted in the taking of captives for use as slaves.

Strontium analysis of a young female, 'Hallonflickan' from the Falbygden area of Västergötland, western Sweden, suggests that she may have come from southern Sweden (Sjögren *et al.* 2017). Movement of captured people over long distances could have been part of a widespread ritualised practice, but also provides evidence of increasing levels of conflict.

In general, ritual sacrifice of captured people is also a sign of a social stratification, in which certain people control the lives of others. Such control could be practised in life as well as after death, as in the burying and reburying of individuals, or parts of individuals (*e.g.*, Moen & Walsh 2021). It is quite clear that violence occurred throughout the Neolithic in southern Scandinavia, where 32 out of 154 adult male individuals, primarily from passage grave contexts and bogs, show signs of violence (corresponding to 21%), whereas ten out of 83 women show evidence of violence (corresponding to 12%) (Fibiger *et al.* 2013). Many of the injuries to women do not show signs of healing, whereas the opposite applies to the males. Perhaps the injuries to the males were inflicted in ritualised conflicts that did not result in the killing of enemies, which could also explain the large number of healed trepanations on Neolithic individuals (Bennike 2006, 108). The injuries on the back of the skulls observed on the Neolithic women, however, indicate that they were lying prone when they suffered the blow, thus perhaps suggesting this is evidence of raids on enemies, although other interpretations could include the ritualised execution of rivals' families.

Concluding remarks

Again, human sacrifices are difficult to identify amongst the archaeological materials. In the case of hunter-gatherer burials, the interpretation of human sacrifice is seldom considered and other natural causes of death are instead preferred. But we should be open to the possibility that human sacrifices may have occurred in diverse ways, such as mercy killings and infanticide, in which children and disabled or older family members followed the deceased to the grave. The critical approach to the appearance of human sacrifice is not questioned to the same degree when interpreting sacrificed individuals from the Neolithic in southern Scandinavia. The appearance of human sacrifice as a symbolic behaviour within agrarian societies is part of a convincing narrative, which is associated with the emergence of group or individual status hierarchies, and the subsequent exertion of power over lower-ranking individuals. A central question regarding human sacrifices relates to the value of a human life within these societies – a question which still remains unanswered. In some communities a human may have been considered to have the same value as an animal or a specific object, while in other societies human life was valued in relation to a specific deity or some other exceptional unit

of comparison. In hunter-gatherer societies, with their high degree of mobility and exploitation of high and low prestige resources, other considerations of kinship may have been associated with human sacrifice. In Neolithic societies, the appearance of human sacrifice is closely related to the arguments concerning competition and the emergence of surplus production, population growth and increased social stratification, as well as violence and conflicts over agrarian land (Plate 8). More extensive and thorough studies of human remains from the Mesolithic and Neolithic are required in the future in order to investigate contextual details, as such information can alter the interpretation from random violence to a human sacrifice. Nevertheless, the individuals from Boelkilde, Sigersdal and Stenstrup with ropes tied around their necks still provide some of the most convincing evidence of human sacrifices dating to the Stone Age of southern Scandinavia.

Note

1   Since this chapter was written, new ^{14}C dates have separated Graves A and D in the long barrow at Bygholm Nørremark in time. Thus, it is difficult to uphold the assumption that the four individuals in grave D were subjected to retainer sacrifice.

References

Aaris-Sørensen, K. 2009. Diversity and dynamics of the mammalian fauna in Denmark throughout the last glacial-interglacial cycle, 115–0 kyr BP. *Fossils and Strata* November 2009: 57.

Adams, R.L. 2019. Building workforces for large stone monuments: The labour dynamics of a living megalithic tradition in Eastern Indonesia. In *Megaliths-Societies-Landscapes. Early Monumentality and Social Differentiation in Neolithic Europe*, edited by J. Müller, M. Hinz and M. Wunderlich, vol. 3, 1113–1132. Bonn: Habelt.

Ahlström, T. 2008. An early example of scalping from the Mesolithic cemetery Skateholm, Sweden. In *Traumatologische und pathologische Veränderungen an prähistorischen und historischen Skelettresten – Diagnose, Ursachen und Kontext. Interdisziplinärer Workshop in Rostock-Warnemünde, 17.–18. November 2006*, edited by J. Piek and T. Terberger, 59–66. Archäologie und Geschichte im Ostseeraum 3. Rahden: Verlag Marie Leidorf.

Albrethsen, S.E. & Brinch Petersen, E. 1977. Excavation of a Mesolithic cemetery at Vedbæk, Denmark. *Acta Archaeologica* 47, 1976, 1–28.

Andersen, S.H. 2015. Den voldsomme Jæger-fisker-stenalder. In *Krig og vold I fortiden*, edited by N.B. Thomsen, P. Hoffmann, B. Staal, J. Petersen, A. Tomlinson, I. Skibsted Klæsøe and F. Arntsen, 10–22. Sammenslutningen af Danske Amatørarkæologers 25-års-jubilæum. Højby: Nordvestgrafik.

Andersen, N.H. 1997. *The Sarup Enclosures. The Funnel Beaker Culture of the Sarup site including two causewayed camps compared to the contemporary settlements in the area and other European enclosures*. Jysk Arkæologisk Selskabs skrifter XXXIII:1. Højbjerg.

Andersen, N.H. 1999. *Saruppladsen. Sarup* vol. 2. Jysk Arkæologisk Selskabs Skrifter XXXIII(2). Højbjerg: Moesgård Museum.

Andersen, N.H. 2000. Kult og ritualer i den ældre bondestenalder. *Kuml* 2000, 13–57.

Beck, M.R. 2013. Højensvej Høj 7 – en tidligneolitisk langhøj med flere faser. *Aarbøger for nordisk Oldkyndighed og Historie* 2011–2012: 33–117.

Becker, C.J. 1952. Skeletfundet fra Porsmose ved Næstved. *Fra Nationalmuseets Arbejdsmark* 1952: 25–30.

Bennike, P. 1985. *Palaeopathology of Danish Skeletons. A Comparative Study of Demography, Disease and Injury*. København: Akademisk Forlag.

Bennike, P. 2006. Ancient trepanations and differential diagnoses – a re-evaluation of skeletal remains from Denmark. In *Frühe Spuren der Gewalt – Schädelverletzungen und Wundversorgung an prähistorischen Menschenresten aus interdisziplinärer Sicht. Workshop in Rostock-Warnemünde vom 2.-30. November 2003*, edited by J. Piek and T. Terberger, 107–114. Beiträge Zur Ur- Und Frühgeschichte Mecklenburg-Vorpommerns 41.

Bennike, P., Ebbesen, K. & Jørgensen, L.B. 1986. Early Neolithic skeletons from Bolkilde bog, Denmark. *Antiquity* 60: 199–209.

Bennike, P. & Ebbesen, K. 1987. The bog find from Sigersdal. Human sacrifice in the Early Neolithic; with a contribution by Lise Bender Jørgensen. *Journal of Danish Archaeology* 5, 1986, 85–115.

Bertemes, F. 1991. Untersucungen zur Funktion der Erdwerke der Michelsberger Kultur in Rahmen der kupferzeitlichen Zivilisation. In *Die Kupferzeit als historische Epoche. Symposium Saarbrücken und Otzenhausen 6.–13.11.1988*, edited by J. Lichardus, 441–464. Saarbrücker Beiträge zur Altertumskunde 55, Bonn: Rudolf Habelt.

Biel, J., Schlichtherle, H., Strobel, M. & Zeeb, A. (eds) 1998. *Die Michelsberger Kultur und ihre Randgebiete – Probleme der Entstehung, Chronologie und des Siedlungswesens. Kolloquium Hemmenhofen, 21–23.2. 1997*. Materialhefte zur Archäologie in Baden-Württemberg, Heft 43. Stuttgart: Konrad Theiss Verlag.

Brinch Petersen, E. 1990. Nye grave fra jægerstenalderen. Strøby Egede og Vedbæk. *Nationalmuseets Arbejdsmark*, 9–31.

Brinch Petersen, E. 2001. Mesolitiske grave og skeletter. In *Danmarks Jægerstenalder – status og perspektiver*, edited by O. Lass Jensen, S.A. Sørensen and K.M. Hansen, 43–58. Hørsholm: Hørsholm Egns Museum.

Brinch Petersen, E. 2006. Manipulation of the Mesolithic body. In *Frühe Spuren der Gewalt – Schädelverletzungen und Wundversorgung an prähistorischen Menschenresten aus interdisziplinärer Sicht. Workshop RostockWarnemünde 2003*, edited by J. Piek and T. Terberger, 43–50. Beiträge zur Ur- und Frühgeschichte Mecklenburg Vorpommerns 41.

Brinch Petersen, E. 2015. Diversity of Mesolithic Vedbæk. *Acta Archaeologica* 86(1) (Acta Archaeologica Supplementa XVI): 19–202.

Brinch Petersen, E. 2016. Afterlife in the Danish Mesolithic – the creation, use and discarding of 'Loose Human Bones'. In *Mesolithic Burials – Rites, Symbols and Social Organisation of Early Postglacial Communities. International Conference Halle (Saale), Germany, 18th–21st September 2013*, edited by J. Grünberg, B. Gramsch, L. Larsson, J. Orschiedt and H. Meller, Band 13/I, 47–62. Tagungen des Landesmuseums für Vorgeschichte Halle.

Brinch Petersen, E., Meiklejohn, C. & Alexandersen, V. 1993. Vedbæk. Graven midt i byen. *Nationalmuseets Arbejdsmark*, 61–68.

Chapman M. 1980. Infanticide and fertility among Eskimos: a computer simulation. *American Journal of Physical Anthropology* 53(2): 317–327.

Christensen, C. 1993. Land and sea. In *Digging into the Past. 25 Years of Archaeology in Denmark*, edited by S. Hvass and B. Storgaard, 20–27. The Royal Society of Northern Antiquaries & Jutland Archaeological Society. Aarhus: Aarhus University Press.

Christensen, J. 2004. Warfare in the European Neolithic. *Acta Archaeologica* 73: 129–156.

Degerbøl, M. 1942. Om Kannibalisme i Danmarks Stenalder. Dyr i Natur og Museum. *Aarbog for Universitetets zoologiske Museum* 1941: 25–43.

Donald, L. 1997. *Aboriginal Slavery on the Northwest Coast of North America*. Berkeley: University of California Press.

Earle, T. 2011. Chiefs, chieftaincies, chiefdoms, and chiefly confederacies: Power in the evolution of political systems. *Social Evolution & History* 10(1): 27–54.

Ebbesen, K. 1993. Simple, tidligneolitiske grave. *Aarbøger for Nordisk Oldkyndighed og Historie* 1992: 47–102.

Ebbesen, K. 2011. *Danmarks Megalitgrave* Bind 1,1–2. København: Forfatterforlaget Attika.

Ember, C.R. & Ember, M. 1994. *Cultural Anthropology*. 7th edition. New Jersey: Prentice Hall.

Eriksen, P. & Andersen, N.H. 2014. *Stendysser. Arkitektur og funktion*. Aarhus: Ringkøbing Skjern Museum/Moesgaard Museum/Jysk Arkæologisk Selskabs Skrifter 85.

Fahlander, F. 2008. A piece of the Mesolithic. Horizontal stratigraphy and bodily manipulations at Skateholm. In *The Materiality of Death, Bodies, Burials, Beliefs*, edited by F. Fahlander & T. Oestigaard, 29–45. Oxford: British Archaeological Report IS 1768.

Fibiger, L., Ahlström, T., Bennike, P. & Schulting, R.J. 2013. Patterns of violence-related skull trauma in Neolithic southern Scandinavia. *American Journal of Physical Anthropology* 150: 190–202.

Fitzhugh, B. 2003. *The Evolution of Complex Hunter-gatherers: Archaeological Evidence from the North Pacific*. Interdisciplinary Contributions to Archaeology. New York: Springer Science & Business Media.

Freeman, M.M.R. 1971. A Social and Ecologic Analysis of Systematic Female Infanticide among the Netsilik Eskimo. *American Anthropologist*, New Series, 73(5): 1011–1018.

Gronenborn, D. 2001. Zum (möglichen) Nachweis von Sklaven/Unfreien in prähistorischen Gesellschaften Mitteleuropas. *Ethnographish-Archäologische Zeitschrift* 42: 1–42.

Gronenborn, D., Strien, H.-C. & Lemmen, C. 2017. Population dynamics, social resilience strategies and adaptive cycles in early farming societies of SW Central Europe. *Quaternary International* 446: 54–65.

Grünberg, J.M. 2000. *Mesolithische Bestattungen in Europa. Ein Beitrag zur vergleichenden Gräberkunde* I–II. Internationale Archäologie 40. Rahden/Westfalen: Verlag Marie Leidorf.

Grünberg, J.M. 2016. Mesolithic burials – rites, symbols and social organization of early postglacial communities. In *Mesolithic Burials – Rites, Symbols and Social Organisation* of Early Postglacial Communities. International Conference Halle (Saale), Germany, 18th–21st September 2013*, edited by J. Grünberg, B. Gramsch, L. Larsson, J. Orschiedt and H. Meller, Band 13/I, 13–24. Tagungen des Landesmuseums für Vorgeschichte Halle.

Hallgren, F. & Fornander, E. 2016. Skulls on stakes and skulls in water. Mesolithic mortuary rituals at Kanaljorden, Motala, Sweden 7000 BP. In *Mesolithic Burials – Rites, Symbols and Social Organisation of Early Postglacial Communities. International Conference Halle (Saale), Germany, 18th–21st September 2013*, edited by J. Grünberg, B. Gramsch, L. Larsson, J. Orschiedt and H. Meller, Band 13/I, 161–174. Tagungen des Landesmuseums für Vorgeschichte Halle.

Hallgren, F., Berggren, K., Arnberg, A., Hartzell, L. & Larsson, B. 2021. *Kanaljorden, Motala. Rituella våtmarksdepositioner och boplatslämningar från äldre stenålder, tngre stenålder och järnalder*. Väserås: Stiftelsen Kulturmiljövård. Rapport 2021: 12.

Hayden, B. 2014. *The Power of Feasts, from Prehistory to the Present*. New York: Cambridge University Press.

Holten, L. 2000. Death, danger, destruction and unintended megaliths. An essay on human classification and its material and social consequences in the Neolithic of South Scandinavia. In *Neolithic Orkney and its European Context*, edited by A. Rithie, 287–297. Cambridge: McDonald Institute Monographs.

Holten, L. 2009. Åbninger til en anden virkelighed. Megalitanlæg som mediatorer mellem her og hisset. In *Plads og rum i tragtbægerkulturen. Bidrag fra Arbejdsmødet på Nationalmuseet, 22. september 2005*, edited by A. Schülke, 159–177. Nordiske Fortidsminder Ser. C, bind 6. Det Kongelige Nordiske Oldskriftselskab, København.

Jeunesse 2010a. Die Michelsberger Kultur. Eine Kultur ohne Friedhöfe. In *Jungsteinzeit im Umbruch. Die 'Michelsberger Kultur' und Mitteleuropa vor 6000 Jahren*, edited by C. Lichter, 90–95. Karlsruhe: Badisches Landesmuseum.

Jeunesse 2010b. Das Erdwerk von Mairy und seine grossen Gebäude. In *Jungsteinzeit im Umbruch. Die 'Michelsberger Kultur' und Mitteleuropa vor 6000 Jahren*, edited by C. Lichter, 62. Karlsruhe: Badischen Landesmuseum.

Jeunesse, C., Le Roux, P. & Boulestin, B. (eds) 2016. *Mégalithismes vivants et passes: approches croisées* (Living and Past Megalithisms: Interwoven Approaches). Oxford: Archaeopress Archaeology.

Jørgensen, E. 1977. Brændende langdysser. *Skalk* 5: 7–13.

Jørgensen, L.B. 1987. The string from Sigersdal Mose. *Journal of Danish Archaeology* 5, 1986, 105–106.

Jørgensen, T. & Hagedorn, L. 2015. Salpetermoseliget. *Alle tiders Nordsjælland. Museum Nordsjællands årbog* 2015, 118–122.

Kannegaard Nielsen, E. & Brinch Petersen, E. 1993. Burials, people and dogs. In *Digging into the Past. 25 Years of Archaeology in Denmark*, edited by S. Hvass and B. Storgaard, 76–81. The Royal Society of Northern Antiquaries & Jutland Archaeological Society. Aarhus: Aarhus University Press.

Karsten, P. 1994. *Att kasta yxan i sjön. En studie över rituel tradition och förändring utifrån skånska neolitiska offerfynd*. Stockholm: Acta Archaeologica Lundensia Series in 8°, No. 23.

Karsten, P. & Knarrström, B. 2003. *The Tågerup Excavations*. Lund: National Heritage Board, Archaeological Excavations Department.

Klassen, L. 2004. *Jade und Kupfer. Untersuchungen zum Neolithisierungsprozess im westlichen Ostseeraum unter besonderer Berücksichtung der Kulturentwicklung Europas 5500–3500 BC*. Jutland Archaeological Society Publications 47. Aarhus: Moesgård Museum.

Klassen, L. 2014. *Along the Road. Aspects of Causewayed Enclosures in South Scandinavia and Beyond*. East Jutland Museum/ Moesgaard Museum. Aarhus: Aarhus University Press.

Koch, E. 1998. *Neolithic Bog Pots from Zealand, Møn, Lolland and Falster*. Nordiske Fortidsminder Ser. B, Vol. 16, Det Kgl. Nordiske Oldskriftselskab, København.

Kosse, K. 1990. Group size and societal complexity: Thresholds in the long-term memory. *Journal of Anthropological Archaeology* 9: 275–303.

Larsson, L. 1988. *Et fångstsamhälle för 7000 år sedan*. Kristianstad: Signum.

Larsson, L. 2016. Some aspects of mortuary practices at the Late Mesolithic cemeteries at Skateholm, southernmost Sweden. In *Mesolithic Burials – Rites, Symbols and Social Organisation of Early Postglacial Communities. International Conference Halle (Saale), Germany, 18th–21st September 2013*, edited by J. Grünberg, B. Gramsch, L. Larsson, J. Orschiedt and H. Meller, Band 13/I, 175–184. Tagungen des Landesmuseums für Vorgeschichte Halle.

Lass Jensen, O. 2006. Stenalderjægernes hytter og grave ved Nivå. *Hørsholm Egns Museum, Årbog* 2005–2006: 6–31.

Lass Jensen, O. 2009. Dwellings and graves from the Late Mesolithic site of Nivå 10, eastern Denmark. In *Mesolithic Horizons. Papers presented at the Seventh International Conference on the Mesolithic in Europe, Belfast*, edited by S. McCartan, S. Schulting, G. Warren and P. Woodman, 465–472. Oxford: Oxbow Books.

Lass Jensen, O. 2016. Double burials and cremations from the Late Mesolithic site of Nivå 10, eastern Denmark. In *Mesolithic Burials – Rites, Symbols and Social Organisation of Early Postglacial Communities. International Conference Halle (Saale), Germany, 18th–21st September 2013*, edited by J. Grünberg, B. Gramsch, L. Larsson, J. Orschiedt and H. Meller, Band 13/I, 95–108. Tagungen des Landesmuseums für Vorgeschichte Halle.

Madsen, T. 1993. Barrows with timber-built structures. In *Digging into the Past. 25 Years of Archaeology in Denmark*, edited by S. Hvass and B. Storgaard, 96–99. The Royal Society of Northern Antiquaries & Jutland Archaeological Society. Aarhus: Aarhus University Press.

Meiklejohn, C. & Zvelebil, M. 1991. Health status of European populations at the agricultural transition and the implications for the adoption of farming. In *Health in Past Societies: Biocultural Interpretations of Human Skeletal Remains in Archaeological Context*, edited by H. Bush and M. Zvelebil, 129–145. Oxford: British Archaeological Report IS 567.

Meiklejohn, C., Brinch Petersen, E. & Alexandersen, V. 2000. Anthropology and archaeology of Mesolithic gender in the western Baltic. In *Gender and Material Culture: from Prehistory to the Present*, edited by M. Donald and L. Hurcombe, 227–237. London: Macmillan Press.

Miller, B. 2007. *Cultural Anthropology*. 4th edition. Boston: Pearson.

Moen, M. & Walsh, M. 2021. Agents of death: Reassessing social agency and gendered narratives of human sacrifice in the Viking Age. *Cambridge Archaeological Journal* 31(4): 597–611.

Newell, R.R. & Constandse-Westermann, T. 1988. The significance of Skateholm I and Skateholm II to the Mesolithic of Western Europe. In *The Skateholm Project I. Man and Environment*, edited by L. Larsson, 164–174. Acta Regiae Societatis Humaniorum Litterarum Lundensis. Stockholm: Almqvist & Wiksell International.

Nielsen, P.O. 1977. Die Flintbeile der frühen Trichterbecherkultur in Dänemark. *Acta Archaeologica* 48: 61–138.

Nielsen, P.O. & Sørensen, L. 2018. The formation of social rank in the Early Neolithic of Northern Europe. *Acta Archaeologica* 89: 15–29.

Nielsen, P.O. & Nielsen, F.O.S. 2020. *First Farmers on the Island of Bornholm*. Nordiske Fortidsminder vol. 32. Copenhagen: The Royal Society of Northern Antiquaries/University Press of Southern Denmark.

Nilsson, L.S. 2003. Embodied rituals and ritualized bodies. Tracing ritual practices in Late Mesolithic burials. *Acta Archaeologica Lundensia* 46. Stockholm: Almqvist & Wiksell International.

Persson, P. & Sjögren, K.-G. 2001. *Falbygdens gånggrifter. Del 1. Undersökningar 1985–1998*. GOTARC, Series C, Vol. 34. Göteborg: Institutionen för Arkeologi.

Price, T.D. & Gebauer, A.B. 2017. The emergence of social inequality in the context of Early Neolithic Northern Europe. In *Rebellion and Inequality in Archaeology*, edited by S. Hansen and J. Müller, 135–152. Human Development in Landscapes 11. Universitätsforschungen zur prähistorischen Archäologie 308. Bonn: Habelt.

Rønne, P. 1979. Høj over høj. *Skalk* 5: 3–8.

Sahlins, M.D. 1963. Poor man, rich man, big man, chief: Political types in Melanesia and Polynesia. *Comparative Studies in Society and History* V(3): 285–303.

Sheridan, A. 2010. The Neolithisation of Britain and Ireland: The big picture. In *Landscapes in Transition*, edited by B. Finlayson and G. Warren, 89–105. Oxford: Oxbow Books.

Sjögren, K.-G., Ahlström, T., Blank, M., Price, T.D., Frei, K.M. & Hollund, H.I. 2017. Early Neolithic human bog finds from Falbygden, western Sweden: New isotopic, osteological and histological investigations. *Journal of Neolithic Archaeology* 27(December): 97–126. doi:10.12766/jna.2017.4.

Skaarup, J. 1975. *Stengade. Ein langeländischer Wohnplatz mit Hausresten aus der frühneolithischen Zeit*. Rudkøbing: Meddelelser fra Langelands Museum.

Skaarup, J. 1985. *Yngre stenalder på øerne syd for Fyn*. Rudkøbing: Meddelelser fra Langelands Museum.

Skaarup, J. 1993. Megalithic graves. In *Digging into the Past. 25 Years of Archaeology in Denmark*, edited by S. Hvass and B. Storgaard, 104–109. The Royal Society of Northern Antiquaries & Jutland Archaeological Society. Aarhus: Aarhus University Press.

Strömberg, M. 1968. *Der Dolmen Trollasten in St. Köpinge, Schonen*. Acta Archaeologica Lundensia, Series in 8°, N° 7, Lund.

Strömberg, M. 1971. *Die Megalithgräber von Hagestad. Zur Problematik von Grabbauten und Grabriten*. Acta Archaeologica Lundensia, Series in 8°, N° 9, Lund.

Sørensen, L. 2014. *From Hunter to Farmer in Northern Europe. Migration and Adaptation during the Neolithic and Bronze Age*. Acta Archaeologica Supplementa Vol. XV. Oxford: Wiley.

Sørensen, L. 2020. Monuments and social stratification within the early Funnel Beaker Culture in South Scandinavia. In *Monumentalising Life in the Neolithic: Narratives of Change and Continuity*, edited by A.B. Gebauer, L. Sørensen, A. Teather and A.C. de Valera, 73–87. Oxford: Oxbow Books.

Sørensen, S.A. 2009. Lollikhuse, a site from the transitional phase between the Mesolithic and Neolithic in Denmark. In *Mesolithic Horizons. Papers Presented at the Seventh International Conference on the Mesolithic in Europe, Belfast*, edited by S.B. McCartan, R. Schulting, G. Warren and P. Woodmann, 541–547. Oxford: Oxbow Books.

Sørensen, S.A. 2016. Loose human bones from the Danish Mesolithic. In *Mesolithic Burials – Rites, Symbols and Social Organisation of Early Postglacial Communities. International Conference Halle (Saale), Germany, 18th–21st September 2013*, edited by J. Grünberg, B. Gramsch, L. Larsson, J. Orschiedt and H. Meller, Band 13/I, 63–72. Tagungen des Landesmuseums für Vorgeschichte Halle.

Tilley, C. 1996. *An Ethnography of the Neolithic. Early Prehistoric Societies in Southern Scandinavia*. New Studies in Archaeology. Cambridge: Cambridge University Press.

Van Beek, R., Quik, C., Bergerbrant, S., Huisman, F. & Kama, P. 2023. Bogs, bones and bodies: The deposition of human remains in northern European mires (9000 BC–AD 1900). *Antiquity* 97(391): 120–140. doi:10.15184/aqy.2022.163.

Vang Petersen, P. 1990. Eksotiske faunarester i Kongemose- og Ertebølletid et resultat af udveksling? *Hikuin* 16: 17–30.

Vang Petersen, P. 2016. Papooses in the Mesolithic? A reinterpretation of tooth and snail shell ornaments found in grave 8 at Bøgebakken and other Mesolithic burials. In *Mesolithic Burials – Rites, Symbols and Social Organisation of Early Postglacial Communities. International Conference Halle (Saale), Germany, 18th–21st September 2013*, edited by J. Grünberg, B. Gramsch, L. Larsson, J. Orschiedt and H. Meller, Band 13/I, 109–124. Tagungen des Landesmuseums für Vorgeschichte Halle.

Wahl, J. 2010. Wenige Knochen, viele Fragen. Auf der Suche nach den Menschen der Michelsberger Kultur. In *Jungsteinzeit im Umbruch. Die 'Michelsberger Kultur' und Mitteleuropa vor 6000 Jahren*, edited by C. Lichter, 96–101. Karlsruhe: Badisches Landesmuseum.

Societies that sacrifice? Examining the potential for attendant sacrifices in the Nordic Bronze Age

Matthew J. Walsh and Samantha S. Reiter

Abstract

This chapter investigates the possibility of attendant sacrifices in graves from the Nordic Bronze Age. In particular, we look at a sample of double graves from the period in which a single, primary inhumation appears to be accompanied by a secondary burial of an individual(s) that appears to have been treated in death in a manner different from that of the primary burial (e.g., the secondary individual was cremated at a time at which cremation was not the norm and placed in a subordinate position to the primary burial). We suggest that this may point to the practice of attendant sacrifices made as part of the funerary rites of elite individuals during the Nordic Bronze Age. We discuss possible logics for such sacrificial practices in relation to Nordic Bronze Age social and wealth hierarchies and the exceptional disparities between the treatments of individuals of differing social classes which appeared during this period. We suggest, for example, that human victims may have been seen as valuable graves goods for use in the afterlife, or that such sacrifices may have been sanctioned by the elite as conspicuous acts used to signal and affirm wealth and power.

Keywords: attendant sacrifice, Nordic Bronze Age, social hierarchy, status inequality, double graves, *herostratic* offerings

Introduction

Research across the social sciences links periods of socio-political upheaval with intra-societal violence (Osella & Osella 2003; Broch-Due 2004). Although that violence can take many forms, there seems to be a distinct link particularly between sacrificial violence and the emergence of wealth- and hierarchical status-based social identities as by-products of polity formation (Shulman 2003; Pacheco-Forés *et al.* 2021). While scholars have pointed to the European Bronze Age as a potential point of origin for modern Europe (Demakopoulou *et al.* 1998; Tarschys 1998) due to the emergence of Europe's first economic World System (Wallerstein 1974; Sherratt 1993; Kristiansen 1994; Harding 2013) and the complex and widespread social and political networks which united disparate groups across the continent (Rowlands 1980; Kristiansen & Larsson 2005; Bentley *et al.* 2009; Holst *et al.* 2013; Nosch *et al.* 2013; Vandkilde 2016; 2017; Kaul 2017; Kristiansen 2017; Ling *et al.* 2018; Mittnik *et al.* 2019; Kristiansen *et al.*

2020; Johnston 2021), archaeologists have nonetheless noted a marked dearth of evidence suggesting beyond reasonable doubt that human sacrifice was practised during this period (Glob 1969; Becker 1971; Ebbesen 1993; Green 2001).

This paper addresses the Bronze Age sacrifice question by examining Danish and north German material from a specific temporal phase, namely the Nordic Bronze Age (henceforth NBA), which ranged from *c.* 1800–500 BCE (Jensen 1982; Vandkilde 1996; Hornstrup *et al.* 2012). While in many cases the sometimes acidic soils of Scandinavia do not support bone preservation on their own (Hedges 2002; Turner-Walker & Peacock 2008; Kibblewhite *et al.* 2015; Snoeck *et al.* 2015), other preservation conditions (especially for organic remains) are often exceptional. Conditions such as those promoting the preservation of remains from wetland depositions recovered from Neolithic and Iron Age contexts (Bennike *et al.* 1986a; 1986b; Ebbesen 1993; van der Sanden 1996; Breuning-Madsen & Holst 1998; Breuning-Madsen

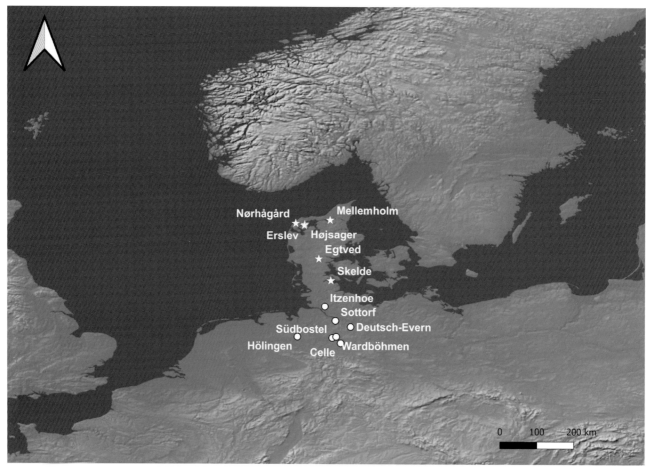

Figure 2.1. Map showing locations of the Danish (white stars) and German (white dots) graves discussed in the text. Map generated using QGIS with Natural Earth basemap.

et al. 2003) make it more likely that evidence for human sacrifice would survive within those contexts, should it have been present.

There are numerous finds of NBA votive offerings in wetlands (including war-booty, hoards of bronze artefacts and the remains of animal sacrifices; Müller 1886; Becker 1947; Lund 2002), but paradoxically little suggests the presence of the same or similar types of human sacrifice traditions in this period as can be observed in both earlier and later historical phases. Here, we present that what seems at first to be a lack of human sacrifice in the region during this period may be more a question of comparative perspective and how different forms of sacralised human killings or the ritual use of human bodies are interpreted. In the following, we first present a discussion of human sacrifice and some key characteristics of societies that practice it before applying this framework to a consideration of the NBA evidence from Denmark and northern Germany. To this end, we have selected a subset of NBA graves which have heightened sacrificial connotations: namely, those in which inhumation burials of high-status individuals were accompanied by the deposition of cremated human remains, seemingly

as grave goods rather than burials in the normative sense. These include graves from the Danish mainland (Jutland) and from northern Germany (see Figure 2.1).

Sacrifice and attendant sacrifice in context

By definition, 'sacrifice' means 'to make sacred' (Hubert & Mauss 1964 (1899); Insoll 2011). However, it is understood to also include the dedication of an object, animal or person to a specific higher purpose (Beattie 1980). For this reason, there has been a significant amount of debate about the difference between 'sacrifice' and 'offering' (*e.g.*, Firth 1963; Henninger 1987; Schwartz 2007; Oras 2013). Although there are many permutations of human sacrifice across space and time (see *e.g.*, Hubert & Mauss 1964 (1899); Bourdillon & Fortes 1980; Lincoln 1991, 204; Bloch 1992; McClymond 2008; Murray 2016), for the purposes of this paper, we concentrate on a specific variety of sacrificial practice: so-called attendant (or 'retainer') sacrifices (for discussion, see Testart 2004). We define attendant sacrifice as the ritualised killing of a secondary living being (animal or human) in direct relation to the burial of a high-status individual, with the killing of the attendant meant as a supplementary obligation of some sort towards the deceased. Survey of the available data indicates that such attendant sacrifices seem to have been widespread throughout the ancient world (Trigger 2007, 88–89).

Folklore, myth and historical accounts hint at various goals associated with what seems to have become well-established practices of attendant sacrifice in prehistoric Northern Europe (Green 1998; Aldhouse-Green 2001). For example, in the highly animistic cosmology of pre-Christian Northern Europe (see *e.g.*, Ahlqvist & Vandkilde 2018; Kveiborg *et al.* 2020), it is entirely feasible that the recently deceased could have been seen to be transformed into any number of *transempirical*, metaphysical entities (Geertz 1999, 460) – such as ancestor guardian spirits or even demigods – to be expiated, appeased or adored through sacrifice. By contrast, within ancient Norse religion, the concept of providing servants for elites recently departed to the afterlife (*i.e.*, through human sacrifice) may have been *de rigueur* (see *e.g.*, Davidson 1964; Turville-Petre 1964; Lincoln 1986; Hedeager 1999; Nässtrom 2002; Price 2002; Andrén *et al.* 2006).[1] Whether or not the intentions of these sacrifices were similar or dissimilar, we hypothesise that the societies which practised them embodied distinct technological, socio-political and even cultural similarities, which we have termed 'characteristics of societies that sacrifice'.

Characteristics of societies that sacrifice

Where sacrifice has become a research topic for social scientists, its presence tends to be viewed on a very local or regional scale, perhaps due to the quite specific denominations which sacrifice takes in accordance with the unique demands of a society that practices it. Most recent studies have tended to focus on human sacrifice as a potential means of asserting social and political control (*e.g.*,Watts *et al.* 2016). However, survey of the relevant literature addressing cross-cultural sacrificial practices has allowed us to identify several overarching hallmarks which build upon these ideas (see Table 2.1).

Thematic debate concerning the European Bronze Age in general, as well as the NBA specifically, illustrates significant societal concern with all of the aspects detailed above:

1. heightened symbolic thinking associated with representations of regional belonging especially concerning

Table 2.1. *Characteristics of societies which practice sacrifice and appropriate literature.*

	Characteristic	Reasoning	References
I.	Social complexity	Etymologically, the term 'sacrifice' means 'to make sacred'. Therefore, by sacrificing some thing or someone, that offering becomes a symbol. It transcends its prior identity and takes on a potential myriad of re-understood symbolic meanings and values. In a very real sense, it is transformed from the actual to the abstract. Although abstract thinking may have been present across the human timeline, theorists have made associations between more complex symbolic thinking and developed, more sedentary (agrarian) societies, probably due to the heightened amount of social interactions therewith associated (Gillespie 2011).[1]	(Bremmer 2007; Smith 2015; Westermarck 2016)
II.	Centralised power/ rise of urbanism	The emergence of centralised power structures and establishment of social hierarchies (however they may arise) ultimately stem from differences in resource management and the arrival of communities robust enough to support professional specialisation, *e.g.*, a priestly class. Invariably, this leads to societies defined to varying degrees by 'haves' and 'have nots'. In order for a sacrifice to have meaning, it must have value, and that value must be perceived as 'sacred' within the given society. But the sacred and its associated values are inherently measured on the sliding scale of social, economic and cosmological difference, and must be weighted in culturally relative terms.	(Beattie 1980; Conte & Kim 2016; van Dijk 2007; Frankfort 1948, Frazer 2017; Mumford 1961; Watts *et al.* 2016; 2016; Winkelman 1998; 2014)
III.	Collective identity	In order for hierarchical societies (*i.e.*, those with complex social hierarchies, wealth inequality, *etc.*) to function, internal differences are balanced against a sense of collective identity; and series of inter- and intra-group boundaries between an 'us' and a 'them' must be established and maintained (*i.e.*, the formation of the 'Other').	(More 1895; Hubert & Mauss 1964; Beattie 1980; Shulman 2003; Pacheco-Forés 2020)
IV.	Outside threat	The collective identity described above is often maintained and reinforced by common goals: *e.g.*, fighting famine and/or enemies (*e.g.*, rival city states/imperial competitors real or perceived). A common cause or foe(s) goes a long way towards enshrining in-group social cohesion.	(Tacitus 1811; Todorov 1992; Whitehouse 2013, 2017; Winkelman 1998)

[1]   Here we should acknowledge Frazer's (1925) contention that the annual necessity to set aside seed for seed crops to ensure the next year's harvest was conceptualised as a sort of 'offering' and may also have played a formative role in associations within agrarian societies and their sacrificial traditions relating ritualised destruction and loss to the fertility of the land and by natural proxy to the fecundity and prosperity of humankind.

elite females (Wels-Weyrauch 1989b; Jockenhövel 1991; 1995; Brück 2009) and males (Jockenhövel 1980; Kristiansen 1984; Wels-Weyrauch 1989a; Treherne 1995);

2. the emergence of social hierarchies and centralised power as 'culture and society demonstrably changed from a backward-looking, ancestral focus to one which projected outwards from the individual' (Renfrew 1974; Shennan 1982; Clarke & Cowie 1985; Reiter 2014, 17);

3. an increase in displays of individual identity and status in funerary contexts (*e.g.*, individual barrow burial as opposed to *e.g.*, communal identity, such as would be visible in megalithic tombs), especially as relating to costume and the expression of wealth (see above; also discussions in Sørensen 1992; 1997; 2000; 2006; 2010; Sofaer & Sørensen 2002; Bergerbrant 2007; Sørensen & Rebay-Salisbury 2009; Rebay-Salisbury *et al.* 2010) and of difference (Shennan 1975; Anfinset & Wrigglesworth 2012; Bergerbrant 2012; Holst *et al.* 2013; Bergerbrant *et al.* 2017). We find this same pattern in terms of specialisation within crafting circles (Nørgaard 2017; 2018a; 2018b; Nørgaard *et al.* 2019);

4. a particular cultural emphasis on the practice and ideology associated with raiding and warfare as an important step to power and/or means of maintaining it both at home and abroad (Frankfort 1948; Mumford 1961; Kristiansen 1984; Horn 2013; Horn & Kristiansen 2018).

For these reasons, we suggest that human sacrifice as such may merit further investigation within the NBA. To this end, we discuss a number of graves from southern Scandinavia spanning the period from the Late Neolithic to the Early Nordic Bronze Age (ENBA) in terms of their archaeological context in order to evaluate whether some of them may have a sacrificial element (specifically that of attendant sacrifices buried as grave goods with the primary deceased individual). Below, we discuss the Danish graves from Egtved, Norhågård, Erslev, Skelde, Højsager and Mellemholm and the German graves from Celle, Sottorf, Itzenhoe, Hölingen, Südbostel, Wardböhmen and Deutsch-Evern in relation to possible attendant sacrifices: *cf.*, the burial of Egtved Girl, Plate 9.

The Danish graves

Egtved (FF170601-109; Ke 4357; Aner & Kersten 1990, 39–41)

One of the most iconic burial assemblages from prehistoric Northern Europe comes from a well-preserved grave from Egtved, which included the woman known as 'Egtved Girl' as well as the remains of a cremated child (Thomsen 1929; Frei *et al.* 2015). The principal burial (the 'Egtved Girl') was actually a young woman of between 18 and 25 years of age at the time of her death. Her grave was discovered

in 1921 by a farmer who was ploughing down a dilapidated burial mound on his property. The mound was one of what had been many relatively large Bronze Age burial mounds in the vicinity of the small village of Egtved in south-east Jutland, Denmark. Luckily, upon unearthing what appeared to be the corner of a wooden coffin, the farmer notified the National Museum of Denmark. Excavation of the mound revealed the young woman's remains in a coffin hewn from the trunk of an oak tree, set in place on a furrow of stones. Conditions inside the burial mound had caused the woman's skeleton to disintegrate, while her teeth, fingernails and hair, along with her wool clothing and bronze objects, had all been nearly perfectly preserved (Plate 9, left). From her remarkably well-preserved tree coffin, the burial has been dated by dendrochronology to 1370 BCE. She wore bronze bracelets on each wrist, and an ornate bronze belt-plate among other personal items. She was dressed in a wool costume, comprised of a corded skirt, a double-wrapped belt with tassels and a short blouse. Attached to her belt, tucked partly beneath her belt-disc, was a horn comb. Remarkably, recent strontium isotope analyses of her preserved teeth, hair and fingernails, as well as of the wool from her clothing, were interpreted to indicate that she had been born outside of the boundaries of present-day Denmark (Frei *et al.* 2015). Isotopic analyses of the wool from her clothing have also been interpreted as having been produced using wool from abroad (Frei *et al.* 2015; 2017). A suite of isotopic analyses ($^{87}Sr/^{86}Sr$; $\delta^{15}N$; $\delta^{13}C$) yielded results which were interpreted to indicate that the Egtved Girl had made several long-distance journeys during her relatively short lifetime, including a difficult one during which she experienced malnutrition shortly before her death (Frei *et al.* 2015).

A birch bark vessel at her feet had contained a beverage of honeyed beer (Hald *et al.* 2016). Above her right shoulder was a smaller birch bark container that enclosed wool thread, remnants of various herbs and moss, a bronze awl with a wooden handle and some fragmentary cremated bones from a child. Placed alongside her left leg was a length of wool, folded neatly around the cremated remains of a five- to six-year-old child, presumably the same child whose remains were also in the box at her shoulder. Strontium analysis of the cremated child's remains suggested that the child had also originated from outside of present-day Denmark, possibly from the same location as the young woman herself (Frei *et al.* 2015).

Early on, the original excavator, Thomas Thomsen (1929, 33) noted the possibility that the cremated child accompanying the Egtved Girl was an attendant human sacrifice, writing:

All this suggests and justifies that there was a difference in the social ranking between the two, to the extent that it is reasonable to assume that the child was a servant. The accompanying child was the woman's servant or slave. Naturally, it cannot be ruled out that master and servant could have died at the same time due to a contagious disease. However, far more likely, is the possibility that the child had been a sacrificial offering in the woman's grave, so that after death she [the child] could fulfil her role, lie at her feet, and give her the drink when she wanted it – thus, the child is to be regarded as a death sacrifice in the woman's honor.

Flemming Kaul (1998, 45) has approached the subject of human sacrifice in the Egtved Girl's grave with caution, noting other possible scenarios for the conditions of the burial. These include the recognition that the two individuals could very well have died of any number of natural causes and been buried together for any number of reasons. However, he also cites other possible examples of human sacrifice, as well as the possibility of ritualised cannibalism in the Scandinavian Bronze Age (drawing principally from Lomborg [1964]). Ultimately, Kaul concludes that, as potential evidence for human sacrifice during the ENBA is scant, if it was practised, then it was likely uncommon at best. This opinion can be taken alongside Thomsen (1929, 34), who noted also other examples from Bronze Age burial contexts in which human sacrifices may have been likely. He pointed out that, in most cases, the victim was cremated while the primary deceased was not (see also Kristiansen & Larsson 2005, 275). Furthermore, it seems that in most potential sacrifice cases, the sacrificial victim was placed at the foot of the primary deceased, implying a subordinate presence in relation to the primary burial. From this line of evidence, Thomsen (1929, 34) concluded that 'The burned bones [from Egtved] wrapped in the fabric can hardly be interpreted as anything but a sacrifice ...'.

Another element within the Egtved grave which is suggestive of an attendant sacrifice is the birch bark vessel which was filled with honeyed beer and placed immediately atop the wrapped-up cremated remains set to the lower left of the young woman's left leg. It appears to have been the last thing placed in the coffin. Importantly, this conspicuous placement and proximity suggest that both 'objects' – the vessel with beverage and the child – were arranged in the grave as offerings meant to serve the deceased in the afterlife. As Thomsen noted, the attendant was set close at hand to the beverage offering, symbolically ready to serve. The child's cremated remains being placed in two separate locations is also curious. Their placement in the birch bark box above the woman's right shoulder – accompanied by the awl, segment of knotted string and an assortment of organic materials (yarrow [*Achillea millefolium*], Fern leaf Beech [*Fagus sylvatica*], heather [*Ericaceae* sp.] and unspecified moss[2]) – echoes a reminder of domestic responsibilities such as plant gathering and mending (Thomsen 1929, 19).

In the century since the discovery of the Egtved Girl and her curious companion, a number of finds have come to light which closely parallel the circumstances offered by Thomsen for the possible evidence of attendant sacrifice in the NBA, namely, 1) the inhumation burial of an elite individual

(usually female), 2) accompanied by the cremated remains of another (usually a sub-adult) 3) placed conspicuously in the grave as if as grave goods rather than as a 'proper' burial for the period (*e.g.*, cremated instead of inhumed), and 4) often placed in a subordinate location relative to the primary burial (at the deceased's feet). While none of the subsequent graves revealed to date are so well-preserved as that from Egtved, a sample of possibly parallel cases are discussed below.

Nørhågård (FF 110304-78; Ke 5176)

Grave A at Nørhågård in Thisted in north-west Jutland (Ke5176; Aner & Kersten 2001, 108), contained a single supine and extended inhumation in a wood coffin set into a stone cist (Figure 2.2). This individual was buried concomitantly with a second adult individual whose cremated remains were discreetly placed into a small niche of limestone slabs constructed at the left foot of the grave (National Museum archive report, Haack Olsen 1982). Notably, the

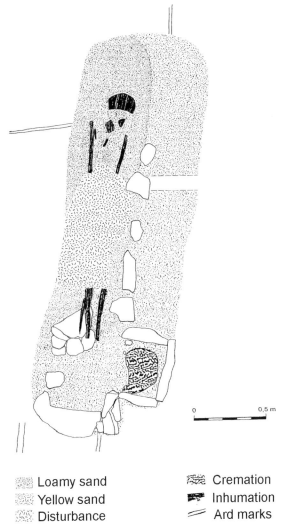

▨ Loamy sand	▨ Cremation
▨ Yellow sand	▨ Inhumation
▨ Disturbance	▱ Ard marks

Figure 2.2. Grave A from Nørhågård (after Aner & Kersten 2001, 108).

partial cremated remains of a sheep (*Ovis aries*) were also recovered in the niche. Interestingly, strontium isotope analyses of the human inhumation (Frei *et al.* 2019) as well as the cremated human and animal were very similar, suggesting that the three individuals may have come from the same place (Reiter *et al.* 2021). This adds a further connotation supporting the possibility of the intermingled human and animal remains as the remnants of a sacrificial offering.

Erslev (FF 110405-26; Ke 5278)

Grave C, from mound no. 26 in Erslev, also in Thisted (Ke5278; Aner & Kersten 2001: 142), contained the inhumation burial of an older woman with well-worn teeth. She had been buried supine and extended in a stone cist. At her feet lay an oval pile of cremated remains and some unburnt cranial bones, all likely from a child. The woman

was buried with a bronze fibula, likely worn on the breast or shoulder, and a bronze dagger with a horn handle and bronze pommel. Less than a metre beyond the foot of her grave was a round feature of blackened and charred earth, 2–3 cm thick of charcoal and burnt bones – presumably the remnants of the pyre upon which the cremated child had been reduced, suggesting that the child may have been put to flame on the spot, perhaps as a part of the funerary rite itself (Figure 2.3).

Skelde (FF 230301-37; Ke 3295)

Grave B at mound no. 37 near Skelde, Broager Land in Sønderjylland (Ethelberg 1994; 2000), was that of a woman interred in a tree coffin with rich grave goods. These included gold ear spirals, a twisted bronze neck-ring, a

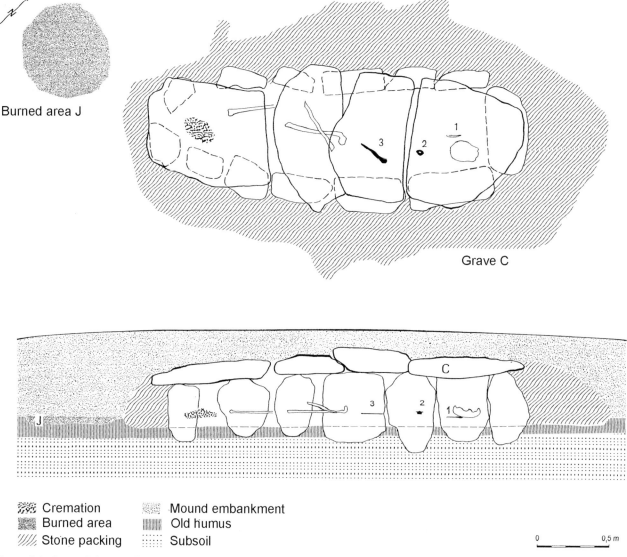

Figure 2.3. Grave C from Erslev, showing the close proximity of the possible cremation pyre at the foot of the burial cist (after Aner & Kersten 2001, 142).

bracelet worn on the left wrist, an anklet on each ankle, a fibula worn at the centre of the chest, as well as a circular belt-box, each of bronze, and what appear to have been two hanging belt-fittings of coiled gold wire interspersed with at least one blue glass bead. Beads of this type in Nordic Bronze Age graves have been found to have originated in Egypt and Mesopotamia and traded through the Mediterranean (Varberg *et al.* 2015). In addition, the cremated remains of a second individual (possibly an adult male) were wrapped up in textile and placed at the woman's feet. Unfortunately, there is no image available.

Højsager (FF 110402-61; Ke 5272)

In a series of low, sandy mounds at Højsager in north-west Jutland (Thisted Amt, Morsø Nørre Herred, Bjergby Søgn SB No. 61), P.C.O. Nørgaard discovered three graves of which two included several individuals (Graves B and C) (Ke 5272; Aner & Kersten 2001, 138; Nørgaard 1967). Grave B seemed to contain a principal inhumation of a man from the Late Neolithic with the remains of a second individual placed near his legs. Grave C contained a primary inhumation from ENBA Period II, at whose feet a cremated individual also appears to have been placed at a later date (Figure 2.4).

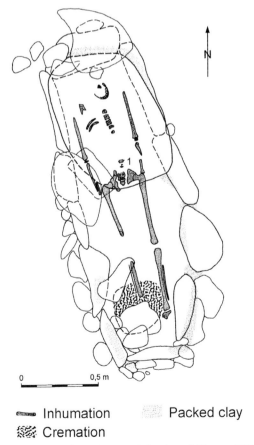

Inhumation

Cremation

Packed clay

Figure 2.4. Grave B from Højsager (after Aner & Kersten 2001, 138).

Mellemholm (FF 120508-13; no Ke number)

A remarkable set of graves from the site of Mellemholm in northern Jutland comprised two double graves and one single grave. In both of the multiple graves, the 'secondary' individual was placed in the grave in a 'sharply contracted' position at the foot of the primary, supine inhumation. In each case, the secondary individual seems to have been placed in a similar place and manner, as were the grave goods. One grave included a woman as the primary deceased who was buried extended and with typical elite women's grave offerings, including a belt-plate, finger ring and bracelet, each of bronze. At her feet was another individual set in a tight hocker position.

Curiously, the other multiple grave was that of a child, who was buried as the primary inhumation, with a 'secondary' adult in a crouched position at the child's feet (Grantzau *et al.* 1953, 123). This child also possessed an armband and a coiled ring, both of bronze, which may be indications that s/he was likely a member of a wealthy family. A man's grave with grave goods in the same vicinity did not appear to contain a similar attendant offering. These contexts led the original authors to conclude succinctly that 'it was the custom on Mellemholm to accompany burials with a human sacrifice' (Grantzau *et al.* 1953, 135). Here, social status, rather than sex or age, appears to have been the main consideration regarding the possible inclusion of an attendant sacrifice. Unfortunately, again no image is available of this grave.

The German graves
Celle Mound 16

Beate Siemoneit (1996, 357–360) describes three Bronze Age graves from northern and north-central Germany of women with the remains of children. Only one of these (Kat-Nr. 2) from Celle mound 16 represents an adult inhumation with a cremated child. In that case, the woman wore a bronze Lüneburg wheel-headed pin and two bronze bracelets, indicating that she was of high wealth and status. The child's remains were placed besides the woman's right calf. Two other children were also recovered at the site. One of these was an infant (Nr. 12, Kat-Nr. 48; Siemoneit 1996, 355–356) that was buried with a miniature ceramic vessel. The other (a child aged 1–2 years old; Kar-Nr. 38) was in the grave of a woman of *c.* 20–39 years of age. Both woman and child were cremated. Thus, we presume that these latter two cases indicate, respectively, a deceased child provided with its own grave offering, and a probable mother-child burial in which both individuals were cremated. In other words, these represent children that did not die as attendant sacrifices. However, the first example does fit our criteria given the differential treatment of the deceased and the placement of the child's cremated remains at the foot of the high-status adult's inhumation.

Similar graves in Sottorf, Itzehoe, Hölingen, Südbostel, Wardböhmen and Deutsch-Evern

Günther Haseloff (1938, 61) also describes similar women's inhumation graves from Sottorf and Itzehoe in northern Germany which included cremated children. Likewise, Bergmann (1962) identified similar cases: *e.g.*, in mound 9 at Hölingen, he (pp. 67–68) reports on one grave in which 'a child who had been cremated beforehand was added to the male burial at its feet'. Bergmann (1962, 78–79) also cites H. Piesker (1958) and G. Körner (1959, 13) regarding Grave 4 from Mound 17 from Deutsch-Evern as well as graves in Südbostel and Wardböhmen in the southern Lüneburg Heath in which the remains of infants were placed next to the lower legs of inhumed ENBA women. Further to this point, in his study of central German contexts, B. U. Fischer (1957) noted that sacrificial offerings of children occasionally occurred in ceramic vessels.

Körner (1959, 19) interprets yet another grave from Deutsch-Evern within a sacrificial schema (Grave VII, also from Mound 17). This included one male individual as well as what seemed to be two female graves (sex determined from the accompanying grave goods). He suggests that the principle male burial may have been accompanied by his primary and secondary wife, reflecting a possible suttee scenario (*ibid.*).

Discussion

As can be seen from the above examples, there are several cases which suggest that we may consider taking a fresh look at the possibility that Nordic Bronze Age societies were societies which practised at least one form of human sacrifice. The disparity between the age and sex profiles of these secondary funerary inclusions suggests that there were many different kinds of persons who may have been included as potential victims for attendant sacrifices. Although both adults and children appear to have been possible sacrifices, in at least one case it appears that a sacrificed adult may even have accompanied a child. In most cases, it seems that children may have accompanied adults. The presumption is that lower status and therefore more vulnerable individuals were selected as 'expendables'.

The predominance of children has been interpreted in various ways. As concerns the grave of the Egtved Girl, the cremated child who accompanied her may have come from the same far-off place from which the Egtved Girl herself travelled before she was interred in present-day Vejle County, Denmark (Frei *et al.* 2015). Positing an alternative to the attendant sacrifice scenario, specifically focused on the cremated children placed in inhumation graves, Kaul (pers. comm.) has suggested that the co-occurrence of children alongside adults may have been the result of Bronze Age religious practices or cosmology insofar as the remains of a dead child may have had to 'wait' for the funeral of an adult in order to have a companion or guide on the journey to the afterlife (Schmidt 1993; Wehlin 2013). The uptake of cremation as a funerary practice may have made such practices more feasible, moving on towards the later part of the NBA, as cremation provides a greater degree of flexibility for final funerary arrangements for human remains, as opposed to the deposition pressure brought about by the putrefaction of non-cremated remains.

However, one may also consider that, particularly in the early part of the NBA, there are numerous graves of children in which the child *was* given an otherwise 'proper' individual burial, which included both coffin as well as grave goods. This suggests that the children included as secondary deceased individual may have had another purpose. Interestingly, while we can recognise that human sacrifice is a well-documented archaeological phenomenon in many parts of the world, importantly for most of the cases presented here, we must likewise observe that across times and places it also has involved the use of children as victims (*e.g.*, Harner 1977; Benson & Boone 1979; Bourdillon & Fortes 1980; Davies 1981; Bloch & Parry 1982; Hughes 1991; Carrasco 1999; Hill 2003; Bremmer 2007; Fischer 2007; Sutskover 2014; Arbel *et al.* 2015).

The differential treatment of the dead is a telling phenomenon when considering the possibility of attendant sacrifices. For the ENBA, typical elite burials were made in tree coffins and/or stone cists. We can see oak-coffin burials of children elsewhere at, for example, Grave B at Guldhøj (mentioned above), Grave C at Trindhøj (Aner & Kersten 1986, 24–28) and Grave F at Strandfogedgård (Aner & Kersten, 1976, 196–198). There, the deceased youths were not cremated and were afforded appropriately sized coffins. Even at Trindhøj, where there is a clear association by proximity between an adjacent adult burial – Grave C – and the child's Grave B, each was laid in their own separate coffin (Plate 10). Yet another example, the child's burial from Guldhøj, was also in its own small oak coffin which was even lined with a black sheepskin. In other words, in each case, the sub-adult deceased was provided a 'proper' burial for the period: in their own coffin, with their own grave goods and in their own grave.

In other cases, there are examples (such as those set out by Siemoneit given above) of women's graves in which a child is present. But in these cases the woman and child are positioned in a way suggestive of a more intimate (*e.g.*, mother-child) relationship; in no such case is the child's body treated differently (*i.e.*, cremated) than the adult. Rather, generally, where the adult is cremated, so too is the child. Thus, we may presume that cremated individuals placed at the feet of inhumation burials possibly represented for those performing the burial rite an active delimitation of the social statuses of the deceased – the transformation of one individual's remains into the material possessions of another for use in the afterlife. In further support of this notion, during ENBA Period III when cremation became the norm, we also see evidence of women and children being cremated together, as in Grave B from the double-burial of 'a family' at Trappendal (Aner & Kersten 1990, 50–52).

In the NBA, it seems that children may have been prescriptively targeted as attendant sacrifices for use at the funerals of high-status individuals. We imagine that such children may have been slaves or low-born members of local or neighbouring communities with no one to stand for them, *e.g.*, children taken in raids or perhaps orphans. Within NBA society such individuals may not have been perceived of as persons in their own right, but as commodities to be expended as such. Thus, what these cases potentially illuminate is yet another example of the disparities evident between classes of people and notions of personhood and individual value during this period – a time in prehistory in which wealth and status hierarchies appear to have been exceptional.

What can sacrifices tell us of the significance of children as victims in the contexts of prehistoric traditions of institutionalised violence? Indeed, what do such sacrifices suggest about the societies in which they occurred? Children play a pivotal but often underrepresented role in family, community and overall social structures and their dynamics, from subsistence to language, but also feature in ritual traditions such as sacrifice (Lillehammer 1989; see also Baxter 2008; Crawford *et al.* 2018). It should come as no surprise that as a sacrificial victim, the selection of a child must have been a significant, value-laden decision, regardless of whichever side of the spectrum of value the lives of children were afforded within NBA societies. Whether children were selected because they were considered special to the purpose of serving the dead in the afterlife, or because they may have been easy to procure and take advantage of, is likely to remain unclear. Either scenario is telling. ENBA society appears to have been highly stratified. Different lives likely had very different values to those making such value judgements. One point in relation to this as it pertains to the possibility of attendant or retainer sacrifice is that what we know about ENBA society fits very well within the characteristic criteria outlined by Van Dijk (2007, 151) for societies in which such sacrifices might emerge.

For example, during this period, wealth and power were remarkably pronounced by those of elite status in what Holst *et al.* (2013) have observed as '*herostratic*' performative acts of symbolically excessive resource use. They cite the construction of highly costly burial mounds which significantly detracted from the agrarian potential of the landscape, as well as the construction of large timber longhouses which eventuated extensive deforestation. They observe that these extensive and probably ritualised forms of conspicuous consumption were likely integrated into every aspect of everyday life (*cf.*, Brück 1999; Bradley 2005). Within such an arena, the expression of wealth and status through the consumption of human lives is well attested, especially as it comes to accompany emotionally charged eschatological rituals. Of note, the preserved contexts of the graves in which we observe

the possible evidence for attendant sacrifices in elite burials date from Periods II–III of the ENBA (*c.* 1500–1150 BCE), the same 350-year phase in which the greatest concentration of barrows and longhouses described by Holst *et al.* (2013) appear to have been undertaken. We suggest that attendant sacrifice may have been yet another such excessive expression of power illustrating and exercising the will of the elite social class.

Based on this conspicuous feature, we take a stance *contra* Girard's (1977) theory of sacrificial violence as both product of and mediatory device for social crises stemming from what he referred to as unchecked 'memetic desire'. Being activated as a feature of funerary ritual, the NBA attendant sacrifices do not appear to correspond to the looming social crises to which Girard refers. Rather, we see NBA attendant sacrifices as comprising two key aetiologies: 1) a direct manifestation of social control borne out of the proclivities of elites as a means of perpetuating the social status of the deceased in the afterlife by providing them with a servant, but which 2) also had the added bonus of reinforcing the *status quo* in the minds of all who partook in, witnessed or merely heard later about such events. Thus, the spectacle of sacrificing and cremating an individual at the funerary rite, sending them as smoke to follow the already deceased into the afterlife, would likely have resonated deeply with all involved; the attendant's death and physical transformation by fire 'transubstantiating' (Siebers 2003, 15) the victim's death onto all those in attendance; the act constituting

> an excess of communication that arcs specific objects or individual bodies to responses related to collective emotions … A particular and ordinary object [*e.g., a slave*] becomes the subject of intense focus, with the result that it changes into another object, but an object of a special kind, one that maintains a peculiar materiality while achieving a universal and communicable meaning beyond materiality.

Such *herostratic* acts would have been powerful indeed as means of extorting a dominant position of one social class over another, both physically and symbolically.

Conclusion

Whether the cases provided here actually reflect human sacrifices in the late prehistory of southern Scandinavia remains to be seen. The existing evidence can certainly be interpreted in different ways. However, we suggest that the graves herein described share common features that can be argued to point to an attendant sacrifice tradition. These include: 1) inhumation burials (the 'proper' form of burial for this time and place) 2) accompanied by the cremated remains of another individual (often a sub-adult) (with cremation being uncommon treatment of the dead during this time period), 3) placed in the grave apparently as grave offerings rather than as a stand-alone burial, and 4) placed in a position within the grave as to suggest the second individual's subordination to the primary burial (such as at the deceased's feet). Further, all of these examples come to us from a period of prehistory in which exceptional social inequality appears to have been the norm, and in which status elites regularly engaged in *herostratic* consumption of vital resources. Human lives may have been one such resource.

Set against this backdrop, we believe that the notion that high-status elites may have used the ritual taking of lives not only as a means of furnishing their deceased loved ones with retainers in the afterlife, but also as a means of signalling their control over life and death is not a large interpretive leap to make.

Acknowledgements

We wish to thank the editors and one anonymous peer-reviewer for their constructive comments on this manuscript. Funding for this research was provided by the Norwegian Research Council's generous support of the 'Human Sacrifice and Value' project (FRIPRO HUMSAM 275947; PI Rane Willerslev), as well as from the Carlsberg Foundation's 'Semper Ardens' research grant CF18-0005 'Tales of Bronze Age People' and grant CF15-0878 'Tales of Bronze Age Women' (both projects PI Karin M. Frei).

Note

1   We note that, though this last set of references relate to the Iron Age, we do not suggest that equivalence be made between NBA and later prehistoric Northern European pagan cosmologies, as indeed NBA 'religion' appears to have been quite nuanced from later Celtic and Germanic Iron Age 'religions' (Kaul 2004; 2020).

References

Ahlqvist, L. & Vandkilde, H. 2018. Hybrid beasts of the Nordic Bronze Age. *Danish Journal of Archaeology* 7(2): 180–194.

Aldhouse-Green, M. 2001. *Dying for the Gods: Human Sacrifice in Iron Age and Roman Europe*. Stroud: Tempus.

Andrén, A., Jennbert, K. & Raudvere, C. (eds) 2006. *Old Norse Religion in Long-Term Perspectives: Origins, Changes and Interactions. An International Conference in Lund, Sweden, June 3–7, 2004*. Lund: Nordic Academic Press.

Aner, E. & Kersten, K. 2001. *Die Funde der älteren Bronzezeit des nordischen Kreises in Dänemark, Schleswig-Holstein und Niedersachsen, Vol. 11*. Copenhagen: Verlag Nationalmuseum.

Anfinset, N. & Wrigglesworth, M. (eds). 2012. *Local Societies in Bronze Age Northern Europe*. Sheffield: Equinox.

Arbel, V.D., Burns, P.C., Cousland, J.R.C., Menkis, R. & Neufeld, D. (eds) 2015. *Not Sparing the Child: Human Sacrifice in the Ancient World and Beyond. Studies in Honor of Professor Paul G. Mosca*. London: Bloomsbury.

Baxter, J.E. 2008. The Archaeology of Childhood. *Annual Review of Anthropology* 37: 159–175.

Beattie, J.H.M. 1980. On understanding sacrifice. In *Sacrifice*, edited by M.F.C. Bourdillon and M. Fortes, 29–44. London: Academic Press.

Becker, C.J. 1947. Mosefundne Lerkar fra yngre Stenalder. *Aarbøger for Fordisk Oldkyndighed og Historie* 1947: 1–318.

Bennike, P., Ebbesen, K. & Bender Jørgensen, L. 1986a. The bog find from Sigersdal: Human sacrifice in the Early Neolithic. *Journal of Danish Archaeology* 5: 85–115.

Bennike, P., Ebbesen, K. & Bender Jørgensen, L. 1986b. Early Neolithic skeletons from Bolkilde bog, Denmark. *Antiquity* 230: 199–209.

Benson, E.P. & Boone, E.H. (eds) 1979. *Ritual Human Sacrifice in Mesoamerica. A Conference at Dumbarton Oaks, October 13th and 14th, 1979*. Washington, D.C.: Dumbarton Oaks Research Library and Collections.

Bentley, R.A., Layton, R.L. & Tehrani, J. 2009. Kinship, marriage and the genetics of past human dispersals. *Human Biology* 81(2–3): 159–179.

Bergerbrant, S. 2007. *Bronze Age Identities: Costume, Conflict and Contact in Northern Europe 1600–1300 BC*. Stockholm Studies in Archaeology 43. Lindome: Bricoleur Press.

Bergerbrant, S. 2012. The Nordic Bronze Age and the Lüneburger Culture: Two different responses to social change. In *Local Society in Bronze Age Northern Europe*, edited by N. Anfinset and M. Wrigglesworth, 169–184. New York: Routledge.

Bergerbrant, S., Kristiansen, K., Allentoft, M.E., Frei, K.M., Price, T.D., Sjögren, K-G. & Tornberg, A. 2017. Identifying commoners in the Early Bronze Age: burials outside barrows. In *New Perspectives on the Bronze Age*, edited by S. Bergerbrant and A. Wessman, 37–64. Oxford: Archaeopress Archaeology.

Bergmann, J. 1962. Hügelgräber der älteren Bronzezeit bei Hölingen, Gemeinde Reckum, Kreis Grafschaft Hoya. *Die Kunde* 13: 53–100.

Bloch, M. 1992. *Prey into hunter. The politics of religious experience*. Cambridge: Cambridge University Press.

Bloch, M. & Parry, J. (eds) 1982. *Death & the Regeneration of Life*. Cambridge: Cambridge University Press.

Bourdillon, M.F.C. & Fortes, M. (eds) 1980. *Sacrifice*. London: Academic Press.

Bradley, R. 2005. *Ritual and Domestic Life in Prehistoric Europe*. New York: Routledge.

Bremmer, J.N. 2007. *The Strange World of Human Sacrifice*. Leuven/Paris/Dudley, MA: Peeters.

Breuning-Madsen, H. & Holst, M.K. 1998. Recent studies on the formation of iron pans around the oaken log coffins of the Bronze Age burial mounds of Denmark. *Journal of Archaeological Science* 25(11): 1103–1110. doi:10.1006/jasc.1998.0288.

Breuning-Madsen, H., Holst, M.K., Rasmussen, M. & Elberling, B. 2003. Preservation within log coffins before and after barrow construction. *Journal of Archaeological Science* 30(3): 343–350. doi:10.1006/jasc.2002.0845.

Broch-Due, V. 2004. *Violence and Belonging: The Quest for Identity in Post-Colonial Africa*. London: Routledge.

Brück, J. 1999. Ritual and Rationality: Some problems of interpretation in European Archaeology. *European Journal of Archaeology* 2(3): 313–344.

Brück, J. 2009. Women, death and social change in the British Bronze Age. *Norwegian Archaeological Review* 42(1): 1–23. doi:10.1080/00293650902907151.

Carrasco, D. 1999. *City of Sacrifice: The Aztec Empire and the Role of Violence in Civilization*. Boston, MA: Beacon Press.

Clarke, D.V. & Cowie, T.G.F.A. 1985. *Symbols of Power at the Time of Stonehenge*. Edinburgh: National Museum of Antiquities of Scotland.

Crawford, S., Hadley, D. & Shepherd, G. (eds) 2018. *The Oxford Handbook of the Archaeology of Childhood*. Oxford: Oxford University Press.

Davidson, H.E. 1964. *Gods and Myths of Northern Europe*. Baltimore: Penguin Books.

Davies, N. 1981. *Human Sacrifice: In history and today*. New York: William Morrow & Company, Inc.

Demakopoulou, K., Jensen, J., Kemakopoulous, K., Eluère, C., Jockenhovel, A. & Mohen, J-P. (eds) 1998. *Gods and Heroes of the European Bronze Age*. Copenhagen: National Museum of Denmark.

Ebbesen, K. 1993. Sacrifices to the powers of nature. In *Digging into the Past: 25 Years of Archaeology in Denmark*, edited by S. Hvass and B. Storgaard, 122–125. Aarhus: Aarhus University Press.

Ethelberg, P. 1994. Høj over høj. *Broagerland VIII*, 152–169. Gråsten: Lokalhistorisk Forening for Broagerland.

Ethelberg, P. 2000. En fornem kvinde af højfolket. In *Vor skjulte kulturarv: Arkæologien under overfladen: til Hendes Majestæt Dronning Margrethe II 16. April 2000*, edited by Hvass, S., 74–75. København: Det kongelige Nordiske Oldskriftselskab, Jysk Arkæologisk Selskab.

Firth, R. 1963. Offering and sacrifice: Problems of organization. *The Journal of the Royal Anthropological Institute of Great Britain and Ireland* 93(1): 12–24.

Fischer, Z. 2007. Sacrificing Isaac: A new interpretation. *Jewish Bible Quarterly* 35(3): 173–178.

Frazer, S.J.G. 2017. *The Golden Bough*. Place of publication not identified: Independently published.

Frei, K.M., Bergerbrant, S., Sjögren, K.-G., Jørkov, M.L., Lynnerup, N., Harvig, L., Allentoft, M.E., Sikora, M., Price, T.D., Frei, R. & Kristiansen, K. 2019. Mapping human mobility during the third and second millennia BC in present-day Denmark. *PLoS ONE* 14(8): e0219850. doi:10.1371/journal.pone.0219850.

Frei, K.M., Mannering, U., Kristiansen, K., Allentoft, M.E., Wilson, A.S., Skals, I., Tridico, S., Nosch, M.L., Willerslev, E., Clark, L. & Frei. R. 2015. Tracing the dynamic life story of a Bronze Age Female. *Nature* 5: 10431. doi:10.1038/srep10431.

Frei, K.M., Mannering, U., Vanden Berghe, I. & Kristiansen, K. 2017. Bronze Age wool: Provenance and dye investigations of Danish textiles. *Antiquity* 91(357): 640–654.

Fyllingen, H. 2003. Society and violence in the Early Bronze Age: An analysis of human skeletons from Nord-Trøndelag, Norway. *Norwegian Archaeological Review* 36(1): 27–43.

Geertz, A.W. 1999. Definition as analytical strategy in the study of religion. *Historical Reflections/Réflexions Historiques, The Definition of Religion in the Context of Social-Scientific Study* 25(3): 445–475.

Gillespie, S.D. 2011. The archaeology of meaning. In *Encyclopaedia of Life Support Systems: Archaeology*, 273–294. London: Eolss Publishers/UNESCO.

Girard, R. 1977. *Violence and the sacred*. Baltimore, MD & London: Johns Hopkins University Press.

Grantzau, M., Marseen, O. & Riismøller, P. 1953. Mellemholm: En stenalderboplads over broncældergrave. *KUML* 1954: 121–136.

Green, M. 1998. Humans as ritual victims in the Later Prehistory of Western Europe. *Oxford Journal of Archaeology* 17(2): 169–189.

Hald, M.M., Henriksen, P.S. & Mortensen, M.F. 2016. Food, economy and society: Multi-faceted lessons to learn from ancient plant remain. In *Food, Population and Health – Global Patterns and Challenges*, edited by L. Jørgensen, N. Lynnerup, A. Løkke and H. Balslev, 169–178. Viborg: Det Kongelige Danske Videnskabernes Selskab.

Harding, A. 2013. World systems, cores and peripheries in prehistoric Europe. *European Journal of Archaeology* 16(3): 378–400.

Harding, A. 2018. Bronze Age encounters: Violent or peaceful? In *Warfare in Bronze Age Society*, edited by C. Horn and K. Kristiansen, 16–22. Cambridge: Cambridge University Presss. doi:10.1017/9781316884522.003.

Harner, M. 1977. The Ecological Basis for Aztec Sacrifice. *American Ethnologist* 4(1): 117–135.

Haseloff, G. 1938. Der Galgenberg von Itzehoe. *Offa*: 18–84.

Hedeager, L. 1999. *Skygger av en Annen Virkelighet: Oldnordiske myter*. Oslo: Pax forlag.

Hedges, R.E.M. 2002. Bone diagenesis: An overview of processes. *Archaeometry* 44(3): 319–328.

Hill, E. 2003. Sacrificing Moche Bodies. *Journal of Material Culture* 8(3): 285–299.

Holst, M.K., Rasmussen, M., Kristiansen, K. & Bech, J-H. 2013. Bronze Age 'Herostrats': Ritual, political, and domestic economies in Early Bronze Age Denmark. *Proceedings of the Prehistoric Society* 79: 265–296. doi: 10.1017/ppr.2013.14.

Horn, C. 2013. Weapons, fighters and combat: Spears and swords in Early Bronze Age Scandinavia. *Danish Journal of Archaeology* 2(1): 20–44. doi:10.1080/21662282.2013.838832.

Horn, C. & Kristiansen, K. 2018. *Warfare in Bronze Age Society*. Cambridge: Cambridge University Press.

Hornstrup, K.M., Olsen, J. Heinemeier, J., Thrane, H. & Bennike, P. 2012. A new absolute Danish Bronze Age chronology as based on radiocarbon dating of cremated bone samples from burials. *Acta Archaeologica* 83(1): 9–10. doi:10.1111/j.1600-0390.2012.00513.x.

Hubert, H. & Mauss, M. 1964. *Sacrifice. Its Nature and Functions*. Trans. by W.D. Halls. Chicago: The University of Chicago Press.

Hughes, D.D. 1991. *Human Sacrifice in Ancient Greece*. London & New York: Routledge.

Insoll, T. 2011. Sacrifice. In *The Oxford Handbook of the Archaeology of Ritual and Religion*, edited by T. Insoll, 151–165. Oxford: Oxford University Press.

Jensen, J. 1982. *The Prehistory of Denmark*. London & New York: Routledge.

Jockenhövel, A. 1980. *Die Rasiermesser in Westeuropa*. Munich: Prähistorische Bronzefunde.

Jockenhövel, A. 1991. Räumliche Mobilität von Personen in der Mittleren Bronzezeit des westlichen Mitteleuropa. *Germania* 69: 49–62.

Jockenhövel, A. 1995. Zur Ausstattung von Frauen in Nordwestdeutschland und in der Deutschen Mittelgebirgszone Während der Spätbronzezeit und Älteren Eisenzeit. In *Festschrift für Hermann Müller-Karpe zum 70 Geburtstag*, 195–212. Bonn: Habelt.

Johnston, R. 2021. *Bronze Age Worlds: A Social Prehistory of Britain and Ireland*. Oxon: Routledge.

Kaul, F. 2004. *Bronzealderens religion*. København: Det Kongelige Nordiske Oldskriftselskab.

Kaul, F. 2017. The xenia concept of guest-friendship. Providing an elucidatory model for Bronze Age communication. In *North Meets South: Theoretical Aspects on the Northern and Southern Rock Art Traditions in Scandinavia*, edited by P. Skoglund, J. Ling and U. Bertilsson, 172–198. Oxford: Oxbow Books (Swedish Rock Art Series).

Kaul, F. 2020. The Possibilities for an Afterlife. Souls and Cosmology in the Nordic Bronze Age In *Between the Worlds. Contexts, Sources, and Analogies of Scandinavian Otherworld Journeys*, edited by Egeler, M. & Heizmann, W., 185–202. Berlin: Walter de Gruyter.

Kibblewhite, M., Tóth, G. & Hermann, T. 2015. Predicting the preservation of cultural artefacts and buried materials in soil. *Science of The Total Environment* 529: 249–263. doi:10.1016/j.scitotenv.2015.04.036.

Körner, G. 1959. Ein bronzezeitlicher Mehrperiodenhügel bei Deutsch-Evern im Landkreis Lüneburg. *Nachtrichen aus Niedersachsens Urgeschichte* 28(96): 3–19.

Kristiansen, K. 1984. Krieger und Häuptlinge in der Bronzezeit Dänemarks. Ein Beitrag zur Geschichte des bronzezeitlichen Schwertes. *Jahrbuch des Römisch-Germanischen Zentralmuseums Mainz* 31: 187–208. doi:10.11588/jrgzm.1984.0.58781.

Kristiansen, K. 1994. The emergence of the European World System in the Bronze Age: Divergence, convergence and social evolution during the first and second millennia BC in Europe. In *Europe in the First Millennium BC*, edited by K. Kristiansen and J. Jensen, 7–30. Sheffield Archaeological Monographs 6. Sheffield: Sheffield Academic Press.

Kristiansen, K. 2013. Households in context: Cosmology, economy and long-term change in the Bronze Age of Northern Europe. In *The Archaeology of Households*, edited by M. Madella, G. Kovacs, B. Kulscarne-Berzsenyi and I. B. Godino, 235–268. Oxford: Oxbow Books.

Kristiansen, K. 2017. Interpreting Bronze Age trade and migration. In *Human Mobility and Technological Transfer in the Prehistoric Mediterranean*, edited by E. Kiratzi and C. Knappet, 154–181. Cambridge MA: Cambridge University Press.

Kristiansen, K. & Larsson, T.B. 2005. *The Rise of Bronze Age Society: Travels, Transmissions and Transformations*. New York: Cambridge University Press.

Kristiansen, K., Melheim, L., Bech, J-H., Mortensen, M.F. & Frei, K.M. 2020. Thy at the crossroads: A local Bronze Age community's role in a macro-economic system. In *Contrasts of the Nordic Bronze Age: Essays in Honour of Christopher Prescott*, edited by K.I. Austvoll *et al.*, 269–282. Turnhout: Brepols.

Kveiborg, J., Ahlqvist, L. & Vandkilde, H. 2020. Horses, fish and humans: Interspecies relationships in the Nordic Bronze Age. *Current Swedish Archaeology* 28: 75–98.

Lillehammer, G. 1989. A child is born. The child's world in an archaeological perspective. *Norwegian Archaeological Review* 22: 89–105.

Lincoln, B. 1986. *Myth, Cosmos, and Society: Indo-European Themes of Creation and Destruction*. Cambridge: Harvard University Press.

Lincoln, B. 1991. *Death, War, and Sacrifice: Studies in Ideology and Practice*. Chicago: University of Chicago Press.

Ling, J., Earle, T. & Kristiansen, K. 2018. Maritime mode of production: Raiding and trading in seafaring chiefdoms. *Current Anthropology* 59(5): 488–524. doi:10.1086/699613.

Lomborg, E. 1964. Gravfund fra Stubberup, Lolland. Menneskeofringer og kannibalisme i bronzealderen. *KUML*: 14–32.

McClymond, K. 2008. *Beyond Sacred Violence: A Comparative Study of Sacrifice*. Baltimore: Johns Hopkins University Press.

Mittnik, A., Massy, K., Knipper, C., Wittenborn, F., Friedrich, R., Pfrengle, S., Burri, M., Carlichi-Witjes, N., Deeg, H., Furtwängler, A., Harbeck, M., von Heyking, K., Kociumaka, C., Kucukkalipchi, I., Lindauer, S., Metz, S., Staskiewicz, A., Thiel, A., Wahl, J., Haak, W., Pernicka, E., Schiffels, S., Stockhammer, P. & Krause, J. 2019. Kinship-based social inequality in Bronze Age Europe. *Science* 366: 731–734. doi:10.1126/science.aax6219.

More, T. 1895. *Utopia*. London: Constable.

Müller, S. 1886. Votivfund fra Sten- og Bronzealderen. *Aarbøger for Nordisk Oldkyndighed og Historie* 1886: 216–250.

Murray, C.A. (ed.) 2016. *Diversity of sacrifice. Form and function of sacrificial practices in the ancient world and beyond. IEAM Proceedings*, Vol. 5. Albany: State of New York University Press.

Näsström, B.-M. 2002. *Blot. Tro och offer i det förkristna Norden*. Stockholm: Norstedt.

Nørgaard, H.W. 2017. Bronze Age metal workshops in Denmark between 1500–1300 BC: elite-controlled craft on Zealand. In *New Perspectives on the Bronze Age: Proceedings from the 13th Nordic Bronze Age Symposium, held in Gothenburg 9th June to 13th June 2015*, edited by S. Bergerbrant and A. Wessman, 127–142. Oxford: Archaeopress

Nørgaard, H.W. 2018a. *Bronze Age Metalwork. Techniques and Traditions in the Nordic Bronze Age 1500–1100 BC*. Oxford: Archaeopress.

Nørgaard, H.W. 2018b. The Nordic Bronze Age (1500–1100 BC): Craft mobility and contact networks in metal craft. *Prähistorische Zeitschrift* 93(1): 89–120.

Nørgaard, H.W., Pernicka, E. & Vandkilde, H. 2019. On the trail of Scandinavia's early metallurgy: Provenance, transfer and mixing. *PLOS ONE* 14(7): e0219574. doi:10.1371/journal.pone.0219574.

Nørgaard, P.C.O. 1967. *Højsager MHM x 44*. Thisted. Nationalmuseet Arkiv. 110402–61.

Nosch, M.L.B., Strand, A., Birgitta, E., Mannering, U. & Frei, K.M. 2013. Travels, transmissions and transformations – and textiles. In *Counterpoint: Essays in Archaeology and Heritage Studies in Honours of Professor Kristian Kristiansen*, edited by S. Bergerbrant and S. Sabatini. Oxford: British Archaeological Report SI 2508, 469–476.

Oras, E. 2013. Sacrifice or offering: What can we see in the archaeology of Northern Europe? *Folklore* 55: 125–150.

Osella, F. & Osella, C. 2003. Migration and the commoditisation of ritual: Sacrifice, spectacle and contestations in Kerala, India. *Contributions to Indian Sociology* 37(1–2): 109–139. doi:10.1177/006996670303700106.

Pacheco-Forés, S.I. 2020. Ritual violence and the perception of social difference: Migration and human sacrifice in the Epiclassic Basin of Mexico. In *ASU Electronic Theses and Dissertations*. Arizona State University. Available at: http://hdl.handle.net/2286/R.I.57026 (accessed 9 June 2021).

Pacheco-Forés, S.I., Morehart, C.T., Buikstra, J.E., Gordon, G.W. & Knudson, K.J. 2021. Migration, violence, and the 'other':

A biogeochemical approach to identity-based violence in the Epiclassic Basin of Mexico. *Journal of Anthropological Archaeology* 61: 101263. doi:10.1016/j.jaa.2020.101263.

Price, N.S. 2002. *The Viking Way: Religion and War in Late Iron Age Scandinavia.* Uppsala: Department of Archaeology and Ancient History.

Randsborg, K. 2006. Opening the oak coffins. New dates – new perspectives. In *Bronze Age Oak Coffin Graves: Archaeology and Dendro-Dating*, edited by K. Randsborg and K. Christensen. Vol. 77, 3–162. Copenhagen: Blackwell Munksgaard Acta Archaeologica Supplementa.

Rebay-Salisbury, K., Sørensen, M.L. & Hughes, J. 2010. *Body Parts and Bodies Whole: Changing Relations and Meanings.* Oxford: Oxbow Books.

Reiter, S.S. 2014. A choreography of place: Globalisation and identity in the Bronze Age. In *Rooted in Movement: Aspects of Mobility in Bronze Age Europe*, edited by S.S. Reiter, H. Wrobel Nørgaard, Z. Kölcze and C. Rassmann, 15–22. Aarhus: Jutland Archaeological Society.

Reiter, S.S., Møller, N.A., Nielsen, B.H., Bech, J.-H., Olsen, A.-L.H., Jørkov, M.L.S. *et al.* 2021. Into the fire: Investigating the introduction of cremation to Nordic Bronze Age Denmark: A comparative study between different regions applying strontium isotope analyses and archaeological methods. *PLoS ONE* 16(5): e0249476. doi:10.1371/journal.pone.0249476.

Renfrew, C. 1974. Beyond a subsistence economy: The evolution of prehistoric Europe. In *Reconstructing Complex Societies*, edited by C.B. Moore, 69–95. Bulletin of the American Schools of Oriental Research 20. Cambridge, MA: Henry N. Sawyer (for the A.S.O.R.).

Robertson Smith, W. 2015 [1889]. *Lectures on the Religion of the Semites.* London: Creative Media Partners, LLC.

Rowlands, S.M. 1980. Kinship, alliance and exchange in the European Bronze Age. In *Settlement and Society in the British Later Bronze Age*, edited by J.C. Barrett and R. Bradley, 15–55. Oxford: British Archaeological Reports.

Schmidt, J.P. 1993. *Studien Zur Jüngeren Bronzezeit in Schleswig-Holstein Und Dem Nordelbischen Hamburg*, vol. 15. Universitätsforschungen Zur Prähistorischen Archäologie. Bonn: Habelt.

Shennan, S. 1975. The social organization at Branc. *Antiquity* 49(196): 279–288.

Shennan, S. 1982. Ideology, change and the European Early Bronze Age. In *Symbolic and Structural Archaeology*, edited by I. Hodder, 155–161. Cambridge: Cambridge University Press.

Sherratt, A. 1993. What would a Bronze Age World System look like? Relations between temperate Europe and the Mediterranean in later prehistory. *Journal of European Archaeology* 1(2): 1–58.

Shulman, S. 2003. Exploring the economic basis of nationhood. *Nationalism and Ethnic Politics* 9(2): 23–49. doi: 10.1080/13537110412331301405.

Siebers, T. 2003. The return to ritual: Violence and art in the media age. *Journal of Cultural and Religious Theory* 5(1): 9–33.

Siemoneit, B. 1996. Das Kind in der Bronzezeit. Archäologische und anthropologische Befunde aus Niedersachsen. *Die Kunde N.F.* 47: 341–371.

Snoeck, C., Lee-Thorp, J., Schulting, R., de Jong, J., Debouge, W. & Mattielli, N. 2015. Calcined bone provides a reliable substrate for strontium isotope ratios as shown by an enrichment experiment. *Rapid Communications in Mass Spectrometry* 29(1): 107–114. doi: 10.1002/rcm.7078.

Sofaer-Derevenski, J.S. & Sørensen, M.L.S. 2002. Becoming Cultural: Society and the Incorporation of Bronze. In *Metals and society: papers from a session held at the European Association of Archaeologists sixth annual meeting in Lisbon 2000*, edited by B.S. Ottaway and E.C. Wager, 117–121. Oxford: British Archaeological Reports.

Sørensen, M.L. 1992. Gender archaeology and Scandinavian Bronze Age studies. *Norwegian Archaeological Review* 25(1): 31–49.

Sørensen, M.L. 1997. Reading dress: The construction of social categories and identities in Bronze Age Europe. *Journal of European Archaeology* 5(1): 93–114.

Sørensen, M.L. 2000. *Gender Archaeology.* Cambridge: Polity Press.

Sørensen, M.L. 2006. Gender, things and material culture. In *Handbook of Gender Archaeology*, edited by S.M. Nelson, 105–135. Berkeley: Altamira Press.

Sørensen, M.L.S. 2010. Bronze Age bodiness – maps and coordinates. In *Body Parts and Bodies Whole: Changing Relations and Meanings*, edited by K. Rebay-Salisbury, M.L.S. Sørensen and J. Hughes, 54–63. Oxford: Oxbow Books.

Sørensen, M.L. & Rebay-Salisbury, K. 2009. Landscapes of the body: Burials of the Middle Bronze Age in Hungary. *European Journal of Archaeology* 11(1): 49–74.

Sutskover, T. 2014. The Frame of Sacrificing in Judges. *Vetus Testamentum* 64: 266–278.

Tacitus, C. 1811. *The Works of Cornelius Tacitus.* Edited by A. Murphy. London: J. Stockdale.

Tarschys, D. 1998. Foreword by the Secretary General of the Council of Europe. In *Gods and Heroes of the European Bronze Age*, edited by Demakopoulou, K., Jensen, J., Kemakopoulous, K., Eluère, C., Jockenhovel, A. & Mohen, J-P. London and New York: Thames and Hudson.

Testart, A. 2004. *Les Morts d'accompagnement. La servitude volontaire I.* Paris: éditions Errance.

Thomsen, T. 1929. *Egekistefundet fra Egtved fra den Ældre Bronzealder.* Kjøbenhavn: H.H. Thieles Bogtrykkeri.

Todorov, T. 1992. *Nous et les Autres.* Paris: Éditions du Seuil.

Treherne, P. 1995. The warrior's beauty: The masculine body and self-identity in Bronze Age Europe. *Journal of European Archaeology* 3(1): 105–144.

Trigger, B. 2007. *Understanding Early Civilizations: A Comparative Study.* Cambridge: Cambridge University Press.

Turner-Walker, G. & Peacock, E.E. 2008. Preliminary results of bone diagenesis in Scandinavian bogs. *Palaeogeography, Palaeoclimatology, Palaeoecology* 266(3): 151–159. doi:10.1016/j.palaeo.2008.03.027.

Turville-Petre, E.O.G. 1964. *Myth and Religion of the North: The Religion of Ancient Scandinavia.* Westport: Greenwood Press.

van der Sanden, W. 1996. *Through Nature into Eternity. The Bog Bodies of Northwest Europe.* Amsterdam: Batavian Lion International.

Vandkilde, H. 1996. *From Stone to Bronze. The Metalwork of the Late Neolithic and Earliest Bronze Age in Denmark.* Aarhus: Jysk Arkaeologisk Selskab/Aarhus University Press.

Vandkilde, H. 2016. Bronzization: The Bronze Age as pre-modern globalization. *Praehistorische Zeitschrift* 91(1): 103–123.

Vandkilde, H. 2017. Small, medium, large: Globalisation perspectives on the Afro-Eurasian Bronze Age. In *Routledge Handbook of Globalization and Archaeology*, 506–521. London: Routledge.

Van Dijk, J., 2007. Retainer sacrifice in Egypt and Nubia. In *The Strange World of Human Sacrifice*, edited by J.N. Bremmer, 135–155. Leuven: Peeters Publishers.

Varberg, J., Gratuze, B. & Kaul, F. 2015. Between Egypt, Mesopotamia and Scandinavia: Late Bronze Age glass beads found in Denmark. *Journal of Archaeological Science* 54: 168–181.

Wallerstein, I. 1974. *The Modern World System: Capitalist Agriculture and the Origins of the European World-Economy in the Sixteenth Century*. New York: Academic Press.

Watts, J., Sheehan, O., Atkinson, Q.D., Bulbulia, J. & Gray, R.D. 2016. Ritual human sacrifice promoted and sustained the evolution of stratified societies. *Nature* 532: 228–234. doi:10.1038/nature17159.

Wehlin, J. 2013. Östersjöns Skeppssättningar. Monument Och Mötesplatser under Yngre Bronsålder, GOTARC 59. Gothenburg: University of Gothenburg.

Wels-Weyrauch, U. 1989a. Fremder Mann. *Germania* 67: 162–167.

Wels-Weyrauch, U. 1989b. Mittelbronzezeitliche Frauentrachten in Süddeutschland. In *Dynamique du Bronze Moyen en Europe Occidentale Actes du 113e Congrès National des Sociétés Savantes*, 117–134. Strasbourg: Congrès National des Sociétés Savantes.

Westermarck, E. 2016. *The Origin and Development of the Moral Ideas*. Available at: https://www.gutenberg.org/ebooks/52106 (accessed 8 June 2021).

Winkelman, M. 1998. Aztec human sacrifice: Cross-cultural assessments of the ecological hypothesis. *Ethnology* 37(3): 285–298. doi:10.2307/3774017.

Winkelman, M. 2014. Political and demographic-ecological determinants of institutionalised human sacrifice. *Anthropological Forum* 24(1): 47–70.

Human sacrifices and human remains – ultimate sacrifices?

Pernille Pantmann

Abstract

The topic of bog bodies is far from being a closed subject. Bog bodies are still mostly associated with the most iconic mummified examples. These are often understood in the light of human sacrifice. The sacrificial offering of human lives is often conceptualised as the so-called 'ultimate' sacrifice. But how do we understand sacrifice? Can a human sacrifice even be archaeologically identified? The approach to bog bodies is often biased, as the mummified examples are separated from other finds, thus creating an image of human sacrifice as a rare undertaking. By integrating the bog skeletons and the loose human bones from all contexts – including the non-sacrificial – a more complete impression of ancient societies' treatment of human remains appears. Thus, I suggest here that future bog body research could benefit by moving in new directions, where human value is debated based on the contexts of the many diverse finds of human remains, from the ritual deposition of complete bodies to the deposition of loose human bones, to depositions, e.g., among household waste and in other contexts.

Keywords: mummified bog bodies, bog skeletons, human remains, Loose Human Bones (LHB), ultimate sacrifice

Introduction

This article seeks to question how human sacrifice is still perceived in Danish archaeology, especially regarding Iron Age studies, which Løvschal *et al.* exemplify – that is, to associate this topic with bog bodies and the early Iron Age (*c.* 500 BC–AD 400) (Løvschal *et al.* 2019a, 3). The setting of the discussion is, however, often too narrow. For example, it is still debatable whether all (or any) bog bodies reflect human sacrifice. The bog body studies are furthermore uneven as the mummified examples continue to be favoured. Despite several examples from other periods (*e.g.*, Nielsen *et al.* 2020), Iron Age is still considered to be 'the age of the real bog bodies' (Fischer 2007, 169). Furthermore, the discussion of human sacrifice only partly takes single human bones from unexpected contexts into account. The latter is particularly important as these bones could potentially contribute to an insight into prehistoric views on human value and ethics towards human remains, which by all accounts make the essence of the human sacrifice discussion. Today, human sacrifice is often considered the *ultimate sacrifice*, but did this apply in prehistory as well?

So, how is human sacrifice archaeologically defined and understood, and most importantly, how is it archaeologically identified? And where do single human bones fit in? Within Mesolithic research such bones are acknowledged and named Loose Human Bones (LHB). A universal term would ease the possibility to take a *longue durée* perspective on the prehistoric ethics regarding human remains, which furthermore could broaden the archaeological understanding of human value during prehistory. This article suggests that a universal term is used in all period studies describing single human bones – LHB, for instance.

Sacrifice as opposed to offering from an archaeological viewpoint

Within the archaeological definition of *human sacrifice* lies both a definition of *sacrifice* in general and more specifically the *human sacrifice*.

The concept of *sacrifice* is widely debated within anthropology (*e.g.*, Hubert & Mauss 1964; Insoll 2011) and history of religion (*e.g.*, Eliade 1959; Carter 2003). The archaeological discussions of the subject are deeply inspired by these disciplines, but given that written sources are few, and eyewitness accounts from Danish prehistory are non-existent, we must rely on the fragmented archaeological material. Within archaeology, *sacrifice* is typically associated with religious actions in the sacred sphere, originally in the understanding of a division between the sacred and the profane spheres, inspired by Hubert and Mauss (who themselves were deeply inspired by Durkheim's discussion on that dichotomy). They defined the sacrifice to be the act of communication between the sacred and the profane worlds (Hubert & Mauss 1964). But the dichotomy between the sacred and profane has been widely debated during the last decades and is by many scholars considered to be false, with the two concepts rather intertwined across much of human experience (*e.g.*, Brück 1999; 2007; Bradley 2005).

The *sacrifice* tends very often to be associated with the violent death (and often destruction) of living creatures that are subsequently placed in contexts that differ from typical deposition practice of a particular society (Schwartz 2017, 228). The act of destroying the living is by some scholars understood as a specific element of the sacrifice (*e.g.*, Insoll 2011, 151). Thus, sacrifice would be in opposition to offerings and apparently related to non-living objects (Bradley 1990). The latter has, however, been rejected by Lund and Schwartz, who argue that non-living objects can also be sacrificed (Lund 2010; Schwartz 2017, 224). Schwartz (2017) provides an overview of where the debate on the matter stands today. According to Hubert and Mauss the destruction is the physical transformation from one state to another, and this transformation was sacred (Hubert & Mauss 1964). The problem is that deliberate acts of destruction occur on all types of objects, even the non-human (Lund 2010).

If killing can be part of both the sacrifice and the offering, and we furthermore have very poor documentation of the actions prior to the depositing (*i.e.*, the killing), then a sacrifice appears very difficult, perhaps even impossible, to identify archaeologically. Although killing is identified on some cases of Danish bog bodies: *e.g.*, the Tollund Man from pre-Roman Iron Age (Fischer 1999; 2007), and the Neolithic Sigersdal Girls (Bennike 1999; Bennike & Ebbesen 1987), it is impossible to establish whether they were sacrificed or executed. This dilemma leads to the next: can we distinguish a sacred act of killing from an execution, or can it be both simultaneously (see Walsh *et al.* 2020)? Apparently, they can, according to Campbell's studies of the Chinese Shang Culture (Campbell 2012, 315).

An archaeological distinction between the two terms, *sacrifice* and *offering*, remains to be a matter of subjective and personal preference of the terms. In my view, the broader context is the most important aspect when identifying a deposit of sacred nature (Pantmann 2020, 120). Whether or not there is a difference between a sacrifice or an offering is a discussion I prefer to avoid, as I agree with Oras, who states that the terms are usually used and understood based on an individual understanding of the terms (Oras 2013, 126). I agree with those who express concerns that within the distinctions between the terms lies a more or less hidden rating of deposited items or individuals, where a sacrifice is considered more valuable than an offering (*e.g.*, Oras 2013, 133). Thus, I prefer general terms such as *sacred act* or *sacred deposit*, rather than *sacrifice* or *offering*. As sacred deposits may contain both living and non-living objects in the sense of killed and/or exposed to destruction, it seems unreasonable to rate the living and the non-living against each other by using the terms sacrifice and offering. And if it is generally acknowledged that both humans and non-humans can be destroyed, then how can we decide whether a human was more valuable than a cow, wagon parts or flint axes, all known as offered/sacrificed items from Danish prehistory spanning the Neolithic into the Iron Age? Since the differences in value cannot be archaeologically recognised, then a human sacrifice should not maintain a status as the 'ultimate' sacrifice, as it is frequently described (see below).

The problems of identifying human sacrifice archaeologically

The choice between the terms *sacrifices* and *offerings* is somehow rarely debated when it comes to humans. Maybe this is because sacrifice traditionally entails violence and destruction, both considered parts of the human sacrifice. Løvschal *et al.* stress that human sacrifice is defined 'as any kind of violence that people inflict on one another when sanctioned or sanctified, *e.g.*, by social authority, and with explicit reference to a higher purpose or higher authority' (Løvschal *et al.* 2019a, 2). Lately, the Danish site Alken Enge has been published (Løvschal *et al.* 2019b). This site is particularly known for the deposition of numerous human skeletons exposed to violence in what was a lake during the 1st century AD. The bodies were excarnated before deposition, thus they were not deposited as individual, complete humans. Although the human bodies were obviously subject to killing and destruction, this find is not classified as human sacrifice, which illustrates the paradoxes of the choice of archaeological terms. The complexity lies in the archaeological proofs of sanctioning or sanctification. According to Schwartz, sacrifice is a possible interpretation if 'a body subjected to violence was not placed in a conventional locus for disposed humans or animals', and furthermore '... there is evidence of persons of specific ages being chosen for sacrifice' (Schwartz 2017, 229).

Another problem is that we cannot always identify violence, as many bog body skeletons have no indications of the cause of death. Thus, the unconventional placement of bodies remains an important factor in establishing whether these bodies reflect human sacrifices. Peaty environments are, in Danish archaeology, traditionally considered sacred areas, hence bodies in these environments have traditionally been equated with sacred activities (see below), although this somewhat unilateral view has recently been questioned (Pantmann 2020). Household waste without sacred countenance, for instance, is often uncovered from peaty environments as well (Pantmann 2017, 36; 2020, 266–267), occasionally with human body parts included (see below). Based on the context, these bones could just as well represent punished criminals, murder victims or simply the last remains of excarnations. The point is that the definitions of human sacrifice can easily be rejected, indicating that an overall definition of how to archaeologically identify a sacrifice must be assessed in each case based on the individual context.

Within the discussion of the human sacrifice, the general prehistoric view on human value is rarely debated concurrently, thus there is a general understanding that the encounter of human bones outside grave contexts must either be remnants of disturbed graves or human sacrifices (Stjernquist 1997, 40; 2001, 18, 21; Hansen 2006, 130–131; Holdgaard Nielsen 2011, 210; Thilderkvist 2013, 28; Henriksen 2015, 183; Sørensen 2016, 65), whereas in Britain such bones may be considered reflecting various ritual purposes (Cunliffe 1993, 105). Furthermore, it appears to be commonly accepted within Iron Age research that a human sacrifice is the *ultimate* sacrifice (*e.g.*, Stjernquist 1997, 40; 2001, 18, 21; Chapman 2000, 140; Oestigaard 2000, 42; Carlie 2004, 137; Asingh 2009, 227; Nieuwhof 2015, 89). However, Carlie has noted that not all human bones are necessarily evidence of human sacrifice, they could also represent redeposited persons in an ancestor cult (Carlie 2013, 59). The problem is, how to distinguish between a human sacrifice and other sacred practices that include human body parts?

This question is relevant as single human bones are occasionally discovered from peaty environments, but do they reflect bog bodies, subsidiary human sacrifices, other sacred acts of depositing (a final stage of excarnation, burial custom, ancestor cult, *etc.*), or something else entirely? The complexity increases as most of the bog bodies have been unprofessionally uncovered resulting in uncertainty regarding the completeness of the human remains. Are complete bodies required for a human sacrifice classification? If not, do all human bones express human sacrifice, even if their context does not imply so? According to Moen and Walsh human skeletal remains may represent sacrifice which however does not make them *human sacrifice* (Moen & Walsh 2022, 11). The discussion of the interpretation of human remains is furthermore complicated by the encounter of human remains from cultural layers with household waste. Considering how context otherwise is defining for the interpretation, it would be reasonable to consider human bones from refuse layers to be part of the refuse. Before

the subject is further elaborated, the concept of bog bodies is briefly discussed as, in Scandinavian research, they are often associated with human sacrifice.

The bog body discussion

In 1952 E. Thorvildsen introduced the human sacrifice theory in relation to the bog bodies, which was new, as they were otherwise associated with punishment and shame, inspired by Tacitus (Thorvildsen 1952). Since 1952, the sacrifice theory has been the most preferred theory within Scandinavian bog body research (*e.g.*, Glob 1965; Sellevold *et al.* 1984; Bennike and Ebbesen 1987; Fischer 1999; 2007; Asingh 2009; van der Sanden 2013, 409); for a complete overview of the early research history of bog bodies, see van der Sanden (1996). Thorvildsen based her theory on the understanding of wetlands as prehistoric sacred places, thus bog bodies should be seen in the light of this (Thorvildsen 1952, 44). A few attempts to challenge this theory have been attempted; M. Ravn, for instance, has suggested that some of the bog bodies should simply be understood as graves (Ravn 2010; 2011). Still, it appears that Danish research maintains a veneration for the human sacrifice theory, particularly related to the Iron Age bog bodies, apparently still based on the common perception of wetlands as sacred places (*e.g.*, Frei *et al.* 2015, 99; Nieuwhof 2015, 139; Løvschal *et al.* 2019a, 3), despite many examples of multiple functions of the wetlands as lately presented (*e.g.*, Johannesen 2016; Mortensen *et al.* 2020; Pantmann 2020). According to Chapman, the human sacrifice theory is linked to the Iron Age bog bodies because: 'Whilst bog bodies are known from a range of different periods, those dating to the later prehistoric/Roman periods have attracted particular attention, perhaps due to apparent patterns in the circumstances of and brutality associated with their deaths' (Chapman 2015, 110). Still, it is surprising that bog bodies continue to be associated with the Iron Age (Aldhouse-Green 2015, 9, 35; Løvschal *et al.* 2019a, 3), when it has been known for a long time that placing human bodies in wetlands spans a long chronological range from the Mesolithic to the sub-recent (van der Sanden 2013, 404; Giles 2020, 2–3). Several of the Danish bog bodies, for instance, are dated to the Neolithic (Thorvildsen 1952, 47; Bennike & Ebbesen 1987, 104; Koch 1998; Bennike 1999, 29; van der Sanden 2013, 404).

Many studies rate the mummified bog bodies above the skeletons or simply disregard the skeletons (Aldhouse-Green 2015, 8–9; Fischer 2007; Frei *et al.* 2015, 93, 96), despite numerous arguments for the inclusion of the skeletons in the understanding of the bog bodies (*e.g.*, Moen & Walsh 2022); 'the strong focus on bog mummies has led to an incomplete, biased picture' (van der Sanden 2013, 414). In my view this continued biased approach creates a false story of the low frequency of the bog body phenomenon, because the total number of bog bodies will increase if skeletal remains are included. True, the cause of death of many of the skeletons is unknown to us, which makes the human sacrifice theory more difficult to establish, but some skeletons do have traces of lethal trauma. Recently, a Neolithic bog body from Salpetermosen, in North Zealand, was discovered, and it shows an undisputable cause of death (Jørgensen & Hagedorn 2015; Plates 11–13). Furthermore, the one-eyed focus on the mummies also maintains the false impression that the phenomenon is related to the Iron Age.

Despite a general lack of interest in the skeletons, there have been a few published works over the years (*e.g.*, Bennike and Ebbesen 1985; 1987; Koch 1998; Sjögren *et al.* 2017; Nielsen *et al.* 2020; Moen & Walsh 2022). One of the greatest problems of the skeleton bog bodies is that they are not systematically ^{14}C dated, making the chronological span much more invisible, which the few campaigns of ^{14}C datings have already shown (Koch 1998; Monikander 2010; Nielsen *et al.* 2020). Of the approximately 50 bog bodies of Museum Nordsjælland, so far only eight have been ^{14}C dated, and nine bog body skeletons from Roskilde Museum have been dated. The results of these efforts, given in Table 3.1, provide an idea of the timespan. Whatever interpretation we apply to the bog bodies, we must begin with a revision of the understanding of the temporal aspect of the concept. Bog bodies are not restricted to the pre-Roman or early Roman Iron Age. Although this fact has been noted before (see above), the implications apparently need to be stressed once again.

The next issue is that many of the bog bodies are incomplete, which is a challenge. If a complete body is needed in the argument of a human sacrifice, only a few can fulfil this criterion, though it could be due to unprofessional excavations. But based on the professional excavations, it appears that some bodies were deposited in an incomplete state (*e.g.*, Ferdinand & Ferdinand 1961; Kunwald 1970). The questions are, then, whether the skeletons, both incomplete or single human bones, express human sacrifices simply due to their contexts in wetlands and/or in their relation to other deposits of sacred character? Or whether incomplete skeletons and single human bones might reflect other activities entirely? These questions bring us back to the previous discussion of the recognition of human sacrifices in the archaeological records. But the questions are also relevant in the general discussion of the meaning of single human bones deposited in wetlands. If these bones are perceived as human sacrifices, then a similar interpretation might be applied to single human bones from other contexts as well. In that case, human sacrifice was perhaps more common than we generally anticipate. In either case, all human remains should be considered when discussing topics such as ethics, human value and, of course, the ultimate status of the human in the *human sacrifice*.

Single human bones in other period studies and definition of LHB

So, what then might single human bones reflect? Are they part of a sacrificial phenomenon or are they part of a diverse find group? I will get back to the Iron Age examples below, but first the Mesolithic discussion of the subject will be briefly introduced.

Within Mesolithic research, the significance of single human bones has been discussed since the mid-1800s (Sørensen 2016, 64). However, it is only recently that these single bones have been referred to as *Loose Human Bones* (LHB). According to Brinch Petersen, LHB are defined as one or several bones that are not part of a burial (Brinch Petersen 2016, 47). They are not a homogenous group, some are possibly related to a complex burial ritual, while others are related to acts of violence (*ibid.*, 48). Brinch Petersen furthermore raises the question of whether LHB should be understood as acts of inauguration of certain sacred sites using the remains of ancestors; an interpretation that has also been suggested concerning some Mesolithic graves (*ibid.*, 53). Apparently, none of the Danish Mesolithic LHB are found in graves, and nearly all of them come from

Table 3.1. An overview of the ^{14}C dated bog body skeletons.

Source	Total ^{14}C dated individuals	Early Neo.	Early/ Mid. Neo.	Late Neo.	Early BA	Late BA	Late BA/ PRIA	PRIA	Early RIA/ Late RIA	Late RIA/ Early Migration Period	Late Migration Period	Viking Age	Published/ unpublished
Koch	17	4	8	1			4						Koch 1998, 155
Monikander	13							4	1		7	1	Monikander 2010, 87
Roskilde Museum*	9	2		2	2					1	1	1	unpublished
Museum Nordsjælland	8	2		2		1		2	1				unpublished

(*I thank Ole Kastholm, Roskilde Musuem, for sharing this information with me.)

dwelling sites with or without burials (*ibid.*, 49; Sørensen 2016, 65). Interestingly, the discussion and choice of terms in the Mesolithic research regarding human bones appear to be different from the Iron Age tradition, human sacrifice is rarely mentioned. This remains true even in the case of the site at Mortala in Sweden, where 10 human skulls, two with stakes in them, were found in a former shallow wetland. This find is referred to as parts of 'mortuary rituals' (Hallgren & Fornander 2016). I will not enter a discussion of whether these finds could be interpreted as human sacrifices, but we must wonder if the understanding of this site would have been different were it dated to the Iron Age.

Although the LHB phenomenon is mostly associated with Mesolithic research, the discussions and inclusions of single human bones are also known from the Neolithic. But as opposed to the Mesolithic studies, human sacrifice is also a well-known interpretation from the Neolithic research (Bennike & Ebbesen 1987; Andersen 2000). While Andersen agrees that human sacrifices are evident in the Neolithic, he also mentions other practices involving the manipulation of human bones (Andersen 2000, 24). Kaul elaborates, suggesting this manipulation to be the result of excarnation in both the Neolithic and the Bronze Age (Kaul 1994, 11, 35–36). Kaul's idea is not typical of Danish research, where the idea of excarnation is not widespread in the same manner as in European research (*e.g.*, Cunliffe 1993; Nieuwhof 2015; 139–140; Louwe Koojimans *et al.* 2016, 605).

In short, LHB are typically seen and understood in the light of the other ritualised activities of the periods, which in my opinion makes the concept applicable to other periods such as the Iron Age. By using the same term in different period studies would furthermore offer the opportunity to apply a *longue durée* perspective on the phenomenon LHB in unexpected contexts.

The LHB phenomenon applied to the Iron Age finds

Bog bodies are not the only examples of unconventionally treated human beings compared to the concurrent burial custom in the Danish Iron Age. As mentioned above, LHB (though not known as such) are known from Iron Age contexts, though the topic has not been widely explored in the Danish literature. When LHB are occasionally mentioned, it is typically in publications of specific settlements or finds, where their presence is only briefly mentioned and generally not recognised as perhaps part of a larger phenomenon.

On the Iron Age settlement site at Nørre Hedegård in northern Jutland, a human long bone was discovered in the chalk floor, west of the entrance of house A227, hence it was suggested to be a 'house offering' (Runge 2009, 87). On the same site a complete human skeleton was placed on the abdomen. The skeleton is stratigraphically dated to Late Bronze Age or Early pre-Roman Iron Age when cremation was the common burial practice (*ibid.*, 120–121). The find is compared to the bog bodies, referring to theories of punishment and human sacrifice (*ibid.*, 122). At the settlement site Nørre Tranders, also in northern Jutland, several finds of body parts, particularly skull fragments, were apparently related to the houses, and are thus interpreted 'house offerings', not human sacrifices (*ibid.*, 122).

At the Roman Iron Age settlement site of Lindved, on Funen, a cooking pit contained the remains of a 20–25-year-old woman. Although the entire skeleton was represented, it was incomplete. Some of the bones were articulated, suggesting that the body was deposited with connective tissue still partly preserved. Some bones had signs of cutmarks, and the bones also showed signs of heating while still covered with flesh. No indication of genuine cremation was visible. Cannibalism is mentioned as a possibility, although it cannot be proven. It has also been suggested that this person's fate was comparable to the fate of the bog bodies, but human sacrifice is not mentioned as a possible interpretation in the descriptive literature (Henriksen 2005, 95).

Brudager Mark, on Funen, is one of several examples of burial sites from the early Roman Iron Age, where the cremation burials often do not contain the complete amount of cremated material from a complete individual (Henriksen 2009, 108). This phenomenon must reflect a selection of human bones/body parts, either before or after the cremation.

The site of Ramløse Bakker,[1] North Zealand, revealed a pit which contained uncremated human bones dated to 200–1 BC, where the custom of cremation was universal. The context of the pit is unclear, as it was discovered during private gardening. At first the pit was unprofessionally excavated, and it was initially believed to be a matter for local police. It later became an archaeological concern, with some information lost during the process. The bones appeared unarticulated, suggesting a deposition after excarnation. The questions mount up. Does the find represent an executed or sacrificed person? Does the deposit express household waste or a ritualised ceremony?

These Danish examples show how the variety of unexpected treatments of human bones during the Late Bronze Age through to the Early Iron Age. They all reflect practices and perhaps even aspects of the prehistoric perception of human value, which may have differed dramatically from current principles. Yet, these perspectives ought to be included in the discussion of the significance of human sacrifice or the general sacred practice with human remains.

These Danish examples might have parallels in various European sites: on several Dutch sites like the Englum site, human skulls without mandibles were deposited within the settlement, often accompanied by animal parts. Apparently, the skulls have been removed from graves to be deposited elsewhere within the settlement (Nieuwhof 2015, 130–131).

Nieuwhof does not regard them as human sacrifices but relates them to excarnation along with other examples of LHB within the settlements (*ibid.*, 139–140). The British site of Danebury has demonstrated complex depositions of humans, both complete and incomplete bodies, which according to Cunliffe could represent human sacrifice as well as a variety of ritual activities including excarnation related to burial rituals (Cunliffe 1993, 105). Excarnation is also used to explain both the lack of graves in Scotland from 700 BC–AD 800, and the LHB on settlements/domestic contexts (Shapland & Armit 2012, 100). Based on the Scottish Iron Age finds, Shapland and Armit emphasise that prehistoric ethics towards human remains must have been considerably different to the current ethics as human bones were also used as raw material (*ibid.*, 111).

Returning to Denmark, recent excavations of dwelling sites from North Zealand have, as previously mentioned, revealed prehistoric cultural layers in former wetlands. These cultural layers contain a combination of artefacts that are generally described as household waste, such as ceramics, faunal remains, fire-cracked stones and charcoal, but occasionally LHB are also included. On the Hareholm site[2] a human humerus was found in a fen containing a refuse layer dating to the Early Iron Age, but there were also skull fragments from another, nearby fen and from a pit both ^{14}C dated to the Early Neolithic (Poz-80899). Another example is the lately excavated site called Hvidelandsgård[3] where a human humerus (Plate 13) was found in a Bronze Age refuse layer in a small, drained fen. This bone is ^{14}C dated to Late Bronze Age (Poz-124893). The Landlyst site[4] also revealed a small fen containing a refuse layer from the Roman Iron Age which included a piece of a human skull. Recently, human skull fragments have also been discovered in the cultural layers on Salpetermosen Syd site.[5] Nothing in these examples indicates that the LHB reflected sacred deposits. They could be remnants of disturbed graves, however no inhumation graves have been discovered in any of the cases.

As previously mentioned, excarnation is suggested both in the Mesolithic and Neolithic, whereas the phenomenon is only rarely mentioned within Danish Iron Age literature. LHB are equally not much discussed in Danish Iron Age contexts, as these are typically associated with remnants of disturbed graves or more vaguely defined cult practices (see above). However, LHB in settlement contexts such as refuse layers could be a result of excarnation practices, even though this is rarely proposed. Another explanation could be that human bones were used as raw materials, which finds from the Netherlands and Scotland might indicate (Shapland & Armit 2012; Nieuwhof 2015, 266–269). According to Shapland and Armit the worked human bones have a chronological wide range which indicates that this practice must be seen in a *longue durée* perspective (Shapland & Armit 2012, 104–105).

The implications of including the LHB in the human sacrifice discussion

The wide range of contexts in which human bones appear indicate that there are many aspects of prehistoric understanding of human value and indeed the related ethics thereof. The discussion of human sacrifice is traditionally centred around the common definition of sacrifice as the act of destroying a life for sacred means under ritualised circumstances, which is subsequently adopted into the archaeological lexicon. Although the variations on this definition are vague, there is one aspect which has retained broad appeal: that the *human sacrifice* is the *ultimate sacrifice*, which is accepted as largely implicit.

This idea is probably rooted in the western Christian anthropocentric view on human superiority, which also influences the human-animal relationship (Aldhouse-Green 2015, 186; Jennbert 2002, 116–117; Zachhuber & Meszaros 2013, 4) as well as on ethnographic studies of human sacrifices in other cultures (Jansen & Jiménez 2019, 7). The idea of human superiority is difficult to maintain, when the LHB with all their diversities of contexts and implications are considered. It is equally difficult to maintain the idea of the human sacrifice as an expression of human superiority, when there are so many examples of human and animal remains being treated uniformly on numerous sites and in varied contexts (*e.g.*, Jennbert 2002, 113–114; Nilsson 2009, 82). This idea is furthermore challenged by the examples of LHB from household waste contexts. Finally, the notion of human superiority requires further justification in the situations where human bones were evidently used as raw materials. Perhaps the answer to several of these dilemmas is ancestor worship, or that some humans were considered more valuable than others. But we still need to accept that humans and animals were often treated the same, which is already debated by those concerned with the so-called *animal turn* (Jennbert 2014; Boyd 2017; Salzani 2017). In short, it is thought-provoking how the treatment of many human bones contradicts the common idea of human superiority. Even though human bones are used in many ritual activities they also appear in many cases to have been handled like those of animals, or even as non-living objects. As Moen and Walsh point out, '… divides between animals, objects, and humans are not universal and static but culturally determined' (Moen & Walsh 2022, 4). It appears that ideas surrounding the value of human bodies, in parts and in whole, in blood and in bone, were diverse and laden with meanings, the likes of which we may only hope to gain a glimpse of through the archaeological record.

Conclusion

Did human sacrifice really take place in prehistory? There is ample evidence to suggest that it did. Should we abolish the idea of human sacrifice as a phenomenon within prehistoric archaeology? No. The phenomenon is an indisputable part of iconography and literature from many different cultures. But can human sacrifice be identified archaeologically, and is it truly the ultimate sacrifice? The status of the *human sacrifice* as the *ultimate sacrifice* is an assumption that does not necessarily sit well when juxtaposed against a wide variety of other finds of human remains in and out of ritual contexts. Thus, it is very important to include all human remains in the human sacrifice debate, as this contributes to a more nuanced understanding of ancient societies' view on what human value was.

As both living and non-living things can be sacrificed, and the sacred treatment of human and animals in general are alike and, in some cases, identical to the treatment of objects, then the whole idea of human superiority as an offering – and thus the human as the *ultimate sacrifice* – is difficult to maintain. In my view, we should be much more aware of the many sacred aspects that human remains could be parts of, and recognise that human remains could be disposed of in ways that may appear as offerings because they had served their purpose – for instance, after a period of excarnation. The elevated status which Iron Age research in particular forces upon the ancient view of the human being is both anthropo- and Eurocentric and under severe influence of the legacy of Christianity. But if one includes the many LHB and bog bodies, including those remains which are only preserved as skeletons, then a scenario appears in which human life may have had vastly different kinds of values attributed to it than we may even conceive of or imagine from our modern perspectives. And we might notice an element of a *longue durée* perspective which would also add to other current ideas of human ethics during prehistory. Consequently, we should consider altering our perception of human sacrifice as the *ultimate sacrifice*.

Notes

1 GIM3937 SB 010109-141.
2 NFHA 2616 SB 010506-44.
3 MNS50527 SB 010509-211.
4 NFHA2838 SB 010301-145.
5 MNS 50005 SB 010301-230, MNS 50010 010301-173.

References

Aldhouse-Green, M. 2015. *Bog Bodies Uncovered. Solving Europe's Ancient Mystery*. London: Thames & Hudson.

Andersen, N.H. 2000. Kult og ritualer i den ældre bondestenalder. *Kuml* 2000: 13–57.

Asingh, P. 2009. *Grauballemanden*. Højbjerg: Moesgård Museum.

Bennike, P. 1999. The Early Neolithic Danish bog finds: A strange group of people! In *Bog Bodies, Sacred Sites and Wetland Archaeology*, edited by B. Coles, J. Coles and M.S. Jørgensen, 27–32. Exeter: Wetland Archaeology Research Project.

Bennike, P. & Ebbesen, K. 1985. Stenstrupmanden. *Fra Holbæk Amt* 1985: 28–39.

Bennike, P. & Ebbesen, K. 1987. The bog find from Sigersdal. Human sacrifice in the Neolithic. *Journal of Danish Archaeology* 5: 85–115.

Boyd, B. 2017. Archaeology and human-animal relations: Thinking through anthropocentrism. *Annual Review of Anthropology* 46: 299–316.

Bradley, R. 1990. *The Passage of Arms. An Archaeological Analysis of Prehistoric Hoards and Votive Deposits*. Cambridge: Cambridge University Press.

Bradley, R. 2005. *Ritual and Domestic Life in Prehistoric Europe*. New York: Routledge.

Brinch Petersen, E. 2016. Afterlife in the Danish Mesolithic – the creation, use and discarding of 'Loose Human Bones'. In *Mesolithic Burials – Rites, Symbol, and Social Organization of Early Postglacial Communities*, edited by J.M. Grünberg, B. Gramsch, L. Larsson, J. Orschiedt and H. Meller, 47–62. Tagungen des Landesmuseums für Vorgeschichte Halle 13/1.

Brück, J. 1999. Ritual and rationality: Some problems of interpretation in European archaeology. *European Journal of Archaeology* 2(3): 313–344.

Brück, J. 2007. Ritual and rationality: Some problems of interpretation in European archaeology. In *The Archaeology of Identities – a Reader*, edited by T. Insoll, 281–307. Abingdon: Routledge.

Campbell, R. 2012. On sacrifice: An archaeology of Shang sacrifice. In *Sacred Killing. The Archaeology of Sacrifice in the Ancient Near East*, edited by A.M. Porter and G.M. Schwartz, 305–325. Winona Lake, Indiana: Eisenbrauns.

Carlie, A. 2004. *Forntida byggnads kult*. Stockholm: Riksantikvarieämbetets förlag.

Carlie, A. 2013. Archaeology and ritual: A case study on traces of ritualization in archaeological remains from Lindängelund, southern Sweden. *Folklore* 55: 49–68.

Carter, J. 2003. *Understanding Religious Sacrifice. A Reader*. London & New York: Continuum.

Chapman, J. 2000. *Fragmentation in Archaeology*. London: Routledge.

Chapman, H. 2015. The landscape archaeology of bog bodies. *Journal of Wetland Archaeology* 15(1): 109–121.

Cunliffe, B. 1993. *Book of Danebury*. London: B.T. Batsford, English Heritage.

Eliade, M. 1959. *The Sacred and the Profane*. New York: Harcourt Publishing Company.

Ferdinand, J. & Ferdinand, K. 1961. Jernalderofferfund i Valmose ved Rislev. *Kuml* 1961: 47–90.

Fischer, C. 1999. The Tollund Man and the Elling Woman and other bog bodies from Central Jutland. In *Bog Bodies, Sacred Sites and Wetland Archaeology*, edited by B. Coles, J. Coles and M.S. Jørgensen, 93–97. Exeter: Wetland Archaeology Research Project.

Fischer, C. 2007. *Tollundmanden. Gaven til guderne. Mosefund fra Danmarks forhistorie*. Silkeborg: Hovedland.

Frei, K.M., Mannering, U., Price, T.D. & Iversen, R.B. 2015. Strontium isotope investigations of the Haraldskær Woman – a complex record of various tissues. *ArcheoSciences, revué d'archéométrie* 39: 93–101.

Giles, M. 2020. *Bog Bodies. Face to Face with the Past*. Manchester: Manchester University Press.

Glob, P.V. 1965. *Mosefolket – Jernalderens mennesker bevaret i 2000 år*. København: Gyldendal.

Hallgren, F. & Fornander, E. 2016. Skulls on stakes and skulls in water. Mesolithic mortuary rituals at Kanaljorden Mortala, Sweden 7000 BP. In *Mesolithic Burials – Rites, Symbol, and Social Organization of Early Postglacial Communities*, edited by J.M. Grünberg, B. Gramsch, L. Larsson, J. Orschiedt and H. Meller, 161–174. Tagungen des Landesmuseums für Vorgeschichte Halle 13/1.

Hansen, J. 2006. Offertradition og religion i ældre jernalder i Sydskandinavien – med særligt henblik på bebyggelsesofringer. *Kuml* 2006: 117–176.

Henriksen, M.B. 2005. Danske Kogestensgruber og kogegrubefelter fra yngre bronzealder og ældre jernalder. In *De gåtefulle kokegroper*, edited by L. Gustafson, T. Heibreen and J. Martens, 77–102. Oslo: Varia 58.

Henriksen, M.B. 2009. *Brudager Mark – en romertidsgravplads nær Gudme på Sydøstfyn*. Fynske Jernaldergrave bd. 6,1. Fynske Studier 22. Odense: Odense Bys Museer.

Henriksen, M.B. 2015. Kenotafer, ødelagte grave eller ofringer? Deponeringer og andre aktiviteter på ældre jernalders gravpladser. In *De dødes landskab. Grav og gravskik i ældre jernalder i Danmark*, edited by P. Foss and N.A. Møller, 183–214. Saxo Instituttet Københavns Universitet, Arkæologiske Skrifter 13.

Holdgaard Nielsen, M. 2011. Offerfund og religiøse forestillinger. In *Fyn i Fortiden. Det levede liv 500 f.Kr.–150 e.Kr.*, edited by M.H. Nielsen, 173–213. Odense: Odense Bys Museer.

Hubert, H. & Mauss, M. 1964 (1899). *Sacrifice: Its Nature and Function*. Chicago: University of Chicago Press.

Insoll, T. 2011. Sacrifice. In T. Insoll (ed.) *The Oxford Handbook of the Archaeology of Ritual and Religion*, edited by T. Insoll, 151–165. Oxford: Oxford University Press.

Jansen, M.E.R.G.N. & Jiménez, G.A.P. 2019. *Deconstructing the Aztec Human Sacrifice*. Centre for Indigenous America Studies. Leiden: Leiden University.

Jennbert, K. 2002. Djuren i nordisk förkristen ritual och myt. In *Plats och Praxis – studier av nordisk förkristen ritual*, edited by K. Jennbert, A. Andrén and C. Raudevere, 105–133. Vägar til Midgård. Lund: Nordic Academic Press.

Jennbert, K. 2014. Certain humans, certain animals, attitudes in the long term. In *Exploring the Animal Turn. Human-Animal Relations in Science, Society and Culture*, edited by E.A. Cederholm, A. Björck, K. Jennbert and A-S. Lönngren, 183–192. Lund: Pufendorfinstitutet.

Johannesen, K. 2016. *Rituals of Common Things. The Ritual and Religion of the Mixed Wetland Deposits in the Early Iron Age of Southern Scandinavia* (unpublished Ph.D. thesis, Moesgård University).

Jørgensen, T. & Hagedorn, L. 2015. Salpetermoseliget. *Alle Tiders Nordsjælland*. Museum Nordsjællands Årbog 2015: 118–122.

Kaul, F. 1994. Ritualer med menneskeknogler i yngre stenalder. *Kuml* 1991–1992: 7–52.

Koch, E. 1998. *Neolithic Bog Pots from Zealand, Møn, Lolland and Falster*. Nordiske Fortidsminder. Serie B, Vol. 16. København: Det Kongelige Nordiske Oldsskriftselskab.

Kunwald, G. 1970. Der Moorfund im Rappendam auf Seeland. *Prähistorische Zeitschrift* 45: 42–88.

Louwe Kooijmans, L., Hamburg, T. & Smits, L. 2016. Burial and non-burial at Late Mesolithic Hardinxveld (NL). In *Mesolithic Burials – Rites, Symbol, and Social Organization of Early Postglacial Communities*, edited by J.M. Grünberg, B. Gramsch, L. Larsson, J. Orschiedt and H. Meller, 593–607. Tagungen des Landesmuseums für Vorgeschichte Halle 13/1.

Lund, J. 2010. At the water's edge. In *Signals of Belief in Early England. Anglo-Saxon Paganism Revisited*, edited by M. Carver and S. Semple, 49–66. Oxford: Oxbow Books.

Løvschal, M., Gullbek, S.V., Johansen, M.-L., O'Neill, S., Walsh, M. & Willerslev, R. 2019a. Human sacrifice and value. *Antiquity* 93: 1–4. doi:10.15184/aqy.2019.104.

Løvschal, M., Iversen, R.B. & Holst, M.K. (eds) 2019b. *De dræbte krigere i Alken Enge. Efterkrigsritualer i ældre jernalder*. Jysk Arkæologisk Selskab. Højbjerg: Aarhus Universitet, Museum Skanderborg, Moesgaard Museum.

Moen, M. & Walsh, M.J. 2022. Under the skin: Norwegian bog skeletons and perceptions of personhood, value and sacrifice. *European Journal of Archaeology* 25(4): 483–503. doi:10.1017/eaa.2021.65.

Monikander, A. 2010. *Våld och vatten. Våtmarkskult vid Skedemosse under järnåldern*. Stockholms Studies in Archaeology 52. Stockholms Universitet.

Mortensen, M.F., Christensen, C., Johannesen, K, Stidsing, E., Fiedel, R. & Olsen, J. 2020. Iron Age peat cutting and ritual depositions in bogs – new evidence from Fuglsøgaard Mose, Denmark. *Danish Journal of Archaeology* 9: 1–30. doi:10.7146/dja.v9i0.116377.

Nielsen, B.H., Christensen, T. & Frei, KM. 2020. New insights from forgotten bog bodies: The potential of bog skeletons for investigating the phenomenon of deposition of human remains in bogs during prehistory. *Journal of Archaeological Science* 2020: 1–13. doi:10.1016/j.jas.2020.105166.

Nieuwhof, A. 2015. *Eight Human Skulls in a Dung Heap. Ritual Practice in the Terp Region of the Northern Netherlands 600BC–300AD*. Groningen: Barkhuis.

Nilsson, L. 2009. Häst och hund i fruktbarhedskult och blot. In *Järnålderens rituella platser*, edited by A. Carlie, 81–99. Femton artiklar om kultutövning och religion från en konferens i Nissaström den 4–5 oktober 2007. Halmstad: Kulturmiljö Halland.

Oestigaard, T. 2000. Sacrifices of raw, cooked and burnt humans. *Norwegian Archaeological Review* 33(1): 41–58.

Oras, E. 2013. Sacrifice or offering: What can we see in the archaeology of Northern Europe? *Folklore* 55: 125–150.

Pantmann, P. 2017. Vådbundsgravninger i Danmark. Integrér nu vådbundsområderne i den almene arkæologiske praksis. *Arkæologisk Forum* 37: 35–44.

Pantmann, P. 2020. *Defining Wetlands. New Perspectives on Wetland Living with Case Studies from Early Iron Age on North Zealand, Denmark* (unpublished Ph.D. thesis, Copenhagen University).

Ravn, M. 2010. Burials in bogs. Bronze and Early Iron Age bog bodies from Denmark. *Acta Archaeologica* 81: 106–117.

Ravn, M. 2011. Bog bodies – a burial practice during the Early Iron Age? In *The Iron Age on Zealand – Status and Perspectives*, edited by L. Boye, 81–87. Copenhagen: The Royal Society of Northern Antiquities.

Runge, M. 2009. *Nørre Hedegård. En nordjysk byhøj fra ældre jernalder*. Jysk Arkæologisk Selskabs Skrifter 66. Aarhus: Aarhus Universitetsforlag.

Salzani, C. 2017. From post-human to post-animal. Posthumanism and the 'Animal Turn'. *Lo Sguardo – Revista di Filiosofia* 24 (II): Limiti E Confini del Posthumano, 97–109.

Schwartz, G.M. 2017. The archaeological study of sacrifice. *Annual Review of Anthropology* 2017: 223–240.

Sellevold, B.J., Hansen, U.L. & Jørgensen, J.B. 1984. *Iron Age Man in Denmark*. København: Det Kongelige Nordiske Oldskriftselskab.

Shapland, F. & Armit, I. 2012. The useful dead: Bodies as objects in Iron Age and Norse Atlantic Scotland. *European Journal of Archaeology* 15(1): 98–116.

Sjögren, K.-G., Ahlström, T., Blank, M., Price, T.D., Frei, K.M. & Hollund, H.I. 2017. Early Neolithic bog finds from Falbygden, western Sweden: New isotopic, ostelogical and historical investigations. *Journal of Neolithic Archaeology* 19: 97–126. doi:10.12766/jna.2017.4.

Stjernquist, B. 1997. *The Röekillorna Spring. Spring-cults in Scandinavian Prehistory*. Stockholm: Skrifter utgivna av Kungl. Humanistiska Vetenskapssamfunet i Lund. LXXXII.

Stjernquist, B. 2001. Offerplatsen och samhällsstrukturen. In *Uppåkra. Centrum och Sammanhang*, edited by B. Hårdh, 3–28. Uppåkrastudier 3. Acta Archaeologica Lundensia series 8, no. 34.

Sørensen, S.A. 2016. Loose human bones from the Danish Mesolithic. In *Mesolithic Burials – Rites, Symbol, and Social Organization of Early Postglacial Communities*, edited by J.M. Grünberg, B. Gramsch, L. Larsson, J. Orschiedt and H.

Meller, 63–72. Tagungen des Landesmuseums für Vorgeschichte Halle 13/1.

Thilderkvist, J. 2013. *Ritual Bones or Common Waste. A Study of Early Medieval Bone Deposits in Northern Europe*. Groningen: Barkhuis.

Thorvildsen, E. 1952. Menneskeofringer i Oldtiden. Jernalderligene fra Borremose i Himmerland. *Kuml* 1952: 32–48.

van der Sanden, W. 1996. *Udødeliggjorte i mosen. Historien om de vesteuropæiske moselig*. Amsterdam: Batavian Lion International.

van der Sanden, W. 2013. Bog bodies. Underwater burials sacrifice and executions. In *The Oxford Handbook of Wetland Archaeology*, edited by F. Menotti and A. O'Sullivan, 401–418. Oxford: Oxford University Press.

Walsh, M., Moen, M., O'Neill, S., Gullbekk, S.H. & Willerslev, R. 2020. Who's afraid of the S-word? Deviants' burials and human sacrifice. *Norwegian Archaeological Review* 53(2): 154–162. doi:10.1080/00293652.2020.1850853.

Zachhuber, J. & Meszaros, J. 2013. Introduction. In *Sacrifice and Modern Thought*, edited by J. Zachhuber and J. Meszaros, 1–10. Oxford: Oxford University Press.

4

Naked or clothed? Bog bodies and the value of clothing in the Late Iron Age

Ulla Mannering

Abstract

This chapter provides a brief overview of the Danish bog bodies, bog textiles, bog skin objects and other associated finds. Due to quite special preservation conditions and the changing understandings of the contexts of many such finds, it is important to be critical of previous interpretations, such as the prevailing notion that many of the bog bodies were deposited naked. Textiles and skin clothing objects were basic necessities in the Early Iron Age, just as clothing and garments are today. But it is vital to consider for prehistory that these resources required access to different, often high-investment and valuable raw materials. They also required exceptional crafting skills and a great deal of time and effort to produce. As such, these objects represent a much greater value than they are often assigned. Based on the Huldremose find, the chapter outlines new ways to interpret and estimate the social, symbolic and economic value of bog textiles and skin clothing objects.

Keywords: bog bodies, Early Iron Age, clothing, textiles, skin objects

Introduction

Bog bodies have for many centuries scared and fascinated laymen and professionals, as they offer a unique chance to come close to and visualise individuals who lived many thousands of years ago. The term 'bog bodies' is used for both complete bodies or body parts with preserved soft tissues, while the term 'bog skeletons' is reserved for skeletal parts lacking intact soft tissue. It is estimated that several hundred bog bodies and skeletons have been found in the Danish bogs covering most archaeological periods from the Stone Age to the Viking Age or Early Medieval period (Hald 1980; van der Sanden 1996; Ravn 2010, 106).

While often presented as naked, going through the original find descriptions it is apparent that the majority of the Danish bog bodies are in fact found together with a wealth of clothing items made of textiles, skins and leather. For a long time, it has been ignored that these items represented an exceptional value in a prehistoric society where most goods were produced from locally available resources on individual farmsteads (Frei *et al.* 2015; 2017). In this article I challenge the traditional view that bog bodies are placed

low on a social chain of value and demonstrate that they in fact represent the opposite in Early Iron Age society. The largest group of well-preserved bog bodies in Denmark are the ones dated to the Early Iron Age which cluster in the period between 500 BC and AD 200 (Mannering *et al.* 2010). An important result of the many new datings conducted on the associated textile and skin items is that finds previously linked to either a Late Bronze Age or a Roman Iron Age context have now been securely placed in the pre-Roman Iron Age culture, 500–1 BC. For example, the Borremose I (1946), II (1947) and III (1948) bog bodies that were earlier believed to have ranged between 920–390 BC (Asingh & Lynnerup 2007; Fischer 2007) are now dated to the much narrower period of 416–209 BC. Likewise, the Huldremose Woman which has traditionally been seen as belonging to the Roman Iron Age has now a similar precise dating of 350–41 BC. Secure Late Bronze Age bog finds are the single finds of a pair of shoes from Ørbækgård, a shoe from Vivsø and a shoe from Undelev found together with a male bog body in the late 18th century (Mannering *et al.* 2010; Andersen *et al.* 2011). Altogether, these new dates open up the opportunity for renewed studies of the bog bodies, including their clothing and other objects in a much more precise context than previously possible.

The Danish bog bodies are primarily found in Jutland, where the special acidic environment of the bogs has had a crucial influence on the preservation condition of these finds and other organic objects placed in the bogs (van der Sanden 1996). Among the public, the Tollund Man and the Grauballe Man are probably the most well-known bog bodies. The Tollund Man with his beautiful and peaceful face and the noose around his neck and the Grauballe Man with his crushed face and cut-open throat open a fascinating gateway to prehistoric life in all its complexity and horror (Asingh & Lynnerup 2007; Fischer 2007). But seen from a clothing perspective, the completely naked Grauballe Man and the Tollund Man with his odd outfit consisting of nothing but a fur cap and the leather belt around his waist are neither very exciting nor represent the norm of bog bodies preserved in the Danish wetlands. It is obvious that something vital is missing: their clothing. This raises the question: were either of these two men wearing clothing items which have not survived the long centuries in the bog?

The random retrieval

The first bog body recorded in modern times from a Danish bog was found in Raunholt on Funen in 1773 (Henriksen 2008). Today the find is lost, but from then on, more and more bog bodies and bog finds of textiles and skins have been reported to the authorities and sometimes also incorporated into museum collections.

Another find story of a bog body found during peat cutting in Rørbæk in North Jutland exemplifies their complex and often random discovery. In 1963, during ploughing, a wooden box appeared which turned out to contain the remains of a bog body, including cranial parts and various bones, some still with flesh and skin, part of a hand and human hair, some skin scraps and the remains of a skin cap (NM journal 317/63). The authorities were informed, and by talking to the local farmers it was discovered that the body had already been found in 1893, 70 years earlier, but was secretly reburied in the box close to the find spot in order not to create any disturbance in the peat cutting, and disrupt the income of the peat workers. Right after the recovery it was exhibited at Ålborg Historiske Museum, attracting many spectators. But, after arriving at the National Museum of Denmark, it lived a dull life, placed in the cantina of the conservation department until in 1976 it was finally deemed unworthy of registration and was eventually thrown away. The find from Rørbæk is thus an excellent example of the strangely ambivalent attitude towards some bog bodies, not only in the local community, but also within academia.

A likewise complicated find story is linked to the bog body of the so-called Huldremose Woman, found in eastern Jutland in 1879. In this case the whole find, body and objects, was immediately sent to the National Museum of Denmark in Copenhagen where the exceptionally well-preserved clothing items were included in the museum collection and exhibitions as particular highlights (Hald 1980, 47–54; Mannering 2010). The body, on the other hand, was treated in a quite different way: kept in the museum basement for 25 years until, in 1904, it was given away to the Normal Anatomical Institute in Copenhagen. Here it rested until 1976 when it was rediscovered and returned to the museum (Brothwell *et al.* 1990). For almost 100 years, the body was virtually unseen and untouched by human hands. It was not until 2008, during a careful study of the clothing items, that it was discovered that traces of a linen clothing item was preserved on the woman's back and in skin folds on the lower part of the legs (Frei *et al.* 2009; Mannering 2010). What this clothing item looked like is unknown, but it definitely covered most of the body and was worn underneath the well-known wool and skin clothing items that were removed from the body in 1879.

Therefore, we must consider that bog bodies and materials found in bogs are even more biased by find and preservation conditions than finds from other archaeological contexts. These important but often maltreated remains have undergone changing understandings of their value, as sources of information to both museums (and thus the public) and to academic research.

The Huldremose Woman

Apart from the linen gown, the Huldremose Woman also wore two skin capes, a woven scarf and a skirt (Hald 1980, 47–54; Nørgård 2008). In this way, she represents one of the most well-dressed women from an Early Iron Age context (Plate 14).

The wool scarf, measuring 139–144 cm in length and 49 cm in width (Plate 15), with fringes at both short ends, was placed around the head and neck of the woman, and was pinned together with an 8 cm long pointed bird bone, *i.e.*, a 'primitive' dress pin (Plate 16A). The wool skirt around her waist measures 220–252 cm in circumference and 81–84 cm in height. These textiles each represent a considerable value in terms of raw materials and working hours, not to mention crafting skill and technological knowhow.

The two skin capes, constructed in a less common asymmetrical pattern, are made of several well-prepared curly fleeces. The outer cape is the largest, measuring 82 cm in height and 170 cm in width (see Plate 14). It is constructed of five primary dark sheepskin pieces, but has the unique detail of an insertion of four light goat skin pieces placed around the shoulder line and an inner front lining covering the flesh side. The inner cape is slightly smaller, measuring 80 cm in height and 150 cm in width, and is made similarly of 7–8 primary curly sheep fleeces (Plate 17, top). While the outer cape seems almost new, the inner cape is rather worn and has been repaired several times, with altogether 22 quite different looking patches of goat and deer skin (Plate 17, bottom). Thus, the capes represent, each in their way, an early and late stage of use, and exemplify the care with which skin clothing was treated and hint at the possibility also of their high value.

In the find description it is further stated that a horn comb, a leather thong and a narrow tabby woven band were found in a pocket in the outer skin cape, wrapped in a bladder skin (Plate 16B). An X-ray examination of the capes made in 2009 revealed that the items were in fact not placed in the outer but rather in the inner cape, in a large three-dimensional patch, which was closed on all four sides, thus making the objects inaccessible. Although the patch could have been opened occasionally, nothing in the stitching indicates this more flexible use. The band measures 74 cm in length and only 1.5 cm in width and has two cords attached perpendicular to the length of the band, which are 77 and 78 cm long respectively. Most likely this item had at some point been used as a hairband, or it could have been sewn on to a sprang cap, as is seen in the cases of the Haraldskær and Bredmose Women. The band is not exceptional in any way, except that it is dyed in a blue colour (Vanden Berghe *et al.* 2009). According to the latest research results, plant dyes were introduced in Danish prehistory during the pre-Roman Iron Age, and colours, apart from those of natural wool, were not part of design preferences of earlier periods (Frei *et al.* 2017). Thus, the introduction of yellow, blue, green and sometimes red plant-dyed colours must have made the many dyed textile items even more attractive and visually appealing, but in this context the hairband takes on an extra symbolic dimension, well beyond mere practicality.

Altogether, the Huldremose outfit in all its different parts offers a fascinating insight into pre-Roman Iron Age clothing technology and design, but also shows the high value of different raw materials and aesthetics. In this way clothing may shed light on the capacity of these garments as means of symbols and a way of advertising both group connections and individual identities.

The textile and skin data

The Huldremose Woman is not the only find with many and complete clothing items. Going through the archives at the National Museum of Denmark, it is possible to find data about more than 50 finds, constituting clothing items of textile and skin with or without a connection to a bog body (Table 4.1). Altogether, these represent more than 80 individual items of complete or nearly complete size. From a prehistoric context this is an unprecedented bulk of material, which offers a firm statistical base for evaluating and interpreting the value of the Early Iron Age bog body individuals and their clothing. Like Huldremose, the Haraldskær, Krogens Mølle and Bredmose bog women were

similarly clad in many textiles and skin clothing items which underline their individual status.

Based on Table 4.1 it can be seen that approximately half of the recorded Danish clothing finds from wetland contexts are associated with body bodies. The others are single finds. Of the bog bodies, the distribution of sex is almost even, and only in a few cases has the sex of the individual not been recorded. All bodies are adults, except for the Thorup I find, which was reported as an infant wrapped in a textile. Similarly, it is further possible that the Møgelmose bog body was a very young girl. Unfortunately, neither of these particular bog bodies have survived to the present day, so these descriptions cannot be confirmed.

From Table 4.1 it is further apparent that the bog finds contain almost as many skin objects as textiles. More than 45 individual and almost complete textiles have been recorded together with a bog body or as single finds. Basically, the textiles can be divided into three different size categories which help us consider their function as garments or value as clothing items. The first category consists of textiles in a size of about 50 × 150 cm often with fringes at both short ends. A prime example of this comes from the Huldremose find (Plate 15). The second group consists of larger rectangular textiles with typical measurements of around 100 × 150 cm. An example of this type was found wrapped around the body of the Borremose III Woman (Plate 18). The third group consists of even larger pieces of approximately 150 × 200 cm, such as the textile from Skærsø (Plate 19). This type could have served different purposes, such as blankets or cloaks worn draped around the body. Textile pieces could also be wrapped around the lower legs as in the case of the Søgård II Man (Plate 20).

Likewise, the skin capes were produced in standard designs. These typically comprise either asymmetrical (like the ones from Huldremose) or symmetrical cape designs. More than 15 complete symmetrical skin capes have been found in the Danish bogs, and it is not uncommon for individuals to have more than one cape. For example, in the find from Karlby, four skin capes were found together with a male individual.

Other skin garments consist of caps, wrap-around garments, belts and even a tunic. Further, more than 20 shoes have been found in Danish bogs, either in connection with a body or as single finds (Hald 1972; Mannering & Lynnerup 2013; Mannering 2017). Interestingly, and in spite of her very complete outfit, the Huldremose Woman was not wearing shoes. The Undelev Man, on the other hand, was wearing a pair of shoes, while the Søgård I Man had a pair of shoes lying next to him (Plate 21). Of the single shoe finds, it is especially worth mentioning the Borremose V, St Borremose and Havndal finds, which each contain single worn-out shoes placed in a vessel. No doubt these shoes had little practical value at this stage, but judging by the careful and deliberate placement in the bog, they must

Table 4.1. Bog bodies and single finds of clothing found in the Danish bogs.

Find	Find year	Bog body sex	Textile pieces	Skin capes	Other clothing items	Other artefacts	Date
Arnitlund	>1902	Single find			1 shoe		AD 600–775
Auning	1886	F	1	1	Skin wrap	Sticks	200 BC–AD 140
Baunsø	1927	M/lost		3			AD 20–220
Borremose I	1946	M	1	2		Bast fiber cord	365–116 BC
Borremose II	1947	M	3			Amber bead, vessel, bronze disc, leather cord (sticks)	483–95 BC
Borremose III	1948	F	1			Leather cord	401–209 BC
Borremose IV	1947	Single find			1 shoe in	Vessel	46 BC–AD 115
Borremose V	1950	Single find	1				370–180 BC
St Borremose	1941	Single find			1 shoe in	Vessel	171 BC–AD 2
Bredmose	1942	F	4		Sprang cap		370 BC–AD 10
Corselitze	1843	F/ lost	2		Tablet-woven band	Fibula, 7 beads	AD 210–410
Elling	1938	F		1	Textile belt	Leather rope, skin wrap	390–160 BC
Finderup	?	Single find			Pair of shoes		805–545 BC
Fræer	1842	M?	1		1 shoe (pair)		110 BC–AD 60
Grathe Hede	1933	Single find	1				190 BC–AD 10
Grauballe	1952	M					400–200 BC
Haraldskær	1835	F	3	1	Sprang cap	Wool cord (sticks)	347–42 BC
Havndal	1886	Single find			1 shoe in	Vessel	353–107 BC
Horreby Lyng	1940	?/lost		1?		Wooden spade	385–203 BC
Huldremose I	1879	F	3	2	Textile hair band	Comb, 2 amber beads, leather cord, wool cord	350–41 BC
Huldremose II	1896	Single find	1				350–30 BC
Karlby	1900	M	1	4?			200 BC–AD 90
Krogensmølle	1878	F	c. 5	2		Leather rope, (belt)	399–207 BC
Møgelmose	1857	F/lost			Skin tunic	(sticks)	AD 252–402
Oksenbjerg	1946	Single find				Leather bag	AD 258–532
Rebild	1946	Single find	1			Wooden statue	360–110 BC
Refstrup	>1912	Single find		1			AD 130–630
Rise Hjarup	>1888	Single find			1 shoe		AD 53–229
Roum	1942	F		1			50 BC–AD 80
Rønbjerg II	1891	?/lost	1	2		Leather strap	360–50 BC
Rønbjerg III	1921	M			Pair of shoes		355–47 BC
Skibelund	1944	Single find			1 shoe		47 BC–AD 123
Skærsø	1944	Single find	1				350 BC–AD 90
Skærum	1913	?		1			200 BC–AD 250
Stidsholt	1859	F			Textile hair band		392–204 BC
Stokholm	1894	Single find	1				360–50 BC
Søgårds I	1942	M	1	3	Skin cap, pair of shoes	Bast fibre cord	352–51 BC

(Continued)

Table 4.1. (Continued)

Find	Find year	Bog body sex	Textile pieces	Skin capes	Other clothing items	Other artefacts	Date
Søgårds II	1944	M?		2	Leg wraps, leather wrap		AD 130–340
Søvsø	?	Single find?			1 shoe		1041–851 BC
Thorup I	1887	Infant/lost	1 (leg wraps)				360–50 BC
Thorup II	1951	Single find	1				400–200 BC
Tollund	1950	M			Skin cap	Leather rope, belt	410–210 BC
True	1941	Single find		1			350 BC–AD 70
Tvedemose	1942	?		1?		Stone	350–40 BC
Undelev	1797/1810	M/lost		(2)	1 shoe (pair)	(Sticks)	900–770 BC
Unknown	?	Unknown	1				400–200 BC
Vesterris	1944	Single find			Leather bag	Sticks, other objects	750–100 BC
Vester Torsted	1913	M		1		?	AD 120–330
Viborg I	>1951	Single find?			Pair of shoes		AD 5–124
Viborg II	?	Single find?			1 shoe		388–194 BC
Vindum	1883	F?	(1?)	1			386–203 BC
Vivsø	1946	Single find			1 shoe		900–798 BC
Ømark	1940	Single find	1				390–200 BC
Ørbækgård	>1892	Single find			Pair of shoes		920–807 BC
Ålestrup	1940?	Single find	1				520–380 BC
Årdestrup	1946	Single find		1		Oar and vessels	350–40 BC

have had a different use. Here we see a strong indication that even worn-out clothing objects possessed symbolic meaning and value.

The value of clothing

The majority of the recorded skin objects are produced of skins from domesticated animals such as sheep, goats and cattle (Brandt *et al.* 2014). There are only a few examples of skins from wild mammals such as deer, otter and wolf. This is an interesting identification result, as numerous fur-bearing animals were living close to most inhabited areas during the Early Iron Age, and hunting, although small-scale, was a common aspect of the subsistence economy (Kveiborg 2008). Nevertheless, it appears that fur from wild species was not an important resource when it comes to pre-Roman Iron Age clothing, although it certainly was by the later Viking Age (Mannering 2015). It is estimated that in order to produce a skin cape, approximately six complete animal skins were required. This means that six animals were taken out of production. While these were probably eaten, how often could this be done in the case of an average small Early Iron Age farm in order to create one clothing item? How large a sheep flock did each farm maintain in order to produce both skins for clothing, other utensils and wool for textiles for a whole family? No doubt the amount of resources used for producing the clothing items is impressive and shows

that these clothing items represented a considerable value in Early Iron Age society (Jensen 2013).

To date, the largest textile found in a bog is the single find from Thorup II, which measures 141 × 262 cm (Plate 22). For the manufacture of this single textile it would have been necessary to spin no less than 4400 metres of yarn. It is estimated that an experienced spinner can spin 400 metres of yarn per day (Olufsson *et al.* 2015, 84). Thus, it would have taken at least 11 days to spin the yarn, and another 10 days to weave the textile, not to mention the collection and processing of the wool. All in all, the production would have taken at least 20 days working full-time. Clearly, the fact that so much time, effort and material was taken out of circulation is worth reconsidering when we talk about bog sacrifices and the value of their accompanying clothing.

Textiles and skin clothing objects were basic necessities in Early Iron Age society, and represent a much greater value than we are able to imagine today where common clothing has a relatively low value. This may also be the reason why it is often quoted that bog bodies do not have any personal belongings (Munksgård 1974; van der Sanden 1996). The Huldremose Woman was placed in the bog clad in three textiles and two skin capes, and within her clothing were concealed a comb and a dyed blue hairband: a sign that these objects most likely had a symbolic connotation, similar to magical amulets or fetishes. This is a feature which is well known in, *e.g.*, arctic clothing (Rasmussen 1931,

271–274; Issenman 1997, 184), but has never before been connected to a Northern European clothing tradition. The Huldremose Woman also had two small amber beads on a wool cord around her neck (Plate 16A). Also, the Borremose II Man had an amber bead and small bronze disc on a cord around his neck. Neither of these finds can be described as insignificant objects, as the disc is quite small – little more than a bead itself – and amber was one of the major trade commodities in the preceding periods and possibly still in the Early Iron Age.

Conclusion

Based on the recordings of the many textiles and skin clothing items from Danish bogs, it can be concluded that similar clothing items were placed together with both male and female bog bodies. For instance, the same type of cape is linked to both sexes, likewise are shoes of a similar design observable with both men and women, as are merely smaller versions for children. Also, the various rectangular textile wrap-around garments occur with both males and females, showing that the same design was in fact used by both. The clearest gender-specific garments are the woven skirts for women, which have been found in Huldremose I and Krogens Mølle, while leg-wraps and skin caps are specifically connected with males. Based on this evidence it can be concluded that Early Iron Age clothing design was generally influenced by an interchangeable, unisex concept, or the notion that clothing items were indeed so valuable that they were not subjected to any strict personal ownership customs.

The fact that some of the bog bodies may have been wearing clothing items that have not survived the long stay in the acidic bog environment, as shown for the disintegrated linen gown of the Huldremose Woman, or the odd combination of naught but a belt and cap for the Tollund Man, cannot be ignored. For too long, the focus has been placed on the importance of the human body as the greatest sacrifice. Here, I advocate for the fact that bog bodies and bog deposits are much more complicated phenomena that cannot be subjected to any single explanation. Instead, they require multiple interpretative angles, and when we evaluate clothing items and other attached objects in relation to their value bog bodies provide a whole new understanding of the prehistoric societies of which they were a part.

References

Andersen, S.W., Mannering, U. & Rasmussen, K.L. 2011. Undelevmanden, – et moselig fra yngre bronzealder. *Aarbøger for Nordisk Oldkyndighed og Historie* 2009: 7–18.

Asingh, P. 2007. The Bog People. In *Grauballe Man: An Iron Age Bog Body Revisited*, edited by P. Asingh and N. Lynnerup, 291–314. Aarhus: Jutland Archaeological Society.

Bender Jørgensen, L. 1986. *Forhistoriske Textiler i Skandinavien. Prehistoric Scandinavian Textiles.* Nordiske Fortidsminder Serie B, bd. 9. København: Det kongelige Nordiske Oldskriftselskab.

Brandt, L.Ø., Schmidt, A.L., Mannering, U., Sarret, M., Kelstrup, C.D., Olsen, J.V. & Cappellini, E. 2014. Species identification of archaeological skin objects from Danish bogs: Comparison between mass spectrometry-based sequencing and microscopy-based methods. *PLOS ONE* 9(9): e106875: 1–10.

Brothwell, D., Liversage, D. & Gottlieb, B. 1990. Radiographic and forensic aspects of the female Huldremose body. *Journal of Danish Archaeology* 9: 157–178.

Fischer, C. 2007. *Tollundmanden. Gaven til guderne. Mosefund fra Danmarks forhistorie.* Silkeborg: Hovedland.

Frei, K.M., Skals, I., Gleba, M. & Lyngstrøm, H. 2009. The Huldremose Iron Age textiles, Denmark: An attempt to define their provenance applying the strontium isotope system. *Journal of Archaeological Science* 36: 1965–1971.

Frei, K.M., Mannering, U., Price, T.D. & Iversen, R.B. 2015. Strontium isotope investigations of the Haraldskær Woman – a complex record of various tissues. *ArcheoSciences, revue d'archéometrie* 39: 93–101.

Frei, K.M., Mannering, U., Berghe, I.V. & Kristiansen, K. 2017. Bronze Age wool; provenance and dye investigations of Danish textiles. *Antiquity* 91(357): 640–654. doi:10.15184/aqy.2017.64.

Hald, M. 1972. *Primitive Shoes. An Archaeological-Ethnological Study Based upon Shoe Finds from the Jutland Peninsula.* Publications of the National Museum, Archaeological-Historical Series Vol. XIII. København.

Hald, M. 1980. *Ancient Danish Textiles from Bogs and Burials.* Publications of the National Museum, Archaeological-Historical Series Vol. XXI. København.

Henriksen, M.B. 2008. Forsvundne moselig. *SKALK* 4: 8–13.

Issenman, B.K. 1997. *Sinews of Survival. The Living Legacy of Inuit Clothing.* Vancouver: UBC Press.

Jensen, J. 2013. *The Prehistory of Denmark, from the Stone Age to the Vikings.* Copenhagen: Gyldendal.

Kveiborg, J. 2008. Fårehyrder, kvægbønder eller svineavlere. En revurdering af jernalderens dyrehold. *KUML*, 59–100.

Mannering, U. 2010. The Huldremose find. An Early Iron Age woman with an exceptional costume. *Fasciculi Archaeologiae Historicae* XXIII: 9–18.

Mannering, U., Possnert, G., Heinemeier, J. & Gleba, M. 2010. Dating Danish textiles and skins from bog finds by by means of ^{14}C AMS. *Journal of Archaeological Science* 37: 261–268.

Mannering, U. & Lynnerup, N. 2013. From foot to fact: New light on the Fræer bog find. In *Counterpoint: Essays in Archaeology and Heritage Studies in Honour of Professor Kristian Kristiansen*, edited by S. Bergerbrant and S. Sabatini, 207–211. Oxford: British Archaeological Report IS 2508.

Mannering, U. 2015. Skin and fur in the Viking Age. In *Refashioning Viking Age Garments. Texts for a Seminar in the Seedmoney Network 'Vikingetid i Danmark'*, edited by H. Lyngstrøm, 27–34. The Saxo Institute, University of Copenhagen, 20 February 2015. Copenhagen: University of Copenhagen Press.

Mannering, U. 2017. Forhistoriske sko. In *Arkæologisk tekstilforskning. Baggrund og ny viden*, edited by U. Mannering, 112–117. Copenhagen: The National Museum of Denmark, Denmark's Basic Research Fund Center for Textile Research (DNRF 64).

Munksgård, E. 1974. *Oldtidsdragter*. Copenhagen: The National Museum of Denmark.

Nørgård, A. 2008. A weaver's voice: Making reconstructions of Danish Iron Age textiles. In *Dressing the Past*, edited by M. Gleba, C. Munkholt and M.-L. Nosch, 43–58. Ancient Textiles Series Vol. 3. Oxford: Oxbow Books.

Olofsson, L., Andersson Strand, E. & Nosch, M.-L. 2015. Experimental testing of Bronze Age textile tools. In *Tools, Textiles and Contexts. Investigating Textile Production in the Aegean and Eastern Mediterranean Bronze Age*, edited by E. Andersson Strand and M.-L. Nosch, 75–100. Ancient Textiles Series Vol. 21. Oxford: Oxbow Books.

Rasmussen, K. 1931. The Netsilik Eskimos. *Report of the Fifth Thule Expedition 1921–24*, 8 (1–2). Copenhagen: Gyldendal.

Ravn, M. 2010. Burials in bogs. Bronze and Early Iron Age bog bodies from Denmark. *Acta Archaeologica* 81: 112–123.

Vanden Berghe, I., Gleba M. & Mannering, U. 2009. Towards the identification of dyestuffs in Early Iron Age Scandinavian peat bog textiles. *Journal of Archaeological Science* 36(9): 1910–1921.

van der Sanden, W. 1996. *Through Nature to Eternity. The Bog Bodies of Northwest Europe*. Amsterdam: Batavian Lion International.

Human sacrifice and execution? A brief forensic medical and archaeological perspective on some of the Danish bog bodies

Niels Lynnerup and Pauline Asingh

Abstract

Here we present a summary of the newer analyses of the Danish Iron Age bog bodies. Much has been learned from recent work. For example, by applying medical imaging techniques on 14 of these bodies, we have been able to ascertain more about their lesions. We argue that at least in some cases, the deceased individual was executed in a premediated fashion, and that the execution was performed in such a manner that it led to quick loss of consciousness and death, rather than a drawn-out and deliberately painful death. Furthermore, the executions and body deposition took place in special, dedicated settings. We offer that this use of setting and performed violence may support the hypothesis that these executions reflect specific rituals, including a priesthood administering the deadly undertakings, arguably situating many of these deaths as indeed sacrificial.

Keywords: bog bodies, Iron Age, cause of death, execution, CT scanning, sacrifice

The Danish Iron Age bog bodies, spanning from 500 BC to AD 200, have often been seen as evidence for human sacrifice in Early Iron Age Northern Europe (500 BC–AD 400). The grand old man of Danish archaeology, Professor P.V. Glob, discussed this in depth in his famous book on the subject *The Bog People* (Glob 1965). This book was also a summary of Glob's enquiries into the Danish bog bodies, which for him started when he excavated the Grauballe Man, and subsequently arranged for the bog body to be investigated scientifically, including conservation and exhibition (Plate 23).

Arguably, this excavation, and that of the Tollund Man (Thorvaldsen 1951), another famously well-preserved Iron Age bog body, were the first real archaeological excavations of Danish bog bodies (Figure 5.1).

Of course, across the region of southern Scandinavia, bog bodies had been found before, but in the 18th and 19th century, their remains, if secured at all, were basically left to dry out in museum stores or were reburied in a bog or in consecrated ground in a churchyard. In most cases, notes and records were often lacking (*cf.*, Mannering, this volume). With his painstaking work, and with invaluable help from his conservator, Glob felt reasonably sure that he could establish that their deaths, and subsequent committal to the bogs, were meant as a religious sacrifice, rather than, *e.g.*, a consequence of execution for crimes. To reach this conclusion, he also drew on writings about the Germanic people by the Roman writer Tacitus, hypothesising that Tollund Man and Grauballe Man specifically were executed priests, sacrificed to the Germanic goddess Nerthus (Stewart 2021). However, Glob also drew upon forensic medical methods to investigate the bog bodies. While those examinations certainly were diligent, they naturally relied upon the methods available in the 1950s (Figure 5.2) (Munck 1956).

Specifically, radiography was used as a non-invasive method (Glob 1965). Due to the taphonomic action and chemical composition of the bog, which leaches calcium salts from the bones as well as exerting an immense amount of pressure over time, the skeleton does not show up as fresh bones do in radiographs. Rather, osseous materials have a 'glassy' look, and it is very difficult to discern skeletal trauma, such as fracture lines, from post-mortem

Figure 5.1. The Grauballe Man in situ *during excavation in 1956.*

taphonomic alterations. Furthermore, without the calcium mineral structure to the bones bog bodies become soft and pliable. This in turn leads to the bones warping and bending as a reaction to taphonomic conditions such as soil pressure. Lastly, certain structures in the bodies, especially sinews, fasciae and tendons experience conversely an uptake of soil iron minerals, making them much more visible on radiography. This in effect makes the bone detail less distinguishable. One of the major advances in the forensic medical studies of bog bodies has been the advent of high-resolution computer tomography (CT) which allows for a slice-by-slice view, in either of the three planes (coronal [a-p], transversal and longitudinal) of internal structures (Plate 24). Importantly, the three-dimensional data also allows for a voxel-by-voxel (the smallest unit visible, akin to the pixels of a two-dimensional view) delineation and marking. With this so-called post-processing of the images, it becomes possible to perform a 'virtual' dissection of the bodily structures, thus greatly augmenting the possibilities to ascertain pathological changes and lesions (Gregersen *et al.* 2007).

Over the last 20 years we have examined the remains of 14 Danish Iron Age bog bodies by CT-scanning (Table 5.1), with a focus on forensic pathological interpretations of the observed lesions and trauma. We here discuss how some of our finds and interpretations may fit with archaeological hypotheses of bog bodies being victims of ritual violence, sacrificial or otherwise. Specifically, we seek to address whether, at least in some cases, there is significant evidence suggestive of premediated execution. And, if so, whether the execution was performed in such a manner that it led to quick loss of consciousness and death, rather than drawn-out and deliberately painful death.

Archaeological find circumstances and 'victim' demographics

It is probably not a coincidence that these corpses were placed in a bog. It is likely that it was known that the bogs could have a preservative effect (see discussion in Walsh, Pantmann and Moen, this volume). This may well have

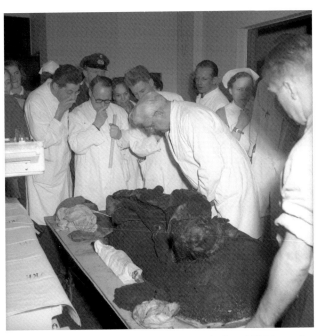

Figure 5.2. The Grauballe Man being studied in 1956 just after excavation and retrieval from the bog.

Table 5.1. Preserved and non-preserved bog bodies included in the present study.

Find	Found	Sex	Estimated age	Date
Auning	1886	F	Adult	200 BC–AD 140*
Borremose I	1946	M	Adult	365–116 BC
Borremose II	1947	F	Adult	483–95 BC
Borremose III	1948	F	Adult	401–209 BC
Elling	1938	F	Adult	381 BC–AD 10*
Fræer	1842	M?	Adult	110 BC–AD 60
Grauballe		M	Adult	190 BC–AD 80*
Haraldskær	1835	F	Adult	347–42 BC
Huldremose I	1879	F	Adult	350–41 BC
Krogensmølle	1878	F	Adult	399–181 BC
Roum	1942	F	Adult	50 BC–AD 80
Stidsholt	1859	F	Adult	392–204 BC
Tollund	1950	M	Adult	400–110 BC*
Vester Torsted	1913	M	Adult	AD 120–330

been first seen when animals ventured into a mire and drowned. The preservation in still water may have led to the corpse being visible from above – eerily pristine below the dusky surface. The fastening of the Borremose Woman (Borremose III) to the bog bed may indicate a precaution to this effect, so that post-mortem bloating due to putrefaction would not cause the body to float. Numerous bog bodies have been found which appear to have been secured into place with stakes, stones or branches. Such a dramatic effect, which could well indicate a ritual feature of a public sacrifice, may just as likely indicate a form of display, *e.g.*, providing a powerful and preternaturally long-lasting visual reminder of the dire consequences of aberrant behaviours, in the case of an executed criminal.

The majority of the bog bodies (*cf.*, Table 5.1) date to the Iron Age (500 BC–AD 400). Other finds are dated to a transitional period between the pre-Roman Iron Age and the Roman or Late Iron Age. The 14 bog bodies number nine females and five males (Table 5.1). These represent adults of various ages, but due to the rather poor state of preservation in many cases it is difficult to accurately determine the age at the time of death. The majority appear to have died between the ages of 20 and 40 years old. In terms of stature, most individuals do not seem to physically differ from the statistical averages for the Danish Iron Age population (Sellevold *et al.* 1984). Researchers have long noted that many bog bodies possess physical characteristics – such as un-worn hands and fingertips – suggesting that the individuals did not live the difficult agrarian lifestyle of hard work presumed for most of the Iron Age population. This has led many scholars to postulate that the bodies interred

into Northern European wetlands are those of individuals of high social status and/or wealth. For example, it was speculated that the fine skin patterns of Grauballe Man's palm and fingertips indicated that he was perhaps of noble birth, since it was presumed that an average Iron Age man should be expected to have hands showing the effects of years of manual labour. However, subsequent interpretations favour that this is more the result of the degenerative processes in the bog which result in the desquamation of the outer epidermal layer.

Cause of death

Some of the Early Iron Age bog bodies show forensic evidence of violent death such as by decapitation (*e.g.*, Roum Man, Stidsholt 'Woman'), strangulation by hanging[1] (*e.g.*, Tollund Man, Elling Woman, Borremose Man [Borremose I]) or having their throat slit (*e.g.*, Grauballe Man) (Fischer 1999; Nielsen 2014). In the former cases, a noose was found around the neck; regarding Tollund and Elling, an inverted 'V' skin fold, corresponding to how the noose would have suspended the body, was found by the forensic pathologists at the find time. Such causes of death are quite expeditious and deliberate. They also point to premeditation. For example, if an individual is to be hanged, a noose must be procured – perhaps even manufactured for the task. If a person is to have their throat cut, then not only must a suitable sharp instrument be at hand, but as our forensic reconstruction of the death of the Grauballe Man has shown (Asingh & Lynnerup 2007), this likely occurred in a controlled setting where the roles of those involved were well defined. For example, the person handling the knife would have been standing behind the individual to be executed. He or she would have to make sure that the head of the victim was bent back to sufficiently expose the throat. The individual to be executed would probably be kept on their knees and/or otherwise controlled or restrained (Gregersen *et al.* 2007). In the case of Grauballe Man, this *may* have been accomplished by a strike to his left shin. Comparatively, other deliberate causes of death, also known historically for the same period, could be crucifixion (the crucified individual dies of exhaustion and exposure due to an extended period of neglect, as well as other complications, see *e.g.*, Maslen & Mitchell 2006). In either case, such means of dispatch are obviously not so expeditious as strangulation, beheading or cutting of the throat.

The causes of death observed for the bog bodies – when they can be ascertained with some degree of certainty – also point to a degree of deliberation or premeditation.

Other forms of dispatch can be imagined. The Borremose Woman, found lying face down, was originally assumed to have had her face crushed. It was speculated that this was the mechanism of execution, pointing to a rather gruesome series of blunt blows *en face* (Ry Andersen & Geertinger 1984). Our renewed forensic analyses, including a CT scan of the cranial bones with emphasis on fracture lines and patterns, showed that the cranial fractures resulted from a single powerful blow, not to the facial region, but to the back of the head. As a result, fracture lines extend basally and frontally, which, together with massive taphonomic changes due to the pressure of the bog, result in a rather crushed facial cranium (Villa *et al.* 2011)

We think this possible single fatal blow to the back of the head also may point to a controlled setting, albeit still violent, but less so than a series of frontal blows. The former can be achieved by the victim kneeling and receiving the blow from above and behind. A powerful blow to the back of the head may result in immediate loss of consciousness, while facial blows potentially may result in much more diffuse wounding, including the nose, orbital regions, maxilla, mandible and dentition. This would not necessarily result in immediate loss of consciousness. Further, this diffused wounding would likely result in pronounced bleeding, which could potentially lead to slow suffocation or drowning. To effectively achieve facial blows of this sort would hypothetically require the victim to lie face-up on the ground, with blows struck from above at roughly a 90-degree angle.

We thus conclude that – when we can ascertain a cause of death with some confidence – there was a rapid loss of consciousness and hence limited sensation of pain. We also conclude that if this was the case, it was premeditated, at least to the degree that rope or sharp instruments were at hand and a controlled environment was established.

Even if the cause of death ultimately was quite quick, it does not necessarily rule out that other traumas were incurred ante-mortem. Indeed, some of the first analyses of the bog bodies pointed to other traumas, and thus a sequence of violence leading up to the final cause of death. As an example, scientists in the 1950s found that the Grauballe Man had sustained a blow to his head in the right-side temporal region, resulting in a cranial fracture. There had also been a blow to his left leg, resulting in a fracture of his tibia. Archaeologists, including P.V. Glob, thus considered that the Grauballe Man likely had his leg broken before his execution in order to incapacitate him and that the blow to the head may have been made to pacify him before his throat was cut (Glob 1965). However, when we CT scanned Grauballe Man in 2001, we were able to render the skull in much more detail. It was clear that the skeletal changes were due to taphonomic influences: the head was not fractured due to a blow, but it had rather basically been squashed (Plate 25) by the pressure of the bog over time.

Bending or warping of the cranial bones inward can also be seen in the skull of the Tollund Man, indicating that soil pressure, along with the bog-induced softening of the bones, had led to this effect. When we scanned the Borremose Woman, we found that she had a femoral fracture that was clearly post-mortem in nature, as her other leg lay intact just across the broken femur. This shows that the soil pressure on the underlying femur broke the bone over time (Villa *et al.* 2011). Indeed, this fracture pattern was very similar to the tibial fracture pattern observed for Grauballe Man, and we thus hypothesise that his tibial fracture may also be due to post-mortem processes rather than acute violence at the time of death.

Thus, in these cases, the bone fractures previously described as ante- or peri-mortem trauma may in fact be due to the effects of taphonomic activities in the bog (*e.g.*, Asingh & Lynnerup 2007; Lynnerup 2007; Fischer 2012). Casting aside previously proposed 'overkill' theories, or other hypotheses of ritually inflicted ante-mortem wounds, we are left with a series of corpses with an immediate cause of death. But what does this actually indicate?

Discussion: Meeting the gods in wetlands

The practice of making offerings in wetlands arrived in Denmark at the very end of the Mesolithic, rather more than 6,000 years ago. During Neolithisation, the transition from hunting and gathering to farming and herding in southern Scandinavia around 4000 BC, early farmers deposited foreign and exotic stone axes as ritual offerings in lakes and bogs. With this came the beginnings of a votive tradition that acquired great significance for the farming cultures of subsequent millennia across the region. Reflections of this are, in all probability, the reason why Grauballe Man was interred in the bog. They may even have been the explicit reasoning for his death. Since the Mesolithic, the bogs continued as a place of offering well up until the introduction of Christianity, and perhaps even after. In pre-Christian farming communities, wetlands in general, and bogs in particular, played a special role in people's encounters with the supernatural, as the place for depositing gifts or offerings to the powers who had an influence over – or even controlled – life and death.

The term 'bog pot' is used to describe the thousands of pottery vessel and sherd deposits on the edges of lakes and bogs made during the Neolithic, the Bronze Age and, particularly, in the subsequent time of the Grauballe Man – the Iron Age (*e.g.*, Becker 1972; Lund 2002). The bog pots were probably placed in the cold, still and reflective waters filled with food offerings. Whether their contents were intended for people or gods we will never really know for sure. We must simply recognise that these types of wetlands played a major, but far from unequivocal, role in prehistoric society. For example, during the Neolithic, oversized polished stone axes manufactured solely for ritual use, along with large amounts of amber and even human sacrifices, were deposited in bogs and lakes. In the Bronze Age, valuable offerings such as gold bowls and bronze weapons and ornaments were often placed in wetlands. Perhaps of significance, from the end of the Bronze Age around 800 BC and reaching a maximum around 500 BC with the onset of the Early Iron Age the climate in the region became more cool and wet. The water table rose, and many low-lying areas became transformed into bogs. As such, in the course of the first centuries of the Iron Age, a quarter of the area of modern-day Denmark became covered by wetlands – with wide rivers cutting through the landscape, which became peppered with lakes, meadows and bogs. Bogs were no longer outlying areas, as many settlements now lay lower in terrain in very close association with low-lying wetlands. Offerings were taken in great numbers to these still waters and diverse sacred offering celebrations were held on their margins (see, *e.g.*, Walsh, Pantmann and Moen, this volume). Besides great amounts of bog pots and bronze ornaments, also more everyday objects such as agricultural tools, animal sacrifices and human remains were lowered into the water as well.

Also around this time, bogs are found to begin playing a new and important role as an energy source. As early as the Bronze Age, farmers had begun to cut peat in the bogs. It is well known from historical times that peat is a significantly less resource-demanding heat source to obtain than wood, which already by the Late Neolithic in Demark had become a somewhat limited resource in many places. Add to this that the Iron Age's definitive technology – *i.e.*, iron production – required enormous amounts of fuel for iron extraction and smithing. The farmers' activities in the bogs were more than sacral – they were intrinsically economical, and these two considerations probably went hand in hand.

For example, at Fuglsøgård bog, south of Hadsund in Jutland, there was a small kettle-hole bog similar to the one at Nebelgaard where the Grauballe Man was found.

Peat was extracted here in the Early Iron Age. It was obtained from several hundred peat cuttings, each up to a couple of metres deep and up to 4 metres wide. The peat cuttings at this site are densely placed, just a few metres apart along the edge of the 3,000 square metre outline of the bog. With time, water-filled pools riddled the surface of the area. Farmers had already lived in the vicinity for generations, cultivating the soil, sending their cattle out to graze and cutting peat from the bogs. At some time between 500–300 BC, they returned to Fuglsøgård bog, but this time with yet another purpose in mind, commanded by tradition and cosmology. In the water-filled peat cuttings they placed pottery vessels filled with grain, and slaughtered and butchered animals. The heads of cattle and horses were placed around the pottery vessels. Tethering stakes used to secure the cattle in the fields during the summer were now driven to secure the animals at the edge of the water before their sacrifice. All of these were deposited together with wooden clubs and finely crafted wooden items, intermingled among the various pots and pot sherds. It is perhaps within the extreme edges of this sort of broadly agrarian ceremonial activity that violent human sacrificial deaths are also manifest.

Where possible, the Iron Age people made their way across the bog on fallen tree trunks to reach the water-filled peat cuttings. Precisely where a trunk divided to form two thinner branches, they submerged pots full of grain. These scenes did not occur on just one day, but extended over months, perhaps years, as recurrent offering rituals were performed according to various events in the farmers' annual rhythm: the return of light and midwinter, the growth of spring and the germination of seeds in the soil, the benevolence of sun and rain and the harvest, the fertility of animals, people and land. Between the pots and the newly butchered animals, they placed small pieces of white quartz that gleamed and twinkled through the surface of the water in both sun- and moonlight (see Walsh, Pantmann and Moen, this volume). The bog was two organisms in one – a place where raw materials were obtained and a place where the supernatural reigned supreme. It was where offerings were taken in intercession for the continuation of the family line. It was a magical and solemn place intrinsically linked with the great mysteries of life. It was not one or another, but both. In other words, wetlands were complex consecrated spaces, filled with everyday meaning.

With this in mind, if we adopt the meaning of human sacrifice as 'the act of killing a human being for the sake of collective well-being, which is consecrated by the divine' (Tiesler & Olivier 2020), can we place the bog bodies in a setting of divine consecration? Fischer (2012) has linked the sacrificial execution by hanging to emerging Asa beliefs with the god Óðinn (or rather with an Óðinn precursor) as an important figure. Thus, violence in consecration to the divine may have gone hand in hand.

We do know that, for whatever reason, human victims of often violent death were deposited in peat cuttings and in open water that subsequently became peatlands. Certainly, these people attract attention when they emerge. We hypothesise that as offerings, and as human beings executed deliberately and premeditatedly, these individuals reflect contributions to the maintenance of human life and society, whether their deaths were penal, sacral or any combination of both.

Conclusion

The human sacrifices known from Danish Iron Age as presented here seem to reflect a quick, execution-style death. These took place in special, dedicated settings. Aldhouse-Green (2001) has argued that this must reflect specific rituals, including a priesthood administering the deathly undertakings in controlled settings. Not only do our more recent anthropological re-analyses not fully support the ideas of 'overkill', they also indicate that the bog people were not overtly physically different from the general Iron Age population. Perhaps the most salient, and the most frustrating, conclusion to make about bog bodies is that all bog body finds thus far have been made by chance. They have never been discovered as a result of focused archaeological excavations. Further, since the finds of bog bodies have also been directly correlated with the industrial extraction of peat, then the ongoing drainage of bogs and the decrease in peat use make it unlikely that many (if any) 'new' bog bodies will be found henceforth. Thus, the Danish bog bodies, as inventoried and described here, will remain unique archaeological specimens from which we may hope to focus continued, intensive and technologically advanced investigations that may provide novel interpretations and findings in the future.

Note

1   From a purely forensic point of view strangulation could theoretically also indicate suicide.

References

Aldhouse-Green, M. 2001. *Dying for the Gods. Human Sacrifice in Iron Age and Roman Europe*. Stroud: Tempus Publishing.

Asingh, P. 2009. *Grauballe Man-Portrait of a Bog Body*. Copenhagen: Gyldendal.

Asingh, P. & Lynnerup, N. (eds) 2007. *Grauballe Man: An Iron Age Bog Body Revisited*. Moesgård: Jutland Archaeological Society.

Becker, C.J. 1972. 'Mosepotter' fra Danmarks jernalder. Problemer omkring mosefundne lerkar og deres tolkning. *Aarboger for Nordisk Oldkydighed og Historie* 1971: 5–60.

Fischer, C. 1999. The Tollund Man and the Elling Woman and other bog bodies from Central Jutland. In *Bog Bodies, Sacred Sites and Wetland Archaeology*, edited by B. Coles, J. Coles and M.S. Jøregensen, 93–98. Exeter: Wetland Archaeology Research Project.

Fischer, C. 2012. *Tollund Man. Gift to the Gods*. Stroud: The History Press.

Glob, P.V. 1965. *Mosefolket*. Copenhagen: Gyldendal.

Gregersen, M., Jurik, A.G. & Lynnerup, N. 2007. Forensic evidence, injuries and cause of death. In *Grauballe Man: An Iron Age Bog Body Revisited*, edited by P. Asingh and N. Lynnerup, 234–258. Aarhus: Aarhus University Press.

Lund, J. 2002. Forlev Nymølle: En offerplads fra yngre førromersk jernalder. *KUML* 2002: 143–195.

Maslen, M.W. & Mitchell, P.D. 2006. Medical theories on the cause of death in crucifixion. *Journal of the Royal Society of Medicine* 99(4): 185–188. doi:10.1258/jrsm.99.4.185.

Munck, W. 1956. Patologisk-anatomisk og retsmedicinsk undersøgelse af moseliget fra Grauballe. *Kuml* 1956: 131–137.

Nielsen, O. 2014. *Tollund Man and Elling Woman*. Skabertrang: Silkeborg Bogtryk.

Ry Andersen, S. & Geertinger, P. 1984. Bog bodies investigated in the light of forensic medicine. *Journal of Danish Archaeology* 3(1): 111–119.

Sellevold, B., Lund Hansen, U. & Balslev Jørgensen, J. 1984. *Iron Age Man in Denmark*. Nordiske Fortidsminder, serie B, Bind 8. Copenhagen: Det Kgl Nordiske Oldskriftselskab.

Stewart, L. 2021. Heaney and bog bodies narratives literary translation as archaeology. *Neke The New Zealand Journal of Translation Studies* 4(1): 1–19.

Thorvaldsen, K. 1951. Moseliget fra Tollund. *Aarbøger for Nordisk Oldkyndighed og Historie* 1950: 302–310.

Tiesler, V. & Olivier, G. 2020. Open chests and broken hearts: Ritual sacrifices and meanings of human heart sacrifice in Mesoamerica. *Current Anthropology* 61(2): 168–193.

Villa, C., Møller Rasmussen, M. & Lynnerup, N. 2011. Age estimation by 3D CT-scans of the Borremose Woman, a Danish bog body. In *Yearbook of Mummy Studied. Vol. 1*, edited by H. Gill-Frerking, W. Rosendahl and A. Zink, 165–169. Munchen: Verlag Dr. Friedrich Pfeil.

6

Six human skulls in a bog:
Svennum – a 1st to 3rd century AD sacrificial bog

Sidsel Wåhlin

Abstract

Svennum bog is a small sacrificial bog in the middle of Vendsyssel, Denmark. In 2013 a farmer unearthed two human skulls. Archaeological excavations in 2013 and 2015 documented a complex ritual site with different areas of ritual deposits where distinct offerings took place, among these the sacrifice of six human skulls. The sacrificial setting dates to the 1st to 3rd century AD via ceramics and ^{14}C dating of animal bones, but one human skull is dated to the 1st century BC. Thus, the human skulls were old objects at the time of sacrifice. The site was abandoned in the 4th century AD. Extensive Iron Age peat cutting took place in the bog and thus it was not a remote site but located centrally in the community. The skulls were defleshed at the time of deposit. Analysis of the six skulls indicate that they were curated from a larger group of people or an exogamic society. They all have signs of infection, however, no pre- or perimortal trauma, nor are post-mortem modifications evident, suggesting a period of natural decay preceded their deposition. Svennum bog has several seemingly parallel Iron Age finds from Vendsyssel stored in the Vendsyssel Historiske Museums (VHM) Collection. The excavation of the Svennum bog suggests that at least some of these skulls were defleshed skulls at the time of deposition. However, further research will be needed in order to address whether this was a South Scandinavian phenomenon and why skulls were selected for wetland deposition.

Keywords: Svennum bog, human crania, skulls and skeletonised offerings, skull/head cult, Danish Iron Age, ritual and sacrificial landscapes

Introduction. The discovery and excavation of six human skulls

> … But footballs do not have teeth.
>> (Finder Finn Jørgensen on the phone reporting the find
>> of two human skulls while repairing drains in 2013,
>> author's translation)

The site of Svennum sacrificial bog was, as with most wetland sites, found by chance. Two skulls rolling in the peat provided the landowner and his assistant quite a fright. Upon archaeological inspection of the skulls and the cleaning of profiles in the trenches where they were discovered, it was clear that the finds were not modern and that the skulls had not been placed in open water but in peat-cutting pits. A cleaning of the northern profile revealed

animal bones and a third human skull *in situ*. After the initial discovery in 2013, VHM conducted a small excavation that same year, funded by the Danish Agency of Culture and Palaces (ACP). Ten Iron Age peat pits were excavated in a small trench some 80 square metres in total. The excavation revealed a complex ritual setting with offerings of stones, sticks, ceramics, various animal bones and six human crania (Plate 26). However, the excavation almost opened more questions than it answered. Were there other finds in the bog in other pits? Why were the pits so hard to detect on the surface? Most importantly, where were the remaining parts of the six humans and were there other human remains sacrificed nearby? Additionally, we needed to address the preservation condition of the bog as the ACP wanted to safeguard the Svennum bog from agricultural activity as a Registered National Monument if the rest of the bog was well preserved. Thus, in 2015, VHM launched a larger project. Funded by the ACP, the new excavation covered 815 square metres (see site plan, Plate 27). The method of the excavations was the usual for this type in Denmark: a hydraulic 18-ton excavator with a 2-metre-wide shovel slowly peeled off the top layers in the trenches. As soon as the archaeologists noted artefacts or features, they excavated by hand from then on. All documentation was digital with high precision GPS and photometric in 2D and 3D. This proved both time-efficient and precise. VHM initiated a collaboration with The National Museum, Department of Environmental Archaeology and Materials Science (NMDEAM) and they participated in the planning and execution of the fieldwork in both campaigns. The details of field methods will be addressed in a forthcoming article (Wåhlin & Maring, in prep). The 2015 campaign did not unearth additional human remains but added to the complexity of the Svennum bog.

The amphitheatre

> It is a natural amphitheatre.
> (Lars Jørgensen, 2015, upon arrival at the Svennum bog)

Svennum lies in an intensive cultural landscape; 150 metres south of the bog an Early Roman Iron Age burial was located (*c.* AD 1–174). A small but prominent burial mound dated to the Bronze Age is situated *c.* 400 metres to the south. On the slopes just north of the Svennum bog a trial trench and surface field survey did not yield traces of settlement or other activities, but 100 metres to the west a fast track across the ploughed field by the author and the landowner revealed shards of Iron Age household ceramics. Further to the west, under the present farm buildings settlement traces were excavated (Wåhlin 2015, 5–6). They could not be dated but are likely from the Late Bronze Age/Early Iron Age, or possibly later. Thus, the bog was a busy place in the 1st and 2nd century AD, situated within easy reach of the nearest settlement and not tucked away in a peripheral landscape or on the outskirts of everyday experience (see Plate 28).

The bog sits in a narrow east–west oriented valley that extends for several kilometres and connects to a network of other narrow Ice Age valleys, some with an open brook but many, like Svennum, overgrown in the Middle to Late Mesolithic with wood peat and alkalic groundwater streaming through the peat (Plate 28). The excavated section of the bog, at the find location of the skulls, was *c.* 40 metres in width, and the north and especially the south banks of the valley are steep, thus creating a very clear natural boundary of the site. The bog itself is a focal point when one stands at the hills either north or south of it. Sounds carries well from the bog to the steep slopes and the site resembles an amphitheatre of sorts where large groups may have come

to oversee and participate in rituals and ceremonies (see Plate 28).

In this setting, the rituals took place. A cluster of 14 pits were selected for a sequence of different sacrifices, ending with the grand sacrifice of six human skulls and a few later deposits of animal bones. It should be noted that the author uses the term sacrifice not as specifically 'ritual killing' but in the broader etymological sense of making something or someone sacred by giving it up (*e.g.*, oblation). At the bottom but above a thin layer of regrowth of the pits hand-to head-sized stones were placed singularly, in rows and in small cairns; the latter served as a form of altar where pot sherds and raw clay lumps were sacrificed. Shortly after the stones, simple wooden sticks with a sharpened end and some touched lightly by fire were sacrificed. Some regrowth took place, then the first animal bones were sacrificed. The final touch before the grand sacrifice was the black polished ornamented ceramic sherds selected from two pots; these were placed in the pits. Most likely, the two pots were smashed for the occasion as refitting between sherds from different pits could be made. Shortly after, the six human skulls were sacrificed. A stallion's skull and bone heaps belong to the same strata, but regrowth is evident between the deposits, thus there is a short time span between deposits. A birch branch held the stallion down, and another one of the human skulls. A sacrifice of animal bones and some sticks were the last deposited in the pits. Thus, until the pits were covered in peat, the six human skulls were visible from the edge of the pits. The ornamented sherds date part of the sacrifice to 1st century AD; this is supported by a ^{14}C date of a wisp of straw placed in the small pot x52 (see Figure 6.1). However, the dated animal bones are younger; VHM00500x38 is particularly interesting as it is from the 2nd century but found below the skull VHM00500x22 (see Figure 6.1).

At the same time, the bog was a place of everyday use in the 1st to 3rd centuries AD. During this time, peat was cut in the bog, as this is a well-known feature in several other sacrificial wetland sites such as Fuglsøgård (Johannesen 2017, 33–40). There are two modes of peat cutting observed at Svennum. The first involved the cutting of pits. ^{14}C dates place the peat regrowth in the pits to the Early Roman Iron Age, and the lowest layers to perhaps the pre-Roman (see Figure 6.1). The pits are small, oval, with steep sides, and deep. At Svennum, they stop just short of the underlying greyish sandy clay, except in peat pit A245 at the south edge of the bog. These pits could be dug in a day and would fill up with water overnight. This extraction strategy left the surrounding bog intact, thus managing water was not necessary. The other mode of peat extraction was large-scale surface cutting where vast areas of the bog surface were lowered. Thus, water would be an issue. Water was managed by cutting two deep east–west-oriented ditches at the south and north sides of the bog, drawing water away towards the

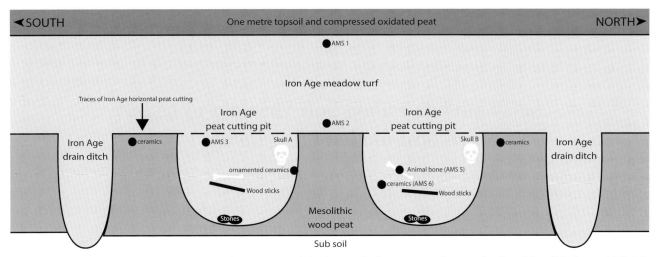

Figure 6.1. A not-to-scale simplified interpolar transect of the bog with the stratigraphy visualised and key ^{14}C dates. AMS lab, University of Aarhus provided all ^{14}C dates. Skull AMS 1: A211 AAR 26057 ^{14}C age 1523±29, 95.4% probability AD 428–605. AMS 2: A211 AAR 26059, ^{14}C age 1805±32, 95.4% probability AD 128–326. AMS 3: skull VHM00500x0002 AAR: 31797, 95.4% probability BC 164–AD 4, 68, 68.2% probability 108–2 BC. AMS 5: VHM00500x38 AAR, ^{14}C age 1889±23, 95.4% probability AD 82–222. AMS 6 Plant material from inside ceramic vessel VHM00500x52 AAR 26056 ^{14}C age 1989±29, 95.4% probability 47 BC–AD 70 (profile created by Mads Lou Bendtsen).

west (Wåhlin, in prep; Mortensen & Wåhlin in prep). The community recut the ditches regularly thus managing and maintaining both the natural and culture landscape. The two ditches also seem to define a border of the ritual site, as no deposits are found outside them.

The decline in activity at the site is dated to the 3rd century AD by ^{14}C dates of the Iron Age regrowth of peat (labelled A211) which covers the preceding Iron Age surface cut and the pits. Thus, it appears that the bog was disused from the 3rd century and left undisturbed until recently (see Figure 6.1).

Pits in other parts of the bog were also selected for sacrifices of stones and animal bones. For example, in feature A245 an incisor from a horse was wedged between two light-coloured stones placed on top of substantial regrowth in the pit. Each of the small wood-deposit pits, features A213, A222, A226, and A238, were used for the deposition of animal bones, stones and wooden objects.

Six human skulls

The six skulls from the Svennum bog (Plate 29) are unusual as they are only the second find of wetland human sacrifice archaeologically excavated in Vendsyssel; the other being the excavation of a 4th–5th century AD bog skeleton from Tollestrup Mose excavated by H. Friis in 1942. VHM00500-x1, -x2, -x22, -x73, -x77 and -x81 are the designations for the six human skulls excavated during the 2013 campaign; -x1 and -x2 are the two skulls the farmer initially found while repairing drains at the site. The four others were unearthed during the following proper excavation. All six skulls were

deposited in a close group of oval peat pits, situated near the northern edge of the bog just east of its narrowest section.

The six human skulls are each in excellent preservation condition. After excavation the skulls were kept wet at 8° C and uncleaned until we could extract a molar for DNA work. The conservation laboratory conducted careful and mechanical cleaning: no chemicals were applied nor were they necessary. Then the skulls were dried very slowly at 8° C. The Anthropological Laboratory KU, did an anthropological analysis and a full CT scan of the skulls (Lynnerup *et al.* 2015). All six skulls are missing the mandible and all the upper incisors. There were no other human bones or teeth found in the excavated parts of Svennum. Mandibles and incisors tend to loosen faster than the premolars and molars as part of natural processes. The method of excavation would have located at least some of the incisors had they fallen out at the find location. We did find half of a molar that had broken off from one of the skulls when the excavator unearthed it the day before. Thus, the Svennum skulls were deposited as skulls and had most likely been defleshed for some time before their final deposition. Thus, the skulls represent an allochthonous deposition of human body parts.

The juveniles

The skulls x1 and x2 are those of children (x1 aged around 12 years old, and x2 aged around 10–15 years old) (Lynnerup *et al.* 2015). Tooth eruption, wear, skull size and suture closing were used to estimate the age. Both skulls are very fine-boned and gracile; x1, with a high forehead, also shows signs of physical stress, infection of the palate and has been sexed by DNA as male.

Table 6.1. Order of deposits in the central pit area. W = wood, S = stone, C = ceramic, CO = black polished ornamented ceramic, AB = animal bone, HS = human skull. The layers are not a fixed level or a distinct peat layer; but the layers where documentation was conducted. However, the top of layer one in all of the pits is the same growth horizon.

Layer	A5	A7	A11	A9	A10	A12	A13	A14	A15
Top		Sx90 Wx60 Cx70	Cx47	ABx39	ABx133	Sx140	Sx144,		Sx143 (Wx181, x182, x187, 192)
Intermedia		Wx82, ABx45 Cx44			(Cx135, x136, x137)	(Cx170, x171)			
Layer 1 last deposits	ABx19	(ABx72 x55)	ABx80 Wx89						
L1 middle deposits	HSx22,Wx25	x82	(HSx73,x77)	HSx81 Wx129	(Cx135, x136, x137, x150) Sx141 (Wx138, x142, x148)	(Cx151, x152, x153)(Wx155, x186)	(Cx149, x150) Wx139	Wx173	Sx156, x185, x191(Wx188, x189)
L1 first deposits		Cx52 COx75 x87	COx98,						
L1 undetermined	(ABx18,x20,x38)	x53, x54, x58, x57, x59, x61, x62, x63, x64, x65, x66, x68, x69, x71	(Cx93,x99)(Sx110, x111)(Wx94, x95)						
Intermedia		(Wx82, x56) (Cx67, COx86)	Sx112				Sx154		Wx189
Layer 2		Wx82 (Sx83, x84, x85, x103)	COx100, ABx101, Wx104	Wx129					Sx169 (Wx157, x158, x159, x160, x161, x162, x163, x164, x165, x166, x167, x168)
Intermedia		Wx82	(Wx104, x97)	Wx129					Sx172
Layer 3		Wx82	(Cx104, x105, x106, x107, x108, x113, x115, x193)Wx104, Sx114, Wx116	Wx134, (Sx130,x131)					
Intermedia									
Layer 4			(Sx118, x120, x121, x122, x123, x124, x125, x126, x127, x128)Wx104, Wx145						
Intermedia									
Bottom	Sx146					Sx184	Sx147	Wx173 Sx183	Wx189

Skull -x2 was damaged. The relatively fresh edges with no patina indicate that this was the result of a recent event. It is likely that the missing cranial bones – among them the maxilla and facial bones – had been dislodged and subsequently lost around ten years prior when the original draining was conducted (Maring 2014). The ^{14}C date of x2 dates the individual to the 1st century BC (AAR: 31797, 95.4% probability BC 164–AD 4, 68.2% probability 108–2 BC). Thus, the skull precedes the overgrowth, indicating the end of human activities by more than two centuries, and as displayed in Figure 6.1 it is older than the animal bones in the pits.

The young adults

The skulls x22, x73 and X77 are those of young adults aged between 18 and 25, as determined from tooth eruption. They are each fine-boned and gracile with high foreheads (Lynnerup *et al.* 2015). They are very light in comparison to the bulk of other skulls found in Vendsyssel. Each had signs of stress in varying degrees (see Table 6.2). It is noteworthy that three individuals, x22, x73 and x77, seem to have been around the same age at their time of death. Skulls x22, x73 and x77 were tentatively suggested to be female (Lynnerup *et al.* 2015) but skulls especially without mandibles are not highly reliable for anthropological sex determination, and the young ages of the individuals makes it even harder, as sex characteristics such as brow ridges may not develop fully before an individual reaches their 20s. In fact, DNA analysis of the five with teeth showed that x22 was male.

A mature man

Skull x81 is that of a mature male (above 30, most likely 30–40 years old) and is somewhat more robust than the other skulls (Lynnerup *et al.* 2015). A more exact age range is not established, as crania are not as useful for age estimation after full tooth eruption, as there are few age markers to

Table 6.2. All anthropological data in the table provided by anthropological report, Anthropological Laboratory KU, Lynnerup et al. (2015). DNA data provided by Globe Institute, Section for GeoGenetics, Willerslev Group, University of Copenhagen, in emails to the author from Peter de Barros Damgaard, 23 June 2015 and Hugh McColl, 6 June 2020.

Find number	Weight of skull	Skull and Teeth	Age, Sex Anthropological estimation	DNA and ^{14}C	Signs of stress Anthropological
VHM00500x1	321g	Incomplete skull face and mandibula missing Molar and premolar, little surface wear	approximately 12 years old	SampleID 793_794_mt.cns Endo% 3,35199793 Haplogroup H5a1g1 Male, DNA	Cribra orbitalia and frontalis and porous palate
VHM00500x2	Incomplete skull 268g	Incomplete skull face and mandibular missing None present	10–15 size and fusing of sutures	No DNA sample taken ^{14}C AAR: 31797 BP age 2054 95.4% probability BC 164–4 AD, 68, 68.2% probability 108–2 BC	None registered, but face and mandibular are missing, and so is the eye sockets, in effect all areas where the other skulls had signs of stress
VHM00500x22	350g	Complete skull mandibula missing Molars premolars	Adultus, 20-30. Tentatively sexed as female	SampeID 801_802_mt.cns Endo% 28,5250586 Haplogroup U5a1a2b Male, DNA	Cribra orbitalialis, porous palate, CT scan shows chronic otitis media
VHM00500x73	397g	Complete skull mandibula missing Molars premolars	Adultus, approximately 18 years old. Tentatively sexed as female	SampeID 795_796_mt.cns Endo% 1,07395762 Haplogroup H1b DNA sex undetermined	Reformation of bone on face and forehead, Cribra orbitalialis, porous palate. Wormian bone formation in the back of the skull (lambda)
VHM00500x77	448g	Complete skull mandibula missing Molar promolar	Adultus, 18–20 Tentatively sexed as female	SampeID 797_798_mt.cns Endo% 0,40293764 Haplogroup H1a3 DNA sex undetermined	Severe Cribra orbitalialis porous palate and area around nasal cavity. Light periodontitis Wormian bone formation in the front, (bregma)
VHM00500x81	475g	Complete skull mandibula missing Molar and premolar	Maturus +30, most likely 30–40 years old. Male shape of skull	SampeID 799_800_mt.cns Endo%1,66998069 Haplogroup H3h Male, DNA	Light Cribra orbitalialis most likely healed, porous palate Wormian bone formation in the back (lambda, known as Inca bone)

go on (Milner *et al.* 2019). DNA analysis unsurprisingly sexed x81 as male.

Life and health

Physically, the six skulls from Svennum are relatively delicate and light (see Table 6.2) compared to *c.* 50 other bog find skulls from Vendsyssel, where the weight for complete adult skulls ranges between 475 and 790 g (Wåhlin in prep). Even excluding the children x1 and x2 from the argument, the four adult skulls from Svennum still weigh less than skulls of similar circumference also dating to the Iron Age in the region. Whether this is a local genetic trait,

Table 6.3. List of finds at Svennum.

Artefact type	Find counts
Stone – some find numbers contain more than one stone	
Light grey/white/blue	279
Green	10
Reddish	6
Flint	15
Stone totals	310
Wood – some find numbers from 2013 contain more than one piece of wood	
Sticks/branches/poles	134
Broken wood objects identified and unidentified	27
Planks/boards	62
construction timber	6
worked	16
Pieces of wood logs?	4
Holk	1
Natural wood bog, small branches etc	52
Wood totals	302
Ceramics – some find number contained ceramics from unornamented and black polished ceramic shards and thus is counted in both categories	
Common ceramics	213
Black polished ornamented	10
Ceramics totals	220
Animal bones/teeth a find number can be a bone heap or a single bone	59
Human skulls	6
White metal lead/silver: ten small bits and one small melt lump	2
Small iron object	1
Leather scrap	1
Total find numbers, samples etc not included in this table	901

due to physical stress or some product of Iron Age curation of nicely gracile skulls for use in the Svennum sacrificial ritual is at present open for discussion.

As mentioned, each of the six individuals suffered from some symptoms of what is commonly referred to as physical stress (see Table 6.2, column 6). Cribra orbitalia is often associated with some sort of malnutrition or malabsorption; however, a recent study concludes that anaemia and marrow hyperplasia are not connected with Cribra orbitalia and that the cause is vascular (Rothschild *et al.* 2021).

Thus, at present it is prudent not to infer from Cribra orbitalia to the individual's health. Chronic otitis media is well documented in ancient populations and can lead to permanent hearing impairment (Homøe *et al.* 1996, 1114–1119). All these stress signs are known from prehistoric populations, but it is notable that all were prominently affected. The affected palates of the five individuals are noteworthy, especially in that child x1 was also afflicted, which indicates an infection of the mouth. Infection in the mouth, here transferred into the palate bone from mouth bacteria, is also quite common and this can spread to other parts of the bone. Thus, the infection that is the cause of the rather severe regrowth into a more porous bone structure and holes in the bone seen especially on x73 and x77 might stem from the mouth originally. Seen as a group, it could seem that the Svennum individuals were more physically unwell than the Iron Age population as presented in Bennike 1985. On the other hand, six skulls are a small sample and none of the observed signs of physical stress would have rendered any of the Svennum individuals incapable of taking part in everyday life. Without the postcranial skeleton, it is hard to evaluate if this group showed signs of hard work or injuries that could be connected to neglect or violence, discussed further below.

DNA and society

The haplogroups suggest that four of them were of common Scandinavian stock whereas x22 had a haplogroup that in the modern population is rarely detected in a Scandinavian context (email to author from Peter de Barros Damgaard, 23 June 2015; see Table 6.2 for haplogroups and reference for the work). As the primary work on the aDNA is still in progress, just one point shall be drawn on the DNA here. The five DNA samples tested all have different maternal lineage, mostly of typical Scandinavian origin. This indicates that a small endogamic group with few ties to the outside world did not orchestrate the deposits but rather were conducted either by a larger community, a number of settlements or a patrilocal exogamic group with marriage ties to other communities. Even if the skulls were not local individuals but outsiders, it stills shows a high interaction with a larger community and/or long-distance interaction.

The skulls on stage

It is not clear which pits skulls x1 and x2 were dislodged from. However, features A235, A5, A7, A10, A13 and A16 are all possible sources as they were all disturbed by the placement of the drainpipe (see Plate 29). The four skulls excavated *in situ* were all deposited on top of extensive regrowth in the peat pits, around 20 cm of peat regrowth separates them from the bottom cut of the pits. As previously mentioned, stones and wooden poles and branches were found on or near the bottom of the pits (Table 6.3). The excavators documented animal bones lower in the same strata as, and just above, the human skulls. Ceramics lay lower and in the same strata as the skulls; most noteworthy, these consist of black ornamented sherds of a type of vessel associated with high-status individuals or households. Thus, it appears that the local community offered the six skulls in a well-established sacrificial setting. In the up to 50 cm of preserved peat atop the skulls only a few poles and branches were found immediately on top of them or separated by just a thin layer of turf. The stratigraphy and the ceramic refits suggest that the human skulls were placed during a single event (see Figure 6.1). This, event also appears to signal the final use of the pits. The regrowth surrounding the skulls and covering them shows that the peatland after the event became an undisturbed grassy meadow with little or no debris from the original wood peat. The pits grew in over time; they were not filled up manually. Hence, the pits would have been open after the sacrificial offerings, putting them on display for a time until they slowly disappeared into the bog.

From head to skull and skull to people

The individuals from whom the skulls originated were not recently deceased at the time of deposition. However, the question of how the local society curated them for the sacrificial ceremony and the closing of the site's use-life must be addressed. The skulls evince no cut marks. Nor are there any other peri-mortem or post-mortem damages to the skulls. So, we have no way of determining the cause of death, except that the individuals did not suffer trauma to the head nor was head severed from body between the base of the skull and the atlas vertebra, which says little as head-severing often occurs between two vertebrae.

That said, the individuals were not in the best of health as a group. They seem to have experienced more stress symptoms than the average Iron Age population as a whole. Most of them lived with some sort of infection that set its mark as skeletal pathologies. However, there is nothing to suggest that these infections were the cause of death, nor would they render a person so ill that they could not participate in everyday activities. Nor is there any evidence that they were mistreated. Thus, there is not enough evidence to suggest slow violence, as suggested on

the Swedish bog skeletons from the area around Gullåkra (Fredengren 2018).

As we presume that the skulls were not 'fresh' heads at the time of deposition, it is possible that the individuals to whom they belonged had quite different and unrelated lives, deaths and even post-mortem experiences up until they were deposited in the bog. It is perfectly feasible that one of the skulls could have been a trophy brought back from battle, while another could have died from natural causes. Nevertheless, the six skulls are connected by the environment in which they ended up, and the physical state of being 'only' skulls, and their role (whatever it may have been) in the final ritual which saw their placement into the peat pits at Svennum.

There are almost no other well-preserved human bones preserved in the numerous contemporary Roman Iron Age graves in Vendsyssel due to the regional geology with low calcium sand and gravel subsoil, and a high surface water flow which tends to decalcify bones. The good preservation of the skulls at Svennum is due to their placement in the alkaline, waterlogged environment of the bog, with low stable temperature and little oxygen. From a preservation standpoint it is possible that the skulls were placed for a time in an alkaline bog with calcium rich ground water flow, then retrieved, possibly even in a naturally skeletonised state or otherwise somehow defleshed without the use of sharp tools. The absence of all incisors could suggest that for a time the skulls were kept in a dry environment where the bones dried out and the teeth fell out prior to the skulls being deposited in Svennum bog. As the skulls are unmarred, it is likely that such a period took place indoors or at least somehow protected from scavengers. For example, skulls are found at some Iron Age settlements in Scandinavia deposited in houses; skulls did have a place in the context of settlements, although many such skulls have been rather violently modified and are often incomplete (Eriksen 2020, 5). Nieuwhofs thorough analysis of eight skull fragments found in a settlement but ritual setting and her analysis of older finds of human remains in settlement context in terp region of the Netherlands is also interesting in this context (Nieuwhof 2015).

Other skulls in other bogs

Other finds in Vendsyssel do indicate that the redepositing of skulls from one bog to another may be a likely scenario. From Lille Thirup, east of Hjørring, one bog skeleton was originally recorded (068/1931 VHM archive, FF 100612-105). But the author's recent review of those bones shows that these were actually from two individuals, although the skulls are missing, along with most of the small bones and the mandibles. A number of other finds from bogs sport skulls with no mandibles. Rather precise notes in the VHM archive support that nothing more of the remains was unearthed in the process of peat cutting. Vibsig

Mose situated 18 km from Svennum is another such a site with three skulls placed among ceramic sherds, stones, sticks and animal bones (016/1947 in VHM archive, FF 100113-192). It is noteworthy that one of the skulls was that of a child (Wåhlin in prep B). Formerly these finds were mostly viewed as incomplete bog skeletons where the peat workers simply did not recognise or bother with the post-cranial remains, assuming them not of academic interest (letter from the National Museum to Try Museum, 23 May 1932, Archive of the National Museum). However, Holger Friis at Vendsyssel Historiske Museum recognised the very significant amount of finds of just skulls (Bidstrup 1975, 180). The collection and records in VHM and the National Museum demonstrate that with at least 50 skull deposits out of a total of 80 known human bog sacrifices, skull sacrifices are more common than body deposits in the early Iron Age in Vendsyssel (some finds have rather poor registrations and thus to be on the safe side only certain crania-only finds are counted as such, those from uncertain areas are at present categorised).

Other scenes and props – the other sacrifices in the bog

Svennum bog is not littered with stray deposits. They are placed in well-defined spots and in between are areas with surface peat cutting as the only noticeable Iron Age human activity. The deposits differ greatly from the central area of the 14 pits.

The wood deposit

Feature A239 that includes A246 and A252 is primarily a wood deposit. It is situated either in a deep surface cut area or in a pit area where the dividing walls between the pits have been cut to the bottom. Both would leave a larger area covered by shallower and more dynamic water than the small pits. The deposits consist of a mix of sticks, poles and smaller wear-broken objects, poorly preserved animal bones and stones. On the bottom of this offering area, a few very large stones were placed. A number of long poles inter-crossed over the central part of the deposit, perhaps having held the skin, skull and extremities of the animals found.

At present most of the 304 numbered wood objects are not identified and await further study. Some heavy rectangular timber pieces are interpreted as building materials. In addition, a possible unfinished part of a small wheel was found. A number of finds are broken peat spades of the T-type (find lists in the excavation report Wåhlin unpublished, T-spades, see Lerche 1985). One of these was in its broken state pushed into the underlying peat. The best-preserved item is the wooden bottom of a basket likely used for carrying heavy loads. However, the most noteworthy wooden objects are in fact the sticks that are, for the most part, of quite specific lengths and widths. A number of sticks

were interpreted as tools as they had a shoulder with clear signs of wear and well-cut ends. These resemble a historic peat-cutting tool used to pre-cut the peat before the spade was applied to lift free the turf from the bog, thus reducing wear on the spade. Thus, the wood objects fall into categories of everyday activity within the local settlement: peat cutting and perhaps also land transport. These objects are worn but not broken intentionally.

Broken pots

The ceramic deposit, feature A234, was placed directly on the peat cutting surface and thus it is more dispersed, with the sherds of two to three pots themselves defining the perimeter of the offering. The sherds were all with fresh edges with small light-coloured stones among them, indicating a dynamic onsite 'smashing' of the pots likely by throwing stones at them (*cf.*, Walsh, Pantmann and Moen, this volume).

Ceramics were only found in the 14 pits and in feature A234. In total 221 finds of ceramic are listed. Generally, the sherds are typologically of everyday household ceramics from the Early Iron Age. The only exception are the sherds of black, polished ceramics found in connection with the skulls.

Signs of other areas of deposit

Some 150 metres to the west of the excavations, drain repairs in 2018 unearthed extremity bones of horse, and in 1897 a bog pot came to light during small-scale peat cutting in this part of the bog (located in the VHM archive, Wåhlin then entered it in FF).

Animal bones

The bones of dog, sheep, cattle and especially horse are present in the Svennum bog (Jacob Kveiborg, in prep, pers. comm., 10 June 2020). The animal bones (especially those from horses) are deposited in different ways. All deposits in the pits were dismembered or special parts were selected, such as the skull of an old stallion (-x87). The largest diversity of species and mode of deposition is in the same setting as the human skulls, where all animal bones appear to have been placed deliberately. The other animal sacrifices are mainly poorly preserved skulls and extremity bones seemingly scattered, perhaps suggesting that these may have been the result of a displayed hide that eventually fell into the bog.

A short note on stones

Stones are present amidst all the offerings, and more than 310 are documented in the excavation. A number of stones have been located when the transect sample drilling of the bog was conducted prior to the 2015 excavation, indicating that more offerings are likely present in the bog (Mortensen 2015). Deposited stones in bogs are a well-known phenomenon in most wetland finds (see Pantmann 2020; Walsh, Pantmann and Moen, this volume), but often not one much elaborated on; however, distinct patterns in stone depositions are documented from among others Fuglsøgård Mose (Johannesen 2017, 33, 38–39, 126). Recently, Pantmann's thorough analysis of stones in the Saltpeter bog demonstrated that they were selected for their light colour. She argues that even though the meaning of the stones is elusive they are nonetheless an elaborate offering and should be included in interpretations relating to sacrificial offerings (Pantmann 2020, 12–15). Like those described by Pantmann, the Svennum stones are selected and placed with intent and purpose. First, they are in the bog and thus placed there by humans. Secondly, at Svennum they are light- to medium-bluish and greyish, which is not common in the surrounding fields, which tend to consist of stones of reddish/brownish hues (Maring 2014; Wåhlin in prep). The reason for this might be practical, as white(ish) stones are easier to see at the bottom of pits, but I would suggest so too would light red stones. Thirdly, as described earlier, the stones are placed in rows and as cairns. These stones were generally not used for weights or any other practical purpose, but are instead part of the offerings themselves. Their exact meaning or purpose remains elusive and beyond the scope of this article, but they must have held some meaning to those placing them into Iron Age wetlands.

The skeletonised offerings

Studies of oracle bones from Bronze Age Chinese Shang Dynasty mention a human sacrifice practice in which the receiver and the intent of the sacrifice had a direct influence on the demography of victims and on the method of death (Wang 2008). Some gods preferred female victims and others male. Some needed multiple victims, while others sought just one or few (Wang 2008). Of course, one should not draw direct parallels between the Shang Dynasty and Iron Age Denmark. That said, within a general approach to the archaeological interpretation of human sacrifice, the demography, gender and/or physical traits of victims is of great importance, both as to what kinds of ritual offerings may have been made and how the practical sacrifices may have been conducted, and thus also reflect different intended recipients and intents behind the offering. Exploring this can help present a more coherent view of the sacrificial practice evident at Iron Age Vendsyssel.

Despite the skulls from Svennum representing all age groups and perhaps both sexes, the sacrificial practice there clearly emphasises the heads, and thus differs from offerings of complete bodies. So, too, the skeletonising process may be telling, indicating different approaches to the sacrificial offerings themselves. The old age of the skulls at the time

of deposit indicates that they had a long post-mortem function prior to the deposit. The emphasis on the head where thought, sight and speech originate could indicate that the heads had a function as media – clairvoyance between the living and the supernatural prior to the final deposit – and it was the vessel of clairvoyance that was transferred from the house to the ritual site. However, further studies on more human bog sacrifices in Denmark are needed before these questions can be adequately addressed. Whether certain demographics were more likely to end up as clean skulls or as full bodies used for sacrificial purposes remains a fascinating conundrum (*cf.* Moen & Walsh 2022).

The cleaned skull

Finally, the skull is quite simply the most unique and easily recognisable human bone(s). Defleshing a skull does not necessarily dehumanise the victim; in a way it accentuates them from other votive offerings, whilst perhaps also symbolically representing what it is to be human in a very general sense. Also, cleaning the skull is a way to ensure long-term preservation, as soft tissue is difficult to conserve. A clean skull is easier to handle and sturdier than a decomposing head.

Classical literature told Roman readers of barbarians such as the Gauls who practised not only human sacrifice but also beheading, embalming and displaying (Diodorus Siculus 1939, 175). The heads of slain enemies were precious and powerful objects. Tacitus describes how delinquents were sacrificed in wetlands (Tacitus 12.2, Bruun & Lund 1974, 46–47). But such sources are problematic to use as direct modes of interpretation for several reasons. Most noteworthy is that classical ethnographica is a literary genre written to speak to a Roman or Greek audience, who, in their own eyes were 'civilised'. The genre describes societies which were the opposite of Greek or Roman civility – *i.e.*, the 'savage' (Müller 1980, 1–25).

Further, recent studies of the soft tissue of bog bodies demonstrates that the 'over-kill' hypothesis or the 'threefold death' often suggested for the Iron Age finds is not supported empirically, as much of the blunt force trauma seems to be due to pressure in the bog and damage done in the process of excavation (Lynnerup 2015, 1010; Lynnerup *et al.* 2007, 254–258). That is not to say that any number of the human victims found in the bogs did not suffer a painful death, but there is, in my mind, little direct correlation to the detailed descriptions in the Classical texts. Also, the finds from Svennum bog display a lack of displayed violence and the context of the skulls is one of common wetland deposits found all over Denmark. This does not fit well with the rather blatant displays of violence in the early literature or the excavated ritual sites in Gaul such as Ribemont-sur-Ancre and Roquepertuse where human bodies and heads were modified and displayed (Cadoux 1984; Armit 2012, 148–157). Thus, other modes of analogy, interpretation and theory must be applied.

It is quite possible that society did not recognise the skulls deposited at Svennum as named individuals. However, it is also quite possible that that society at least believed that they knew exactly who they were and as such they perhaps reflect an equivalent to Medieval relics – representing a potent medium between the living and the supernatural. The lack of visible and thus displayed ritual violence could indicate that these heads were venerated and likely curated from society's own deaths rather than the result of headhunting as defined by Armit (Armit 2012, 12).

Beyond Svennum

Research into the Svennum bog has just begun with the most prominent sacrifice evident being the six human skulls presented here. Detailed studies of the context will in the coming years most likely add new layers to the interpretation. Offering six human skulls at once is a powerful ritual statement. If the skulls were indeed clairvoyant media formerly placed in the hall or house to be displayed and of which society could interact, then removing them from this social engagement and placing them in a central permanent ritual setting would have had implications for both those places and for the ritual practice involved. The power of the skulls as sacred objects was transferred to a new setting perhaps closer to the supernatural world that they helped society to communicate with. Svennum's primary contribution to the study of human sacrifice in the Danish Iron Age is an empirical one. Here we can without doubt state that the skulls were in fact skulls at the time of the final ceremony and not the result of poor preservation or modern disturbances. Thus, a ritual practice where human heads played a key role was indeed at work at least in the centuries before and after the birth of Christ in Vendsyssel. It is this practice that is the focus in the next leg of this study. Why sacrifice skulls, humans and body parts in the wetlands of Vendsyssel? And especially why select these skulls for sacrifice and permanent deposition in local wetlands? What special meaning did the head hold to Iron Age people? The debate continues.

References

Armit, I. 2012. *Headhunting and the Body in Iron Age Europe*. New York: Cambridge University Press.

Bidstrup, K. 1975. *Holger Friis Fortæller*. Copenhagen: Gyldendal.

Bruun, N.W. & Lund, A.A. (eds) 1974. *Tacitus Germania*, I og II. København: Wormianum.

Cadoux, J.L. 1984. Le sanctuaire gallo-romain de Ribemont-sur-Ancre (Somme), état de rechearches en 1983. *Revue du Nord* 66: 125–45.

Diodorus Siculus. 1939. *Library of History, Volume III: Books 4.59–8*. Translated by C.H. Oldfather. Loeb Classical Library 340. Cambridge, MA: Harvard University Press.

Eriksen, M.H. 2020 'Body-objects' and personhood in the Iron and Viking Ages: Processing, curating, and depositing skulls in settlements. *World Archaeology* 52(1): 103–119.

Fredengren, C. 2018. Becoming bog bodies. Sacrifice and politics of exclusion, as evidenced in the deposition of skeletal remains in wetlands near Uppåkra. *Journal of Wetland Archaeology* 18(1): 1–19.

Homøe, P., Lynnerup, N., Skovgaard, L.T & Rasmussen, N. 1996. Estimation of otitis media in ancient populations. 'A study of past and present Greenlandic Inuit'. *J. Laryngol Otol.* 110(12): 1114–1119. doi:10.1017/s0022215100135911.

Johannesen, K. 2017. *Rituals of Common Things. The Ritual and Religion of the Mixed Wetland Deposits in the Early Iron Age of Southern Scandinavia* (Ph.D. dissertation, Aarhus University).

Lerche, G. 1985. Wooden T-Shaped Spades and Double Paddle-Spades. In *Archaeological Formation Processes. The representativity of archaeological remains from Danish Prehistory*, edited by K. Kristiansen, 207–214. København: Nationalmuseet.

Lynnerup, N. 2015. Bog bodies. *The Anatomical Record* 298(6). Special Issue: The Anatomy of the Mummy: 1007–1012. doi:10.1002/ar.23138.

Lynnerup, N., Boldsen, J.L. & Jurik, A.G. 2007. The biological anthropology of Grauballe Man. In *Grauballe Man. An Iron Age Bog Body Revisited*, edited by O. Asingh and N. Lynnerup, 254–258. Aarhus: Jutland Archaeological Society Press.

Lynnerup, N., Jørkov, M.L., Villa, C., Primeau, C. & Alexandersen, V. 2015. *Antropologisk undersøgelse af skeletmateriale fra Svennum Offermose*, VHM 00500 Vort jr. nr. AS 07/15. Antropologisk Laboratorium.

Maring, R. 2014. *VHM00500 Svennum Offermose*. Udgravning efterår 2013. Excavation Report. VHM.

Milner, G.R., Boldsen, J.L. & Ousley, S.D. 2019. *Adult Age Estimated from New Skeletal Traits and Enhanced Computer-Based Transition Analysis*. National Institute of Justice (NIJ) Award # 2014-DN-BX-K0.

Moen, M. & Walsh, M.J. 2022. Under the skin: Norwegian bog skeletons and perceptions of personhood, value and sacrifice. *European Journal of Archaeology* 25(4): 483–503. doi:10.1017/eaa.2021.65.

Mortensen, M.F. 2015. *Mosegeologiske Undersøgelser af Svennum Mose*. Miljøarkæologi og Materialeforskning. Copenhagen: The National Museum.

Müller, K.E. 1980. *Geschichte Der Antiken Ethnographie und Ethnologischen Theoriebildung*. Von den Anfängen bis auf die Byzantinischen Histographen. Teil II. Wiesbaden: F. Steiner.

Nieuwhof, A. 2015. *Eight Human Skulls in a Dung Heap. Ritual Practice in the Terp Region of the Northern Netherlands 600BC–300AD*. Groningen: Barkhuis.

Pantmann, P. 2020. *Defining Wetlands – New Perspectives on Wetland Living with Case Studies from Early Iron Age in North Zealand, Denmark* (Ph.D. dissertation, University of Copenhagen).

Rothschild, B., Zdilla, M.J., Jellema, L.M. & Lambert, H.W. 2021. Cribra orbitalia is a vascular phenomenon unrelated to marrow hyperplasia or anemia: Paradigm shift for cribra orbitalia. *The Anatomical Record* 304(8): 1709–1716.

Wang, P. 2008. Methods of killing human sacrifice in Shang-dynasty oracle-bone inscriptions. *Minima Sinica* 1: 11–29.

Haraldskær Woman under a new light: Bog bodies, martial rituals and value

Mads Ravn

Abstract

This chapter approaches understandings of the deposition of bog bodies with a perspective on social governance and value in relation to how and why bog bodies were deposited. New results and dates for the Haraldskjær Woman are presented and contextualised in order to situate her within a different value perspective than previously considered. In this approach she is compared to other contemporaneous wetland offerings in Northern Europe. Entangling archaeological data and textual sources, the chapter also seeks to outline an Iron Age worldview wherein wetlands seem to represent the dangerous, queer, and other-worldly, thus accounting for a less valuable part of the agricultural worldview. Offerings to control this dangerous otherworld could explain the long continuous offering practices evident in wetlands, stretching back into the Stone Age.

Keywords: bog bodies, wetland deposits, Haraldskjær Woman, social governance, value, otherworld

Introduction

Humans found in bogs date back 8,000 years and in Europe are found from Norway to Crete. Over the years, focus has been on the 'CSI perspective': that is, on applying new forensic analyses to the individual bodies under the auspices that natural sciences offer an analogy to crime scene investigations such as those in popular television shows. A substantial amount of new knowledge has been generated on that account. What, however, has been lacking in the abundance of new data has been the wider context in which the bog bodies occur. Additionally, it seems that the theoretical perspective on the dead people has rested on a more than 150-year-old power-related value perspective, endlessly discussing whether the deposited bodies were criminals or chiefs, rich or poor. Recently, Løvschal and Holst (2018), with a focus on larger post-martial deposits in lakes and bogs in the Iron Age, have suggested a different theoretical approach, while including a larger empirical sample of materials set into broader context. Their study transcends the traditional, national boundaries that have also limited much of the research on bog bodies, because national

narratives and traditions in schools of scholarship have long forced researchers to reinvent the wheel when attempting to synthesise findings on individual cases together (*e.g.*, van der Sanden 1996).

Aim of the Paper

This paper focuses on the wider contexts and reasons as to why bog bodies were deposited in the lakes and bogs of Northern Europe. It explores the framework developed from the theoretical perspective of ritual governance in post-martial depositions (Løvschal & Holst 2018) and takes a broader view towards understanding their value as performative acts. The focus is on the last centuries before our era, as it is from this period that the majority of bog bodies have been deposited.

The mainstream view is that most of the bodies from the Iron Age were part of ritual acts such as ceremonial offerings (Mestorf 1871; Glob 1956; 1965; van der Sanden 1996; Giles 2009; Mulhall 2010; Ravn 2010; 2011a; Aldhouse-Green 2015). The difference of opinion lies in what these acts were all about. This paper includes recent contemplations about, firstly, ritual governance, which has been suggested for post-conflict martial rituals and attempts to adapt this term to the sphere of the bog bodies. Secondly, it discusses the definition and problem of sacrifice from a value perspective. In a value perspective it is irrelevant whether the deposited bog bodies were rich or poor, slaves or free, as have concerned many of the discussions of the last 150 years.

The bog people

Due to exceptional preservation conditions in Northern Europe, we find a number of well-preserved artefacts, animal remains and human bodies, sometimes as skeletons, other times as preserved bodies, especially from the Late Bronze Age and Iron Age (for a review for Denmark, see Glob 1965; Mannering *et al.* 2010; Aldhouse-Green 2015, 50). In 1965 P.V. Glob coined this mysterious find category and called them the 'Bog People', further suggesting that they had been sacrificed. Many before Glob had suggested similar things, mainly inspired from written sources, such as the Roman historian Tacitus, and supported a perspective where the deposited people were seen as criminals or low-status persons, who had been executed (Mestorf 1871). Grauballe Man and Tollund Man, two of the most prominent bog bodies in Denmark, seem to have suffered violent deaths, suggesting execution. Grauballe Man had his throat slit from ear to ear (Asingh 2007, 27). Also, he seemed to have trauma on his leg and skull (but see Lynnerup and Asingh, this volume). Tollund Man was found with a noose around his neck, suggesting a hanging (Fischer 2012, 12). The latter find made connotations to Tacitus' account of how the *Semnones*, a Germanic tribe of the 1st century AD, practised ritual hanging of criminals and other victims.

As a result, a majority of researchers see the bog bodies as sacrificial offerings of humans (Thorvildsen 1952; Glob 1956; 1965; van der Sanden 1996, 178; Fischer 2012; Aldhouse-Green 2015), and the bogs in which they are found could support a contention of a special setting. This is because we find many other things and animals deposited in wetlands, going back as far as the Stone Age. This suggests that the bogs – or water – served over thousands of years as a long-term medium for communicating with the other world through offerings, as a sort of 'gate to the other side' (Asingh 2009, 193).

Lynnerup (2010), Mannering *et al.* (2010) and Ravn (2010; 2011a) made recent surveys of the 560 known bog bodies in Denmark. They suggest that there is no clear pattern as to why they were deposited. Some may have been sacrificed while others may be considered burials. In addition, each of these studies has cast doubt on the idea of 'overkill' evident for some of the bog bodies, as many fractures are suspected to be due to post-depositional

pressure from the bog itself, rather than from peri-mortem violence. This discussion remains ongoing (*e.g.*, Lynnerup and Asingh, this volume; Walsh *et al.*, this volume).

However, the main focus of the latter researchers has been on the *actual bodies* and new scientific approaches which have opened many doors to better understanding the condition, origin and dates of the individuals themselves (see also Frei *et al.* 2015; Nielsen *et al.* 2020). The wider find context, or exactly where in the landscape the bog bodies were placed, has been less in focus. In my view, the wider context of the bog body, *together with* enhanced forensic evidence, may lead us to a firmer idea of what was really going on; if we also include other sources, such as written evidence and landscape studies, intertwining the evidence across disciplines, we may come to a more substantial argument for explaining these enigmatic bodies (Wylie 1989; Ravn 2011b).

It has for long been evident that the landscape in which Glob's 'Bog People' and other things were deposited was mysterious (Hedeager 1999; 2003). I will suggest that, on top of this, from an agricultural value perspective it may be seen as a liminal place, a place the agriculturists of the Iron Age had no control of or use for growing their crops or feeding their animals. This was suggested by myself 20 years ago (Ravn 2003, 9), but others have also developed this hypothesis (Løvschal *et al.* 2020). Here, I will develop this thesis further by using the Haraldskær Woman as an apt example.

The Haraldskær Woman

The Haraldskær Woman was discovered by peat diggers in Juthe bog in 1835, between Haraldskær Copper Factory and Ruhe Mark in the Vejle river valley of Jutland, Denmark (Hvass 1998, 8; Plate 30).

She was placed in the bog with her body secured by stout branches that skewered her elbows and knees and also lay across her chest and abdomen. Close to her, some textiles were found, as well as a leather cloak, probably of sheep or goat hide (Plate 31).

From the notebooks of the original excavators it seems that some of the textiles were located after the body was recovered. Additionally, later ^{14}C analyses suggests that the textiles are not contemporary. The Haraldskær bog is located approximately 13 kilometres to the south of Jelling, the well-known Viking seat of Harald Bluetooth. The national romantic historian Niels Matthias Petersen (1791–1862) promoted the hypothesis of the body being Queen Gunhild, suggesting that *Juthe* bog could have developed from *Gunhild*'s bog. At the time, and perhaps eager to see a mythic piece of Danish history come to life, King Frederik the Sixth (1768–1839) was easily convinced. Therefore, a large ceremonial public burial was instigated. The bog body from Haraldskær was reburied in an ornate, oak coffin and honoured with a proper

Christian burial, fit for a queen. She was laid to rest in the 12th-century Medieval church of Saint Nicholas in the provincial town of Vejle. Here, without further chemical preservation, she remained until 2012, when she was transferred to the Vejle Museums. In 1842, the archaeologist J.J.A. Worsaae opposed the Queen Gunhild hypothesis by deconstructing the myths around the written sources concerning the Gunhild legend. He concluded that it must have been a person from an earlier age, who had perhaps been drowned, as also mentioned by Tacitus in AD 98 in his work *Germania* (*e.g.*, Tacitus 12; Worsaae 1842).

Forensic analyses

At the time of discovery in 1835, the body of the Haraldskær Woman was subjected to an autopsy at Vejle Hospital. Most of her lower intestines were removed and she was sewn back together. The pathologists concluded that she had been pinned down alive in the bog, and there slowly drowned. In a second post-mortem investigation in 1979, CT scans confirmed that the bog body was in fact a well-nourished, Early Iron Age woman of about 40 years of age (Hvass 1998, 56). Further CT scans, X-rays and endoscopy revealed in 2005 that her upper intestines, tongue, lungs and much of her muscle tissue were still quite well preserved, despite the lack of conservation (Plate 32).

The woman from Haraldskær was 150 cm tall, a smaller stature than her female contemporaries, with an average height for females of the time of 161.7 cm (Bennike 1985). Also, a fine line of ligature impression was found around her neck, looking like a mark that would be left after a garrotting process, suggesting that she was strangled before she was placed in the bog (see Plate 30). Apart from this, her general medical condition was fine. She appeared to have been a healthy middle-aged woman at the time of her death. Furthermore, she had none of the degenerative maladies caused by a life of heavy labour that one might expect from hard-working farmers in the Early Iron Age. She also had fine hands, with only signs of arthritis in one of her thumbs (Plate 33). Due to exposure and desiccation, today she is only 133 cm tall and weighs only 2 kilograms.

In 2011, remains associated with the body were subjected to advanced isotopic analyses of strontium, and Frei *et al.* (2015) suggested that the woman had been on a long journey, perhaps to Central Europe, shortly before her death. In 2016, an attempt to remove the *pars petrosa* from her left temporal bone and a section of one of her teeth was undertaken with the aim of acquiring aDNA analysis by the Centre for GeoGenetics at Copenhagen University. This latter enterprise was, however, unsuccessful.

Dating the Haraldskær Woman is also problematic. So far there have been no direct, successful ^{14}C dates on her body itself. Associated finds, such as a lock of hair assumed to belong to the body, dates to approximately 160 cal BC. One

of the pointed branches found holding the body down dates to 490 cal BC. A skin cloak dates to 365 cal BC, whereas woollen textiles date to 158 cal BC. In addition, a hairnet found close by dates to 117 cal BC. Therefore, there are at least two variants to the dates, one pulling towards the early pre-Roman Iron Age around 400 BC, which is the one that is recorded in older publications (*e.g.*, Hvass 1998; Jensen 2003, 184). The other, dated from the hair, is pulling towards the late pre-Roman Iron Age, around 160 cal BC (Mannering *et al.* 2010, 263; Frei *et al.* 2015, 94). Three recent ^{14}C dates made in 2020 on the actual tissue of the inner ear of the Haraldskær Woman revealed that she is more likely to date to 247±17 cal BC (AAR 30881-x2, AAR 30882-x3 and AAR 30883-x4), placing her in between the older and younger extremes (Figure 7.1).

If the dates of the textiles and the skin cloak stand, they may not be contemporary with the body. If that is the case, it implies that the bog body was completely naked. Unfortunately, the body was revealed in 1835, and so far there is no positive contextual evidence confirming that the body was dressed at the time of deposition. Here I will thus rely on the ^{14}C dates of the various items, which indeed seem to disagree with each other, suggesting that they are not contemporary. Even if she was not found naked the context still implies that she was subjected to a deviant ritual act, as a normal contemporary burial at this period is most often that of cremation, where the dead are burnt with their clothes

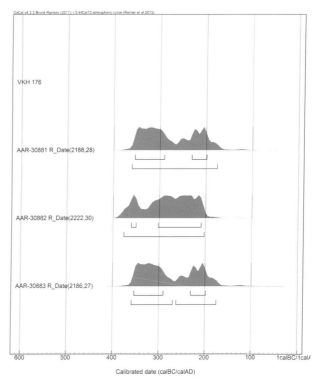

Figure 7.1. Recent dates from the tissue at the inner ear of the Haraldskær Woman (graphics: Aarhus AMS Centre, Aarhus University).

and jewellery. The varied ^{14}C dates of the items could be construed as if people were coming back to the place, again and again, because the other finds were deposited earlier and later, which is also the case at post-conflict martial places of deposition (Løvschal & Holst 2018). This suggests that the bog was an *important* and *significant* place, where potential rituals may have been enacted using sometimes humans or fragmented salient parts and leftovers of humans and things related to humans in a special ritual exegesis. I shall return to the content of this hypothesis below. First, we need to discuss the issue of ritual governance.

Ritual governance

According to Løvschal and Holst (2018, 29), ritual governance may be defined as '... the social structures and dynamics responsible for transferring, sustaining, and reproducing particular social behaviours and knowledge forms'. In such a perspective, ritual governance offers insights into how norms and patterns can self-organise and evolve into complex decentralised social systems. Also, they suggest that emerging social norms may refer back to existing normative structures, constituting an indirect connection between the culture–historical context within which the norms themselves emerged and the existing normative structures in place. A framework of ritual structures thus may consist of A) a group of people, B) being at a place, C) deploying salient symbols and practices, in D) a special ritual exegesis, or the way in which the ritual acts and meanings are organised in the understandings of those participating (Holst *et al*. 2018, 30). As far as the bog bodies are concerned, A and D are the most difficult to reach from an archaeological point of view.

As Løvschal and Holst (2018, 34) suggest by comparing a large amount of material in Northern Europe between 200 BC to AD 200, the emphasis on certain variables change according to time and place. In terms of location (B), rituals are performed in enclosures, bogs and lakes, rivers, grounds and settlement sites. In terms of salient symbols (C), there are appearances of human remains, animal remains, weapons, tools, ceramics, metalwork and coins. Additionally, salient practices may encompass intentional damage and dismantling, human corporal decay, intentional damage inflection and bone modification, including fragmentation, skeletonisation and corporeal selection, including dismemberment and post-mortem composite recombination.

Three tentative groups appear. The first group in Northern Gaul tends to contain rituals carried out in association with enclosures, sanctuaries and settlement sites. Here the emphasis is on cauldrons, chariot pieces, wheels, brooches and coins. Also, human corporeal remains are also frequently present, as is post-mortem manipulation associated with animal bones.

In the other group, rituals are carried out at open sites in association with wetlands and rivers. Sites include damaged and undamaged weapons. Here human corporeal remains are rarely present and there is little or no post-mortem manipulation. Also, local ceramics, white stones (see Walsh, Pantmann and Moen, this volume) and agricultural tools, stakes and poles are present.

A third group has a large quantity of weapons and human remains, revealing a creative ritual latitude in the post-conflict attitudes towards deliberate deposition. But here we have incidences of practices carried out on weapons and human remains, such as the mutilation, folding and disarticulating of both weapons and humans. There is a certain overlap and relatedness between the sites. It is probably within this latter group that we should place the bog bodies, though we need to look at the scale.

Though ritual governance may seem a useful framework to apply to interpretations of the bog bodies, because they appear in similar contexts, the analysis by Løvschal and Holst is, however also different because their emphasis is on the martial aspect, which is not present among the depositions of bog bodies. On the other hand, trauma on some of the bodies seems to concur with the trauma inferred on some of the weapons and things in martial depositions (see Lynnerup and Asingh, this volume). Also, the submerging in wetlands suggest contextual similarity and concurring ritual governance practices that, however, point to a smaller demographic scale of local leaders, family groups and local communities at different frequencies. Additionally, it seems with the bog bodies that a more secluded group are involved, suggesting at least a slightly different meaning implied by the ritualised events. But in order to understand what this is, we need also to discuss the issue of value.

Value

Recent discussions in anthropology have suggested that there are other hierarchies in non-Western societies than merely or predominantly power-related hierarchies. One example is Dumont (1986; see also Iteanu 2009), who stressed that Indian society maintained an ancient caste system of the Hindu religion in tandem with a power-related hierarchy. Here it is cleanness and purity that matter. For example, in this perspective a brahman is higher in the hierarchy than a prince, though it is the prince who holds the power.

I therefore suggest that we consider looking into whether the human depositions really need to reflect a hierarchy of power, as it seems that graves and settlements do. Indeed, from a governance perspective and a value perspective of purity, depositing the poor, criminals, slaves or the rich need not be opposites, nor meaningful for that matter. In an alternative perspective, all could be included in an overall perspective of cleanness, wholeness or fragmentation, the latter also suggested by Lund (2020). The peripheral location of the bog bodies and the possibility that some may, as is the case with the Haraldskær Woman, have been ritually killed and naked adds to the hypothesis that they were something out of the normal sphere. But now we should address the concept of sacrifice in relation to all of this.

Sacrifice or burial?

Here sacrifice is following the definition 'any kind of violence that people inflict on one another when sanctioned or sanctified, *e.g.*, by social authority, and with explicit reference to a higher purpose or higher authority' (Løvschal *et al.* 2019a, 3). Looking at a larger sample of 560 bog bodies, Ravn (2010; 2011a[1]) suggests that the majority interpretation of bog bodies does seem to be that they were sacrificed, although he also opens up the possibility that they may have been alternate burials as also proposed by Mannering *et al.* (2010). One problem with the latter approach is that, as mentioned above, the predominant burial custom at the time was cremation and those that were not cremations were well-furnished graves with set combinations of grave goods, suggesting that they were buried with clothes on (Ravn 2003, 10). In this context, the absence of the same set of combinations and the different context-deposition in wetlands suggests that the bog bodies were treated quite differently than the majority of deceased people at the time.

From current available data, which needs to be quality tested further (catalogue from Aldhouse-Green 2015, 202; Mannering *et al.* 2010), it may be possible to group the bodies in the following way. A majority of the bog bodies were found naked or with few clothes associated (however, see Mannering, this volume). Also, many were subjected to what seems a violent death (however, see Lynnerup and Asingh, this volume). From a general European perspective, the majority of the bodies were of men, although in Denmark men and women are equally distributed (Ravn 2011a). In Denmark 34% of the bog bodies found in the pre-Roman period were dressed, but many only partially, meaning by implication that the majority were at least not fully dressed (Ravn 2010, 109). Additionally, the majority of the deposited bodies were adults. Out of those that suffered a violent death, the majority were strangled. Second are those who had their throats cut. Third and fourth are those who were hanged and/or decapitated. This survey needs a more thorough follow-up before conclusive arguments can be made (see Walsh *et al.*, this volume).

Other sources – written sources

A few written sources may be relevant for this discussion even though these are problematic in terms of date and authenticity. Together with the archaeological contextual information they substantiate a pattern that may have been present in a general form for centuries (see also Lund 2008). Others have argued for the relevance of those sources (*e.g.*, Glob 1965, 136) suggesting that there seems to be a correspondence between the practice outlined by Tacitus' *Germania*, an almost

contemporary source about the *Reudignes, Aviones, Angels, Varines* and *Eudosos, Suarines* and *Nuitones*. Common to those peoples is that they celebrated the goddess Nerthus, and by the end of ceremonies dedicated to her, a wagon was pulled around. After the ceremony, slaves that cleaned the wagon were sacrificed in a remote and secret lake (*Secreto Lacu*, Tacitus 40.5). This passage has made the mainstream bulk of scholars suggest that the bodies in the bogs were sacrificed slaves (*e.g.*, Glob 1965, 136).

What fewer scholars have noticed is the description of the lake itself. It is mentioned that it is '*secreto*', which from the Latin may translate as 'remote' or 'secret'. The use of this word is important because it is less likely to be a product of propaganda on the part of Tacitus. Thus, the word 'secreto' which is the locative, dative inclination of *secretus* meaning 'in a remote lake' is important to bear in mind when in the following we contextualise bog bodies within the landscape. Also, the description coincides spatially with the general view of the archaeological and topographical observations suggesting that the bog bodies are located in what, from an agricultural locus, are liminal and remote places of wetlands (see also Lund 2020, 210). In terms of the Haraldskær Woman, she was located in a wet river valley between 400–500 metres from the nearest Iron Age sites and graves, all of which were placed on higher and drier ground. This corroborates from a spatial perspective that she was placed peripherally in a wetland area. But why was she and many bog bodies placed in remote places? In order to answer this, we must now look at the interplay between sacrifice and value.

Sacrifice and value

From a value perspective, I propose that power was not reflected within the deposition of the bog bodies. Rather power and ownership were used in the burial customs and settlement structures in the 'real' agricultural world of the farmers and their halls (Ravn 2003, 24; Løvschal 2014). The peripheral spatial position of the Haraldskær Woman and the bog depositions in general, from an agriculturist's perspective, will be explored in the contexts of textual sources, landscape observations and archaeological sources. An initial observation suggests that the deposited people were different in the widest definition of the word: possibly even dangerous or impure in the terminology of M. Douglas (1966). Indeed, some may have been social outcasts, as some textual sources such as Tacitus' account indicates.

In this connection, I shall turn to the *Beowulf* poem, which may be going far back into the Migration Period (Newton 1993). Indeed, the fight between the king represented by Beowulf in the hall and the intruding monster Grendel suggests that monsters and 'freaks' came from the remote wetlands to haunt and challenge the 'right' hierarchical world of the king's sovereignty (Ravn 2003, 9). In other words, we have a worldview among ancient Northern

Table 7.1. Some concepts of opposition in ancient Northern European societies.

Our world	Their world
The Hall, settlements, fences and graves	The bog/wetlands
Power and control	Uncontrolled disruption
The domesticated infields	The outfields and the wild
Safe	Dangerous
Agriculture	Unused, barren land
Right	Wrong
Humans	Monsters and freaks
Worldly	Otherworldly
Normative	Queer
Whole, lived lives	Fragmented, terminated lives
Insiders	Outsiders
Pure	Impure

European societies where oppositions and opposing values may be outlined as follows (Table 7.1).

Discussion: Otherness, queerness and fragmentation

If the bodies were treated within a different value hierarchy, the idea of otherness may have surpassed many other values, as also suggested by Lund (2010, 210). Cutting the throat of, for example, the Grauballe Man and strangling the Haraldskær Woman present an element of symbolic mutilation – a fragmentation from and termination of the previous life (Lund 2020, 214). This destruction is also seen in higher resolution in slightly later depositions of bodies at *Alken Enge* (Løvschal *et al.* 2020) and in weapon offerings (Ilkjær 2003). There was a variation of scale to play with for those making such depositions, *e.g.*, where the mutilated remains of martial conflicts and the bog bodies are in opposition to the living but in the same sphere as the more fragmented finds of animals, textiles and other things also placed in wetlands at the time. Only a finer chronology and regional delimitation of each behavioural pattern of the entire depositions in bogs in a larger topographical perspective may reveal a higher resolution of any overlapping pattern (see Walsh *et al.*, this volume).

From a preliminary contextual analysis intertwining several sources and observations, I suggest that the bog depositions were not part of a common burial, because they were less whole than the living; they were placed in a liminal space where they were purposefully and elaborately deposited in areas that were wet, useless, barren, peripheral and perhaps even dangerous from an agrarian perspective. Thus, the overall meaning could be that the wetlands acted

as liminal, dangerous places from where impure and/or queer creatures appeared and to whom one had to deposit equally fragmented, dangerous and impure partial objects and beings (see *Beowulf* 1345–1356). Furthermore, the bogs seem dangerous places:

> mysterious is the region they live in – of wolf fells, wind-picked moors and treacherous fen-paths: a torrent of water pours down dark cliffs and plunges into the earth, an underground flood. (*Beowulf* 1357–1380, see also 1386–1400, translated by Alexander 1973)

Conclusion

In conclusion, by combining a theoretical approach of ritual governance, adjusting it to the scale of the bog bodies and considering an alternative approach to value as well as combining this with textual sources from the same cultural sphere, I have thickened the argument in a contextual analysis where liminal space and a long-term landscape perspective on the wetlands suggest that this area and those placed therein were different in multiple symbolic senses. From this perspective, the bog bodies were part of the same ritual governance sphere as the post-martial rituals. There are, however, also different factors present. Firstly, in scale, as the former seem more singularly made and thus more private. For many bog bodies in general and the Haraldskær Woman in particular mutilation and fragmentation in the form of bodily injury, as well as submerging, seem common factors. Post-conflict martial rituals, on the other hand, highlight long-term exposure to decay, visibility and reorganisation of objects and body parts (Plate 34). But both may have achieved the same or similar purpose – they ritually removed the impure and/or dangerous from view, both in reality and symbolically.

Thus, from a value perspective, it looks like the meaning of depositing bog bodies falls under the value of fragmentation, otherness, dangerousness, nakedness and possibly queerness. They supersede the power-related hierarchies of the living in Iron Age society and its broader domesticated world of power-obsessed chiefs and blood-thirsty gods, especially when one approached the dark waters of the wetlands.

In combination with other observations from archaeology, *Beowulf* and Tacitus' emphasis on 'secret lakes' we find some deeper structures connecting in space with the texts through time, indicating remoteness as strange – even queer (Ravn 2003, 10), like the Haraldskær Woman who was deposited in a lake, away from the settlements and graves. In the two textual sources, Tacitus and *Beowulf*, both seem to substantiate in concert that bogs were liminal undomesticated spaces, as indeed they were considered for more than a millennium before, suggesting long-lived notions that these were queer places, filled with dangerous denizens and settings for the macabre. It is the farmers' wish to control their world, starting already with the earliest Neolithic farmers (*e.g.*, Hodder 2012; see also Sørensen, this volume).

In *Beowulf*, it was from wetlands that the monsters, Grendel and his mother, came to disrupt the balance of the known world, represented by King Hrothgar's fine hall of Heorot. The domesticated world needed to control the feral 'disrupters' symbolically realised in the wetlands. They had to be kept in the right place, as Beowulf does when he slays the monster intruding in the hall. They also had to be kept in a liminal place, like the queer mother of the monster, who Beowulf slays on her own grounds in the moor. Though fanciful, we may envision that this very killing may itself have resulted in a bog body, not so unlike the Haraldskær Woman.

The bog bodies placed to rest in the fens were entered into a non-orderly, fragmented, liminal and dangerous place, parallel to but separate from post-martial depositions. I believe that it is in this similar parallel context that most of the bog bodies and other remains found in the bogs should be seen – as extensions of 'ritual governance' enacted by ancient agrarian Northern European societies.

Note

1   There are two M. Ravns in this paper who are not related, this author and Morten Ravn, which is why I write their full names in the references.

References

Aldhouse-Green, M. 2015. *Bog Bodies Uncovered: Solving Europe's Ancient Mystery.* London: Thames and Hudson.

Alexander, M. 1973. *Beowulf. Verse Translation by Michael Alexander.* London: Penguin Books.

Asingh, P. 2007. The magical bog. In *Grauballe Man. An Iron Age Bog Body Revisited*, 275–289. Højbjerg: Jutland Archaeological Society.

Asingh, P. 2009. *Grauballemanden – portræt af et moselig.* Copenhagen: Gyldendal.

Bruun, N.W. & Lund, A.A. 1974. *Publius Cornelius Tacitus. Germaniens historie, geografi og befolkning*, vols I–II. Aarhus: Wormianum.

Douglas, M. 1966. *Purity and Danger. An Analysis of Concepts of Pollution and Taboo.* Abingdon: Routledge and Kegan Paul.

Dumont, L. 1986. *Essays on Individualism. Modern Ideology in Anthropological Perspective.* Chicago/London: University of Chicago Press.

Fischer, A. 2012. *Tollund Man. Gift to the Gods.* Stroud: The History Press.

Frei, K.M., Mannering, U., Price, T.D. & Iversen, R.B. 2015. Strontium isotope investigations of the Haraldskjær Woman – a complex record of various tissues. *ArcheoSciences, revué d'archéométrie* 39: 93–101.

Giles, M. 2009. Iron Age bog bodies of north-western Europe. Representing the dead. *Archaeological Dialogues* 16: 75–101. doi: 10.1017/S1380203809002815.

Glob, P.V. 1956. Jernaldermanden fra Grauballe. *KUML* 1956: 99–113.

Glob, P.V. 1965. Mosefolket. *Jernalderens mennesker bevaret i 2000 år.* Copenhagen: Gyldendal.

Hedeager, L. 1999. Sacred topography. Depositions of wealth in the cultural landscape. In *Glyfer och arkeologiska rum – en vänbok till Jarl Nordbladh*, edited by A. Gustafsson and H. Karlsson, 229–252. Gotarc Series A, 3. Göteborg: Göteborg University.

Hedeager, L. 2003. Kognitiv topografi: Ædelmetalldepoter i landskapet. In *Snartemofunnene i nytt lys*, edited by P. Rolfsen and F.-A. Stylegar, 147–165. Skrifter, vol. 2. Oslo: Universitetets Kulturhistoriske Museer.

Hodder, I. 2012. *Entangled. An Archaeology of the Relationships between Humans and Things.* Chichester: Wiley-Blackwell.

Hvass, L., 1998. *Dronning Gunhild – et moselig fra jernalderen.* Copenhagen: Sesam.

Ilkjær, J. 2003. *Mosens Skatkammer. Mellem mennesker og guder i jernalderen.* Højbjerg: Jutland Archaeological Society.

Iteanu, A. 2009. Hierarchy and power. A comparative attempt under asymmetrical lines. In *Hierarchy: Persistence and Transformation in Social Formations*, edited by K. Rio and O.H. Smedal, 331–348. Oxford/New York: Berghahn Books.

Lynnerup, N. 2010. Medical imaging of mummies and bog bodies. *Gerontology* 56: 441–448.

Løvschal, M. 2014. Emerging boundaries. Social embedment of landscape and settlement divisions in northwestern Europe during the first millennium BC. *Current Anthropology* 5(6): 725–750.

Løvschal, M. & Holst, M.K. 2018. Governing martial traditions: Post-conflict ritual sites in Iron Age Northern Europe (200 BC–AD 200). *Journal of Anthropological Archaeology*, 27–39.

Løvschal, M., Gullbek, S.V., Johansen, M.-L., O'Neill, S., Walsh, M. & Willerslev, R. 2019. Human sacrifice and value. *Antiquity* 93: 1–4.

Løvschal, M., Iversen, R. & Holst, M.K. (eds) 2020. *De dræbte krigere i Alken Enge. Efterkrigsritualer i ældre jernalder.* Aarhus: Aarhus University Press.

Lund, J. 2020. Alken Enge som rituel plads – Deponeringer i lyset af fragmentering, skelettering og dannelsen af en ny rituel plads. In *De dræbte krigere i Alken Enge. Efterkrigsritualer i ældre jernalder*, edited by M. Løvschal, R.B. Iversen and M.K. Holst, 209–224. Aarhus: Aarhus University Press.

Lund, J. 2008. Banks, borders and bodies of water in a Viking Age mentality. *Journal of Wetland Archaeology* 8: 53–72.

Mannering, U., Possnert, G., Heinemeier, J. & Gleba, M. 2010. Dating Danish textiles and skins from bog finds by means of ¹⁴C AMS. *Journal of Archaeological Science* 37: 261–268.

Mestorf, J. 1871. Über die in Holstein und anderwärts gefundenen Moorleichen. *Globus* 20: 139–142.

Mulhall, I. 2010. The peat men from Clonycavan and Olderoghan. *British Archaeology* 110: 34–41.

Newton, S. 1993. *The Origins of Beowulf and the Pre-Viking Kingdom East Anglia.* Woodbridge: D.S. Brewer.

Nielsen, B.H., Christensen, T. & Frei, K.M. 2020. New insights from forgotten bog bodies: The potential of bog skeletons for investigating the phenomenon of deposition of human remains in bogs during prehistory. *Journal of Archaeological Science* 120. doi:10.1016/j.jas.2020.105166.

Mads Ravn

Porter, J. 1993. *Beowulf.* Text and translation by John Porter. Little Downham: Anglo-Saxon Books.

Ravn, Mads. 1993. Analogy in Danish prehistoric studies. *Norwegian Archaeological Review* 26(2): 59–90.

Ravn, Mads. 1999. Kan vi erkende religion forhistoriske grave? In *Religion og materiel Kultur*, edited by L.B. Christensen and S.B. Sveen, 78–93. Aarhus: Aarhus University Press.

Ravn, Mads. 2003. *Death Ritual and Germanic Social Structure.* Oxford: British Archaeological Reports IS 1164. Oxford: Archaeopress.

Ravn, Mads. 2011b. Ethnographic analogy from the Pacific: Just as analogical as any other analogy. Debates in World Archaeology. *World Archaeology* 43(4): 716–725.

Ravn, Morten. 2010. Burials in bogs. Bronze and Early Iron Age bog bodies from Denmark. *Acta Archaeologica,* 81(1): 106–117.

Ravn, Morten. 2011a. Bog bodies – a burial practice during the Early Iron Age? In *The Iron Age on Zealand. Status and Perspectives*, edited by L. Boye, 81–87. Nordiske Fortidsminder, Series C, 8. Copenhagen: Royal Society of Northern Antiquaries.

Schjødt, J.P. 1993. Det 'hellige' i religionsvidenskaben. *Themata* 5: 4–13.

Schjødt. J.P. 2001. Det 'Hellige' i religionsvidenskaben: En diskussion af det hellige som konstituerende for vor opfattelse af begrebet religion. In *Religionsvidenskabelige sonderinger: Festskrift i anledning af et 10 års jubilæum*, edited by J.P. Schjødt and V. Andersen, 189–198. Aarhus: Aarhus Universitetsforlag.

Thorvildsen, E. 1952. Menneskeofringer i oldtiden. Jernalderligene fra Borremose i Himmerland. *KUML* 1952: 32–48.

van der Sanden, W.A.B. 1996. *Through Nature to Eternity – the Bog Bodies of Northwest Europe.* Amsterdam: Batavian Lion International.

Worsaae, J.J.A. 1842. Hvorvidt man kan antage, at det i Haraldskiærmosen (1835) opgravede Liig er den norske Dronning Gundhildes?, *Historisk Tidsskrift* 1(3): 249–293.

Wylie, A. 1989. Archaeological cables and tacking: The implications of practice for Bernstein's 'Options Beyond Objectivism and Relativism'. *Philosophy of the Social Sciences* 19(1): 1–18. doi:10.1177/004839318901900101.

Figuring out bodies in bogs and other watery places: Posthumanism, figurations and ecological relations

Christina Fredengren

Abstract

This chapter overviews the contributions of the 'Water of the Times' project to research on depositions of bodies and body parts in watery places in Sweden. The project investigates these human and animal remains to trace the changing patterns of when these depositional practices were common, who was deposited, how these bodies were treated in life and death and exactly where in the landscape the depositions occurred. It also deals with what effects such depositions may have had in the formation of relationships between humans, animals and the wet landscapes. The research also makes theoretical contributions and has worked with a critical posthumanist process and ontological approaches, and has dealt with questions around killability, necropolitics, sacrifice and the nature of the inhumane – to highlight how some bodies may have been othered and treated as less than human, but also how bodies may continue to be agential in wetland contexts. This chapter provides a navigational tool through the work in the project, links to that of other research in this field and illuminates how this theory can be used to move from discussing personhood to discuss bodies as figurations, and what interpretations this open up in the analysis of bodies in archaeology and more particularly bodies deposited in watery places.

Keywords: process ontology, critical feminist posthumanism, bog bodies, wetlands, worlding, sacrifice, multispecies archaeology, human-animal-nature relations, personhood of waters, figurations

'Water of the Times' background

The 'Water of the Times' project works primarily with depositions of human and animal remains placed in waters and wetlands and overviews those materials in Sweden. The research has led to novel relational studies of human and animal remains depositions in wetlands with a focus on skeletal remains (compared to the more famous bog bodies preserved in flesh). It engages theoretically with critical feminist posthuman theories (Braidotti 2013; Fredengren 2013; 2018) that throw new light on subject formation and personhood. Hence, the research challenges anthropocentrism at multiple levels. First, it questions the boundedness of individualised bodies and analyses bodies as gatherings of several more-than-human material and immaterial relations. Second, it writes histories around formations of human-animal-nature relations and includes both human and animal remains more symmetrically in the analysis. Third, it deals with how the construction and the ring-fencing of a 'normalised' human can be a tool for political othering that regulates social and ideological notions of killability, which in turn may have played an integral role in sacrificial and depositional practices. Hence, the project deals with how violence and sacrifice may have contributed to the forming of exclusive ideas about humanity, which allowed for the othering of selected parts of the population. As such, these othered others may have been chosen for depositions in watery places under practices that designated them as less-than-humans. In short, their bodies may not have been considered as having full personhood in the context of society, allowing for their inhumane treatment. Thus, this work deals with the *nature of the inhumane*, which is also the title of a planned monograph that will synthesise the work of the 'Water of the Times' project.

The project investigates Swedish human and animal remains depositions from watery places in order to see when these depositional practices were common, who was deposited, how they were treated in life and death and where in the archaeological landscape the depositions took place. It has also explored commonalities expressed in practice and place lore relating to sacrifice and waters by comparing so-called Celtic and Nordic traditions (see Fredengren 2016; 2018a; 2019b). This has led to research that deals with how entities than other human, such as rivers, wetlands and lakes, may also have been acknowledged as living entities and persons (Fredengren 2018).

This work has also gathered several researchers and formed the basis for the European Bog Body Network (https://bogbodynetwork.wordpress.com/), a forum that connects bog body researchers internationally (Fredengren & Bergerbrant 2011; Farley *et al.* 2019). Furthermore, 'Water of the Times' research has contributed to artistic productions (https://signejohannessen.se/posthumous-dialogue/) as well as writings that connect studies of wetlands to the wider field of the environmental humanities inspired by Haraway's (2016) speculative storytelling methods. It was formerly thought that the bad air from bogs - miasma, spread disease. Through speculative writing (Fredengren 2019b) an artistic intervention was made on the topic of miasma, which connects it to the decay of cut wetlands, that in turn emits greenhouse gases. This could be captured as a Miasma 2.0 that consist of the next to imperceptible greenhouse gases that gather up to cause climate change. Furthermore Johannessen & Malmström (2023) have through artistic research folded out the transtemporal relations of the hybrid wetland find from Kvarntorp, mid Sweden, which is connected to an extractive landscape.

Theory work has also been carried out in order to wrestle with some of the terms often used in archaeology, such as 'bog bodies', 'depositions', 'sacrifice', 'personhood' and 'identity' (and this is an ongoing endeavour). The project has also worked with renewing the relationship with natural science methods to explore bodily relations in archaeology (Fredengren 2013). With a base in posthuman/new materialist theories the 'Water of the Times' project has dealt with issues around how such methods can be used to investigate the deposited bodies' relationships with other human and non-human actors both in life and death (Fredengren 2018b). The overall aim of the work has been to get a better understanding of how depositional phenomena were produced and what effects these depositions would have had for building relations between humans and the wider environment, particularly during the Late Bronze and Iron Ages. It investigates the changing and entangled relationships between humans, animals and nature during these periods, but also considers technology and science in relation to

watery depositions and seeks to move beyond leaving this as an analysis of entanglement only (Fredengren 2021a; 2021b) to identify and acknowledge variously situated and power-laden relationships evidenced in wetland depositions.

What follows showcases some of the project results and presents continuing avenues of work still to be done. This chapter is intended to highlight and extend the project's work to make explanatory connections between the concepts of identity and personhood so often used in works of archaeological interpretation (*e.g.*, Farley *et al.* 2019; Giles 2020; Moen & Walsh 2022) and that of figurations, used in the theoretical field of critical feminist posthumanism. Overall, these concepts and theories have been explored within the 'Water of the Times' project in an attempt to better understand the subjectivities of prehistoric wetland depositions (see Haraway 1997; 2008; 2016; Barad 2007; Braidotti 2013; 2017; Fredengren 2013; 2015; Fredengren & Löfqvist 2015).

This chapter illustrates what this theoretical/methodological package can offer to the subject of archaeological body theory and more specifically on watery depositions in prehistory, outlining how the research methods connected to figurations make a difference when mapping bodies in bogs (and other watery places) and comparing this with how personhood works as a heuristic analytic device. Studying bog bodies as figurations opens the analysis to examinations of how such bodies are produced by a confluence of processes both in the past and present, but with effects that also project into the future. This chapter gives a reflection on how not only the bodies themselves but also the bog body phenomenon is a co-production of differently situated sources and forces. For example, several natural science apparatuses contribute to the production of archaeological materials; these have their own entanglements with other practices, bodies and environments in the past. With a base in this reasoning, the paper continues with a discussion on killability, sacrifice, power and subjectivity. Following on from this, the chapter moves onto the question of depositions as ecological relata where different waters might have been endowed with and recognised as living entities with a persona. This also highlights some of the future trajectories of research with a start in such depositions. Hence, it opens up for the archaeological study of ecological and/or burials, *i.e.*, the linking up of 'death' with regenerative practices within the environment.

Overview of project results

The Swedish material has been presented in numerous 'Water of the Times' publications. As a result of searches in museum stores and archives, many formerly unpublished sites have been recognised. The project has gathered over 130 wetland sites with human and animal remains finds in Sweden. These range in date from the Mesolithic period to the Modern (and this compares with the Irish material that has dates starting in the Early Neolithic and continuing on in time). However, and not surprisingly, there is a particularly high concentration of wetland depositions in the Early Iron Age. Hence, the dates in Sweden correspond to those of the more common bog body dates in North-western Europe that also reach a maximum in the Early Iron Age (Fredengren 2011; 2015; 2018a; Fredengren & Löfqvist 2019). This material has been discussed in several research overviews on the phenomenon of bog bodies, and the related question of sacrifice has been a subject of discussion at meetings within the Bog Body Network (Farley *et al.* 2019; Giles 2020).

'Water of the Times' has mapped and published numerous geographically differently situated depositions in Sweden. These publications have dealt with depositions in the wider Mälaren Valley (Fredengren 2015; Fredengren & Löfqvist 2015), sites in Scania, such as the wetlands around Uppåkra (Fredengren 2018) and on Öland, in particular those of Mossberga Mosse (Fredengren & Karlsson 2018). Furthermore, sites with skeletal depositions in Co. Gotland have been published together with researchers in another project (Bergerbrant *et al.* 2013). 'Water of the Times' has also carried out excavations at the depositional site at Lake Bokaren, north of Uppsala, together with Susanna Eklund and Andreas Hennius. There, both human and animal remains from the Roman Iron Age and into the Medieval period were found at what may have been a lake platform used for sacrificial practices (see, *e.g.*, Fredengren 2015; Fredengren & Löfqvist 2019) and the results from these micro-studies will be gathered up for a trend analysis in a coming publication of the project.

Critical feminist posthumanism and process ontological methods have been used throughout the project's work to theorise the relationship between archaeology and the sciences but also to expand on questions of identity, personhood, subjectivity and figurations within archaeological theory (see Fredengren 2013; 2018a; 2018b; 2021a; 2021b; see also Moen & Walsh 2022 for a discussion on bog bodies and personhood). To meet these goals, the 'Water of the Times' project has adapted the theories of Barad (2007) and Braidotti (2013) to the question of *who* was deposited in watery places in prehistory. This question was expanded by asking *how* bog bodies were produced, and hence the project has expanded gender theory in archaeology with these perspectives. This approach (Fredengren 2013; 2018b) allows for a study – and a diffractive vision – of how such bodies are produced in the present using scientific measures and how they also were co-produced by several relational actions in the past. However, this has also moved the discussion from an identity-based argument to an investigation of personhood and figurations of bodies, depositions and burials as co-produced phenomena. Thereby, 'Water of the Times' has dealt with questions around subject formations and has used the term 'figurations' more often than that of 'personhood'. Below, I will try to explain how these concepts are

interconnected and what difference they make in the study of depositions of humans and animals in watery places.

From identity to personhood and figurations

A well-known problem in archaeology is that it is quite impossible to read the minds of past peoples and to know their thinking. We may only surmise how they understood themselves and what their possible identities, as in self-views, in fact were. In recent years the concept of personhood has often been used to capture how particular persons may have been constituted by material and relational means (Brück 2004; Fowler 2004; 2016; Jones 2005). Fowler (2004, 4) has defined personhood as 'the condition or state of being a person, as it is understood in any specific context'. A person is someone or something 'conceptualised and treated' as a person (Fowler 2004, 4) and/or if and how they have agency. Such personhood changes both in life and death, through varied and altered relationships with humans, animals, things and/or places. Particularly, personhood comes into being through people's social practices and interpretations of themselves and each other. Hence, there is an element of mutual constitution of personhood that differs from identity that is more connected to self-perception. In archaeology, studies of personhood have increasingly shifted over to the 'exploration of the relational properties of things, persons, places and materials, and the distribution of agency – and in some cases personhood – well beyond human beings' (Fowler 2016, 397). In Fredengren (2013) I developed how to work with 'figurations' as a tool in archaeology, and I would like to expand on how this adds to the discussion on personhood, bodies and bodily relations in archaeology. In particular, it is of interest to show how the analysis of bodies deposited in bogs and other wetlands can be understood differently through such an approach.

While critical feminist posthumanism philosophies have already been used in archaeology to expand the notion of personhood (see Fowler 2016, *etc.*), neither Barad (2007), nor Braidotti (2013) or Haraway (1997; 2016) seem to make much explicit use of that term. One reason for this, as I understand it, is that it is a concept that implies conceptual boundedness of bodies (as in the case of legal persons [Haraway 1997, 80]). Another reason could be that the term implies a focus on how someone is recognised and conceptualised as a person by other human folks, and hence the production of personhood would be connected with anthropocentric viewpoints, more than stemming from an engagement with bodily materialisation processes.

What I would add to this argument on personhood in relation to depositions in water places is that there might have been bodies that would have existed, lived and have had agential capacities regardless of whether they were recognised as individuals, fully human or persons by other humans. This is a particularly important matter when dealing with bog bodies, killings and sacrifices, as their killability (Fredengren 2021a; 2021b; 2022) and their deaths may be connected with them falling outside of being acknowledged as human bodies to be protected from harm. They may have fallen outside the norms of who was regarded as fully human. Such bodies may have been more vulnerable and shaped by being outside networks of care, as evidenced, for example, in signs of malnutrition or their being exposed to violence.

To Braidotti (2019, 34), figurations (borrowed from Deleuze and Guattari) can be seen as conceptual persona, and as 'a theoretically-powered cartographic tool'. Elaborating on this, figurations, as used in the 'Water of the Times' project, imply the use of specific neo-materialist methods to make cartographies of semiotic and material relations that coincide in and emanate from different bodies. Bodies of humans or animals come together as nodes of relations on the move and their subjectivities operate across species boundaries. They (as well as things, places and landscapes) exist as phenomena in transformation, constantly on the way to becoming something else. Hence, to deal with the question of who was deposited in a watery place means to focus in on different parts of this becoming – *who* were these bodies when they grew up, when they grew older, when they were deposited and when they subsequently decayed? Such questions lead to an exploration of what relations the bodies drew together over time.

Furthermore, this approach of tracing figurations involves exercising critical and creative thinking to map humans as entangled more-than-human beings (produced in webs of interdependencies with environment and other phenomena). Figurations can also be used as tools for 'documenting and exposing the sedentary and restrictive structures of dominant subject-formations (power as potestas, or entrapment)' (Braidotti 2017, 11). Hence a figuration has several more purposes geared towards power analysis, as compared to the general concept of personhood. Figurations can work more affirmatively as they can be used to express 'alternative representations of the subject as an ongoing process of transformation (power as potentia, or empowerment)' (Braidotti 2017, 9). Figurations can be understood broadly as 'figures of thought', that in creative and condensed ways capture more than what a definition or classification does, and hence it is of interest for archaeology to work with. A figuration both signifies an entity (as a body) and a doing (to trace how it comes into being and change). However, this doing is not only a verbal exercise by the archaeologist, as a figuration is conditioned on several material-semiotic processes. For example, conceptual carrier bags such as 'the cyborg', 'the posthuman', 'the onco-mouse', 'the bog body', 'the sacrifice' or 'sacrificial masculinity' are figurations that are made through a conjunction of several encounters between archaeological material, scientific and theoretical apparatuses as well as creative practices. Here artistic research collaborations such

as those between the 'Water of the Times' project and Signe Johannessen on hybrid bodies from wetlands has worked with trans-temporal and trans-species figurations (see Posthumous dialogue; Johannessen & Malmström 2023). Thus, to work with figurations in archaeology may also mean to make use of tools that look at the entanglements and apparatuses of bodily production as well as tracing positive and negative power formations over time.

Figurations are described by Haraway (1997, 11) as 'condensed maps of contestable worlds'. One could, with Haraway (2008, 4–5), say that figurations are non-representational 'material-semiotic nodes or knots', and that the bodies we work with in archaeology, such as bog bodies, are *knotted sites* that when mapped bear the signs of the world that produced them. With figurations as a point of origin, situated depositions of human and animal remains can be analysed as atlases that open up to challenged worlds. To work with figurative methods for understanding body parts deposited in watery places therefore implies that we trace which networks produced those bodies in the past, but also recognise those that may not have been acknowledged as fully human by their contemporaries. Further, this also allows us to explore how archaeological knowledge production about the past is situated in a dense present, where analytical categories can be challenged, as they also ethically project into the future. Such figurative methods can be useful for discussing gender and power in archaeology, as an additional analytic tool, with broader and different implications that adds to the work on tracing identity and personhood. Hence, to trace bodies as figurations encompasses more than investigating people's identity or personhood, while personhood is one figuration among many others.

Apparatuses of bog body production

The 'Water of the Times' project has worked theoretically to meet well with and make use of several scientific methods. The osteological analyses carried out by Camilla Löfqvist have looked at, for example, age, sex/gender, trauma, nutritional status and traits of the handling of the deposited remains. We noted that animal remains often are recorded with less precision than humans and amended the osteological methods to come to terms with this othering. Hence both human and animal remains were treated more symmetrically. The project has also worked with both aDNA and istope analyses. These were used to explore the question of who was deposited, to follow the shifting sex/gender and age patterns in the materials, and to investigate how they were treated in both life and in death. Radiocarbon dating was carried out to identify temporal patterns in the distribution of materials, to look at when the practice of watery deposition was most common, and to see if the locations changed over time. However, these standard methods of archaeology needed to be examined through our theoretical lenses described above. Here, critical feminist posthumanism and its connections with science and technology studies (STS) have been particularly useful for framing new insights into what the archaeologically analysed bodily remains are indeed assemblages of. This has allowed the project to bring a deeper awareness of how bog bodies have been produced both now and in the past.

The paper 'Posthumanism, the transcorporeal and bio-molecular archaeology' (Fredengren 2013) provided the theoretical/methodological bases for the project. It also opened up new avenues of inquiry for understanding what scientific methods bring to archaeological analyses, and how such analyses also alter the reasoning around bodies. For example, through scientific methods in archaeology it is possible to map some relations that stitch through bodies, but such foci never fully capture the full set of relations in their 'agential cut' (Fredengren 2013; 2018a; 2021b). Barad (2007, 148) has used the term 'agential cut' to describe how phenomena that exist in the world rise through acts of observation that make cuts into an interconnected reality. Scientific methods therefore separate what is considered in an analysis from that which is disregarded, and thus produce an ethically infused world where choices around which world that will be produced have been made. With this in mind, DNA analysis, osteology or isotope analysis in archaeology each use particular sets of apparatuses and lenses that allow particular phenomena to arise and be let into our interpretations of the past. However, as bodies arise through an excess of relations, the coming about of such phenomena risks overshadowing other relations that are not a part of such analysis. Hence, in archaeology, theoretical and scientific apparatuses perform cuts that temporarily sta-bilise selected relations, for example, human/animal/nature relations or sex/gender phenomena. Osteological and other natural science laboratory measures are not only analysing the archaeological, but rather co-producing its reality by forefronting certain parts of it.

As a case in point, drawing on Alaimo (2010) in Fre-dengren (2013, 53), I argued that 'unnecessary boundaries have been set up between the body and the environment. The concept of the transcorporeal allows for rethinking the connection between bodies and landscape, enabling us to dis-cuss the environment inside'. As such, the body can be seen as a nexus in a vast network of relations and links with the environment and with the landscape, so to say, internalised. Bodies are produced through transcorporeal intra-action with the environment. For example, isotope analyses do not only show the possible provenance, travels or diets of people. They also show how bodies are immersed in the environment and how the environment is immersed in situated bodies, being such knotted sites where several relations meet and entangle. In fact, such scientific measures point to situated relations with animals, plants and even water, revealing a metabolic landscape within the body. Hence, particular bodily remains can be analysed as 'condensed maps of contestable worlds'

that Haraway (1997, 11) mentions and where bodies differ-entiate depending on in what way they participate in such transcorporeal networks.

This work with figurations in the 'Water of the Times' project has led to questions about how bodies were produced through being part of networks of violence or care as well as how they were also co-produced by relationships with animals and environments. The use of such figurations in archaeology allows us to envisage a 'mapping how entan-gled nature-culture webs coincide or dissolve in bodies and how non-human actors are important for the development of various events' for example as evidenced in food-networks detected through isotope analysis (Fredengren 2013, 66). Such a figurative lens on the archaeological evidence both highlights power asymmetries and deals with how scientific apparatuses co-produce such bodies and work beyond tradi-tional personhood as so often assessed archaeologically by looking at, for example, clothing or equipment.

For example, due to exceptional preservation, many well-known bog bodies such as the Grauballe Man (Asingh 2009; Asingh & Lynnerup 2007; Lynnerup and Asingh, this volume) are often the focus of examination through several scientific techniques. They co-become with several natu-ral scientific methods and laboratory apparatuses, such as isotope analysis, macrofossil analysis, DNA analysis, *etc.*, but also through processes of conservation, to the extent that they come to us in the present as some sort of cyborg (which I will return to below). It is worth noting that the use of these natural scientific methods highlights certain aspects of their relationships, but self-evidently not all. Figurative thinking can provide an inquiry and critique on how bodies are produced as human or non-human, and even more-than-human now, but also in the past by tracing entanglements that are knitted together as exercises of power (Fredengren 2021a). As mentioned, certain aspects may be highlighted by use of scientific techniques, others are left to the side in the archaeological analysis of bodies, and a critical inquiry of the apparatuses of bodily production needs to be in place. As a case in point, in a discussion on the use of aDNA, Brück (2021, 228) argues 'that kinship relations are not determined by biogenetic links, but are generated through social practice'. Together with Brück (2017; 2021) I would like to emphasise that several strands of archaeological data need to be brought together to trace the relationalities that brought any particular body into place. Hence, ancestors that produce a human body are always more-than-human and can be found in the food we eat, the water we drink, the material culture uses, and the places we move in between, in addition to being produced through other social practices where both human and more-than-human agencies contribute. Further-more, Brück (2021, 228) highlights several 'androcentric and heteronormative interpretations of aDNA data'. What could be added to this reasoning is a curiosity in how to interpret aDNA data beyond anthropocentrism, in ways that do not take the normative human as point of origin; also anthropocentric narratives need to be critically examined, which may call for analysing more-than-human kin, or the likes of microorganisms such as bacteria, fungi and viruses that compose bodies of both humans and non-humans. These too belong to such ancestry that produces situated bodies.

Ultimately, on this point, the bog body or bog skeleton as analysed in the present can be understood as a cyborg of several pasts, presents and futures that come together through a meeting between bodily tissues, measuring techniques, conservation substances and theories that make cuts into interconnected worlds, worlds that are constantly on the move towards something new. As discussed, bodies are figures that come together through a variety of more-than-human sources, forces and techniques of several temporal belongings. I have alluded to this already (Fredengren 2013). When we talk about bog bodies, they arise and are produced as Baradian phenomena: as cuts into an interconnected world made by practices both now and in the past. To discuss them as figurations can, as Haraway (1997, 11) suggests, be a way 'to make explicit and inescapable the tropic quality of all material-semiotic processes, especially in technoscience', *i.e.*, to pay attention to how the apparatuses of observation in archaeology also alter the world.

Becoming bog bodies

Bog bodies catch the imagination and appear in fiction and art production (see Johannessen & Malmström 2023). One suggestion is that they are figurative carrier bags around which we strike a conversation and build stories. The conversations I would particularly continue dwell on matters of life and death and their relation to sacrifice as well, and to links between nature and culture. To work with figurations of bog bodies may also imply the mapping processes in the past that contributed to their coming about – their becoming. The concept of becoming, derived from Deleuze's and Guattari's critique of identity questions, has been developed further by, for example, Barad (2007) and Braidotti (2013). The reasoning behind this critique is that 'to be' something implies having a stable identity. Contrary to this, becoming implies an impermanence (*e.g.*, Barad 2007, 336). Coupled with body theory, this opens our archaeological interpretations to the idea that bodies are constantly in the process of shifting agential alliances and are inherently on their way to become something else.

Furthermore, as noted above, there are several agencies that produce bodies as phenomena. Such agencies can be relations with other humans, more-than-humans, technologies, politics, ecologies, landscapes, *etc*. Bodies are constantly composed and decomposed by several agentialities, such as the aforementioned landscape or by processes of decay. Thus, the process of becoming bog bodies can be analysed as differently situated flows of life. In the research

undertaken in the course of the 'Water of the Times' project several such situated processes, which brought together bodily remains in watery place, have been mapped. Several more-than-human forces are necessary for a depositional place to come together. For example, the case of the depositions of human and animal remains at Torresta, Co. Uppland, were discussed as co-produced by the agency of waters, contributing to a gathering of bones in particular locations in the wet environments. Moreover, the paths of hoofed animals through the landscape may have focused movement to the wading place where the bodily remains accumulated and eventually were retrieved (Fredengren & Löfqvist 2015).

Similarly, geological movements that caused shorelines and waters to recede in the landscape would also have been among the agencies that enabled or withdrew facilities in the formation of depositional spots, as for example, along the River Fyris, Co. Uppland. There, as former places of deposition were drying out with the isostatic lift of land, one had to find other watery places for depositions (Fredengren 2015). Hence, we can see that several human-animal-nature processes and relations contributed to the becoming of the phenomena of situated bog bodies and other wetland depositions. The tracing of such relations and their effects contributes to the building of a figurative mapping around the depositions.

Furthermore, such processes of becoming could also be observed through carrying out a life-cycle analysis of the skeletal remains from watery places. For example, in the case study from Uppåkra and Scania (Fredengren 2018) the remains retrieved in wetlands were suggested as deriving from what may be interpreted as a long process of othering. Some of the body parts show signs of malnutrition. Other body parts showed damage that indicates that their lives had been hard. Based on this it can be argued that they were exposed to what can be called 'slow violence'. This is violence of the type that does not work as directly as a blow with (which is recorded as trauma in osteology), but violence that breaks down bodies at a slower pace, over longer periods of time. This includes traumas such as starvation, exposure to toxic environments or work-related damage. Furthermore, to become a bog body was in some situated cases conditioned on a long process of decay and/ or dismemberment and handling on land before deposition of selected parts in the wetlands. For example, the skull from Gullåkra bog (Fredengren 2017) was retrieved without any other body parts and it must have decayed and been separated elsewhere prior to being set in the wetland. The osteological analysis shows that the skull has a glossy surface, which suggests that it was handled and touched on several occasions before it was passed onto the wetlands. As evidenced by bog staining, which affected coloration, the skull was placed on the surface of the bog and only eventually sank into the wetland. There it became a part of a larger assemblage of artefacts that had gathered over time, becoming co-depositions with them. One interpretation is that some people were perhaps not only chosen, but also, to some extent, made for the occasion of killing for sacrifice and hence connected to several processes of othering. While they at some stage in this process may have fallen out of recognition as persons *per se*, this does not mean that these body parts did not continue to matter.

With the division of bodies and deposition of body parts in wetlands, there are similarities to the fragmentation processes described by Chapman and Gaydarska (2007). One possibility is that the deposited bones were treated as dividuals. In such cases, their personhood in life was, through their deposition in death, distributed in and becoming one with the living landscape. The wetlands were in effect also gaining different body parts and were expanded with skulls and on occasion also legs, arms, *etc.* that can be interpreted as the waters becoming an increasingly humanised figure. Fowler (2016, 401) has furthered the archaeological notions of personhood and presented the idea that new versions of persons do indeed emerge over time. Such persons may have been involved in different relations and practices and need to be categorised in more dimensions that only individuals or dividuals. Fowler argues that these two concepts are too broad and that in reality persons consist of bundles of relations that are dynamic and non-binary. This reasoning ties well into the discussion of various bog body figurations, and highlights how bodies are produced as interdependent networks of interactions.

Sacrifice and the nature of the inhumane

We must not take the categories of the human or personhood for granted. While some bog body depositions have been referred to as garbage (*cf.*, Pantmann, this volume) or those of highly valued citizens or dethroned kings (Kelly 2006), there is the possibility that some of those bodies deposited in wetlands lacked full recognition as 'humans', 'persons' or 'citizens' within their societies or that they lost their personhood when they failed as kings. What counts as a person and who has a recognised and respected personhood in life and death varies over time. It is important to note that an essentialisation of 'the human' is a political project both then and now. Braidotti (2013, 116) writes about posthumanism and inhumane practices, bringing attention to necropolitics, wherein de-humanising practices abound. Such politics are of the kind where some actors have the power of managing the boundary between life and death over selected others, just as in sacrificial actions. Hence, sacrifice is a tool in the exercise of necropolitics. Necropolitics can run together with processes of humanisation and de-humanisation which may have been at work in the process of making certain bodies killable (Fredengren 2021a; 2021b; 2022) or more suitable as victims of sacrifice (Fredengren 2021a; 2021b; 2022; *cf.*, Walsh and Reiter, this volume).

There is differing and situated evidence in the bog body record where there are several examples of how body parts indicate that some people suffered malnutrition and ill health, while other bodies were of those who had been cared for by their communities (Fredengren 2018c). There is ample evidence for both bodies produced by caring networks and bodies produced by networks of neglect to have been interred in watery places. If taken as figurations, these bodies, regardless of whether they were conceptualised as full persons or not, can be investigated as 'condensed maps of contested worlds' and accounted for in archaeology. In addition, communities in the past may have dealt with tensions around who was to be considered as fully human, and thus treated as a being worthy of care, and those who were deemed as expendable. To get a better idea of such questions the deposited bodies' relations to the landscape may also be traced. For example, depositions such as those at Uppåkra or Toresta took place in locations that had received depositions before. These locations were special and had a particular agency that kept depositional traditions alive over long periods of time. Depositions at such qualified locations add another dissonance. While they may have been places in the landscape that demanded further sacrifices and depositions – both being woven into practices of power over othered bodies – they may also have provided a way to negotiate the use of violence and situate necropolitics with reference to traditional locations and practices.

Killability

By tracing different kinds of relation-making and working with figurations, the 'Water of the Times' project has dealt with how different othering transforms relationships between human-animal-nature(s) and also on occasion has produced death (see Fredengren 2018a; 2018b; 2018c; 2022). The work continues to engage with questions around sacrifice and killability as described above (see Haraway 2008, 77–78; Braidotti 2013; Fredengren & Löfqvist 2019; Fredengren 2021a; 2021b). With a base in the reasoning of Haraway (2008, 77–78) it is important to reflect on the anthropocentrism resting on the notion that when animals are killed, the term murder is reserved for humans. This notion is based on an understanding of animals as mere automata that react to stimuli such as pain, while humans respond. Such rhetoric can also be found in cases of mass-murders where *othered* others have fallen outside politico-historic-temporal frameworks of what or who should be protected or perceived as human. Similar mechanisms may have been at play during some of the time periods discussed here, where the production of killability and sacrifice as phenomena were activated over long periods of time, as for example through the Scandinavian Bronze and Iron Ages. Again, in line with Haraway (2008, 80) it is important to note, 'It is not killing that gets us into extremisms, but making beings killable.' The works referred to here as well as the continued work of the Water of the Times project have tried to map several material and immaterial relations that may have exposed certain lives to suffering and death, making them killable. There are several factors involved in this, such as cases where there seems to have been a gender/age bias in determining who was more killable. In the case of Uppåkra in Skåne, Sweden, this was clearly focused on adult males (Fredengren 2018b) building up a sacrificial masculinity. Also, factors such as inclusion or exclusion from networks of care would situate certain bodies as more killable than others.

Ecological relations and water as kin

> Another approach, much closer to my heart, is to start from those differences of location and, by accounting for them in terms of power, as both restrictive and productive (potestas and potentia). (Braidotti 2013, 141)

While on the one hand, some of the bodies retrieved from wetlands were the result of violent treatment and neglect which indicates the work of entrapping forces, on the other there are also remains where there is no such evidence for violent treatment of the bodies.

The deposition of body parts in watery places could also be understood as releasing productive forces as the parts became a part of the watery ecologies in their afterlife. The placement of depositions in water also establishes a relationship with the environment. This is a new strand of interpretation of depositions from which they can be interpreted as vehicles for establishing and nurturing ecological relations. Such an argument can be made by highlighting how waters of different types were augmented with body parts of both humans and animal, as well as objects. This may have been the case, for example, in Uppåkra where human remains deposition followed on from object depositions in the wetland locations (Fredengren 2018c). Disregarding this was the intent of the actors that carried out the depositions; they became some sort of ecological burials, *i.e.*, bodies deposited in the environment, spreading out the necrogeographies beyond common burial grounds. On occasions these depositions were not anatomically complete bodies, but only body parts. Their bodies were dividable and shareable with the ecologies into which they were inserted. However, disregarding the depositions of bodies as whole or parts, such placements could possibly have contributed to a merging, transformative process making rivers and wetlands more human, and some humans and animals more a part of the environment. Tracing of critical cartographies of sacrifice and depositions suggests that the dead could have co-worked in lively and generative worlding practices (Fredengren 2022) that joined up bodies of the dead with living material.

Brück (2017, 40) comments on how the metalwork found in rivers must have been separated from the bodies of individuals, and that such depositions may have worked to tie

community identities to particular places in the landscape. Also, as such depositions were often of metal weapons placed at political boundaries, they may have been a way of dealing with the transformative and sometimes hazardous potentials of such areas. Tying in with this reasoning, the 'Water of the Times' project has drawn attention to the fact that folklore and documentary sources, not only in Scandinavia and Ireland but also in the rest of Europe, attest that water bodies were seen as being alive. In some cases, they were even deities. This led the project toward a discussion of enchantment effects of wetland materials and how waters may have been approached as animated (Fredengren 2015; 2016). In Fredengren (2018a) it was suggested that some depositions of swords, necklaces or other items may have been a way for people to address watery places as if they were living beings ready to receive gifts of a kind that were suited for human use. Such relationship building may also have framed the receiving partner, the wetlands, as a next to human being or worked to recognise it as a person. Furthermore, adding body parts to the wetland through depositions would have supplemented its being with skulls, arms, legs and other body parts, possibly making it even more creature-like. In this light, depositions of both body parts and objects might have co-produced a composite personhood of the waters.

Brück (2017, 40) also suggests that the models of self in the Bronze Age would have been rather dissimilar and more fluid than those of today. As I have argued (Fredengren 2018a), several depositional practices geared towards wetlands may have worked as such practices to establish relationships with waters. One possibility is that certain waters were understood as more-than-human kin. Depositions of body parts of certain human and animal bodies may have been a way to articulate and produce an ecological kinship with wet environments, extending humans into wetlands and integrating wetlands into humans. Haraway (2016, 102–103) writes about how to make kin with entities other than humans. This would lead to another complex figuration of waters and wetlands as potential ancestors and more-than-human kin, that both works through humans addressing waters as persons and through the landscape inscribing itself in and through our bodies making out humans' more-than-human mottled kin within.

Conclusion – knotted sites

The 'Water of the Times' project has approached the study of bodies and body parts deposited in watery places through critical feminist posthumanism theories on subject formation, personhood and figurations. The benefits of such an approach are to encompass a wider and more complex range of relationalities that may have been of importance for the formation of particular bodily remains depositions and to further the discussion of power and agency differentials.

This has meant working with what may have been fluid conceptions of self, but also moving beyond taking for granted that all bodies, human and more-than-human, may at all times have been recognised as persons. This reasoning highlights how personhood is connected to how some bodies are recognised or misrecognised as such by other humans. To work wider with figurations (that may be steeped in both damaging and enabling power structures) also means to query anthropocentrism in archaeological studies of sacrifice and beyond. By considering how archaeological subjectivities are produced by present-day apparatuses together with the materials of the past and their relations, the boundedness of individualised bodies are challenged. By considering how archaeological subjectivities are produced by present-day apparatuses together with the materials of the past and their relations, the boundedness of individualized bodies is challenged. Instead, bodies can be analyzed as knotted sites, and formed by situated human-animal-nature relations. This is relevant to the study of sacrifice as necropolitics may have rendered both human and animals as non-persons in moves to make them killable.

This chapter has suggested some theoretical methods for working with critical figurations in archaeology, for example, the figurations of bog bodies, sacrifices or waters as kin that may have been related to as living persons. Together with this, the project has explored several points of connection in mythology and practice over larger parts of Northern Europe, particularly tied to Celtic and Nordic literary traditions. Such figurations could also work creatively and affirmatively, as in the artwork of Signe Johannessen that reveals several relationalities around the find of a multispecies body at the bog of Kvarntorp. These kinds of figurations highlight the entanglement of ecological relations that connect across tissue of the inner and the outer bodily worlds and can join company with Haraway's famous critical figurations such as the cyborg and the oncomouse. Here and in further work, I would like to dwell on what type of critical figuration bog bodies could become. It could be moving figuration that draws attention to the trope of sacrifice. It could also be a figuration to investigate different ways of tying ecological relationships with the environment.

References

Alaimo, S. 2010. *Bodily Natures: Science, Environment, and the Material Self*. Indianapolis: Indiana University Press.

Asingh, P. 2009. *Grauballe Man – Portrait of a Bog Body*. Aarhus: Aarhus University Press.

Asingh, P. & Lynnerup, N (eds) 2007. *Grauballe Man – An Iron Age Bog Body Revisited*. Moesgård. Jutland Archaeological Society Publications.

Barad, K. 2007. *Meeting the Universe Halfways*. Durham NC: Duke University Press.

Bergerbrant, S., Fredengren, C., Molnar, P., & Löfqvist, C. 2013. Violent death and wetlands: Skeletal remains from Gotland. In *Counterpoint: Essays in Archaeology and Heritage Studies in Honour of Professor Kristian Kristiansen*, edited by S. Bergerbrant and S. Sabatini, 199–206. Oxford: British Archaeological Report IS 2508.

Braidotti, R., 2013. *The Posthuman*. Cambridge and Malden, MA: Polity Press.

Braidotti, R. 2017. Posthuman critical theory. *Journal of Posthuman Studies* 1(1): 9–25.

Braidotti, R. 2019. A theoretical framework for the critical posthumanities. *Theory, Culture & Society* 36(6): 31–61.

Brück, J. 2004. Material metaphors: The relational construction of identity in Early Bronze Age burials in Ireland and Britain. *The Journal of Social Archaeology* 4: 307–333.

Brück, J. 2017. Gender and personhood in the European Bronze Age. *European Journal of Archaeology* 20(1): 37–40.

Brück, J. 2021. Ancient DNA, kinship and relational identities in Bronze Age Britain. *Antiquity* 95(379): 228–237. doi:10.15184/aqy.2020.216.

Chapman, J.C. & Gaydarska, B.I. 2007. *Parts and Wholes: Fragmentation in Prehistoric Context*. Oxford: Oxbow Books.

Crellin, R. & Harris, O. 2020. Beyond binaries: Interrogating ancient DNA. *Archaeological Dialogues* 27: 37–56. doi:10.1017/S1380203820000082.

Farley, J., Giles, M. & Fredengren, C. 2019. Foreword: Bog Bodies Special Edition. *Journal of Wetland Archaeology* 19(1–2): 1–8. doi:10.1080/14732971.2020.1820769.

Fowler, C. 2004. *The Archaeology of Personhood: An Anthropological Approach*. London: Routledge.

Fowler, C. 2016. Relational personhood revisited. *Cambridge Archaeological Journal* 26(3): 397–412. doi:10.1017/S0959774316000172.

Fowler, C. & Harris, O.J.T. 2015. Enduring relations: Exploring a paradox of new materialism. *Journal of Material Culture* 20(2): 127–146.

Fredengren, C. 2011. Where wandering water gushes – the depositional landscape of the Mälaren valley in late prehistoric periods of Scandinavia. *Journal of Wetland Archaeology* 10: 109–135.

Fredengren, C. 2013. Posthumanism, the transcorporeal and biomolecular archaeology. *Current Swedish Archaeology* 21: 53–71.

Fredengren, C. 2015. Water politics. Wetland deposition of human and animal remains in Uppland, Sweden. *Fornvännen* 111: 161–183.

Fredengren, C. 2016. Deep time enchantment. Bog bodies, crannogs and other worldly sites at disjuncture's in time. Archaeology and Environmental Ethics. *World Archaeology* 48(4): 482–499.

Fredengren, C. 2018a. Personhood of water. Depositions of bodies and things in water contexts as a way of observing agential relationships. *Current Swedish Archaeology* 26: 219–245.

Fredengren, C. 2018b. Archaeological posthumanities: Feminist re-invention of humanities, science and material pasts. In *A Feminist Companion to the Posthumanities*, edited by C. Åsberg and R. Braidotti. Cham: Springer. doi:10.1007/978-3-319-62140-1_11.

Fredengren, C. 2018c. Becoming bog bodies. Sacrifice and politics of exclusion, as evidenced in the deposition of skeletal remains in wetlands near Uppåkra. *Journal of Wetland Archaeology* 18(1): 1–19. doi:10.1080/14732971.2017.1408596.

Fredengren, C. 2019. Att möta våtmarkernas natur, en spekulativ arkeologi om offer, mosslik och klimatfrågor. OEI#84-5 *Våtmarker och Experiment*: 51–56.

Fredengren, C. 2021a. Bodily entanglements: Gender, archaeological sciences and the more-than-ness of archaeological bodies. Special Edition on Posthumanism. *Cambridge Archaeological Journal* 3: 525–531. doi:10.1017/S0959774321000226.

Fredengren, C. 2021b. Beyond entanglement. Keynote + response. *Current Swedish Archaeology* 29: 11–33. doi:10.37718/CSA.2021.01.

Fredengren, C. 2022. Worlding waters with the dead (or the more-than-dead). Necrogeographies. *Norwegian Archaeological Review* 55(2): 140–158. doi:10.1080/00293652.2022.2073910.

Fredengren, C. & Bergerbrant, S. 2011. Dead people in the bogs: Network report. *Journal of Wetland Archaeology* 10: 152–153.

Fredengren, C. & Löfqvist, C. 2015. Food for Thor. The deposition of human and animal remains in a Swedish wetland area. *Journal of Wetland Archaeology* 15: 122–148.

Fredengren, C. & Karlsson, J. 2019a. Mossberga Mosse: Excavating the archives and tracing museum ecologies. *Journal of Wetland Archaeology* 19(1–2): 115–130.

Fredengren, C. & Löfqvist, C. 2019. Finitude – human and animal sacrifice in a Norse setting. *Proceedings of the Old Norse Mythology Conference 2015*. Stockholm: Stockholm University Press. 225–262.

Giles, M. 2020. *Bog Bodies: Face to Face with the Past*. Manchester: Manchester University Press.

Haraway, D. 1997. *Modest_Witness@Second_Millenium.FemaleMan_Meets_OncoMouse*. London: Routledge.

Haraway, D. 2008. *When Species Meet*. Minnesota: University of Minnesota Press.

Haraway, D. 2016. *Staying with the Trouble: Making Kin in the Chthulucene*. Durham NC/London: Duke University Press.

Johannessen, S. & Malmström, C. (eds) 2023. *Hornvännen*. Tallin: Printon.

Jones, A.M. 2005. Lives in fragments? Personhood and the European Neolithic. *Journal of Social Archaeology* 5: 193–224. doi:10.1177/1469605305053367.

Kelly, E. 2006. *Kingship and Sacrifice: Iron Age Bog Bodies and Boundaries*. Archaeology Ireland, Heritage Guide no. 35. Bray: Wordwell.

Mbembe, A. 2003. Necropolitics. *Public Culture* 15(1): 11–40.

Moen, M. & Walsh, M.J. 2022. Under the skin: Norwegian bog skeletons and perceptions of personhood, value, and sacrifice. *European Journal of Archaeology* 25(4): 483–503. doi:10.1017/eaa.2021.65.

Thrown stone for flesh and bone? 'White' stones in sacrificial context in Iron Age Scandinavia

Matthew J. Walsh, Pernille Pantmann and Marianne Moen

Abstract

This chapter looks at the ritual deposition of white and white(ish) stones in wetlands in Danish prehistory. We investigate this phenomenon from two quite different but not opposed perspectives: 1) that the ritual deposition of white stones in wetlands could be an abstract expression of some aspect(s) of prehistoric Nordic cosmology, such as that proposed by the trifunctional hypothesis for Proto-Indo-European cosmology popularised by Dumézil; and 2) that such depositions may have served as substitute offerings, taking the place of human, animal or other sacrificial tender – a practice seen in diverse cultural contexts from the ethnographic record. We also consider that the white stones may reflect more mundane activities nevertheless rooted in everyday ritualised praxis.

Keywords: white stones, wetland depositions, substitute offerings, prehistoric cosmology, ritual praxis, sacrificial offerings

Introduction

This paper considers an interpretative exercise for approaching a prehistoric ritual phenomenon. The aim is in examining what appears to be a repeated ritual behaviour seen in Early Iron Age Scandinavia: namely the presence of white or 'whitish' stones in ritual landscapes (Bradley 2000), here particularly in wetlands. The presence of such stones in these places is the direct result of human agency. Our point of departure is that interpreting ancient religious behaviours is tenuous and in part speculative (*cf.*, Berger 1986), and yet this need not hinder our interpretations so long as this is acknowledged. Inspired by Fahlander's (2001, 41) observation that unique and extinct forms of prehistoric religious expression must have existed, we take a notably playful stance in attempting to explain this little-known and highly enigmatic ancient ritual proclivity from the past, represented by the presence of white stones in 'sacred' settings. In our approach, we offer two interpretative options: one that configures the sacrificial offering of white stones in wetlands as reflecting aspects of Proto-Indo-European cosmology and associated ritual practice (*e.g.*, Ward 1970; Dumézil 1973; Lacy 1980; Lincoln 1986). A second we ground in a post-structuralist framework which takes as its basis an ethnological understanding of substitution logics. Both are discussed as food for thought towards thinking about the vagaries of sacrificial traditions in prehistory. We suggest that one, or both together, can provide useful points for comparison and contrast when seeking to further contextualise this often overlooked, interpretively nebulous, archaeological find group.

Our exploration is intended to highlight a find category which has hitherto seen little explicit focus (though see Pantmann 2020), though it has attracted comment in several studies (*e.g.*, Carlie 1998; Lund 2002; Hansen 2006; Monikander 2010, 35; Johannesen 2016; Løvschal *et al.* 2019; Pantmann 2020). It should be noted that we do not here set out to offer a comprehensive overview of sites which contain white stones, nor do we offer a universal model of interpreting those sites or the stones themselves. Instead, we have chosen to look at a selection of wetland sites, traditionally understood as sacrificial, which contain anthropogenic white stones. We add a caveat here, that by terming these settings as sacrificial, we do not intend to say that this is their *only* attribute of note, nor even the *primary* one. Instead, we understand that these sites may have fulfilled any number of concurrent functions, with sacrificial offerings and rituals being but one.

Our first interpretative level places our material in a similar context to Dumézil's thesis (1973; see discussion in Ward 1970) which posits three functions in relation to Proto-Indo-European cosmology and ideology: 1) sovereignty (sacral), 2) martial (warfare), 3) productivity/ fertility (domestic/economic), where each of these were reflected in diverse but referential sacrificial offerings. Crucially, we recognise that rigid frameworks such as this cannot be used as universal explainers of complex actions and beliefs. However, drawing inspiration from it, we suggest a differentiation in ascribed symbolism to different forms of votive offerings, as below. As will become evident below, we draw some inspiration from Norse pagan religion, though with the crucial stipulation here that we do not extend mythological motifs and symbolism thus far back in time. Rather, we suggest that we may be able to deduce echoes of earlier practices in later motifs, here illustrating the mutable yet persistent nature of ritual over time.

Conversely, viewed from an ethnological perspective, the presence of white stones may be seen to reflect a substitution logic at play in the use of stones as sacred paraphernalia – a logic in which the stones themselves stood in as sacrificial surrogates for other forms of offerings, including (potentially) human or animal lives. We approach this possibility with two ethnographic examples from diverse societies, namely the Chukchi of Far East Siberia and the Nuer of East Africa, both mobile herding societies with well-documented sacrificial substitution logics.

We offer that the white stones in Iron Age sacrificial settings can be considered in a different and possibly more significant light than may at first be apparent. In the following text, we will first introduce the material, followed by a discussion on the nature of wetlands and sampling bias before clarifying our stance on offerings and sacrifices. We thereafter place the white stones into our stipulated frameworks to discuss the untapped potential of this material for thinking about ritual sacrificial behaviours in the past.

White stones in wetland contexts

Across Northern Europe, many wetland sites have been found to contain objects, animal and human remains. Sampling biases aside, it is striking that many wetland sites contain corresponding or comparable types of finds, allowing for cross-regional and indeed temporal comparisons. Within this context of votive wetland sites, a considerable number of these also contain white stones. These are not attributable to natural occurrences.

One such site is Sweden's Käringsjön, where stones were found amongst wooden tools and clay vessels in a wetland used in the 3rd and 4th century AD (Carlie 1998).

Skedemosse, also in Sweden, was in use as a sacrificial site from the 2nd through to the 5th centuries AD. While famed for its massive amounts of weapons, animal and human remains, it also contained numerous stones of local white limestone. Notably, at Skedemosse, these stones were found particularly in areas with human and animal bones (Monikander 2010, 88).

Forlev Nymølle in Denmark, a site known primarily for pottery vessels, wooden effigies and agrarian tools dating to around 200 BC, shows high concentrations of white stones, in both quartzite and white-cortex flint (Lund 2002). Ejsbøl, also in Denmark, shows a large number of stones in between large amounts of weapons, from around 300 AD (Monikander 2010). Similarly, the famous Hjortspring ship was found with large numbers of white stones (Monikander 2010), and the boat deposited at Kvaldsund in Norway from AD 780–880 was also found with several stones, though the colour is not known (Shetelig & Johanesen 1929). At Rislev, large amounts of animal bone were found along with human skeletal remains and other objects – and large quantities of white stones (Ferdinand & Ferdinand 1961). At both Ejsbøl and Hjortspring, white or whitish stones were in addition to, and therefore contextually different from, stone tools such as whetstones and strike-a-lights also purposefully deposited as components of the gear belonging to the ship's retinue. At these sites, white stones were found below, in and on top of the other ritually deposited materials, placing them before, during and after deposition of these.

Furthermore, several of the lesser-known wetland contexts with human remains in Norway contained white stones as well: at Starene, Rytjernet, Hvitberg-tjernet and Råtjernet, all dated to between the 4th century BC and the 1st century AD (Bukkemoen & Skare 2018). These sites have recently been contextualised into a wider European ritual tradition of offerings and sacrifices (Moen & Walsh 2021).

Pantmann (2020, 183) observes that at Salpetermosen Syd, south of Hillerød in northern Zealand, Denmark, concentrations of 'whitish stones' often occur in sacrificial contexts with animal bones and often with another (usually single) stone of an alternate hue, *e.g.*, red, blue or green (Plate 35, top). At Skødstrup, just north of Aarhus, white stones were found in wetland deposits from between 200 BC to AD 150. Here, the stones were scattered conspicuously among the skeletal remains of a young woman, presumed to have been in her 20s, as well as among the remains of eight dogs, along with other domesticated animal remains and a ceramic vessel. In this case, these offerings were placed in exhausted peat-cutting pits in close proximity to a nearby village. The woman's cranium was missing, having been removed at some point prior to her full deposition into the bog. Her body had been pinned down into one of the pits by two wooden stakes.

Notably, the distributions of white stones at some sites, such as, *e.g.*, Forlev Nymølle and Salpetermosen (Plates 35 and 36), there are both broader scatters which could indeed reflect acts of throwing the stones into the water. At other sites (and locations within sites) the stones appear in distinct concentrations and heaps in deliberately placed positions (Plate 35, bottom), as in exhausted peat pits with collections of other objects at Skødstrup. Thus, we have varied distributive systems rather than a singularly proscribed 'use' *per se* of white(ish) stones in these broadly ritualised contexts.

It is clear from the above that white(ish) stones appear in varied contexts and settings. It is to be hoped that the stones occasion more research focus in the future, thus enabling a more comprehensive view of their contexts, functions and the symbolism at play in their presence. As it stands, they appear in contexts of highly varied natures: with human remains in inland Norway, with mixed animal and human deposits in Sweden, Denmark and Norway, with weapon deposits in Denmark and Sweden and with deposits of vessels and agrarian tools, as well as with boats, across southern Scandinavia. In each instance, their presence is anthropogenic and deliberate. Thus, we find them deposited with skeletal remains, ceramics and other objects, and interpret them into the ritual practice involving the deposition of varied offerings.

Wetlands and preservation: a biased view?

At this stage however, it is necessary to take a step back and consider the discussion of white stones in wetlands in a broader sense. By this, we mean to lift the gaze away from wetlands, and consider if the throwing or deposition of stones was a practice peculiar to rituals connected to water (Plate 36), or if the weight of evidence is skewed in favour of wetland deposits due to the nature of those environments.

White stones are in fact known to occur at ritually charged dryland sites as well, such as for instance in burials. Burials, though perhaps not offerings *per se*, are often made up of a considerable amount of earthly riches, *offered* in a sense, in the grave. In an examination of burial rites in a large Iron Age mound on the west coast of Norway, Barbo Dahl recently noticed the presence of white quartz stones prevalent in the mound (Dahl 2016), in particular, the appearance of crushed quartz stones thrown in a layer between two of the mound's main construction layers (Dahl 2016). Furthermore, the well-known Iron Age ritual location at Lunda in Sweden had remnants of crushed stone placed in layers upon the small hill which acted as a ritual foci throughout several centuries from the 2nd century BC until the end of the Iron Age (Andrén 2005).This hints at the presence of rituals wherein throwing or placing stones could configure in many ways.

Another consideration must also be raised here, namely the tendency to equate Northern European wetlands with rituals as a matter of course. That there has been a tendency to deposit offerings in wetlands throughout European

prehistory is established beyond doubt (see *e.g.,* Coles *et al.* 1999), but we also need to recall the peculiar nature of wetland environments over dryland sites (for an insightful discussion on perceptions of wetlands see Giles 2020). Soil is ploughed, stones are moved, sediments are shifted to make way for farming, houses, buildings, roads. Things on land also tend to deteriorate faster than those in water. Water, and especially bogs, preserve in ways that air and soil do not. The result here may be a significant bias, in that wetland sites yield more frequent and more complete vistas of past ritual behaviour, which dryland sites tend to leave only in fragments, if at all.

In further contrast, dryland sites tend not the be seen as inherently sacred in the same ways as wetlands often are. One may ask if this is to do with the fluctuating and unstable conditions of wetlands, their alien nature from the ground on which daily lives are lived. It is worth considering whether or not those in the past who lived in close proximity with wetlands considered them inherently 'sacred' as such, or if they were but another part of daily life, itself inseparable from sublime experiences (*cf.,* Bradley 2005). The answer may be that they can fulfil both functions – much like solid ground can and does. Equating wetlands with ritual behaviour thereby may obscure the real relationship between those who used them – for multiple purposes – and the landscapes themselves. Perhaps the dichotomy between drylands and wetlands is imposed as much by modern eyes as by the material that they yield.

Offerings and sacrifices: the implications of terminology

As we have framed our discussion of white stones as part of ritual behaviour set into sacrificial contexts, a brief discussion of the terminology of sacrifice is necessary before proceeding. Recently, scholars such as Esther Oras (Oras 2013) have insightfully discussed the interpretive significance of the difference between *offerings* and *sacrifices*, particularly as viewed from the archaeological record (see also Firth 1963; Baal 1976; McClymond 2008; Schwartz 2017). Along the same lines, we argue that many of the distinctions which cause so much controversy in discussions of sacrifice (Oras 2013; Walsh *et al.* 2020) are better understood more as classificatory disagreements which bear little relation to the enactment and outcome of ritual acts. In this sense, the terminology of sacrifice is rather complicated by the persistent insistence of several scholars that in order for something to be considered a sacrifice, there must be an overt link with the divine (Reynolds 2009; Edholm 2016). Thus, terms like 'offerings' or 'ritual killings' are often substituted in cases that involve human bodies. And yet, it can be argued that the finer points of for whom such sacrifices were made meant little in the enactment and experience of such acts, both for victims, witnesses and perpetrators.

Furthermore, we need to recognise that any such act may rest on more than one single simple motivation, and though communion with the divine or expiation of the supernatural may have been an important factor in some cases, there may have been other mechanisms of faith or collective action at play simultaneously.

Ultimately, there appears no general consensus on what distinguishes a sacrifice from an offering that can be lifted from academic discourse and unto material expressions without caveats or disagreements. For example, some scholars highlight a destructive element in sacrifices that are not there in offerings (*e.g.*, Hubert & Mauss 1964; Girard 2011; Insoll 2011). Yet, this divide seems somewhat arbitrary and hard to ascertain archaeologically (as discussed in Oras 2013). Indeed, even though something is offered instead of sacrificed, it is ultimately removed from circulation and given up to a higher power: the outcome is arguably much the same, especially when depositing said offering in a wetland environment. To wit, in prehistoric contexts, distinguishing between 'sacrifices' and 'offerings' becomes an interpretive exercise more in the eye of the beholder than in the materials with which we are dealing.

Conversely, the implied meaning of the word *sacrifice* is in itself worthy of some elucidation. Whilst conventional wisdom would have that to sacrifice means to make sacred (Hubert & Mauss 1964), we query the validity of assuming a universal applicability of a strictly etymological application of a specific term, which is situated within western knowledge production, across a wide variety of societies and cultures. As Durkheim recognised early on, that which is held 'sacred' by any given society is entirely culturally relative, subject to change and takes inherently varied forms. Yet, still, embedded in the literal reading of the term lies a western-centric value judgement of what it ought to mean to commune with, or offer oblation to, a supernatural power. Any ritual act involving perceived implications of loss or of the necessity to give something up as proof of devotion or expression of thanks could potentially find explanation through the logic of sacrifice. It depends entirely on the players involved and their understandings and intentions of the undertaking. We hold that when applying such terms to prehistoric archaeological contexts, a wider content of potential meanings ought to be embraced. As a result, we consider the divide between offerings and sacrifices unnecessary in the context of this article, but choose to retain the use of sacrifice as a preferred term, in order to situate our contribution within the wider tradition of knowledge production on the topic. We keep the term in its broad sense of meaning something offered for specific, religiously forefronted motivations (*i.e.*, sacralised), though with explicit recognition that this may only be part of more complex and composite aims and motivations made up of complimentary layers of meaning.

In the context of the stones discussed here, though their function is not immediately apparent, and their symbolism appears obscure, the repeated presence of small(ish) and white(ish) stones in recognised votive contexts means we are justified in considering them as some aspect of distinctly ritual behaviours. In this sense, we place the stones and their find contexts into a ritual understanding (Bell 1997), and recognise that through them being classed as ritual, they also become tied to prehistoric cosmological and 'religious' beliefs and ideas which we may only guess at (*cf.*, Hansen 2006). But this relationship is not a logical tautology. We accept that the act of depositing objects and the bodies of sentient beings into wetlands lends itself to being read as sacrificial regardless of the intents of those undertaking the activities at the time. Here we appreciate that there exist(ed) diverse ways of communing through ritual acts outside of any overtly 'religious' connotation (*cf.*, Saler 1993; Bell 1997).

Introducing the first interpretative framework: ritual re-enactment and collective memorialisation

Carlie (1998, 19) suggests, for the Käringsjön sacrificial bog at in Härjedalen, mid-Sweden, that the many white stones present there could have been cast as offerings – effectively representing what she refers to as 'votive throws' aimed specifically at fertility: sacrificial offerings made by a peaceful agrarian community (see also Johannesen 2016, 171). In some cases, the stones' frequency and distribution do suggest the casting of stones, perhaps at standing targets or at floating targets such as the bundles of flax found at Käringsjön and Forlev Nymølle (*cf.*, Carlie 1998; Lund 2002). While at Fuglsøgard Mose in east Jutland flax bundles were also found, in one case inside a ceramic vessel, and in another as a star-shaped grouping of flax bundles apparently placed at the base of a pre-existing peat-cutting pit, similar to the sacrificial finds observed at Skødstrup (above), and beneath other material offerings such as ceramic sherds, animal bones, wood and stones (Johannesen 2016). Notably, white stones and pebbles of flint at the site were commonly placed into vessels, which Johannesen (2016, 44–45) points out indicates a particular custom at this specific site, perhaps indicative of the stones serving an additional function as weights. Importantly, at Fuglsøgard Mose, deposits were made in dry peat-cutting pits, not in open water as is presumed the case for most wetland depositions: indeed, stones are also related to peat cuts in North Zealand, where deposits were generally related to such cuts. There, the distributions of stones and other objects indicate that they were set down deliberately in concentrations and heaps, not thrown (*cf.*, Hansen 2006, 140). It could be hypothesised that stones thrown as offerings were made as individual acts interacting with other offerings, perhaps in some cases collective (for instance human or animal sacrifices), or they could be read as the expression of individual contributions into larger settings of entangled offerings: both stones, sticks, animals and humans, and other objects.

If we suppose that offerings comprised of ceramics and animal remains represent something akin to Dumézil's 'domestic' category, and likewise that weapons and war-booty made as sacrificial offerings (as at Ejsbøl, Hjortspring and Nydam, or from various locations at Illerup Ådal [Ilkjær 2000]; see overview in Løvschal & Holst 2018) represent a 'martial' category, we propose that the white stones may represent links with the divine. To explore this, we must remove ourselves from a naturalistic perspective (à la Descola 2006; 2013) which sees the inanimate as non-agential and inherently un-sacred. Rather, we must acknowledge that the ordinary and everyday can be much imbued with unseen forces and agency: accepted interpretations of past belief systems highlight how even the mundane was a composite world of 'the sacred' with animistic themes permeating belief systems (cf., Andrén 2005, 108; Bradley 2005; Hansen 2006; Price 2002). This tendency to imbue everyday objects (e.g., a 'lucky coin') or something abstract like a colour with ideas of symbolic value or ritual charge remains persistent. The colour white, for instance, a relevant example for this discussion, is ubiquitously associated with the divine, with purity and with the sacred in myriad cultures across time and place, certainly including among the early Indo-European traditions and in the later Celtic, Germanic and Scandinavian religions of the North. If we take this notion of white as a sacred colour (or shade), we may propose that the conspicuous use of particularly white stones in sacred contexts illustrates more than simply rocks as votive offerings or as the functional architecture of ritual features. Notably, the white stones discussed here do not appear to have been selected based on material, they are of quartzite, limestone, flint and sometimes other material, and generally do not appear to fit a strict morphology besides being commonly fist-sized. It is their colour which seems to have been of primary import in their selection. Thus, they share three basic characteristics: 1) being of a movable and relatively 'toss-able' size; 2) having been placed deliberately in sacrificial contexts during the Scandinavian Iron Age; and 3) being white(ish). Whatever their nature, they seem to have possessed symbolic value for sacrificial purposes.

Substitute and fertility sacrifices in wetlands

Glob (1971, 156) illuminates the iconography of a 'fertility goddess' from the Nordic Bronze Age, exemplified by a bog find of a female figurine from that period: the so-called Veksø goddess, dated to the Late Bronze Age c. 500 BCE. The areas immediately surrounding Veksø are rife with sacrificial significance. For instance, the Neolithic

Sigersdal women (one with a cord still around her neck) were found in a bog a few kilometres away, and the famous Veksø horned helmets were also recovered from a bog at a similar distance. In short, the locality was a sacrificial hot spot spanning the Danish Neolithic through the Late Bronze Age/Early Iron Age.

Seen through the lens in which a substitute victim or offering is made in symbolic place of another, usually more valuable and otherwise proscribed offering, this figurine could be interpreted as an elaborate material surrogate used as a stand-in for a formal human victim (cf., Stanley 2012). The 'double neck ring' evident around the neck of the Veksø figure could very easily be interpreted as showing a rope around her neck (see Figure 9.1) rather than a decorative neck ring. Hence, the Veksø 'goddess' may still represent a fertility figure, but instead of representing a divinity per se, it may show us a sacrificial victim in substitution. As a point of argument, the craftship of the Veksø 'goddess' figurine could suggest a rushed crafting process, perhaps a result of time constraints related to the necessity of a timely sacrificial offering (other small figurines, such as the so-called 'Værebro Woman' figurine from the same area, exhibit similar pose and quality).

The many bog bodies recovered from Northern European wetlands have long been queried as representing some symbolic reference to both fertility (Glob 1971) and sovereignty (Kelly 2006) sacrifices, so too with animal remains, ceramic vessels and war-booty, but what of ritual bog depositions of otherwise anomalous things such as unmodified stones? Nested within archaeological knowledge production lies the fundamental question of what constitutes archaeological remains, and within this what makes an object (as discussed in Ingold 2007; Pantmann 2020). As an example, let us consider ceramic vessels and domesticated animals as representative of the economic/domestic function (i.e., the trappings of sustenance and subsistence, and/or reflections of agrarian and herding activities). If so, then findings such as at Bukkerup and Gummerup, both on the island of Funen in central Denmark, where the complete and sometimes articulated limbs, commonly of cattle found in situ with ceramic vessels, should safely be considered sacrificial offerings. In many cases, the bones were collected together and sometimes even tightly bound by rope, and some evince cut marks indicating that meat was removed prior to deposition (in Concentration 30 at Bukkerup and in Forlev Nymølle Concentration III some bones appear to have been split for marrow extraction, which is otherwise uncommon), suggesting they may have been sacrifices and food offerings.

We may presume from these indications that the bone depositions were the aftermath or part of a feasting ritual in which consumption of the animals in question was a key part, perhaps as part of a form of fertility and/or thanksgiving sacrifice: i.e., the domestic/economic sphere. However, we must be careful to recognise that one purpose

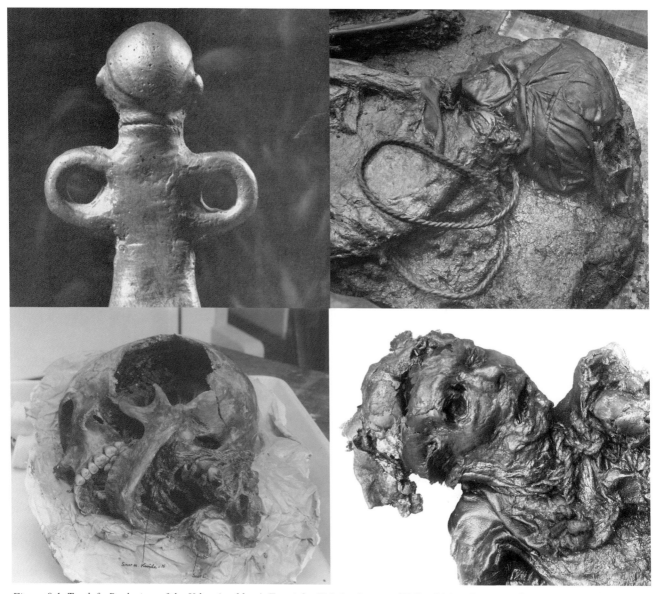

Figure 9.1. Top left: Back view of the Veksø 'goddess'; Top right: Side-back view of Tollund Man; Bottom right: Front view of Borremose Man; Bottom left: One of the young women from Sigersdal. Each individual can be seen with a cord, rope or implement around the neck (photos from the Archives of the National Museum of Denmark. Used by permission).

or function of a sacrifice need not preclude others, as Hubert and Mauss (1964, 97) observe, a singular sacrificial act may provide for '… thanksgiving, a vow, and a propitiation, sacrifice can fulfil a great variety of concurrent functions'. Likewise, the underlying motivations can be multi-layered and opaque.

Not only can the logics of sacrifice therefore be queried, but the enactment of them can also manifest in fundamentally different ways. In this sense, we suggest a platform based on the understanding that seeing sacrifice as a single, repeated phenomenon is too simplistic, and that diversity in expression, motivation, manifestation and indeed expected results must be the starting point for new debates.

Throwing stones at gods?

Lund (2002; *cf.*, Feddersen 1881) suggests that wooden sticks and carved effigies at Forlev Nymølle appear to have possibly been held in a standing position by heaps of stones. As stones outside of and surrounding these heap concentrations appear to dissipate out from them, the possibility that stones may have been thrown targeting the standing wooden objects is at least feasible (Plate 38). Though much later chronologically, there is a potential echo of throwing as a religiously connected motif found in the Old Norse myths: in the story of the death of Baldr (explicitly associated with the colour white), the gods all gathered to play a game of throwing and shooting at the invulnerable god (see syntheses of Norse religion in *e.g.*, Davidson 1964; Turville-Petre 1964; Price 2002; Andrén *et al.* 2006). In Irish mythology, another example springs to mind: Lugh, like Baldr, was strongly associated with the colour white, the sun, invulnerability, purity and kingship, and kills his own grandfather with a magical sling stone (Gwynn 1924, 279; Macalister 1941, 341). Though we cannot and do not wish to connect this myth, written down so much later, and pertaining to a very different time and presumably system of beliefs, directly to the white stones, it is nevertheless possible to suggest an echo of thematic rituals of throwing or slinging, perhaps connected with devotional rituals, or with notions of sovereignty, authority or invulnerability or the like – all explicitly associated with the colour white (Genevra 2020), which may have survived in the collective memory.

Another interpretive angle worth thinking about in this vein is that in Norse cosmology, the mountains of the earth were believed to have been fashioned from the bones of the frost giant Ymir, himself the victim of targeted cosmogonic violence at the hands of Oðinn and his brothers, Vili and Vé. Conceptually, the selections of white (bone-like) stones, whose concentrations may have been visible from the shore's edge of a sacred wetland, hazily visible in the shallow but murky water act as a solemn reminder of offerings necessary, negotiated and made. Such stones, mingled with the bones and debris of previous sacrifices, might even have reflected those of prototypical, primordial beings such as Ymir, or omnipresent animistic powers or the memories and remains of mythological ancestors. Hypothetically, white stones could also have symbolically served as surrogates for or symbols of human bones, thus presenting a particularly potent form of substitute by imitation.

While these remain but musing interpretations, one may imagine that the white stones (and wooden figures) found in some Scandinavian wetlands could reflect some ritualised re-enactment of these or similar narratives, where casting stones formed a liturgical part of ritual behaviour. In other cases, they may represent clever substitutes for bones, representing sacrifices without requiring bloodshed. Collective memory is strong, and ritual features as a binding and crucial component of this in many instances. Though we cannot here see direct lines between the Norse myths as we know them today, we may perhaps glimpse reflections of a common ritual thread, enacted, remembered and re-enacted, and thus constantly reinvented across time.

Stones but not stones: substitution in sacrificial logics and the second interpretative framework

Another potentially fruitful avenue is to consider that the stones were not intended as votive offerings, as fertility-inducing 'tosses' at effigies or as reflecting the material remains of the transempirical, but rather that they may

have represented symbolic stand-ins for other things. For example, wooden anthropomorphic effigies found in wetlands from across Northern Europe and Eurasia have been suggested as possibly representing supernatural entities (see, *e.g.*, the enigmatic early Holocene 'Shigir Idol' from Chelyabinsk Oblast in Russia; see discussions in Coles 1990, 332; Lund 2002, 167–177) to whom sacrifices may have been made. They themselves may also have served as sacrificial substitutes for living victims (see, *e.g.*, the Early Iron Age 'Gortnacrannagh Idol'[1] recently recovered from a bog site in Roscommon Co., Ireland). Specifically, there is a possible analogue to such objects in relation to substitution in sacrificial contexts (Stanley 2012). But not only effigies may have been sufficient stand-ins for human victims. Willerslev (2009, 699) has pointed out that among the Chukchi of Far East Siberia, a stone may be symbolically 'sacrificed' in place of a reindeer, an animal so sacred to the society that its life is conceptually considered on the same value level as that of a human. He points out, within the hierarchy of substitutes in the Chukchi sacrificial system, that a stone is the lowest form of surrogate that might replace some other form of offering in a well-understood graduating system of lesser-valued lives or objects (Plate 39), while all substitutes figuratively stand in for the highest form of offering: that of human life. This substitution logic echoes Evans-Pritchard's (1954, 26) classical example of hierarchical sacrificial substitutions among the Nuer, in which a goat, sheep or even a wild cucumber may be offered in place of an ox or cow, which itself is conceived of as 'shielding' the life of its master. In each case the offering is ultimately a symbolic surrogate for a human life. Thus, within the chain of substitutes in diverse sacrificial logics, it is not unfeasible that special stones or other otherwise mundane objects might symbolically have been offered in place of offering a human (or other animal) life. We may contextualise this with the above suggestion of stones as potentially metaphorical bones, lending strength to such ideas.

In some cases, 'sacrificed' objects were physically altered, as with ritually 'killed' and deposited weapons (as at Alken Enge and Ejsbøl Mose, *etc.*). The Gortnacrannagh Idol mentioned above is thought to have 'originally stood close to the centre of [ritual depositional] activity before being taken down, broken and buried' (Eve J. Campbell, pers. comm., 18 August 2021). In other cases, unaltered offerings are more difficult to interpret in light of their nature as sacrificed offerings. For example, as has often been brought up in regards to how to interpret votive offerings vs. hoards (Johansen 1986) or either types of assemblages from 'proper' sacrifices which conceptually necessitate some form of destruction or loss (Oras 2013). While feasible from the ethnological parallels, we observe that given the frequency and diverse contexts and configurations in which the white stones appear in the Northern European

Iron Age sites, the possibility that white stones may have been cast or placed as symbolic stand-ins for living victims seems ultimately unverifiable.

As Firth (1963, 12–13) noted

> An offering is a species of gift. This means: (a) that the thing given is personal to the giver, his own property, or something over which he has rights of alienation; (b) that the thing transferred must have some value for the person who hands it over; and, (c) that it is transferred with some degree of voluntary initiative – it is not given by compulsion nor does it occur as a technical part of a series of actions dictated by some generally planned end … Sacrifice is a species of offering or oblation, but implies a relation between what is offered and the *availability of resources* … The notion that a sacrifice is involved in the diversion of some valued object from one end to another which is regarded as more pressing, raises the question of alternative response or equivalents to be expected according to the end served.

In this regard, then, we must consider also that when objects entered into votive settings it is likely that the actors' conception of them was changed in this process (*cf.*, Ingold 2007). Just as today when one might make a wish and cast a coin into a fountain, symbolically the coin ceases to be a pecuniary unit of value (its value is transformed). The coin becomes a proxy for the wisher and a ritual 'payment' for the hypothetical receipt of the wish desired – the offering is thus not made as expiation or as oblation, but rather a sacrifice of request (sensu Hubert & Mauss 1964, 14). In this context, *if* stones were cast in ritual contexts as we have imagined, they were not meant as gifts, but rather as much more complex sacraments. This notion is important in light of the relentlessly pessimistic cosmological paradigm of Norse religion (so vividly described by Price 2002, 49–53). Such individual acts of recitation and reflection on Baldr's 'sacrificial' death – which was in the Norse understanding indeed a portent of the end of all things – then we may very reasonably view the casting of stones not just as a ritual act (which it certainly was), but one with the potential to have been perceived as acknowledging the inevitability of time and endings, of cosmogony and cataclysm. Recent evidence does suggest that some pre-Christian Norse communities did ritually engage with and attempt to navigate the potentialities of these apocalyptic events (Smith *et al.* 2021). From this perspective, the casting of stones may have been quite valuable indeed. In this context it also need not signify a particular aspect of a tripartite structure as theorised by Dumézil, but rather the importance of the stones or the act of casting them was in the contemplation of or dedication to a deity or as recognition of some other sacred entity.

Conclusion

It is telling that archaeologists readily use the terminology of sacrifice when referring to depositions of weapons and effigies while at the same time shying away from the term

in relation to less empathic or agential objects, considering rather subjectively that some objects over others ought to be differentiated outside of a sacrificial light, as *e.g.*, 'votive offerings', as if those *mere* objects could not have possibly equated in status to the sacred. Swords and pots can be 'killed' in sacrificial rituals. But what about mere stones? Indeed, the ethnographic evidence suggests that everything from mere cucumbers to pebbles can stand in as substitutes of sacrificial lives within vastly different cultural contexts. In this regard to interpreting prehistoric religion (or ritual praxis), Johansen (1986, 67) iterates that 'We must no longer regard a sword as a weapon of war, an axe as a tool for cutting trees, or clothes as simply means of protecting the body from the elements', since by ritual use or connotation they have ceased to comprise their previous function and taken on symbolic meaning and value; so too we posit with the ubiquitous white stones and stone formations from Iron Age wetland contexts.

If we reconsider the 'making sacred' defining aspect of sacrifice, it becomes clear that we may see sacrifices in offerings well beyond lives and their ritual destruction. This is because we must understand 'the sacred' in its relative context: 'the sacred' need not actually be a religious or cosmological phenomenon but may also be a paradigmatic one. In societies with different understandings of value (*e.g.*, of things, of people, of animals, of concepts and ideas, what have you) the definition of sacred is altered. The sacred may not be religious, ideological or material, it becomes whatever is of primal existential value – whatever is of such importance that one would go to any length in order to associate, engage or commune with it. Thus, perhaps we should not be too concerned with the definition of sacrifice or whether any given evidence is indicative thereof, but instead attempt to understand how different notions of the sacred may have been manifest in what often to us seem mundane.

This exploration of white stones in sacrificial wetland contexts has necessarily been brief and superficial. Yet we hope that it may contribute to a growing debate and awareness of what we consider a largely overlooked but potentially significant manifestation of ritual behaviour(s), present both in wetland and in other known ritually charged contexts. A considerable degree of work lies ahead before we can hope to fully understand what the white stones mean, but we believe there are numerous and rewarding lines of enquiry into the diversity of sacrificial and votive ritual behaviours if we allow ourselves the liberty of casting our ideas about like stones.

Acknowledgements

The authors would like to thank an anonymous peer reviewer for their constructive critiques and comments. We are also grateful to Eve J. Campbell for information and insights into her team's finds surrounding the Gortnacrannagh Idol and related finds. This research was funded by generous support from the Norwegian Research Council for the 'Human Sacrifice and Value' project (PI Rane Willerslev; FRIPRO HUMSAM 275947).

Note

1   https://www.smithsonianmag.com/smart-news/1600-year-old-wooden-idol-found-ireland-180978453/ (accessed 18 August 2021). While this site and finds are still under investigation at the time of this writing, at least a small quantity of unworked anthropogenic white quartz pebbles were found in the vicinity of the idol, animal bones and other finds. White quartz, known in Irish as glocha geala or 'shining/bright stones', has a long history of importance in Irish folklore and ritual, being particularly associated with the Irish sí, a term representative of both supernatural entities and sites (Thompson 2005) (Eve J. Campbell, pers. comm., 18 August 2021). White and rose quartz has also been observed in Early Iron Age burial contexts in Germany, and have been interpreted by Arnold (2012) as 'soul stones', further reflecting their possible ritual significance.

References

Andrén, A. 2005. Behind 'Heathendom': Archaeological studies of Old Norse religion. *Scottish Archaeological Journal* 27: 105–138.

Andrén, A., Jennbert, K. & Raudvere, C. 2006. *Old Norse Religion in Long-Term Perspectives: Origins, Changes and Interactions. An International Conference in Lund, Sweden, June 3–7, 2004.* Lund: Nordic Academic Press.

Arnold, B. 2012. 'Soul stones': Unmodified quartz and other lithic material in Early Iron Age burials. In *Archaeological, Cultural and Linguistic Heritage Festschrift for Erzsébet Jerem in Honour of her 70th Birthday*, edited by P. Anreiter, E. Bánffy, L. Bartosiewicz, W. Meid and C. Metzner-Nebelsick, 47–56. Budapest: Archaeolingua Alapítvány.

Baal, J. v. 1976. Offering, sacrifice, gift. *Numen* 23: 16–178.

Bell, C. 1997. *Ritual: Perspectives and Dimensions.* Oxford/New York: Oxford University Press.

Berger, A. 1986. Cultural hermeneutics: The concept of imagination in the phenomenological approaches of Henry Corbin and Mircea Eliade. *The Journal of Religion* 66(2): 141–156.

Borlase, W.C. 1897. *The Dolmens of Ireland, Vol. III.* London: Chapman & Hall.

Bradley, R. 2000. *An Archaeology of Natural Places.* London/New York: Routledge.

Bradley, R. 2005. *Ritual and Domestic Life in Prehistoric Europe.* New York: Routledge.

Bukkemoen, G.B. & Skare, K. 2018. Humans, Animals and Water The Deposition of Human and Animal Remains in Norwegian Wetlands. *Journal of Wetland Archaeology* 18(1): 35–55.

Carlie, A. 1998. Käringsjön. A Fertility Sacrificial Site from the Late Roman Iron Age in South-west Sweden. *Current Swedish Archaeology* 6: 17–37.

Carlie, A. 2004. *Forntida bygnadskult. Tradition och regionalitet I södra Skandinavien.* Stockholm: Riksantikvarieämbetet Arkeologiska Undersökningar Skrifter nr. 57.

Coles, B. 1990. Anthropomorphic wooden figures from Britain and Ireland. *Proceedings of the Prehistoric Society* 56: 315–333. doi:10.1017/S0079497X0000517X.

Dahl, B. 2016. Haugen som Gravfelt. *AMS Varia* 58: 77–95.

Davidson, H.E. 1964. *Gods and Myths of Northern Europe.* Baltimore: Penguin Books.

Descola, P. 2006. Beyond Nature and Culture. *Proceedings of the British Academy* 139: 137–155.

Descola, P. 2013. *Beyond Nature and Culture.* Trans. by J. Lloyd. Chicago: The University of Chicago Press.

Dumézil, G. *From Myth to Fiction: The Saga of Hadingus.* Trans. by Derek Coltman. Chicago: The University of Chicago Press.

Edholm, K. af. 2016. Människooffer i fornnordisk religion. En diskusjon utifran arkeolgoskt material och källtexter. *Chaos* 65: 124–148.

Evans-Pritchard, E.E. 1954. The meaning of sacrifice among the Nuer. *The Journal of the Royal Anthropological Institute of Great Britain and Ireland* 84(1/2): 21–33.

Fahlander, F. 2001. *Archaeology as Science Fiction: A Microarchaeology of the Unknown.* Gotarc Serie C No. 43. Göteborg: University of Gothenburg.

Feddersen, A. 1881. To Mosefund. *Aarbøger for Nordisk Oldkyndighed og Historie 1881.* Kjøbenhavn: Det Kongelige Nordiske Oldskrift-Selskab.

Ferdinand, J. & Ferdinand, K. 1961. Jernalderofferfund i Valmose ved Rislev. *Kuml* 1961: 47–90.

Firth, R. 1963. Offering and sacrifice: Problems of organization. *The Journal of the Royal Anthropological Institute of Great Britain and Ireland* 84: 21–33.

Genevra, R. 2020. Gods who shine through the millennia: Old Norse Baldr, Celtic Belinos, Old Irish Balar, and PIE *bʰelH-* 'be white, shine'. In *Proceedings of the International Conference of the Society for Indo-European Studies and IWoBA XII, Ljubljana 4–7 June 2019, Celebrating One Hundred Years of Indo-European Comparative Linguistics at the University of Ljubljana, Baar*, edited by L. Repanšek, H. Bichlmeier and V. Sadovski, 189–208. Hambrug: Baar-Verlag Andrea Brendler.

Giles, M. 2020. *Bog Bodies: Face to Face with the Past.* Manchester: Manchester University Press.

Girard, R. 2011. *Sacrifice.* East Lansing: Michigan State University Press.

Glob, P.V. 1971. *The Bog People: Iron-Age man preserved.* New York: Ballantine Books.

Gwynn, E. 1924. *The Metrical Dindshenchas, Part IV.* London: Williams & Norgate.

Hansen, J. 2006. Offertradition og religion i ældre jernalder i Sydskandinavien – med særlig henblik på bebyggelsesofringer. *KUML* 2006: 117–175.

Hubert, H. & Mauss, M. 1964. *Sacrifice: Its Nature and Function.* Chicago: University of Chicago Press.

Ilkjær, J. 2000. *Illerup Ådal – et arkæologisk tryllespejl.* Aarhus: Moesgaard Museum Press.

Ingold, T. 2007. Materials against materiality. *Archaeological Dialogues* 14(1): 1–16.

Insoll, T. 2011. Sacrifice. In *The Oxford Handbook of the Archaeology of Ritual and Religion*, edited by T. Insoll, 151–165. Oxford: Oxford University Press.

Johannesen, K. 2016. *Rituals of Common Things: The ritual and religion of the mixed wetland deposits in the Early Iron Age of Southern Scandinavia.* Aarhus: Museum Østjylland & Aarhus University.

Johansen, Ø. 1986. Religion and archaeology: Revelation or empirical research? In *Words and Objects*, edited by G. Steinsland, 67–77. Oslo: Norwegian University Press.

Kelly, E.P. 2006. Secrets of the Bog Bodies: The enigma of the Iron Age Explained. *Archaeology Ireland* 20(1): 26–30.

Lacy, A.F. 1980. Some Additional Celtic and Germanic Traces of the Tri-Functional Sacrifice. *The Journal of American Folklore* 93(369): 337–341.

Lincoln, B. 1986. *Myth, Cosmos, and Society: Indo-European Themes of Creation and Destruction*. Cambridge, MA: Harvard University Press.

Løvschal, M. & Holst, M.K. 2018. Governing martial traditions: Post-conflict ritual sites in Iron Age Northern Europe (200 BC–AD 200). *Journal of Anthropological Archaeology* 50: 27–39.

Løvschal, M., Birch Iversen, R. & Holst, M.K. (eds) 2019. *De dræbte lrogere o aslken Enge*. Højbjerg: Jyst Arkæologisk Selskap.

Lund, J. 2002. Forlev Nymølle: En offerplads fra yngre førromersk jernalder. *KUML*: 143–195.

Macalister, S.R.A. 1941. *Lebor Gabála Érenn. The Book of the Taking of Ireland, Part IV*. Dublin: Educational Company of Ireland.

Mack, B. 1987. Introduction: Religion and ritual. In *Violent Origins: Walter Burkert, René Girard, and Jonathan Z. Smith on Ritual Killing and Cultural Formation*, edited by R.G. Hamerton-Kelly, 1–70. Stanford: Stanford University Press.

McClymond, K. 2008. *Beyond Sacred Violence: A Comparative Study of Sacrifice*. Baltimore: Johns Hopkins University Press.

Moen, M. & Walsh, M.J. 2021. Agents of Death: Reassessing Social Agency and Gendered Narratives of Human Sacrifice in the Viking Age. *Cambridge Journal of Archaeology* 31(4): 597–633.

Monikander, A. 2010. *Våld och vatten. Våtmarkskult vid Skedemosse under järnåldern*. Unpublished thesis. Stockholm: University of Stockholm.

Oras, E. 2013. Sacrifice or offering: What can we see in the archaeology of Northern Europe. *Folklore (Estonia)*: 125–50.

Pantmann, P. 2020. Lyse sten – en udrofrdende arkæeologisk fænomen med potentiale. *Gefjon* 5: 53–83.

Polomé, E. 1970. The Indo-European component in Germanic religion. In *Myth and Law Among the Indo-Europeans: Studies in Indo-European Comparative Mythology*, edited by J. Puhvel, 55–82. Berkeley/Los Angeles: University of California Press.

Price, N.S. 2002. *The Viking Way: Religion and War in Late Iron Age Scandinavia*. Uppsala: Department of Archaeology and Ancient History.

Puhvel, J. 1970. Aspects of equine functionality. In *Myth and Law Among the Indo-Europeans*, edited by J. Puhvel, 159–172. Los Angeles: University of California Press.

Reynolds, A. 2009. *Anglo-Saxon Deviant Burial Customs*. Oxford: Oxford University Press.

Saler, B. 1993. *Conceptualizing Religion*. New York/Oxford: Berghahn.

Schwartz, G.M. 2017. The archaeological study of sacrifice. *Annual Review of Anthropology* 46: 223–240.

Shetelig, H. & Johannesen, F. 1929. *Kvalsundfundet og andre norske myrfund av fartøier*. Bergen Museums Skrifter. Ny rekke 2 Museum, Bergen: A/S John Griegs boktrykkeri.

Smith, K.P., Ólafsson, G. & Pálsdóttir, A.H. 2021. Ritual responses to catastrophic volcanism in Viking Age Iceland: Reconsidering Surtshellir Cave through Bayesian analyses of AMS dates, tephrochronology, and texts. *Journal of Archaeological Science* 126: 105316.

Stanley, M. 2012. The 'Red Man' or war and death? *Archaeology Ireland* 26(2): 34–37.

Stjernquist, B. 1973. Das Opfermoor in Hassle Bösarp, Schweden. *Acta Archaeologica* 110(XLIV): 19–62.

Thompson, T. 2005. Clocha Geala/Clocha Uaisle: White quartz in Irish tradition. *Béaloideas, Iml* 73: 111–133.

Turville-Petre, E.O.G. 1964. *Myth and Religion of the North: The Religion of Ancient Scandinavia*. Westport: Greenwood Press, Publishers.

Walsh, M.J., Moen, M., O'Neill, S., Gullbekk, S.H. & Willerslev, R. 2020. Who's afraid of the S-word? Deviants' burials and human sacrifice. *Norwegian Archaeological Review* 53: 154–162.

Ward, D.J. 1970. The Threefold Death: An Indo-European trifunctional sacrifice? In *Myth and Law Among the Indo-Europeans*, edited by J. Puhvel, 123–142. Los Angeles: University of California Press.

Willerslev, R. 2009. The optimal sacrifice: A study of voluntary death among the Siberian Chukchi. *American Ethnologist* 36(4): 693–704.

'Better not to pray than to sacrifice too much':[1] Human sacrifice and its alternatives in Northern Europe AD 750–1050

Bo Jensen

Abstract

The ritual killing of humans and animals was a central element in Viking Age paganism. This paper presents a summary of relevant archaeological evidence, and some speculation on its meaning. The paper stresses the poor fit between written sources for sacrifice by hanging and the archaeological finds of decapitated bodies, and suggests that the killings most visible in archaeology were not the sacrifices mentioned in text sources.

Keywords: Viking Age, decapitation, Scandinavia, ritual killing, execution, human sacrifice

Introduction

In 1963, Thorkild Ramskou published the initial results of his excavations at Viking Age Lejre, Denmark, under the headline 'The Vikings sacrificed people'. In 2014, when Loe *et al.* published a Viking Age find from Ridgeway Hill, England, their discussion was stridently secular and political: were these Vikings executed as part of the St Brice's day massacre or, more likely, of some other military conflict? These two examples may highlight a bias in archaeological interpretation: similar finds do not inspire similar interpretations, and writers may be too eager to invoke paganism as an explanation for finds from Scandinavia, even when the evidence has close similarities in contemporary Christian Europe.

Background

From the late AD 700s, communities from South Scandinavia spread overseas. By AD 1000, there were satellite settlements from South Greenland to the Black Sea. They shared a common language, some material culture, artistic and technical developments.

Expansion, trade and Christian missions brought Scandinavians into contact with more literate societies. Viking Age Scandinavians were described by their contemporaries from other cultures, and by their own Christian descendants.

Relevant text sources are rare and very isolated in space and time, and it is unclear how homogenous Scandinavian culture ever was.

During the Viking Age, Scandinavians gradually converted from paganism to Christianity. Scandinavian paganism has been the object of significant public interest, and re-imagined, more or less luridly, in a wide variety of contexts. Human sacrifice has played a central role in some reconstructions, sometimes mobilised as an artistic motif for contemporary agendas independently of any historical or archaeological facts – for example, Stensköld (2006, 205ff.) details how Carl Larsson's famous painting *Midwinter Sacrifice* is far more a metaphor for the painter's controversial understanding of his own role in modern Sweden than any attempt at a reconstruction of history or archaeology. Larsson's self-portrait as king and martyr was provocative, and the painting was received, reviled and eventually celebrated as a comment on early 20th-century Sweden. It uses Viking Age human sacrifice as a metaphor for the present, not as an observation on the past.

Sacrifice in the written sources

Manuscript sources are central to any discussion of Viking Age sacrifice. The idea of pagan Viking Age human sacrifice was well established in historiography long before the first archaeological excavations, and all relevant archaeological finds have been interpreted in the light of the text sources. In general, these texts focus more on myths and abstract beliefs than on those ritual actions that leave archaeological evidence. Here, human sacrifice is something of an exception, an unusually well-described ritual practice. Animal sacrifice seems to have been commonplace, but received much less attention from Medieval writers.

In source-critical terms, all the written sources for Viking Age human sacrifice are problematic. Each text is isolated: no two authors have described the same sites or events. Almost all the authors convey information at second-hand or worse. Only Ibn Fadlan seems to be an eye-witness to some (not all) of the details he reports. Several relevant texts are much later than the events they describe (*e.g.*, the sagas, *Landnámabók*, Dudo). Even leaving aside any discussion of the authors' agendas, isolated reports of old, second-hand information must be vulnerable to mistakes and inaccurate transmission. However, without texts, we cannot recognise sacrifice at all. A few details recur across sources written independently, in different languages, centuries apart, and are likely to be credibly reported.

Morten Warmind (2004, 136f.) identifies a consistent pattern of death by stabbing and asphyxiation: in *Gautrec's saga* (ch. 7), the victim is simultaneously hanged from a tree and hit by a thrown javelin, his killer saying 'I dedicate you to Odin'. In Ibn Fadlan's *Risāla*, the victim is garrotted and stabbed with a dagger. Dedication is not mentioned. In *Hávamál* (138), the speaker recalls hanging on a tree, 'wounded with a spear, dedicated to Odin, myself to myself'. Ibn Rusta mentions hanged sacrifice of men and animals, and Theitmar of Merseburg and Adam of Bremen describe victims hanging from trees, likely dead by hanging; stabbing and dedication are not mentioned. All these texts may reflect one single ritual practice with minor variation, reported in Old Norse, Arabic and Latin. A few isolated narratives describe very different rituals: Dudo of St Quentin describes sacrifices clubbed to death with a yoke; in *Landnámabók* 85 and *Eyrbrygja saga* 1, the pagans on Thórsness, Iceland, break victims' backs over a boulder (the two accounts are identical, so not independent); and Leszek Gardeła reads *Egils saga ok Ásmundar* (ch. 8) to suggest sacrifice by decapitation. With only one source each, these latter rituals cannot be regarded as common or well attested, and *Egils saga ok Asmunds* is set in the Tatar kingdom and is very ambiguously worded.

In *Gautreks saga* and *Hávamál*, sacrifices are dedicated to Odin. In legend, Odin uses the same formula to claim whole armies to himself before battle. This may suggest that sacrificed men were considered the equivalent to fallen warriors. Formulae do not appear in any other text. The Thórsness-narrative describes human sacrifice to Thor, as does Dudo, while *Historia Norwegiae* claims that king Domalde from the Yngling tradition (*Ynglingtal*, verse 5,

Yngling saga, ch. 18) was offered to Ceres, whom Wikstöm (2020, 292) identifies as Freya. I suspect that the Thorsness tradition is a reconstruction from place-names and personal nicknames. Dudo has been regarded with scepticism by historians, his account of paganism more moralistic than ethnographic. Thus, the evidence for human sacrifice to Thor is unconvincing. The Yngling tradition reproduces a trope well known from Irish and Arthurian mythology, where the health of the king ensures the health of the land, and where replacing, if necessary killing, an aging or sick king and installing a young, healthy successor restores fertility to the land (*cf.*, the Fisher King motif, the death of Muichertach mac Erca – Pestano 2011, 79f.). Moreover, the association with Ceres is only made very late in the tradition. It may be a scholarly reconstruction, rather than an ancient, oral tradition. Thus, the evidence for human sacrifice to Freya, too, is unconvincing. Only Odin is consistently named as recipient.

All human sacrifices explicitly dedicated to named gods in the texts are male. They contrast to the ritual killings at funerals in other texts (Ibn Fadlan, Ibn Rusta and several Old Norse texts; see Näsström 2001, 37ff.). These are overwhelmingly female. Nordenström (1994, 286) lists six literary parallels of aristocrats or royals buried with companions. Five are wives killing themselves to accompany husbands, one is a male friend of the dead man. Nordenström (1994, 275f.) and Näsström (2001, 14) stress that the funeral killings are not clearly dedicated to any named god, and may instead aim to provide the buried person with companions. They reserve the word 'sacrifice' for killings with clear dedication. In the texts, ritual killing at funerals is consistently an elite phenomenon, associated with rich grave goods (Ibn Fadlan), leading men (Ibn Rusta), aristocrats and kings (*Flateyjarbók* 63 – see Nordenström 1994, 268 and 286). Causes of death include strangulation and stabbing (Ibn Fadlan), burial alive (Ibn Rusta), grief (the goddess Nanna, *Gylfaginning* 49) and possibly self-immolation (Brynhild in *Volsung Saga* 33; but in *Skáldarskarpamál* 7 she stabs herself).

Writers have assumed that victims were often slaves, on little evidence (*e.g.*, Näsström 2001, 36; Naumann *et al.* 2014). Only one text specifically mentions slave-sacrifice (Ibn Fadlan). Two narratives mention the sacrifice of kings (the Yngling material, and *Gautreks saga*), and one mentions sacrifices of freemen outside the community (*Vita Willibrodii*; see also *Egils saga ok Ásmundar*). Three sources indicate victims chosen by lots (Dudo, *Vita Willibrodi*, *Gautreks saga*), and the rest are extremely vague on the victims' identities (*e.g.*, 'men' in Adam of Bremen, Thietmar of Merseburg, the Yngling tradition). As already noted, I regard the sacrifice of kings as a legendary trope, not a historical fact.

Medieval Christian writers seem to have assumed a hierarchy of sacrifice: in *Yngling Saga 18*, people progress from sacrificing oxen, to generic 'men', to the king himself.

Similarly, Adam of Bremen's and Thietmar of Merseburg's descriptions of centralised, massive human sacrifice in Lejre and Uppsala at nine-year intervals contrast to references scattered across other works, referring to animal sacrifice on local farms, possibly every year. It is unclear whether this hierarchy really existed or whether it is an artefact of Christian interpretation.

The archaeology of ritualised killings

I have argued elsewhere that archaeology is poorly suited to distinguishing between sacrifices and executions, but well suited to distinguish between opportunistic and structured killings (Jensen 2015). Opportunistic violence in war, crime and civil unrest is often unstructured and heterogeneous. It can happen in any place, it can involve a changing repertoire of weapons, and individual injuries are often unpredictable. Structured violence, in sacrifice and executions, is far more predictable: it has favoured places, dates, techniques and results.

Historians stress the difficulties of distinguishing between sacrifice and execution. Thus, throughout Christian history, clergy have been present at executions, to minister to both convicts and executioners, and even the secular officials involved regularly invoke God. Historically, various ecclesial authorities have demanded execution for crimes under ecclesiastic law, including sodomy, blasphemy, heresy and witchcraft, and respected secular authorities' right to execute laymen for secular crimes (for a Roman Catholic apology, see Mansour 2005). Only radical dissenters, notably the Anabaptists, have consistently challenged the state's right to kill. Yet, because Christianity regards killing as at least potentially sinful, the ethics of permissible killings are a Christian theological problem, and the structures, ethics and logics of Western executions are deeply shaped by Christianity (see Floto 2001, *passim*). Theologically, Christian human sacrifice is unthinkable, but in material and practical terms, Western executions could easily be mistaken for sacrifices (*cf.* Jensen 2015). I suggest, then, that 'human sacrifice' is a meta-phenomenon, an interpretation of intentions rather than a description of objective acts, and sometimes an overtly orientalising or even racist interpretation. Thus, the interpretation of structured patterns of violence must rely on historical and ethno-historical sources (see *e.g.*, Campbell 2014b; Swenson 2014; Farnum 2017).

Here, I cannot do justice to the complex archaeology of animal sacrifice. Let me observe in passing that just as human sacrifice and execution may be archaeologically indistinguishable, so may animal sacrifice and slaughter. Both are very structured processes. We have a few famous examples of animal bone assemblies interpreted as structured sacrifices (Frösö, Hofstaðir; see Magnell & Iregren 2010, 237f; Lucas & McGovern 2008; *cf.*, cat. 5, 26, 28

and 30), occasional examples of less dramatic, local sites (*e.g.*, Snævringen, Fyn; Henriksen 2015, 202) and many more of animals included in graves. Given the number of written references, recognisable archaeological finds are surprisingly rare, and the recognised examples are very different from each other. As Magnell (2012) shows for Uppåkra, even in contexts where we would expect animal sacrifice, it can be hard to recognise. My impression is that everyday animal sacrifices did not normally produce characteristic highly structured assemblages, or if they did, these resemble butchery waste. Elsewhere, for example in Greece and Rome, it was certainly possible to both sacrifice an animal and butcher it for meat.

Archaeological evidence for structured homicide in the Viking world

As we have seen, text sources associate human sacrifice with asphyxiation, very difficult to identify in the archaeological record. So far, Gerdrup is the only recognised candidate (Table 10.1, 14). The large-scale mass sacrifices described in the Latin sources are also somewhat elusive, although Swedish archaeologists have identified a few possible sites (Table 10.1, 5, 28, 30; see Wikström 2020, 125ff.). The human remains from these sites are few (13 people total; Table 10.4), mostly very broken down, often poorly dated, and yield little contextual information. Far more study is needed to exploit this material.

Three sites reveal multiple internments of children and sub-adults: at Trelleborg (Table 10.1, 27), four children and several animals were deposited in wells (cat. 27). The deposition of the animals is matched at Tissø (Jørgensen *et al.* 2014). McLeod (2018), interprets the four sub-adults inhumed together at Repton (Table 10.1, 22) as sacrifices, and suggests the same for the four plus cremated sub-adults at Whithorn (Table 10.1, 29). The repeated deposition of sub-adults is sets of four or more is a consistent pattern. It is not, however, a pattern very recognisable from the manuscript sources discussed above. Incidentally, the Whithorn example of cremated remains included in an inhumation resembles a well-documented if poorly understood practice of cremated remains in the fill in Scandinavian graves, discussed *e.g.*, by Ulriksen (2011; see also Salge & Ree 2022). Likewise, the quadruple inhumation at Repton has a number of possible parallels across Scandinavia. However, with no clear cause of death, it remains uncertain whether these three examples are indeed all ritual killings.

A second consistent phenomenon in the archaeological material is decapitation. As I hinted in the introduction, decapitated people have often been interpreted as sacrifices. These finds, too, are a poor fit for the written sources discussed above, but they do throw light on the context and meaning of *all* ritual killings in the Viking Age, including

Table 10.1. Catalogue of Viking era decapitations in graves.

	Site	Description	References
1	Ballateare, Isle of Man	Double grave with one intact man and one woman with heavy injuries to the head, deposited in an unusual position.	Gardeła 2013, 127–128; Williams 2008, 175ff.
2	Birka, Grave A129, 'the elk man', Uppland, Sweden	Double grave with one intact man and one decapitated man.	Gardeła 2013, 116–117 and *ibid.*, cat. 1, Holmquist Olausson 1990, *passim*
3	Birka, Grave Bj. 959, Uppland, Sweden	Single grave with one decapitated woman.	Gardeła 2013, 119–120 and *ibid.*, cat. 1
4	Bogøvej 21, Langeland, Denmark	Single grave with one decapitated woman.	Gardeła 2013, 123–124 and *ibid.*, cat. 3
5	Bokaren, Uppland, Sweden	Lakeshore site with multi-period deposition of human and animal remains, at least two humans and 11 horses. One human, a Viking Age young adult male, had been decapitated. Both cranial and postcranial bones were present. Radiocarbon date (one sigma) AD 985–1040. NB: this unusual site is not exactly a formal burial, and deserves much more discussion.	Eklund *et al.* 2018; Wikström 2020, 131f.
6	Bollstanäs, Uppland, Sweden	Double grave with one intact person and one decapitated person with bound feet, prone.	Hemmendorff 1984, 4–12
7	Dublin, Ireland	Total of 17 skulls: 11 men, one woman, four adults without clear sex, one child.	Ó Donnabhain 2010, 274–275
8	Fjälkinge, Grave 3, RAÄ 18-19, Fjälkinge socken, Scania, Sweden	Double grave with one intact man and one decapitated person with cut-off feet.	Svanberg 2003, 301 and cat. 254:3; Gardeła 2013, 115 and cat. 4
9	Fjälkinge, Grave 776, RAÄ 18-19, Fjälkinge socken, Scania, Sweden	Two skulls, young individuals, in a pit on a grave field.	Svanberg 2003, 305 and cat. 255:776; Gardeła 2013, 117–118
10	Flakstad, Grave 5864, Lofoten, Nordland, Norway	Double grave with one man and one headless man, possibly a third person.	Naumann *et al.* 2014
11	Flakstad, Grave 5865, Lofoten, Nordland, Norway	Double grave with one man and one headless woman.	Naumann *et al.* 2014
12	Flakstad, Grave 5863, Lofoten, Nordland, Norway	Double grave with one woman and one headless man.	Naumann *et al.* 2014
13	Frösö Church, Uppland, Sweden	Layer of animal bones, interpreted as sacrifices. 29 bones from at least four humans, not necessarily sacrifices.	Magnell & Iregren 273–274
14	Gerdrup (or Gjerdrup), Lejre, Roskilde amt, Denmark	Double grave with one intact woman and one man with ? bound feet and ? broken neck. Radiocarbon dated: AD 885–990 (BP 1108±25, AAR-23141, cal. with 2σ. Cranial bones of two sheep/goats.	Kastholm & Margaryan 2021, with extensive references
15	Grydehøj, Roskilde amt, Denmark	Double grave with one ? intact woman and one decapitated man.	Ulriksen 2011, 172–174
16	Høje Kasernes Plads, Næstved, Præstø amt, Denmark	Double grave with two intact persons and one decapitated person. The date is unclear: Viking or Early Medieval. This seems based on the find of Baltic ware in a neighbouring grave. Cf. Cat. 17.	*Fund & Fortidsminder*
17	Kalmargården, Store Fuglede sogn, Holbæk amt, Denmark	Double grave with two decapitated men, both with clear cut marks on the vertebrae. The date has been contested, and Pedersen cites a date to *c.* 1240 AD, but I am informed that this date will be reassessed again presently.	Sellevold *et al.* 1984, 70; Gardeła 2013, 114 and cat. 5, Pedersen 2014, 267
18	Kumle Høje, Grave F, Langeland, Denmark	Double grave with two decapitated men, one with bound feet, prone.	Gardeła 2013, 113 and cat. 7

(Continued)

Table 10.1. (Continued)

	Site	Description	References
19	Lejre, grave 55, Roskilde amt, Denmark	Double grave with one intact man and one decapitated man with cut marks, bound hands and feet, prone.	Sellevold *et al.* 1984, 77; Gardeła 2013, 111f. and cat. 8; Wulff-Andersen 1960, 26; see Fig. 10.2
20	Ljungbacka, Grave 23, Scania, Sweden	Single grave with one decapitated man.	Gardeła 2013, 115 and cat. 9
21	Lockarp grave 1, Lockarp-sogn, Scania, Sweden	Double grave with one intact man and one decapitated man.	Svanberg 2003, 290 and cat. 227:1 – 1976 excavation; Gardeła 2013, 116 and cat. 10
22	Repton, Derbyshire, England	Site of a Viking winter camp; remains include a mass grave, with secondary burial of disarticulated bones of 264+ individuals, and a pit with four articulated children, aged 8 to 17, no obvious evidence for cause of death. Mound. McLeod accepts these four as probable human sacrifices, but with no clear cause of death, they are not comparable to the rest of the catalogue analysed here.	McLeod 2018, 76–78
23	Ridgeway Hill, Dorset, England	40 skeletons and 47 skulls in a pit, estimated at least 52 people. Radiocarbon dated AD 970–1025. Isotope analysis shows that many were not local to the British Isles, but may originate from different places in the Viking world. Most are young adults, and all are male or ambiguous. Interpreted as a Viking raid gone wrong.	Loe *et al.* 2014
24	Rosensgade 17-19, Aarhus, Aarhus Amt, Denmark	Skull, one man, with cut marks, found in a well. The dating on Rosengade is contested; it may be medieval.	Gardeła 2013, 128
25	Stengade II grave FII, Langeland, Denmark	Double grave with one intact man and one decapitated man with bound feet, and possibly hands. Very poor bone preservation.	Sellevold *et al.* 1984, 116; Gardeła 2013, 108–110
26	Ströja, Kvillinge, Östergötaland, Sweden	Multi-period site. Fragments of four skulls, one dated to the 7–800s; from two piles of stones interpreted as a place of sacrifice. Extensive assemblage of animal bones. Still undergoing analysis. Two of these people were female, all skulls separated from the body and broken. Cut marks on (some? all?) skulls. Three of the four may be significantly older than Viking Age.	Wikström 2020, 129–130
27	Trelleborg, Slagelse Amt, Denmark	Two wells, containing the bones of four children and animals, including a reasonably complete billy-goat and large dog, parts of cow and horse. The finds pre-date the famous round fortress on the site. 8th/9th or 10th century. The children are anatomically aged 4, 7, 4 and 4 years old, with no obvious evidence for cause of death; a few bones of an adult person may be accidental inclusions relocated from elsewhere.	Godtfredsen *et al.* 2014; Jørgensen *et al.* 2014
28	Uppåkra, Scania, Sweden	Bones of at least six individuals, weathered through long exposure, found in the so-called cult house. Unclear date. Large assemblage of animal bones.	Wikström 2020, 125–126; Magnell 2012
29	Whithorn, Dumfries and Galloway, Scotland	Christian graveyard; grave with infant (8–12 months old), two beads; disarticulated bones of two adults, male and female, apparently secondary internment; and cremation layer with burnt remains of at least four people, likely young or young adult. No clear evidence of violence or cause of death. McLeod accepts these cremated remains as probable human sacrifices, but with no clear cause of death, they are not comparable to the rest of the catalogue analysed here.	McLeod 2018, 79–80
30	Äverstaån, Närke, Sweden	Multi-period site with human and horse bones, at least some of the human bones Viking Age, at least two people and one horse.	Wikström 2020, 130; Zachrisson 2014, 96

the elusive sacrifices, and they are numerous enough for some quantitative analysis.

I have compiled a catalogue of evidence of highly structured killings (Table 10.1), based mostly on the Danish national database *Fund & Fortidsminder* and older catalogues (Sellevold *et al.* 1984; Svanberg 2003; Gardeła 2013; Wikström 2020). This catalogue is probably most complete for Denmark and South Sweden, less so for Norway and Middle Sweden, and even less so beyond this. I have included two cases with convincing evidence of lethal violence other than decapitation (see below), but not included other examples of multiple internments in the analysis: as Gräslund has convincingly argued, many of these may represent secondary burials, not funeral killings (Gräslund 1980, 74). The catalogue is limited by bone preservation. Thus, no cremations have been included in the analyses (*cf.*, Table 10.1, 29, Withorn) and many early finds are too poorly recorded for analysis. Not incidentally, the three graves from Lofoten were initially interpreted as single graves (see Sandmo 1985, 81). Only much later did aDNA analysis reveal that each of these graves contained at least two people (Naumann *et al.* 2014). Other similar cases may well await identification. I have included the Rosengade skull, the Kalmergård and Høje kasernes Plads graves (Table 10.1, 17), despite controversies over the date. To keep this text readable, I have moved all references to the tables at the end of the paper.

The catalogue lists 20 isolated skulls (Table 10.1, 7, 9, 24) and 18 graves containing a total of 20 victims, 19 of these decapitated (Table 10.1, 1, 2, 3, 4, 6, 8, 10, 11, 12, 14, 15, 16, 17, 18, 19, 20, 21, 25). Cut marks have been observed on 13 individuals in graves and on four isolated skulls, but depend on bone preservation. In their absence, decapitation is inferred from the separation of the skull from the post-cranial skeleton. Some of the 20 isolated skulls without cut marks may reveal different phenomena, including re-deposition of skulls from disturbed graves (*cf.*, Table 10.1, 9). One skull, from a Dublin pit, has injuries congruent with mounting on

a stake. The jaw was present, and Ó Donnabháin (2010, 274) suggests that this head was mounted, taken down and buried before it had decayed much.

Ten graves contain one intact and one decapitated person each (Table 10.1, 2, 6, 8, 10, 11, 12, 15, 19, 21, 25); one contains two intact and one decapitated person (cat. 16); two graves contain two decapitated people each (Table 10.1, 17, 18); and three contain single decapitated individuals (Table 10.1, 3, 4, 20). All these are formal interments. Two isolated skulls have been found in a pit on a grave-field (Table 10.1, 9), one in an urban well (Table 10.1, 24), and three in urban pits, one of these possibly a latrine (Table 10.1, 7). 14 skulls were found in urban infill layers (Table 10.1, 7). The exceptional site of Bokaren falls outside all these categories, being a wetland deposition of an entire decapitated individual without formal burial (Table 10.1, 5), and probably more comparable to the other Swedish open-air sites (Table 10.1, 5, 28, 30).

Many of these remains have been sexed: the 10 double graves with one intact and one decapitated person hold seven decapitated men, seven intact men, one decapitated woman and two intact women (decapitated men: Table 10.1, 2, 10, 12, 15, 19, 21, 25; intact men: 2, 8, 10, 11, 19, 21, 25; decapitated woman: 11; intact women: 12, 14; Table 10.2). Three individuals in these graves have not been sexed (Table 10.1, 6, 8). In the triple grave, no remains have been sexed (Table 10.1, 16). Another two graves contained two individuals each, an intact man and an injured woman (not decapitated; Table 10.1, 1); and an intact woman and a possibly hanged man (not decapitated; cat. 14). In the double graves with two decapitated people, all are men (Table 10.1, 17, 18). The single graves contain two decapitated women and one decapitated man (Table 10.1, 3, 4; 20), with one more decapitated man at Bokaren, not in a grave (Table 10.1, 5). In total, the graves hold 12 decapitated men and three decapitated women. Stray skulls include 12 men and one woman, for a total of 24 decapitated men and four women (Table 10.3).

Table 10.2. Graves with at least one intact body.

	Intact male	Intact unidentified sex	Intact female	SUM
Male victim	Cat. 2, 10, 19[#], 21, 25[#]; total n=5	-	Cat. 12, 14*[#], 15; total n=3	8
Victim of unidentified sex	Cat. 8[□]; total n=1	Cat. 6, 16 (two intact people); total n=2 victims, 3 intact	-	3
Female victim	Cat. 1*, 11; total n=2	-	-	2
SUM	8	3	3	14 intact people, 13 victims

* Not decapitated.
[#] Bound.
[□] Maimed.

Table 10.3. Contexts without any intact bodies.

	Isolated skulls	*Headless bodies*	*SUM*
Male	Cat. 7 (11 people), 24; total n=12	Cat. 18[#] (two people), 20; 23 (47+ people); total n=50+	62+ men
Unclear sex	Cat. 7 (5 people), 9 (2 people); total n=11		11 people
Female	Cat. 7; total n=1	Cat. 3, 4; total n=2	3 women
SUM	24 people (12 men, 1 woman)	50+ people (54+ men, 2 women)	76 + people (62+ men, 3 women)

[#] Bound.

Four decapitated men are interpreted as bound, and one person of unclear sex has had both feet chopped off (Table 10.1, 14, 18, 19, 25; 8). Three men lay prone and one woman lay twisted into an unusual position (Table 10.1, 6, 18, 19; 1). These people may have been thrown into graves, rather than laid down. Where stratigraphy exists, decapitated individuals invariably lie higher (later) than intact individuals. Intact individuals seem to have been carefully laid to rest first, decapitated individuals placed much less carefully in the grave later. Binding may have had symbolic meaning beyond its practical aspects: a number of written sources refer to a belief in a magic technology called loosening runes, supposedly developed by Odin and thought to be shared with a few elite men, which made binding them impossible (*e.g.*, *Hávamál* 149). Regardless of the sex of the intact body, men were killed more often than women, and only men were tied up.

The suggested dates span the Viking Age and vary greatly in precision. Dates have been suggested for four graves with one intact and one decapitated person (cat. 6: [14]C AD 760±100, cat. 2: *c.* AD 800, cat. 19: *c.* AD 850–950 and cat. 8: after AD 900); for an intact woman and likely hanged man (cat. 14: AD 885–990); for single burial of a decapitated woman (cat. 3: *c.* 850–975); for an unburied, decapitated man (Table 10.1, 5: AD 985–1040); for a mass grave (Table 10.1, 23: AD 970–1025); and for three contexts with isolated skulls (Table 10.1, 9: AD 800–1000, 24: AD 900s, 7: AD 900s and 1000s; all references in the Table 10.1 catalogue). These dates may suggest a vague pattern, where double graves with one decapitated person are early, isolated skulls late. Thus, the meaning of decapitation may have changed over time. Christianisation did not limit decapitation, although it may have changed how people deposited the remains of decapitated dead.

Geographically, the evidence is clearly regional, with concentrations in eastern Denmark (Roskilde and the South Funen Sea), Scania and Dublin (map, Figure 10.1), all areas associated with the Danes. There are large areas of Scandinavia with well-known Viking Age gravesites but no evidence of decapitation burials. Neither bone preservation alone nor state formation alone can explain this – bone preservation is fair in the Mälar Valley where the Svear state formed, excellent on Gotland, yet nothing in either region matches Scania. There may be some sense of spatial continuity, with multiple finds from Dublin, Lofoten, Fjällklinge and Birka,

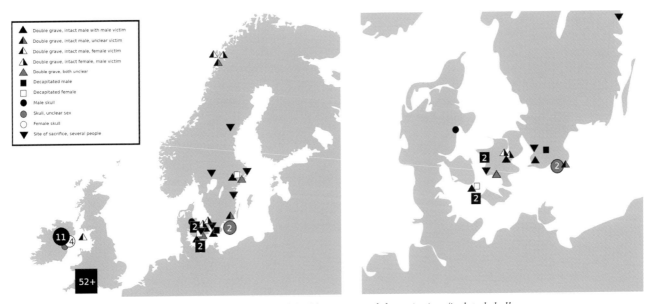

Figure 10.1. Distribution map of double graves and decaptitations/isolated skulls.

but also many sites with just one recognised example. The larger sites with stray finds of human bone interpreted as human sacrifices are exclusively Swedish, and largely concentrated in eastern Sweden, from Örebro to Östergötaland, with an outlier in Uppåkra, Scania (Viking Age Denmark, modern Sweden). This outlier may suggest that discovery and interpretation owe more to national standards of field archaeology today than to past differences. Both the intact men buried with female victims are in the west, on Man and Lofoten. If we add Ibn Fadlan's description, the killing of women at men's funerals might be geographically marginal, perhaps a product of relations between travelling Scandinavian men and local women. The five intact men buried with male victims are eastern, or central if we include Ibn Fadlan's example, and two of the three intact women buried with male victims are from the small region around Roskilde and Old Lejre, but the third is hundreds of kilometres away, at Lofoten. Ritual deposition of multiple sub-adults seems very over-represented in Britain. The numbers are too small for statistics, but do suggest some regional variation.

The grave goods include very poor and moderately wealthy examples. Ballateare contains spear and sword; Grydehøj, horse, dog and a strange bronze-and-iron object; another six graves contain poor to average goods (knives, buckles and brooches, occasional weapons); and four contain no grave goods whatsoever. Conversely, the richest graves in Viking Age Scandinavia do not offer good evidence of ritual violence, although both Oseberg and Hedeby boat-chamber grave contain multiple bodies which may be victims of funeral killings by other means than decapitation (see Holch 2006; Wamers 1994; Wamers offers a very different interpretation of the Hedeby find).

For Flakstad, only, Naumann *et al.* (2014) analysed aDNA and concluded that the people buried together were not close biological relatives. Their istotope analysis reveals that people buried intact and accompanied by sacrifices had a very terrestrial diet, whereas sacrifices, dogs and people buried alone had a more marine diet. On this basis, the researchers suggest that sacrifices were slaves, a bold claim. On the evidence given, they could equally be free people, like those buried alone. However, the difference in diet surely argues against interpreting these double graves as married couples.

At Gerdrup, recent analysis on mtDNA showed that the decapitated man was a close relative to, possibly a son of, the woman with whom he was buried (Kastholm & Margaryan 2021, 9). This is very surprising, but might speak against them being either mistress and slave or wife and husband.

Viking Age ritualised violence: a re-assessment

The structured violence visible in archaeology is a poor fit for the sacrifices described in the text sources. Although archaeology and texts likely reflect a shared, overreaching cultural understanding of violence, they also highlight several different phenomena within it.

Decapitation is not closely associated with human sacrifice in text sources. Only one saga may hint at human sacrifice by decapitation (*Egils saga ok Asmunds*, ch. 8), whereas two unambiguously mention decapitation of prisoners of war (*Jómsvikinga saga ch. 47, Egils saga skallagrímsonar ch. 55*), and one myth mentions the gods decapitating hostages (*Ynglinga saga* 4, 7). Two legends mention cups made of human skulls, both in the context of revenge (the legends of Wayland and of Gudrun and Atli, in *Völundarkviða, Atlaskviða, Atlamál in groenlanzko*; see also Jensen 2017). Based on the text sources, decapitation was more often political than religious.

As noted above, written sources describe the killing of women at men's funerals. The archaeological evidence for ritual violence includes more men buried with men than any other combination (five examples; Table 10.2). These burials cannot reasonably be interpreted as married couples, actual or symbolic. Three graves might suggest men killed at women's funerals, and only two graves can reasonably be interpreted as women killed at men's funerals (Table 10.2). As noted, aDNA and diet also speak against these graves representing married couples. Thus texts and archaeology may reveal quite different phenomena.

Barra Ó Donnabháin (2010, 274f.) interprets the isolated skulls from Dublin as evidence of political, often hostile, relations between Scandinavians and Irish groups. The 47+ decapitated men on Ridgeway Hill, too, have been interpreted in a political context (Loe *et al.* 2014, 211). In the rest of the Viking world, such overt and large-scale political ritual violence is not obvious in archaeology, despite being evident in text sources.

Table 10.4. Sites of sacrifice.

	Bones sexed male	Bones of unclear sex	Bones sexed female	SUM
With lethal injuries	5 (n=1)			1
Without identified, lethal injuries		26 (n=2), 27 (n=4) 28 (n=6)*, 30 (n=2)*	28 (n=2)	16*
SUM	1	14*	2	17 people (1 man, 2 women)

* Unclear dates on sites with long chronologies, not all need be Viking Age.

Figure 10.2. Lejre grave 55 (cat. 19). Cut marks on the third vertebra show that the uppermost of the two dead persons was decapitated. The uppermost body is prone, the lower body supine (photo: H. Andersen, © ROMU, Roskilde Museum, reproduced with permission).

Leszek Gardeła (2013) highlights that in several texts, dead bodies are dug up and decapitated post-mortem, to keep them from rising from their graves and haunting the living. He interprets isolated decapitated women as potential revenants, double graves as human sacrifice of slaves (but *cf.* discussions above). In my catalogue, isolated decapitated women are rare (two examples, cats. 3, 4). In most graves, there is no evidence that decapitation was later than burial.

Lars Jørgensen (2003, 183) interpreted the two decapitated men from Kalmergården (cat. 17) as executed criminals. The interpretation could apply more widely, most obviously to the two decapitated men from Kumle Høje (cat. 18). We have no written sources for juridical decapitation in Viking Age Scandinavia, but this may be due to source bias: Latin and Arabic writers were largely uninterested in Scandinavian legislation. The Old Norse sources are very interested in legislation, but focus on private vendettas on Iceland where no centralised state existed. Thus, absence of evidence for executions is not evidence of their absence further south, and the urban finds of severed heads, especially, are strong candidates for people executed as criminals and even displayed to celebrate the triumph of the law.

Since we have no evidence that decapitation had any privileged religious meaning to pagans, and since it continued into Christian times, I suggest that this is more likely a legal or political practice than a strictly religious and pagan one. I speculate that it reflects a larger, cultural logic.

Old Norse literature was a central inspiration for Marcel Mauss' theory of the gift (Mauss 2011 [1925]) and his theory fits remarkably well with many aspects of that society, including revenge (Jensen 2017), and, arguably marriage, kinship and religion. Ibn Fadlan's description of money offerings in a temple on the Volga reflects the same logic, *do ut des*, giving offerings and sacrifices to gods either to repay past favours or encourage future ones, as does *Hávamál 146* (cited at the start of this paper).

The purpose of *blót*, human or animal sacrifice, is widely given as *ár ok frið*, 'year and peace', prosperity and safety (Näsström 2001, 110). *Ynglinga saga* (ch. 8) separates these purposes by date, but is the only text to do so. One pre-Viking runestone commemorates a man who 'gave a good year' with nine bucks or billygoats and nine stallions, likely by sponsoring a sacrifice (Stentoften, Blekinge, as interpreted by Looienga 2003, 29). On this evidence, animal sacrifices could be reciprocal payments for a year of prosperity and animal fertility, that is, ár. Symmetrically, human sacrifice, especially of adult men, might then aim to secure *frið*, military safety and minimal military losses. As already noted, the dedication used for sacrifices was also associated with warriors in battle, the fallen claimed by Odin. More generally, human sacrifice may have developed in tandem with a culture of constant warfare and one of killing captured enemy combatants after battle, *cf.* also Aztec and Shang Chinese traditions of sacrificing defeated military opponents (for Shang, see Campbell 2014b, 98ff.).

Funerary killing seems to be a different phenomenon. Elsewhere, retainer killings were intended to provide the dead protagonist with loved or trusted companions. However, retainers often had second thoughts, fled and had to be replaced post-haste at funerals (Morris 2013, 84). In Scandinavia, retainer sacrifice has been a popular hypothesis, but the archaeological evidence of people tied up, or, in one case, having their feet cut off, and being thrown carelessly into the pit rather suggests a lack of trust and respect. *Those* funerary killings are unlikely to be trusted retainers. These killings may more closely match yet another phenomenon reported by Morris, of killing enemies to display power (*ibid.*, 72).

I would speculate that all highly structured killings, be they sacrifices or executions, not only reflect order, but also aim to strengthen it – be it cosmic order or social order, or both; *vice versa*, very disorganised violence may aim to actively undermine order, in addition to harming its victims. This would be relevant for, *e.g.*, terrorist attacks, guerrilla warfare, riots and state terror, all of which can be and often are construed as attacks on all of society, and even as affronts to higher values. In this reading, *all* structured killings aim to restore or uphold some order, usually one serving the killers' interests, but not always one overtly religious.

I speculate, then, that these funeral decapitations are structurally similar to the killing of defeated enemy soldiers after battles, often by decapitation. This practice is well documented among contemporary pagans and Christians alike. I suggest that men decapitated at funerals were killed *like* military opponents and were decapitated in *wilful contrast* to the hanged sacrifices to Odin. The small scale of the killings might suggest personal, juridical conflicts, rather than larger, military ones (except, obviously, for Ridgeway Hill). Thus, this may be evidence of a dramatic way of closing a vendetta. I speculate that if and only if an opponent in a vendetta could be completely isolated, leaving nobody to avenge his death, he could be killed without negative consequences. Under those same circumstances, he would have nobody to bury him and get no monument to recall him. If a family could capture their last opponent, decapitate him and include him as a minor element in one of their own funerals, this would solve all these structural problems and demonstrate their power, all in one action. It would effectively erase the potential of future conflict and overwrite it with the recall of ostentatious burial. Building on Gardeła's thesis, the un-avenged dead would be perfect candidates for revenants. If decapitation post mortem was used to end haunting, death by decapitation might be used to forestall it. What we see here, then, might be killing with no legal repercussions, a ritualistic imitation of the battlefield and the state of exception found there. This is not sacrifice, then, but a juridical ritual, a way of killing enemies but escaping the normal legal consequences of their deaths, by transforming them into the equivalent of war causalities.

To summarise on the Viking Age, written sources and archaeological evidence highlight several very different phenomena. The human sacrifices by asphyxiation so evident in the texts are largely invisible to archaeologists; the women killed at men's funerals are very much in minority; the severed heads, mostly in urban contexts, and the men killed at funerals, so evident in archaeology, demand different interpretations. I have offered a first attempt at these here. Despite the enormous attention paid to pagan human sacrifice, Ridgeway Hill illustrates that far more people were likely killed in military conflicts, and executed on orders from rulers, Christian and pagan alike. Here, as everywhere, violence was a means to, and a technology of, political power first and last.

Note

1   I am grateful to Susanna Eklund for giving me access to the not yet published report on Botaren, and to ROMU, Roskilde for the photograph from Lejre. The title is, of course, from *Hávamál* 145: Betra er óbeðit/en sé ofblótit/ ey sér til gildis gjǫf; in a free translation, better not to ask anything of the gods than to sacrifice too much; gifts demand something in return. I follow Larrington's (1996) translation, since revised.

Bibliography

Primary sources

All family sagas are available in Scandinavian and English translations in the collected editions from Saga Forlag (English: V. Hreinsson, ed. 1997: *The complete sagas of Icelanders, including 49 tales*; Danish: A. Lassen, ed. 2014: *Islændingesagaerne, alle sagaer og niogfyrre totter*; Swedish: K. Jóhannesson, G.D. Hansson & K.G. Johansson, eds. 2014: *Isländningasagorna, Samtliga släktsagor och fyrtionio tåtar,*; Norwegian: J.G. Jørgensen, ed. 2014: *Islendingesagaene – Samtlige sagaer og fortini tætter;* all Reykjavik: Saga Forlag).

A treasury of Arabic sources have been collected in P. Lunde and C. Stone, *Ibn Fadlan and the Land of Darkness. Arab Travelers in the Far North.* London: Penguin.

Adam of Bremen: *Gesta Hammaburgensis Ecclesiae Pontificum.* In *Hamburgische Kirchengeschichte, Hannover Monumenta Germaniae Historica.* Scriptores Rerum Germanicarum in Usum Scholarum Separatim Editi (SS rer. Germ) vol. 2. Translated by B. Schmeidler. Berlin: De Gruyter, 1917.

Atlamál in groenlanzko, or The Greenlandic Poem of Atli. In the *Poetic Edda,* translated by C. Larrington. Oxford: Oxford University Press, 1996.

Atlaskviða, or The Lay of Atli. In the *Poetic Edda,* translated by C. Larrington. Oxford: Oxford University Press, 1996.

Dudo of St Quentin. De Moribus et Acti Primorum Normanniæ Ducum, edited by J. LairCaen: Le Blanc Hardel, 1865. The relevant passages are translated in Wikström 2020, 228.

Egils saga ok Ásmundar: Egils saga einhenda ok Ásmundar berserkjabana, translated by G. Horgen. Norrøne Bokverk 49. Oslo: Det Norske Samlaget, 1989.

Egils saga skallagrímssonar. In *Egils saga eller fortælling om Egil Skallagrimsson,* edited by V. Dallerup and translated by F. Jónsson. Kjøbenhavn: Gyldendalske Boghandel, Nordisk Forlag, 1923. See also https://heimskringla.no/wiki/Egils_Saga.

Eyrbyggja saga. Translated by H. Pálsson and P. Edwards. London: Penguin, 1972.

Flateyjarbók. In *En samling af norske Konge-Sagaer sammen med indskudte mindre Fotællinger om Begivenheder i og udenfor Norge samt Annaler*, vol. I, edited by C.R. Unger. Christiania: P.T. Malling, 1860. See also T. Titlestad (ed.) and E. Eikill (trans.). 'Flatøybok'. Hafrsfjord: Saga Bok A/S, 2014.

Gautreks saga. In *En fornaldarsaga. Götriks saga*, translated by M. Malm. Örebro: Samsprok, 1990.

Hávamál, or The Sayings of the High One. In the *Poetic Edda*, translated by C. Larrington. Oxford: Oxford University Press, 1996.

Historia Norwegiæ. Ekrem, I. & Boje Mortensen, L. (eds). Translated by P. Fisher. Copenhagen: Museum Tuscalanum, 2003. Relevant text is quoted in Wikström 2020, 292.

Ibn Rusta (اصفهانی رسته ابن احمد) Aḥmad ibn Rusta Iṣfahānī) 'Kitāb al-A'lāk an-Nafīsa' ('Book of Precious Records'). The relevant passages are translated in Näsström 2003; Nordenström 1994; and in Lunde & Stone 2012. The entire work is published as M.J. De Groeje (ed. and trans.), *Ibn Rusta's Kitāb al-A'lāq al-nafīsa* in *Ibn Rusta's Kitāb al-A'lāq al-nafīsa and Kitāb al-Buldān by al-Ya'qūbī*, M.J. de Goeje's Classic Editions (1892), Bibliotheca Geographorum Arabicorum, Vols 1–7. Leiden: Brill, 2014.

Ibn Fadlan (حماد بن راشد بن العباس بن فضلان بن احمد/ Aḥmad ibn Faḍlān ibn al-'Abbās ibn Rāšid ibn Ḥammād): Rīsala, published in Ibn Fadlān and the Rūssiyya, edited and translated by J.E. Montgomery. In *Journal of Arabic and Islamic Studies* 3: 1–25. Cambridge: Cambridge University Press, 2003. The text can also be found in Lunde & Stone 2012.

Jómsvíkinga saga. In *Jomsvikinga saga og Knytlinge Saga tillige med Sagabrudstykker og Fortællinger vedkommende Danmark*, translated by C.C. Rafn. Copenhagen: Det Kongelige Nordiske Oldskriftsselskab, 1829.

Landnámabók. Edited by F. Jónsson. Copenhagen: Det kongelige Nordiske Oldskriftselskab, 1990.

Skáldskárpamál, or Poetic Diction, in Snorri Sturlasson (n.d., early 1200s): *The Prose Edda*, edited and translated by J. Byock 2005. London: Penguin Classics.

Theitmar of Merseburg, Chronicon: German translation, 1st edition. Berlin: Weidmannschen Verlagsbuchhandlung. See also http://www.mgh-bibliothek.de/thietmar/edition/vorrede.html. Munich: R. Holtzmann, 1935.

Vita Willibrodi: *Vita Willibrordi Archepiscopi Traiectensis Auctore Alcuino*. In *The Anglo-Saxon Missionaries in Germany*, edited by C.H. Talbot. London: Sheed and Ward, 1954.

Volsung saga, or The Saga of the Volsungs, translated by J.L. Byock. London: Penguin, 2013.

Völundarkviða, or The Lay of Volund. In the *Poetic Edda*, translated by C. Larrington. Oxford: Oxford University Press, 1996.

Ynglingatal is available in the original Old Norse and in Danish and Swedish translation here: http://www.heimskringla.no/wiki/Ynglingesaga.

Ynglinga saga is available in the original Old Norse and in Danish, Swedish and Norwegian translation here: http://www.heimskringla.no/wiki/Ynglingesaga.

References

Andersen, H. 1960. Hovedstaden i riget. In *Nationalmuseets arbejdsmark*, 13–35. Copenhagen: Nationalmuseet.

Campbell, R. 2014a. Introduction: Towards a deep history of violence and civilization. In *Violence and Civilization*, edited by R. Campbell, 41–22. Joukowski Institute Publications. Oxford: Oxbow Books.

Campbell, R. 2014b. Transformations of violence: Humanity and inhumanity in Early China. In *Violence and Civilization*, edited by R. Campbell, 94–118. Joukowski Institute Publications. Oxford: Oxbow Books.

Christensen, T. & Bennike, P. 1983. Kvinder for fred?. *Skalk* 1983: 3. Højbjerg: Jysk Arkæologisk Selskab.

Eklund, S., Fredegren, C. & Hennius, A., with Prata, F. 2018. Återbesök vid Bokaren. Arkeologisk forskningsundersökning, Stavby 137:1, Sunnersbol Bolsbyn, Stavby socken, Östhammars kommun, Uppland, Uppsala Län. SAU rapport 2018:14. Uppsala: Societas Archaeologica Upsalaiensis.

Farnum, J. 2017. Gender and structural violence in Prehistoric Peru. In *Archaeolgies of Gender and Violence*, edited by U. Matić and B. Jensen, 247–262. Oxford: Oxbow Books.

Floto, I. 2001. *Dødsstraffens kulturhistorie. Ritualer og metoder, 1600–2001*. Copenhagen: Museum Tuscalanum.

Gardeła, L. 2013. The headless Norsemen: Decapitation in Viking Age Scandinavia. In *Motyw głowy dawnych kulturach/The Head Motif in Past Societies*, edited by L. Gardeła and K. Kajkowski. Motywy przez wieki/Motifs Through the Ages, vol. 1, 88–155. Butów: Museum Zachodniokaszubskie wbytowie.

Godtfredsen, A.B., Primeau, C., Frei, K.M. & Jørgensen, L. A ritual site with sacrificial wells from the Viking Age at Trelleborg, Denmark. *Danish Journal of Archaeology* 2014(3). Copenhagen: The National Museum.

Gräslund, A.-S. 1980. *Birka IV: The Burial Customs: A Study of the Graves on Björkö*. Stockholm: KVHAA (Kungliga Vitterhets Historie och Antikvitets Akademiet).

Hemmendorf, O. 1984. Människooffer: ett inslag i järnåldrens gravritualer, belyst av ett fynd in Bollstanäs, Uppland. *Fornvännen*, 4–12. Stockholm: KVHAA (Kungliga Viterhets Historie och antikvitetsakademien).

Henriksen, M.B. 2015. Kystens kultpladser. In *Odense Bys Museer 2015*, 200–217. Odense: Odense Bys Museer.

Holch, P. 2006. The Oseberg Ship Burial, Norway: New Thoughts on the Skeletons From the Grave Mound. *European Journal of Archaeology* 9(2–3): 185–210. DOI:10.1177/1461957107086123

Holmqvist Olausson, L. 1994. Elgmannen från Birka: presentation av en nyligen undersökt krigargrav with människooffer. In *Fornvännen*, 175–182. Stockholm: KVAA (Kungliga Viterhets Historie och antikvitetsakademien).

Jensen, B. 2015. Sacrifice or execution. In *Beyond War: Archaeological Approaches to Violence*, edited by A. Piquer and A. Vila-Mijà, 1–23. Newcastle upon tyne: Cambridge Scholars.

Jensen, B. 2017. Skull-cups and snake-pits: Men's revenge and women's revenge in Viking Age Scandinavia. In *Archaeologies of Gender and Violence*, edited by U. Matić and B. Jensen, 197–222. Oxford: Oxbow Books.

Jørgensen, L. 2003. Manor and market at Lake Tissø in the sixth to the eleventh century. The Danish 'productive' sites. In *Markets in Early Medieval Europe. Trading and 'Productive' Sites 650–850*, edited by T. Pestell and K. Ulmschnieder, 175–207. Bollington: Windgather Press.

Jørgensen, L., Albris, S.L., Bican, J.F., Frei, K.M., Gotfredsen, A.B., Henriksen, P.S., Holst, S. & Primeau, C.C. 2014. Førkristne kultpladser – ritualer og tro i yngre jernalder og vikingetid. In *Nationalmuseets arbejdsmark 2014*, 186–200. Denmark: Nationalmuseet.

Kastholm, O.T. & Margaryan, A. 2021. Reconstructing the Gerdrup grave: The story of an unusual Viking Age double grave seen in context and in the light of new analysis. *Danish Journal of Archaeology* 10, 1–20. Copenhagen: Nationalmuseet.

Loe, L., Boyle, A., Webb, H. & Scarre, D. 2014. *Given to the Ground: a Viking Age Mass Grave on Ridgeway Hill, Weymouth.* Dorset Natural History and Archaeological Society Monograph Series No. 2. Oxford: DHAS and Oxford Archaeology.

Looienga, T. 2003. *Texts and Contexts of the Oldest Runic Inscriptions.* Northern Worlds 4. Leiden and Boston: Brill.

Lucas, G. & McGovern, T. 2008. Bloody slaughter: ritual decapitation at the settlement of Hofstaðir, Iceland. *European Journal of Archaeology* 10(1): 7–30. https://doi.org/10.1177/1461957108091480.

Lunde, P. & Stone, C. (trans. and ed.). 2012. *Ibn Fadlān and the Lands of Darkness. Arab Travelers in the Far North.* London: Penguin.

Magnell, O. 2012. Sacred Cows or Old Beasts? A taphonomic approach to studying ritual killing with an example from Iron Age Uppåkra, Sweden. In *The ritual killing and burial of animals*: European perspectives, edited by A. Pluskowski, 192–204. Oxford: Oxbow Books.

Magnell, O. & Iregren, E. 2010: Veitsu hvé blóta skal? The Old Norse *blót* in the light of osteological remains from Frösö Church, Jämtland, Sweden. *Current Swedish Archaeology*, 18, 223–250. Stockholm.

Mansour, O. 2005. Not torments, but delights: Antonio Gallino's Trattato de gli instrumenti de martyrio of 1591 and its illustrations. In *Roman Bodies*, edited by A. Hopkins and M. Wyke, 157–166. Rome: British School of Rome.

Mauss, M. 2011 [1925]. *The Gift: The Form and Reason of Exchange in Archaic Societies.* Translated by W.D. Hall. London/New York: Routledge.

McLeod, S. 2018. Human sacrifice in Viking Age Britain and Ireland. *Journal of the Australian Early Medieval Association* 14, 71–88. Melbourne: Australian Early Medieval Association.

Morris, E. 2014. (Un)Dying loyalty: Meditations on retainer sacrifice in Ancient Egypt and elsewhere. In *Violence and Civilization*, edited by R. Campbell, 61–93. Joukowski Institute Publications 4. Oxford: Oxbow Books.

Naumann, E., Krzewińska, M., Götherström, A. & Eriksson, G. 2014. Slaves as burial gifts in Viking Age Norway? Evidence from stable isotope and ancient DNA analyses. *Journal of Archaeological Science* 41, 533–540. Amsterdam/London: Elsevier.

Näsström, B.-M. 2001. *Blót: tro and offer in det førkristne Norden.* Translated by K.A. Lie. Oslo: Pax Forlag.

Nordenström, L. 1994. Dödande vid begravningar: ett inslag i järnålderns gravritualer i komparativ religionshistorisk belysning. *Fornvännen* 89(4): 265–278. Stockholm: KVAA (Kungliga Viterhets Historie och antikvitetsakademien).

Ó Donnabhain, B. 2010. Cultural clashes? The human remains from the Wood Quay excavations. In *The Viking Age: Ireland and the West*, edited by J. Sheehan and D. Ó Corráin, 271–282. Proceedings of the 15th Viking Congress. Dublin: Four Courts Press.

Pedersen, A. 2014. *Dead Warriors in Living Memory.* Copenhagen: Nationalmuseet.

Pestano, D. 2011. *King Arthur in Irish Pseudo-historical Tradition. An Introduction.* Dark Age Arthurian Books.

Ramskou, T. 1963. Vikingerne ofrede mennesker. In *Nationalmuseets Arbejdsmark 1963–1965*, 79–86. Copenhagen: Nationalmuseet.

Reynolds, A. 2009. *Anglo-Saxon deviant burial customs.* Oxford: Oxford University Press.

Salge, L. & Ree, M. 2022: Brændt og destrueret. Sekundære offerlag i vikingetidsgrave. In *Arkæologisk Forum 45*, 31–36. Copenhagen: Foreningen af Fagarkæologer.

Sandmo, A.-K. 1985. Gravfelt og bosetningsområder fra eldre og yngre jernalder på Flakstad i Lofoten. Forløpige gravningsresultater og noen hypoteser. In *Arkeologisk Feltarbeid i Nord-Norge 1984*, edited by Ericka Engelstad and Inger-Marie Holm-Olsen. Tromura, Kulturhistorie no. 5. Tromsø: University of Tromsø.

Sellevold, B., Lund Hansen, U. & Jørgensen, J.B. 1984. *Iron Age Man in Denmark*, Vol. III. Nordiske fortidsminder, serie B, bind 8. Copenhagen: Det Kongelige Danske Oldskriftsselskab.

Stensköld, E. 2006. Flying daggers, horse whisperers and a midwinter sacrifice: Creating the past during the Viking Age and Early Middle Ages. In *Current Swedish Archaeology 14*, 199–219. Stockholm: Svenska Arkeologiska Samfundet.

Svanberg, F. 2003. *Death Rituals in South Scandinavia AD 800–1000 – Decolonizing the Viking Age 2.* Stockholm: Almqvsit and Wiksel International.

Swenson, E. 2014. Dramas of the dialectic: sacrifice and power in ancient policies. In *Violence and civilization*, edited by R. Campbell, 23–27. Oxford: Oxbow Books.

Ulriksen, J. 2011. Vikingetidens gravskik in Danmark: spor af begravelsesritualer i jordfæstegrave. *Kuml*, 161–245. Højbjerg: Jysk arkæologisk selskab.

Wamers, E. 1994. König im Grenzland. Neue Analyse des Bootkammergrabes von Haiðaby. *Acta Archaeologica* 65: 1–56.

Warmind, M. 2004. '… á þeim meiði, er mangi veit, hvers hann af rótom renn': Kosmologi og ritualer i det førkristne Norden. In *Ordning mot kaos – studier av nordisk förkristen kosmologi*, edited by A. Andrén, K. Jennbert and C. Raudvere, 135–144. Lund: Nordic Academic Press.

Wikström af Edholm, K. 2020. *Människoofer i myt och minne. En studie av oferpraktiker i fornnordisk religion utifrån källtexter och arkeologiskt material.* Åbo: Åbo University.

Williams, H. 2008. *Death and Memory in Early Medieval Britain.* Cambridge: Cambridge University Press.

Wulff-Andersen, S. 1960. Lejre, skibsætninger, Grydehøj. In *Aarbøger for Nordisk Oldkyndighed and Historie, 1993*, 7–137. Copenhagen: Det Kongelige Danske Oldskriftselskab.

Zachrisson, T. 2014. De heliga platsernas arkeologi. Materiell kultur och miljöer i järnålderns Mellansverige. In *Den heliga platsen. Handlingar från symposiet Den heliga platsen, Härnösand 15–18 september 2011*, edited by E. Nyman, J. Magnusson and E. Strzelecka, 87–125. Sundsvall: Mittuniversitetet.

Regulated deviancy – ritual executions at Viking Age Tissø as indications of a complex judicial culture

Mads D. Jessen and Jesper Olsen

Abstract

The past 15 years have witnessed an increased effort to study and understand the deviant burials of the Viking Age. The main objective has been to identify and describe instances of burials with irregular arrangement, content or pathologies and group these as deviant burials in one form or the other. The current article will attempt a differentiation of the concept of deviant burials on the basis of scrutinising the dating of the two decapitated individuals at Kalmergården, Tissø, as well as considering a possible connection between the two and the sovereigns of the time and their involvement with inter-regional power struggles and legislative ambition, including capital punishment. Furthermore, we argue that the deviancy detected in Viking Age burials, and especially so for the later period, is best understood not as an arbitrary category, but rather as forming part of a well-regulated regime adhering to a legal machinery that makes use of specific means of punishment and public display.

Keywords: decapitation, Viking Age Tissø, Cnut the Great, reservoir effect, ^{14}C, δ^{15}N, δ^{13}C

Stattu fyrir mer ok hogg mik i hofud mikit saar þviat eigi samir at hogga hofdingia sem þiofa.[1]

(*Orkneyinga Saga* – the beheading of Magnus Jarl)

Introduction

Burials come in many shapes and forms. The more peculiar and bizarre versions exhibit such a large degree of departure from the normative burial practice that they have often been designated as 'deviant burials' (Geake 1992; Aspöck 2010; Murphy 2008; Reynolds 2009; 2013). The numbers and characteristics of Viking Age deviant burials have in particular been debated in the last 15 years (Thäte 2007; Gardeła 2013; 2017, 177–195; see also Toplak 2015). A general conclusion has been that their rather irregular appearance and diverse ritual practices render a single explanation for their occurrence impossible, such that an intrinsic characterisation of the spectrum of non-normative graves would be a 'diversity in deviance' (Gardeła 2013, 110). There is, however, a clear consensus regarding the punitive or deterring character of the majority of

the ritual practices pertaining to these graves (if not all) demanding a mixture of legal and superstitious influences to be clarified. Central to the current paper are the two burials found at Kalmergården in the southern part of the Tissø settlement (see Plate 40) and near the Halleby Stream on Sealand; these have been included in the category of Viking Age deviant burials. The two burials are of particular interest in that they are the latest of the so-called Viking Age deviant burials and dated to a time period which encompasses a redefinition of the status of the king and his legal obligations and opportunities, and also a period in which consolidation of the Christian church takes place. These points are important to include in the debate in order to assess the societal, ideological and the geopolitical conditions for the deviant burials of the Viking Age.

The decapitated

The initial burial, the west grave (see Figures 11.1 and 11.2), was dug into a shallow, natural depression about 45 m north of the old crossing of the Halleby Stream (Poulsen 1980;

Figure 11.1. Excavation from the south. The two men were both placed in simple north–south oriented and shallow graves and had their decapitated heads placed between their legs. Note the depression in the middle stemming from the large stone.

Bennike & Christoffersen 1981). The bottom of the grave was level and rested on the sterile, clayey subsoil. The interred was placed in supine position, on his back with straight legs – the right might have been slightly bent – and the arms rested along the body. Between the legs, the decapitated skull could be found with the face towards the pelvis. Consequently, the placing of the person seems quite orderly and the grave must have been backfilled just after the decapitation. Soon after, a large stone was erected on top of the grave. There can hardly be any doubt that the stone and the content underneath it was known to the wider community when the second burial took place (see below). The skeleton in the west grave had male attributes, is estimated to be between 35–50 years of age at the time of death and approximately 171 cm in height. He had only moderate tooth-wear, was in general good health with almost no osteoarthritis and had an unusually large skull of approximately 1,700 cm^3. He did, however, have enamel hypoplasia, indicating that at a young age he had suffered from malnutrition or some kind of severe illness. He had a distinct underhung jaw which would have made him very recognisable (Lynnerup & Skaarup 2007). The cut to his neck hit right on his second cervical vertebra, and just glanced the lower part of his jawbone. It cut the head clean off.

The second grave, the east grave, clearly had a more unconcerned character to it. The grave pit itself slanted toward the large stone, and the body was almost entirely placed in a natural depression, as a result of which only the upper part of the corpse rested in clayey subsoil. As if almost

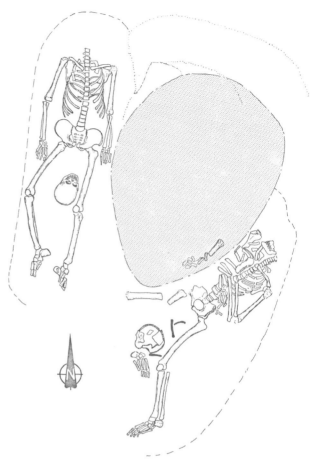

Figure 11.2. Plan of excavation. The large stone (grey shadow) seems to have been placed next to the west grave and would have been clearly visible for the travellers on the nearby north–south road crossing the Halleby Stream right next to the graves.

thrown into the pit, the body lay on its side with the arms flung across the breast and the legs, especially the right leg, bent towards the torso. The head was severely damaged by the decapitation, and the cranium rested by the knees while the jaw, which had been separated by the killing blow, was placed by the neck – presumably as a result of it still being attached to the facial skin (Bennike 1979). Seemingly, the grave-pit was dug close to the large stone, almost under it, and appears very narrow, with hardly any space to contain the body. Placed on the side, the skeleton appears as having been dropped into the pit, indicating a casual and hasty handling of the decapitation as well as the interment. The skeleton has been determined as a male that at the time of death was between 21–35 years old, and approximately 173 cm in height. All teeth were present, but the inside of the upper incisors had visible flat wear, which could indicate them being used for a special purpose and as a 'tool'. The bones appeared normal except for a fusion of the right hip bone and the sacrum resulting in a deterioration of the entire hip and femur and a completely stiff right leg. The leg would have pointed outwards in an almost 90-degree angle. Consequently, the person was severely impaired and would have had an acute limp if he could even walk at all. The top of the skull was cut off from behind in a line from the topmost vertebra and out basically in the middle of the nose (Bennike & Christoffersen 1981, 11). The blow would have been instantly fatal, but the execution was either less professional than the west grave, or else the victim pulled his chin back at the last second. As a consequence, the jaw was left hanging by the skin of the chin, and would presumably have been a rather macabre sight to behold.

During the examination of the skeletal remains it was confirmed that both individuals were beheaded, and as both cut surfaces had very sharp edges, the decapitations must have been carried out with a very sharp tool. In either case, the decapitation was pre-mortem and, as no other trauma was detected, most likely the cause of death. Furthermore, both cuts were single blows and effective, suggesting orchestrated and controlled beheadings (*ibid.*).

Another peculiar feature is a dog skeleton found beneath the individual interred in the east grave. Whether the undisturbed dog skeleton formed part of the grave is not clearly expressed in the excavation report. However, dogs accompanying the deceased are certainly not an uncommon feature of Viking Age burials (Gräslund 2006), and at times have a conspicuous expression such as the halved dog from Grave A505 at the graveyard at Trekroner-Grydehøj, Denmark (Ulriksen 2011, 173ff.), or the dissected dog in the ship burial K/IV grave III at Kaupang, Norway (Stylegar 2007, 96). The placing of a dog underneath a deceased individual is unique to this grave, but could signify the demeaning status of the grave, as the interred would have occupied a secondary position relative to the dog. That the dog's corpse stemmed from an earlier event unrelated to the burials is also a possibility. Such a scenario would not inform us of the (lack of) ritual arrangement of the east grave, but would certainly underline the degrading and deterring character of the location itself; the natural pit where the dog lies is now used for burying the decapitated.

The large stone itself was also examined, but showed no sign of preparation or other recognisable features. It measured roughly 70 × 70 × 150 cm, had an egg-like shape and was of a recognisable greyish granite. As the stone at some point clearly had been dug deeper into the soil, which was a very usual means of clearing away large, troublesome stones in the fields during the Middle Ages and after, it could easily have had a more distinctive posture atop the graves at the time of their establishment. Importantly, as part of the modern restructuring, the course of the southern road on the other side of the Halleby Stream involved the removal of another large boulder. This one was of a reddish granite and with a more edged contour, placed approximately with a similar distance to the stream as its northern counterpart (Poulsen 1980). Seemingly, the twin stones marked the

bridge or perhaps even an older crossing or ford (Jørgensen & Poulsen 1979), and would also have made a tangible denotation of the crossing from the Løve parish to the Ars parish – the Halleby Stream forming the actual border between the two parishes. Whether the dead men were Christian is, of course, unclear, but at the time of their execution it is quite probable that a large proportion of the populace followed a Christian ideology and a non-consecrated burial would have been a complete repudiation of the dead person's redemption. 'Non-consecrated' in this case means a non-delineated cemetery that would not have been inside the area that was marked out as consecrated. Precisely what type of delineation this would entail is uncertain (Nilsson 1989, 71), but some sort of physical demarcation seems to be needed, as burial in consecrated soil figures prominently in the Christian concept of resurrection and has historical roots reaching back into the earliest Christian rituals (Dyggve 1952, 150f.; Andrén 2000). For a Christian, being buried in unholy ground was (and still is) virtually unthinkable and great measures were often taken to fulfil these ideological requirements (Madsen 1991; Brendalsmo 2000). As far as the excavation report can inform us the burials were indeed unmarked and thus unconsecrated.

Dating the dead – back and forth

The position of the two decapitated men – just south of the renowned Tissø central place – obviously made the excavators eager to determine the date of the interment of the men. Consequently, the skeletons were ^{14}C dated the following year, which placed them in the transition from the late Viking Age to the early Middle Ages (see Figure 11.3).[2] This relatively early date came as a big surprise to the excavators and the entire research team, not least because such a date would coincide with the termination of the very large central place at Tissø.

However, due to a better understanding of the problems related to 'older' [14]C dates where knowledge about the often severe misdating a reservoir effect can cause was very limited, the surprising result was several decades later, questioned by the local Kalundborg Museum (now part of Museum of Western Zealand). At the time, a large research project focused on investigating the basic diet of the Danish Stone Age population (especially during the Mesolithic/Neolithic transition) was hosted by Kalundborg Museum and as a side-project the reservoir effect in freshwater fish was investigated. Here, local fresh fish from Lake Tissø were shown to have a ^{14}C date of more than 650 years, because they were 'contaminated' with old carbon washed out from the large peatlands of the Åmosen or local springs (Pedersen *et al.* 2006). The hypothesis therefore was that if locals would have followed a diet depending on fish from Lake Tissø, then a severe reservoir effect would be activated and make the ^{14}C of such individuals appear too old. Such

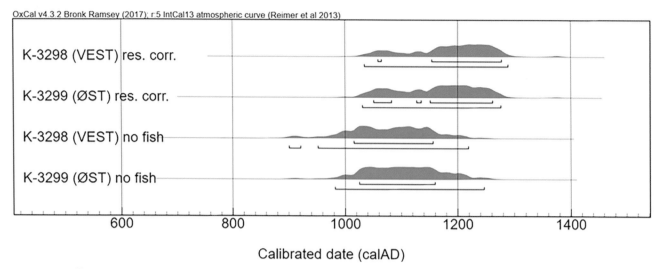

OxCal v4 3 2 Bronk Ramsey (2017); r:5 IntCal13 atmospheric curve (Reimer et al 2013)

Calibrated date (calAD)

Figure 11.3. ^{14}C. The scientific discussion of the two men has been influenced by the ongoing debate concerning the reservoir effect correction of ^{14}C datings. If corrected for the reservoir effect they most likely would have been interred in the High Middle Ages, but the most recent research warrants a non-corrected dating, placing the decapitations in the Late Viking Age.

a diet can be estimated by the $\delta^{13}C$ and $\delta^{15}N$ content of the skeleton and the two interred individuals had an isotopic composition pointing towards a trophic level that might indicate intake of freshwater fish (east grave $\delta^{13}C$ -21.0; $\delta^{15}N$ 10.4), and for the individual in the west grave also marine fish (west grave $\delta^{13}C$ -19.4; $\delta^{15}N$ 12.1), but less than 10% (see Pedersen *et al.* 2006). As a consequence, the two men were regarded as misdated and had to be corrected for reservoir effect. This re-dating deemed them Medieval (*ibid.*, note 6) and the two men were no longer thought to be part of the late Viking Age activities pertaining to the activities of Kalmergården and the larger Tissø settlement.

Nevertheless, the more recent understanding of the impact of diet on ^{14}C-dating has revealed that the data gained from the Mesolithic/Neolithic transition cannot be transferred directly to the dietary situation in the Late Viking Age. In fact, the dietary influence on especially the $\delta^{15}N$ content in the measured samples changes during the Iron Age and more so on the transition from the Viking to the Middle Ages, the reason being an increased manuring of crops during this time period which will lead to enhanced values of $\delta^{15}N$ when compared to human samples from previous periods (*cf.*, Bogaard *et al.* 2013). This interpretation is based on the evidence of intensified manuring that has been found in the field systems and in isotope values of carbonised grain from this period (Kanstrup *et al.* 2014; Nielsen & Dalsgaard 2017; Larsson *et al.* 2019). Accordingly, the elevated $\delta^{15}N$ values of the two decapitated individuals (relative to the Neolithic populace) are probably best explained as a result of the intensive manuring practices indicated by high phosphate levels in the arable soils (*e.g.*, Christensen 1997; Dalsgaard *et al.* 2000; Nielsen *et al.* 2018). Similar explanations can be applied for the $\delta^{13}C$, where a general tendency to incorporate marine foodstuffs into the

diet surfaces in the early Middle Ages of South Scandinavia (*i.e.*, around AD 1100). A prominent reason for this shift is to be found in the dietary restriction an early Christian focus on fasting entailed, whereby fish, and marine species such as cod and herring in particular, were favoured at the expense of meat (Sanmark 2004, 236ff.; Jørkov 2007). In addition, the general change from freshwater to marine diet noted for this period will also entail a less negative influence on the $\delta^{13}C$ (Phillipsen 2013, 9), as a result of which the reservoir effect will statistically be less of a problem the younger the date that is being evaluated (see Plate 41).

Consequently, the idea behind the re-dating of the two men based on the Mesolithic/Neolithic situation is problematic, and the younger dating of the men on the basis of a reservoir-effect correction cannot any longer be upheld. Therefore, the original dating should be regarded as the more accurate. To summarise: the two men were indeed decapitated and interred in the middle of the 11th century, contemporaneously with a significant decline in the activities on the western bank of Lake Tissø.

The social other

Obviously, the placing of two decapitated men just where travellers traverse the stream and the parishes of Løve and Ars meet cannot be a mere coincidence. Just a few hundred metres to the south, at the small hilltop at Bakkendrup, we find a more regular cemetery of 18+ richly furnished graves, which must be seen in conjunction with the Tissø settlement (Albrethsen 2002; 2003). Whether the Bakkendrup cemetery was known to the local community at the time of the executions – it is dated to the latter half of the 9th century – can of course be debated, but it is nonetheless clear that the two men were interred in a location that is displaced in relation to the former burial tradition of the area, and certainly in a spot not usually featured as burial ground. In addition, the exact spot was clearly, almost excessively, demarcated by the large stone, and even matched on the opposing river valley by the similarly placed large stone. Evidently, the locational identification of the decapitated men seemed to have been an aspect that the employer of the executioner wished to accentuate. The men received special treatment not only in punishment and death, but equally in the handling of their corpses and their interment. It should be stressed that the practice of decapitation is not completely absent from the Viking Age record, but has certainly not been a regular enterprise either (Gardeła 2013; see also Jensen, this volume). However, an important characteristic of the earlier Viking Age graves excavated in Scandinavia that contains decapitated persons is that none of these were solitary graves. On the contrary, they all formed part of what must have been regularly used burial grounds with recurring burials of local individuals, and the dead were also accompanied by, often precious, grave goods – such as grave T from Bogøvej (Grøn *et al.* 1994, 17–19) and grave Bj. 959 from Birka (Arbman 1940/43, 384) – or that the decapitated in themselves could be regarded as a sort of potential grave-good in the form of executed slaves accompanying the dead – such as Lejre, grave 55 (Andersen 1960, 26–28; 1995) and Stengade II, chamber grave F (Skaarup 1976, 56–59). In neither of these instances can the positioning of the grave be regarded as different from the other graves comprising the cemeteries of which they form part. In other words, it must be expected that even if the decapitation had ritualistic and possibly legal causes the persons exposed to this unusual treatment were in some way or another still regarded as part of the local community even in their after-life. This post-mortem inclusion of the decapitated stands in stark contrast to the estrangement the men at the bank of the Halleby Stream were exposed to. It is very clear that the decapitation became a sort of spectacle where the need to underline a specific kind of (royal?) authority included the act itself – swinging the axe – and not least the afterlife of dead bodies as part of the process. The situation at Halleby Stream in many ways anticipate later concepts of execution as it has been described by Randall McGowen:

> [T]he punishment of the offender's body had as much to do with a language of community as it did with the mechanics of pain. What has been called the spectacle of suffering turns out on examination to be a spectacle whose meanings stretched beyond the simple infliction of pain. These meanings arose from a series of well-developed analogies to the body and helped to shape the ritual of justice. The execution was a the-atre where belief was made visible … (McGowen 1987, 654)

In this respect, the site of execution became a materialisation of authority, and a physical marker of social justice

prevailing – a characteristic that has been well attested in contemporary English contexts (Williams 2006, 90; Reynolds 2009, 250), where these sites played centre stage in the formation of a deterring legal culture (Reynolds 2013). The ending of a (supposed) criminal's life was thus not necessarily the primary object of concern, but just as much employed in a ceremony that visibly manifested a complex legal machinery being able to exercise its judgments. Another important feature is the repetitive act the two men's burial represent; even if we cannot determine if their decapitation were separated by days, years or even decades their graves are not contemporary, therefore a knowing duplication of the act of decapitation must have occurred. Thus, the executions by Lake Tissø must represent a judicial, if not ritual, event where an authority needed to make an example of their own monopoly of violence as well as to bring into effect this monopoly exactly here, in the former realm of the Tissø magnate.

The act of decapitation

Before considering the social implications of choosing the western shore of Lake Tissø as the place of execution,[3] the act of cutting off a head in public needs to be scrutinised first. Primarily, the act of chopping a human head of is, quite literally, a bloody mess. The possible ritual spectacle of a decapitation would be emotionally charged, and would therefore not be taken lightly, and the effect the executions could have had on the viewers would have been significant. Additionally, this method of punishment could very well contain an echo of pagan superstition and fascination for the head, both as a decorative motif and as a mythological part of the body, and tap into rich symbolic meanings spanning back centuries (Armit 2012, 80–83; Neiß 2013; Gardeła 2017, 116–117). Another central part of the punishment would also have been related to the social degradation that a decapitation would entail. As the quotation in the beginning of the article so vividly illustrates, decapitation was – during the early Middle Ages – obviously regarded as an undignified way of ending your life. Magnus Jarl linked decapitation unequivocally with the lower stratum of social life and in particular the legal means by which the authorities handled thieves and other perpetrators. At this point in time we do not have any written law code for the Danish areas. We do, however, witness a very active and prosperous monarch, King Knud (Cnut) I the Great who ruled England, Denmark and Norway, which in effect made his territorial reign into that of a North Sea empire. For that reason, we also register a marked overlap and interrelation between England and Denmark in the material record, for example in the minting of coins and the persons responsible for it (Jonsson 1994; Bolton 2009, 63; Ruiter & Ashby 2018, 173ff.), and a general comparability between the mentioned areas. Consequently, would it not be a natural process if the king's endeavours followed the same pattern and his judicial ideas and regal proclamations in England affected the behavioural adjustment of the time in the Danish areas? As had almost become a regal ritual during the Anglo-Saxon period, newly crowned kings also made legal proclamation relevant for the territories under their administration. Hence, King Cnut made a proclamation in 1020, where also the use of decapitation as capital punishment is outlined, but seemingly only in specific cases such as in the cases of repeated thievery, disobedient slaves and treason against commander, lord or king (Reynolds 2009, 259–261). Cnut the Great reigned 1016–1035 CE – and was crowned in Denmark in 1019 presumably (Lawson 1993, 89–91) – which is virtually at the same time as the decapitations at Tissø took place. Of importance here is his continuous struggle with the East Danish aristocracy which in many instances formed the richest parts of the Danish realm – especially the region of Scania (Bolton 2009, 203ff.). The Tissø rulers would have belonged to the eastern group of the Danish aristocracy and the relation with other aristocratic sites of eastern Denmark of similar size or layout (such as Lejre and Strøby Toftegaard on Zeeland and Järrestad in Scania) seems inevitable (Söderberg 2005; Jørgensen 2009; 2010; Christensen 2015). That the eastern parts of the realm were the more seditious could very well rest in the dynastic background of Cnut I belonging to the Jelling lineage, which most likely stood in political opposition to the aristocratic centres of eastern Denmark (Jessen in press). Perhaps the need to introduce an English machinery of judicial violence in Denmark piggybacks on the power struggle between ruler and the rest of the upper strata of the east Danish society.

A Viking Age execution cemetery

As mentioned, Ruiter and Ashby (2018, 177) draw attention to an Anglo-Scandinavian hybridisation taking place during the reign of Cnut I, and if a transfer of the framework of judicial violence formed part of this hybridisation, we could perhaps expect a change in the actual appearance of judicial violence as well. With regards to the burials at Tissø, there are a few conspicuous features which seem to set them apart from the other Viking Age deviant burials. Noteworthy is the already mentioned lack of affiliation with more ordinary burials. On the contrary, the two men are placed in a liminal zone in a wetland area, close to a crossing and right at the border between two parishes. This closeness to a main road and the legislative borders seems most significant and follows a recurring locational logic also found in connection with other significant legislative sites such as thing sites (Semple & Sanmark 2013; Iversen 2013), large seasonal markets (Jørgensen *et al.* 2011; Jørgensen 2014) and even parish churches (Wienberg 1993, 101ff.; Brink 2004, 172f.) – where visibility and public access are important for the activities taking place there to have a communal

effect and imprint. The effective and decisive decapitations themselves give, despite the inappropriate placement of the beheading for the east grave, evidence of a skilled and well-equipped executioner and, in combination with the uniform and rudimentary character of the interment, point towards a regime of legal punishment very similar to the early Anglo-Saxon, Christian capital executions (Reynolds 2009, 44–45, 52–60; see also Riisøy 2014 for an account of the Norwegian situation during the early Middle Ages). In this instance the decapitated individuals, even if there are only two, could be seen as comprising a small execution cemetery, and thus far the only one from the Scandinavian Viking Age (contrary to Ruiter & Ashby 2018, 170). For these reasons, we suggest that the notion of Viking Age deviant burials should not be understood as a static and completely heterogeneous group of burials, but a very dynamic concept closely connected to the contemporaneous legal and ritual regime. To this effect, a sort of breakpoint might be recognised with the executions by the Halleby Stream, in which a much more regulated form of deviant burials surfaces and possibly also a regulation rooted in a royal top-down legislative decree and implementation, that might be based on the hybridisation taking place across the North Sea during the reign of Cnut I.

Conclusion

In the article we have attempted to differentiate the Scandinavian Viking Age deviant burials, with particular focus on the latest of these burials, including a confirmation of the dating of the decapitated men from Kalmergården. We believe these burials by the Halleby Stream might be viewed as forming part of a transition to a more close-knit and regulated judicial system (in unison with the establishment of the administrative system of the parishes), where we see the administration of the monopoly of violence and definition of capital punishment being placed at the sovereign level and not left with the local aristocracy. Beforehand, there seemingly was no need to display the position as a legal authority in the same insistent manner, but when a 'new administration' under the Jelling dynasty develops, underlining the legal position of this new authority, it perhaps becomes a prerogative and a priority to do this. Of interest is the subtle closeness of the execution site to a (former) aristocratic residence, yet held noticeably at arm's length from the more active areas in and around the Fugledegård residence. A very similar geopolitical pattern has been shown for the Anglo-Saxon area by Andrew Reynolds, and is believed to demonstrate a shift towards a supra-local system of governance that relies on permanent markers of authority in the landscape (such as large stones) in order to amend the challenges an increase in social distance between sovereign and populace – as well as larger areas of administration – require (Reynolds 2013, 703–707). In that sense, the 'afterlife' of the headless men was just as important as was the spectacle of chopping the head of the convicted, and their bodies were enrolled in a tangible, necropolitical display of power, where the sovereign could demonstrate his political and social power over who should be killed and who not (Mbembe 2003: see also Fredengren & Löfqvist 2019). In death as in afterlife, they were regarded as outcasts and interred in an unconsecrated place of liminality that was neither land nor water, neither one parish nor the other, thus forming part of a social exclusion that was meant to deter the populace from committing similar crimes, but a type of death that could also have helped underline the judicial reach of a far-flung sovereign.

Acknowledgements

We thank the editors and an anonymous reviewer for helpful comments and suggestions on earlier versions of this paper. This study was funded by the Independent Research Fund Denmark grant DFF - 7013-00078, Resilience and breakpoints – exploring linkages between societal, agricultural and climatic changes in Iron Age Denmark.

Notes

1 Stand before me and strike me with a large wound in the head, for it is not fitting to behead rulers like thieves.
2 West grave; K-3298, 970±70 BP, calibrated (2σ) 960–1220 AD. East grave; K-3299, 940±70 BP, calibrated (2σ) 990–1230 AD. Using Oxcal ver. 4.4. and curve IntCal 20.
3 We here infer that the place of burial also was the place of execution, which was also the custom in later periods. Especially the east grave give the impression that the rather mutilated body of the man had not travel far after the decapitation.

References

Albrethsen, S.E. 2002. Hvad landevejen gemte – en gravplads fra vikingetid ved Bakkendrup, Sjælland. In *Drik - og du vil leve skønt, festskrift til Ulla Lund Hansen på 60-årsdagen 18. august 2002*, edited by J. Pind, 227–238. Publications from the National Museum vol. 7. Odense: University Press of Southern Denmark.

Albrethsen, S.E. 2003. Vikingetidsgravpladsen ved Bakkendrup. In *Tissø og Åmoserne - kulturhistorie og natur. Fra Holbæk Amt*, edited by L. Pedersen, 76–79. *Årbog for kulturhistorien i Holbæk Amt 2003*.

Andersen, H. 1960. Hovedstaden i Riget. *Nationalmuseet Arbejdsmark* 1960: 13–35.

Andersen, S.W. 1995. Lejre – skibsætninger, vikingegrave, Grydehøj. *Aarbøger for Nordisk Oldkyndighed og Historie* 1993: 7–142.

Andrén, A. 2000. Ad sanctos – de dödas plats under medeltiden. *Hikuin* 27: 6–26.

Arbman, H. 1940/43. *Birka. Untersuchungen und Studien. Die Gräber. Textband*. Stockholm: Kungl. Vitterhets Historie och Antikvitets Akademien.

Armit, I. 2012. *Headhunting and the Body in Iron Age Europe*. Cambridge: Cambridge University Press.

Aspöck, E. 2010. What Actually Is a 'Deviant Burial'? Comparing German Language and Anglophone Research on 'Deviant Burials'. In *Deviant Burial in the Archaeological Record*, edited by E.M. Murphy, 17–34. (Studies in Funerary Archaeology 2). Oxford: Oxbow Books.

Bennike, P. 1979. *Anthropological Report AS 52/79*. Anthropological Laboratorium, University of Copenhagen.

Bennike, P. and Christoffersen, J. 1981. Et hoved kortere. *Skalk* 1981(3): 10–13.

Bogaard, A., Fraser, R., Heaton, T.H.E., Wallace, M., Vaiglova, P., Charles, M., Jones, G., Evershed, R.P., Styring, A.K., Andersen, N.H., Arbogast, R.-M., Bartosiewicz, L., Gardeisen, A., Kanstrup, M., Maier, U., Marinova, E., Ninov, L., Schäefer, M. & Stephan, E. 2013. Crop manuring and intensive land management by Europe's first farmers. *Proceedings of the National Academy of Sciences* 110(31): 12589–12594.

Bolton, T. 2009. *The Empire of Cnut the Great*. Leiden: Brill.

Brendalsmo, A.J. 2000. De dødes landskap. Måtte man begraves ved sognekirken i middelalderen? *Hikuin* 27: 27–42.

Brink, S. 2004. New perspectives on the Christianization of Scandinavia and the organization of the Early Church. In *Scandinavia and Europe 800–1350: Contact, Conflict, and Coexistence*, edited by J. Adams and K. Holman, 163–175. Turnhout: Brepols.

Christensen, P.M. 1997. Agerbrug i vikingetiden – et studie af fosfor i jorden. *Geologisk Nyt* 4: 12–15.

Christensen, T. 2015. *Lejre bag myten. De arkæologiske udgravninger*. Højbjerg: Jysk Arkæologisk Selskab.

Dalsgaard, K., Karlsen, A.D. & Larsen, L. 2000. Bonden og agerjorden. In *Mellem hav og hede. Landskab og bebyggelse i Ulfbord herred indtil 1700*, edited by K. Dalsgaard, P. Eriksen, J.V. Jensen and J.R. Rømer, J87–103. Aarhus: Aarhus University Press.

Dyggve, E. 1952. The origin of the urban churchyard. *Classica el mediaevalia. Revue danoise de philologie et d'histoire* 13: 147–158.

Fischer, A., Olsen, J., Richards, M., Heinemeier, J., Sveinbjörnsdóttir, Á.E. & Bennike P. 2007. Coast–inland mobility and diet in the Danish Mesolithic and Neolithic: evidence from stable isotope values of humans and dogs. *Journal of Archaeological Science* 34: 2125–2150.

Fredengren, C. & Löfqvist, C. 2019. Finitude: Human and animal sacrifice in a Norse setting. In *Myth, Materiality, and Lived Religion in Merovingian and Viking Scandinavia*, edited by K. Wikström af Edholm, P.J. Rova, A. Nordberg, O. Sundqvist and T. Zachrisson, 225–262. Stockholm: Stockholm University Press.

Gardeła, L. 2013. The dangerous dead? Rethinking Viking-Age deviant burials. In *Conversions. Looking for Ideological Change in the Early Middle Ages*, edited by L. Słupecki and R. Simek, 99–136. Vienna: Fassbaender.

Gardeła, L. 2017. *Bad Death in the Early Middle Ages. Atypical Burials from Poland in a Comparative Perspective*. Collectio Archaeologica Ressoviensis Tomus XXXVI. Rzeszow: Instytut Archeologii Uniwersytetu Rzeszowskiego.

Geake, H. 1992. Burial practice in seventh- and eighth-century England. In *The Age of Sutton Hoo. The Seventh Century in North-western Europe*, edited by M. Carver, 83–94. Woodbridge: Boydell.

Gräslund, A.-S. 2006. Dogs in graves – a question of symbolism? In *Old Norse Religions in Long Term Perspectives: Origins, Changes, and Interactions*, edited by A. Andrén, K. Jennbert and C. Raudvere, 167–176. Lund: Nordic Academic Press.

Grøn, O., Krag, A.H. & Bennike, P. (eds) 1994. *Vikingetidsgravpladser på Langeland*. Rudkøbing: Langelands Museum.

Iversen, F. 2013. Concilio et Pagus – revisiting the early Germanic thing system of Northern Europe. *Journal of the North Atlantic* Special Volume 5: 5–17.

Jessen, M.D. in press. Between worship and representation in the Viking Age – the early Christian buildings in Jelling and South Scandinavia. In *Small Churches and Religious Landscapes in the Norse North Atlantic and Northern Europe c. 900–1300*, edited by J. Arneborg, S.V. Arge and O. Vésteinsson. Brepols: The North Atlantic World.

Jonsson, K. 1994. The coinage of Cnut. In *The Reign of Cnut. King of England, Denmark and Norway*, edited by A. Rumble, 193–230. London: Leicester University Press.

Jørgensen, A.N., Jørgensen, L. & Thomsen, L.G. 2011. Assembly sites for cult, markets, jurisdiction and social relations. Historic-ethnological analogy between North Scandinavian church towns, Old Norse assembly sites and pit house sites of the late Iron Age and Viking Period. *Archäologie in Scleswig Sachsensymposium Haderslev* 2010: 95–112.

Jørgensen, L. 2009. Pre-Christian cult at aristocratic residences and settlement complexes in southern Scandinavia in the 3rd–10th centuries AD. In *Glaube, Kult und Herrschaft. Phänomene des Religiösen im 1. Jahrtausend n. Chr. in Mittel- und Nordeuropa*, edited by U. von Freeden, H. Friesinger and E. Wamers, 329–354. Kolloquien zur Vor- und Frühgeschichte Band 12. Frankfurt: Habelt.

Jørgensen, L. 2010. Gudme and Tissø. Two magnate's complexes in Denmark from the 3rd to 11th cent. AD. In *Trade and Communication Networks of the First Millennium AD in the northern part of Central Europe: Central Places, Beach Markets, Landing Places and Trading Centres*, edited by B. Ludowici, H. Jöns, S. Kleingärtner, J. Scheschkewitz and M. Hardt, 273–286. Neue Studien zur Sachsenforschung Band 1. Hannover: Niedersächsisches Landesmuseum.

Jørgensen, L. 2014. Norse religion and ritual sites in Scandinavia in the 6th–11th century. In *Die Wikinger und das Fränkische Reich. Identitäten zwischen Konfrontation und Annäherung. Unter Mitarb. von Nicola Karthaus*, edited by K.P. Hofmann, H. Kamp and M. Wemhoff, 239–264. München: Wilhelm Fink Verlag.

Jørgensen, M.S. & Poulsen, P. 1979. Arkæologiske udgravninger omkring en vejforlægning ved Halleby Å. *Antikvariske Studier* 3: 224–225.

Jørkov, M.L.S. 2007. *Drinking with the Rich and Dining with the Poor in Roman Iron Age Denmark: A Dietary and Methodological Study Based on Stable Isotope Analysis* (unpublished Ph.D. thesis, Copenhagen University).

Kanstrup, M. 2008. *Gastronomy – Norm and Variation. Dietary Studies Based on Isotope Analyses of Skeletal Remains from Viking Age Graves at Galgedil on Northern Funen* (unpublished MA dissertation, Aarhus University).

Kanstrup, M., Holst, M.K., Jensen, P.M., Thomsen, I.K. & Christensen, B.T. 2014. Searching for long-term trends in prehistoric manuring practice. δ^{15}N analyses of charred cereal grains from the 4th to the 1st millennium BC. *Journal of Archaeological Science* 51: 115–125.

Larsson, M., Bergman, J. & Lagerås, P. 2019. Manuring practices in the first millennium AD in southern Sweden inferred from isotopic analysis of crop remains. *PLOS One* 14(4): 1–24.

Lawson, M.K. 1993. *Cnut. The Danes in England in the Early Eleventh Century*. London: Longman.

Lucas, G. & McGovern, T. 2007. Bloody slaughter: Ritual decapitation and display at the Viking Settlement of Hofstaðir, Iceland. *European Journal of Archaeology* 10(1): 7–30.

Lynnerup, N. & Skaarup, B. 2007. Den halshuggede fra Bakkendrup: Hvordan så han ud? Årets gang 2007 på Kalundborg Museum, 42–43.

Madsen, P.K. 1991. Han ligger under en blå sten. Om middelalderens gravskik på skrift og i praksis. *Hikuin* 17: 113–134.

Mbembe, A. 2003. Necropolitics. *Public Culture* 15(1): 11–40.

McGowen, R. 1987. The body and punishment in eighteenth-century England. *The Journal of Modern History* 59: 651–679.

Murphy, E.M. (ed.) 2008. *Deviant Burial in the Archaeological Record*. Studies in Funerary Archaeology 2. Oxford: Oxbow Books.

Neiß, M.(2013. Viking Age animal art as a material anchor? A new theory based on a head motif. In *The Head Motif in Past Societies in a Comparative Perspective. (International Interdisciplinary Meetings Motifs Through the Ages*, edited by L. Gardeła and K. Kajkowski, vol. 1, 74–87. Bytów: Muzeum Zachodniokaszubskie.

Nielsen, N.H. & Dalsgaard, K. 2017. Dynamics of Celtic fields – a geoarchaeological investigation of Øster Lem Hede, western Jutland, Denmark. *Geoarchaeology – An International Journal* 32(3): 414–434.

Nielsen, N.H., Philippsen, B., Kanstrup, M. & Olsen, J. 2018. Diet and radiocarbon dating of the Tollund Man: New analyses of an Iron Age bog body from Denmark. *Radiocarbon* 60 (Special Issue 5): 1533–1545.

Nilsson, B. 1989. *De Sepulturis. Gravrätten i Corpus Iuris Canonici och i medeltida nordisk lagstiftning*. Bibliotheca Theologiae Practicae, Kyrkovetenskapliga Studier 44. Stockholm: Amqvist and Wiksell International.

Pedersen, L., Fischer, A., Olsen, J. & Bennike, P. 2006. Vikinger på foryngelseskur. *Årets gang 2006 på Kalundborg Museum*, 84–87.

Phillipsen, B. 2013. The freshwater reservoir effect in radiocarbon dating. *Heritage Science* 1(24): 1–19.

Poulsen, P. 1980. *Excavation Report NMI 2654/79*. Copenhagen: National Museum of Denmark.

Reynolds, A. 2009. *Anglo-Saxon Deviant Burial Customs*. Oxford: Oxford University Press.

Reynolds, A. 2013. Judicial culture and social complexity: A general model from Anglo-Saxon England. *World Archaeology* 45(5): 699–713.

Riisøy, A.I. 2014. Deviant burials: Societal exclusions of dead outlaws in medieval Norway. In *Cultures of Death and Dying in Medieval and Early Modern Europe*, edited by M. Kopiola and A. Lahtinen, 49–81. COLLeGIUM: Studies across Disciplines in the Humanities and Social Sciences 18.

Ruiter, K. & Ashby, S.P. 2018. Different strokes: Judicial violence in Viking-Age England and Scandinavia. *Viking and Medieval Scandinavia* 10: 153–184.

Semple, S. & Sanmark, A. 2013. Assembly in North West Europe: Collective concerns for early societies? *European Journal of Archaeology* 16(3): 518–542.

Sanmark, A. 2004. *Power and Conversion – a Comparative Study of Christianization in Scandinavia.* Opia 34. Uppsala: The University of Uppsala.

Skaarup, J. 1976. Stengade II. En langelandsk gravplads med grave fra romersk jernalder og vikingetid. *Meddelelser fra Langelands Museum*, 56–59.

Stylegar, F.-A. 2007. The Kaupang cemeteries revisited. In *Kaupang in Skiringssal. Kaupang Excavation Project Publication Series* (1), edited by D. Skre, 65–128. Aarhus: Aarhus University Press.

Söderberg, B. 2005. *Aristokratisk rum och gränsöverskridande. Järrestad och sydöatra Skåne mellan region och rike 600–1100.* Stockholm: Riksantikvarämbetet Förlag.

Thäte, E.S. 2007. *Monuments and Minds: Monument Re-use in Scandinavia in the Second Half of the First Millennium AD.* (Acta Archaeologica Lundensia Series in quarto 27). Lund: Wallin & Dalholm.

Toplak, M.S. 2015. Prone burials and modified teeth at the Viking Age cemetery of Kopparsvik: The changing of social identities at the threshold of the Christian Middle Ages. *Analecta Archaeologica Ressoviensia* 10: 77–98.

Ulriksen, J. 2011. Spor af begravelsesritualer i jordfæstegrave i vikingetidens Danmark. *Kuml* 2011: 161–245.

Wienberg, J. 1993. *Den gotiske labyrint. Middelalderen og kirkerne i Danmark.* Lund Studies in Medieval Archaeology 11. Stockholm: Almqvist and Wiksell International.

Williams, H. 2006. *Death and Memory in Early Medieval Britain.* Cambridge: Cambridge University Press.

Human sacrifice in Old Norse skaldic poetry

Klas Wikström af Edholm

Abstract

The motif of human sacrifice in Old Norse religion has been used in the skaldic poetry of the Viking Age. Here, I will discuss the references to human sacrifice in the Old Norse poetry from a perspective of history of religions. I will present some examples in the skaldic poetry of human sacrifice and I will argue that this motif mirrors a conception of the Old Norse god Óðinn as the recipient of such ritual practices in Old Norse religion. To mention the killing of enemies as a sacrifice to Óðinn was obviously quite popular among some skalds in Scandinavia during the Late Iron Age; but this begs the question of how we are to interpret this motif, as the mentioning of the slain warriors as a sacrificial gift has not been unanimously concluded. The motif is generally seen as a metaphor, or an aesthetic attribute when describing battle and the killing of enemies. I intend to critically examine this interpretation and I here propose that additional conclusions of the religious conceptions, related to the battle, can be drawn from the texts. My conclusion is that the killing of enemies is not only spoken of metaphorically as a sacred act according to the conception that the slain will receive an afterlife in the presence of Óðinn, but the killings themselves could be conceived of as a sacrifice.

Keywords: Old Norse religion, Skaldic poetry, human sacrifice, Óðinn, Viking Age

The Old Norse skaldic poetry as a source material

A prerequisite for the present analysis is that the use of some poetic metaphors, *e.g.*, Old Norse (ON) *kenning*, and ON *heiti*, are solidly grounded in a specific culture historical context and mirror that context. This means that we are able to trace religious conceptions and ritual practices from the skald's choice of words in the construction of the kennings. The kennings require the audience to have knowledge of the mythic and ritual references, for the kennings to become meaningful and understandable, and by this to fulfil a function in the poem. The knowledge and the conception of human sacrifices as a living practice is in this context a prerequisite for the poetic references to be understandable and gain a meaning. This hypothesis has been doubted within previous research, but I propose that this interpretation gains

new support from a thorough analysis of the skaldic poetry in relation to the martial context in Old Norse society and the mention of human sacrifices in other source materials (see af Edholm 2020). I find the alternative conclusion, that the kennings are just archaic expressions and 'empty' aesthetic references, a less convincing interpretation of the genre as a whole, even though examples of this may be found in some younger poems (see further below for case studies by Males 2010; 2017).

The skaldic motifs are thus created and shaped according to a wider semantic field where the killing and fighting are parts of the cult of the god Óðinn within the Old Norse warrior culture and *comitatus* system (Enright 1996; Herschend 1998; Landholt 1998; Steuer 1998; Timpe 1998; Nordberg 2003; Speidel 2004; Ljungkvist 2006; Price 2019). Central in this cult is the devotion of the participants, where the warrior himself is dedicated to the god. In life, the devotee participates in the battles from which the god is thriving, he dedicates his enemy to Óðinn before the battle begins and the act of the killing becomes a ritual action itself (Nordberg 2003 with references; *cf.*, Halsall 1989). At death, ideally on the battlefield, the devotee unites with Óðinn in the paradise Valhǫll, awaiting the final battle at Ragnarǫk (Nordberg 2003; Hultgård 2017). Thus, the killing of enemies in battle relates to the conceptions where a warrior takes part in the cult of Óðinn both in life and death.

The definition of *sacrifice*

Before we move on to an analyse of the references to human sacrifice in the skaldic stanzas, I will give a short presentation of the analytical term '*sacrifice*', since it is crucial to the interpretation of the skaldic poetry and for the following analysis. A definition of the term that is widely used in comparative religion is the one offered by Henri Hubert and Marcel Mauss already in 1898: 'établir une communication entre le monde sacré et le monde profane par l'intermédiaire d'une victime, c'est-à-dire d'une chose détruite au cours de la cérémonie' (Hubert & Mauss 1898, 133).[1]

This definition is useful as a starting point, but it needs to be specified to be useful in the current analysis. A similar definition of sacrifice is offered by Maurice Bloch (1992) and by Caroline Humphrey and James Laidlaw (2007, 263–64), where the aspect of the sacrifice as a gift to a divine recipient is further stressed (*cf.*, Hultgård 2001; Pongratz-Leisten 2007, 3–10). Bloch clearly adds the gift as a central aspect of the sacrifice: 'Giving something is the lowest common denominator of rituals which have been called sacrifice. ... the importance of gift-giving in sacrifice need not conflict with the idea of self-identification with the victim' (Bloch 1992, 30). The aspect of the gift is important for the analysis, as it helps us recognise the sacrificial motif in the skaldic poetry, and to separate the references to a sacrifice from the eschatological conception of an afterlife in Valhǫll.[2] From this model I resolve to use the category *sacrifice* as the term for a rite where the killing of a living being is used as a communication with a god/goddess, whereby the victim is given as a gift to the divine recipient. The ritual act is stipulated in tradition.[3]

The gift is in the sacrifice equalised with the one offering it. This means that the victim killed in the sacrifice is a substitute for the one offering it. The ideal sacrificial gift in the ritual context of the Old Norse martial culture is thus the donor, *i.e.*, the warrior himself. The devotion of the warrior to the god Óðinn makes the enemies killed into a substitution of the self; enemies killed could be conceived as a gift to Óðinn in order to communicate and influence their relation to this god without the self being slain.

The killing of enemies as a sacrificial act

The killing of enemies could be conceived as a ritual act. It is spoken of (in metaphors) as a sacrifice, in the Old Norse skaldic poetry. The eschatological conceptions and the dedication of the enemy as an offering to Óðinn have been treated in previous research, by for example Gustav Neckel, in a study from 1913 of the conceptions of Valhǫll, and by Andreas Nordberg in his dissertation from 2003. These scholars present the motif that I will analyse as a ritual killing, described as a sacrifice in the metaphors of the poetry. This is certainly correct, but in my opinion, there are further conclusions to be drawn from the material. Some skaldic stanzas refer to the killing as a sacrifice with usual Old Norse sacrificial terms; other stanzas are more implicit. Neckel has shown how the role of Óðinn in the descriptions of the death at the battlefield varies within the sources. This could be used to identify and separate the references to an eschatological conception of the afterlife in Valhǫll from the conception of a sacrifice. The examples that refer to Óðinn as the receiver of ON *valr* 'the battle-slain' refer to a different semantic content than the texts that speak of Óðinn as the one who chooses (who are to be) the slain or that the company of the god(s) has been increased (Neckel 1913, 57–59). When the killing is mentioned as 'Óðinn received the slain' the metaphor refers to the semantic field of sacrifice in contrast to metaphors referring to Óðinn as the chooser of the slain. The latter refers to a semantic field of eschatological conceptions where the battle slain will unite with Óðinn in Valhǫll, and participate in the last battle at Ragnarǫk. I will use this variation to discuss the motif of human sacrifice within the Old Norse skaldic poetry.

The use of human sacrifice as a motif in skaldic poetry demands the idea of this kind of practice as a historical reality and as a living conception. This does not necessarily mean that this is clearly formulated in the material to be discussed. Previous research has not examined systematically the skaldic poetry as a source material for the practice of human sacrifice in Old Norse religion to the degree this material deserves.

An objection against my interpretation of the material could be that the references to human sacrifice therein are just metaphors and are not to be interpreted literally. The poetic expressions are indeed difficult to interpret by themselves, but as long as the poetic language is rooted in the martial ideology of the *comitatus* system, the expressions might mirror central conceptions within this context. This tells us something significant about how the battle and the strife was given meaning within this culture (Birgisson 2007; Price 2019). The experience and conceptualisation of the battle can differ between different individuals and for the same person in different times and contexts. The interpretation of the killing of enemies in battle as a sacrificial act was certainly not equally present or relevant for all individuals at all times. But my point is that this conceptualisation of the killing as a sacrifice is stipulated by tradition. This culturally stipulated conception is part of a wider semantic field, closely connected to the warrior culture and the *comitatus* system.

Another objection that could be raised against my interpretation of the material is that the battlefield ought to have been fairly chaotic, and thus far from the ordered and predictable performance of a typical sacrificial ritual. But rituals are by their nature never totally predictable, and could be conceived differently by different participants (Staal 1979; Bell 1992; 2005; Humphrey & Laidlaw 1994; 2007; Hüsken 2007; Bronkhorst 2012; af Edholm 2016). The partaking in battle could also be conceptualised as a ritual or a sacrificial act on a general level, before and after the fight, even though the actions during the actual battle are not performed with the intention of being a sacrifice – survival might come first and considerations of sacrifice could come later. Neither are the cognitive processes of the individual performing the rite as crucial for the definition given above as the culturally stipulated interpretation and discourse.

Another point in my argument is that this conception of martial acts as offerings to the gods can be categorised as a sacrifice from the definition given above. The killing of enemies is conceptualised as an act where someone is killing a victim as a gift to a divine recipient, in order to communicate and influence their relation to the receiver. The interpretation of the killing as a sacrificial act is stipulated by tradition (see Price 2019). We can thus discuss our potential use of this material as a primary source for the subsequent discussion of human sacrifice in Old Norse religion.

I will not discuss the whole corpus of skaldic stanzas that could be interpreted as referring to the practice of human sacrifice here, but only some clear examples (see af Edholm 2020 for a more complete account). One such skaldic stanza to be used as an example is composed by Þorleifr jarlskáld Rauðfeldarson in his poem *Hákonardrápa* (stanza 1), a praise poem to the Norwegian ruler Hákon jarl Sigurðarson from the middle of the 10th century. The skald praises the ruler for having sent, or sacrificed, nine nobles to Óðinn (*senda Óðni*). It is true that this expression may just refer to Hákon as the man who has killed nine nobles, rather than sacrificed them, but the expression is clearly meant to be associated to the cult of Óðinn and is positioned in the blurry space between sacrifice and other religious conceptions of the battle and death.[4] Kate Heslop (2012) for example argues for a profane intention of the skald when using this expression. But the jarl, Hákon, is also mentioned as a performer of human sacrifices in other narrative sources.[5] One crucial aspect of the stanza is that the Old Norse word *senda* is a well-established term for 'sacrifice' (*cf.*, Liberman 1978; Neff 1980, 58–59). The expression *senda Óðni* is also closely related to, and is to be seen as a variation of, the equal and even more common *gefa*

Óðni, which is generally agreed upon to express a sacrificial gift to Óðinn. The expression *senda Óðni* is probably also to be seen in relation to Hákon as a worshipper of Óðinn, and as a fighter and ruler by his grace. This is clearly expressed in other sources, both in skaldic stanzas and in narrative prose.[6] So, to make a preliminary conclusion about this stanza in *Hákonardrápa*; in this case the expression of the act of Hákon refers to a killing, by which the king is conceived of as thereby making a sacrificial gift to Óðinn. This killing/ gift-giving is formulated as a way of communicating with the god, and by this Hákon improves or upholds his good relationship with the god. In this way, the formulation *senda Óðni* expresses the content of the definition of the term sacrifice, as defined above.

The expression *senda val Óðni* also occurs in Tindr Hallkellsson's poem, also called *Hákonardrápa*, stanza 11, dedicated to the same Hákon jarl Sigurðarson. The stanza describes that the people in Gullmaren in Bohuslän, Sweden, will have trouble to ever again see those warriors who went away, since Hákon has sent them all to Óðinn. The battle that is spoken of is the famous battle of Hjǫrungavágr (*c.* 985 CE). The same motif reoccurs in stanza 9 of the poem, where Hákon is described as giving or delivering the slain to Óðinn. The interpretation of the stanza is not unanimous, it could be read as *Hroptr of náði val nýjum* 'Hroptr [Óðinn] received new *valr* [slain warriors]' (as Finnur Jónsson (1912–1915) has meant), or as *Hroptr hjaldrskýja of náði val nýjum* 'The Hroptr [Óðinn] of the battle skies [Hákon] *of náði* new slain warriors', as Russell Poole (2012b) has meant with the interpretation of the stanza as an expression that Hákon has managed to kill a lot of enemies. This is of course the most fundamental meaning of the stanza, but it does not rule out that Óðinn is meant to be the receiver of those slain. I would say there is another layer in this expression that Poole has not paid attention to. The key for the interpretation of the stanza lays in the words *of náði*, impf. of ON *ná* 'pass (on to), reach (for/to), receive, achieve'. With the meaning 'pass on to' the expression *Hroptr hjaldrskýja* [Hákon] *of náði val nýjum* would be saying that Hákon delivered/passed on new slain warriors (to Óðinn). By delivering new *valr* to Óðinn, Hákon (himself called the Óðinn of the battle) is giving the god a gift, in order to improve their relation. This could be interpreted as a sacrificial act according to the definition given above.

The connection between Hákon jarl and the killing of enemies as a sacrifice is also expressed by the skald Einarr skálaglam Helgason in the poem *Vellekla* from the end of the 10th century. The poem is believed to have been composed during the reign of Hákon. In stanza 31 Einarr dictates that the fallen *valr* filled the field, as Óðinn was given/dedicated the slain (*hlaut Óðinn val*) by Hákon, and that the jarl was guided and aided by the mighty gods. The expression that Hákon is guided and aided by the gods is a further indication of the killing as a sacrifice. The gods are mentioned as ON *rammaukin* 'strengthened in power', possibly meaning that the god(s)' power and strength is increased by Hákon's actions (killing).[7] Einarr ties in this intricate way the killing of enemies in the battle to the motif of Óðinn as the receiver of the slain and the conception that the god thrives and is strengthened by the killing (Nordberg 2003).

That the slain warriors, at one level of consciousness, have been perceived by the participants of this cult of Óðinn as a sacrifice to the god is clearly expressed by several other skalds and it is a motif that reoccurs in the skaldic poetry, as for example in Glúmr Geirasons *Gráfeldardrápa*, stanza 2. The poem is dedicated to the Norwegian king Haraldr gráfeldr, and is probably composed after the king's death, around 970 CE (Finlay 2012, 245). In this stanza it is the expression *senda sverðbautinn her kindar seggja Gauti* 'to send a sword-beaten army of the descendants of men [warriors] to Gautr [Óðinn]' that is of interest as a reference to human sacrifice. This expression can be compared to the very similar one above (*senda ǫðlinga Óðni*). The sacrificial theme is clear, although it may be argued that the skalds only use a metaphor telling us that Haraldr has killed the men who therefore will go to Óðinn in Valhǫll after the battle, and not giving us the information if the killing in itself was considered to be a ritual action (*cf.*, Finlay 2012). Such a conclusion would be disregarding the double meaning and parallel associations used by the skalds in the stanzas mentioned above, and the wider context of the motif that we also find in the comparative material.

This same symbolism can also be discerned in the expression *þorði rjóða vǫll blóði þjóðum* '[Haraldr] braved to redden the field with the blood of the people/men' in the same poem, stanza 8. The ritual layer in the motif is implicit if read by itself, but may be more obvious if seen together with the information that Haraldr himself is inspired or possessed by Óðinn as said twice in stanza 13:

13.	13.
Þar vas – þrafna byrjar þeim stýrðu goð Beima – sjalfr í sækialfi sigtýr Atals dýra. (Finlay *Skaldic Poetry of the Scandinavian Middle Ages*)	There was – the gods steered this Beimi of the staff of the wind [Haraldr] – Sigtýr [Óðinn] himself in the attack-elf of Atall's animal [Haraldr]. (My translation)[8]

The devotion of Haraldr to the cult of Óðinn cannot be disregarded in these cases. This affects our reading and interpretation of the stanzas, in a way that has not always been considered in previous research. The skaldic motifs are created and shaped according to this wider semantic field where the killing and fighting are part of the cult of the god. The theme of human sacrifice is also found in Guthormr sindri's *Hákonardrápa*, stanza 2. The poem is dedicated to

the Norwegian king Hákon góði and probably composed during the king's reign (de Vries 1964 I, 173; Poole 2012a, 156). The poem refers to religious conceptions in several stanzas. In stanza 2, the poet describes Hákon as ON *vandar valsendir* 'the one who sends/sacrifices the slain of the pole/mast (to Óðinn)'.[9] The expression is built up by the components ON *vǫndr*, in this case to be interpreted as the mast of the ship, which defines the next component ON *valr* 'the battle-slain' to mean 'warriors of the mast [seafarers or Vikings]'. These components define the third one, ON *sendir* 'the one who sends/sacrifices' these seafaring warriors. Hákon is in this way described as the one who sends, or sacrifices, the warriors (who through the battle becomes ON *valr*). This demands the idea of a (divine) receiver. I regard this circumstance to strengthen my conclusion that this kind of expression in the skaldic poetry refers to and requires the idea of human sacrifice. The skaldic poems are a primary source category and not interconnected as such. They express the same motif independently of each other.

An even more evident example of this motif is found in Þorbjǫrn hornklofi's poem *Haraldskvæði*, also known as *Hrafnsmál*, composed for the Norwegian king Haraldr hárfagri *c.* 900 CE (Fulk 2012). The subject speaking in the poem is a raven, which describes how it has followed Haraldr ever since it was born and has been well fed with all the corpses from his many battles. An implicit layer in this, not to be overlooked, is that Óðinn in this case probably is speaking through the raven, which underlines the impression that Haraldr is victorious with the grace of Óðinn, and the conception that the god is thriving in Haraldr's vicinity and by his martial living. In stanza 12 the raven even says that:

12.	12.
Valr lá þar á sandi vitinn inum eineygja Friggjar faðmbyggvi; fǫgnuðum dôð slíkri. (Fulk *Skaldic Poetry of the Scandinavian Middle Ages*)	The battle-slain laid there on the sand given/dedicated (*valr lá ... vitinn*) to the one-eyed one who occupies the bosom of Frigg; we welcomed such deeds. (My translation)[10]

The raven thus refers to an act where Haraldr has dedicated or given the slain enemies, possibly as a (sacrificial) gift, to Óðinn. And the corpses will now become food for the carrion crows. It may be argued that the expression that the raven eats from the corpses may be a standardised formulation for the death of warriors, but I want to suggest that this expresses a post-mortem treatment where the bodies are left to carrion-eaters to feed upon. This could also be interpreted as a metaphor that Óðinn, in the shape of the raven, has taken part of the slain, as a (sacrificial) gift or in order to bring them to Valhǫll (Nordberg 2003, 137–149). Regarding the old age of the poem, it is important evidence of the pre-Christian religious background of the motif discussed. That a human sacrifice, in the strict sense of the word, is expressed within these poems is not explicit, of course, but the poetic language builds upon an equivocation that demands the implicit reference to a conception of humans sacrificed to Óðinn. The implicit references in the poems require the audience to be familiar with human sacrifices as a real or ideal practice. The resemblance of the slain enemies to the sacrificial gifts in the skaldic poetry is thus to be interpreted as a reference to human sacrifices as a living idea and a well-known tradition. To regard this as an indication of a real practice of human sacrifices in the Old Norse religion we need comparison with additional sources, but the ideological background of the motif is clear (*cf.*, af Edholm 2020). The conception of a human sacrifice was well established by the time of the composition of the poems, which makes the skaldic poetry a primary source for the study of human sacrifices in Old Norse religion.

The word ON *tafn* and the motif of human sacrifices

A *lausavísa* by the skald Helgi trausti Óláfsson gives us the clearest example of the idea of the killing of an enemy as a sacrifice to Óðinn. In the stanza he twice mentions the killing as a sacrifice to Óðinn, as he praises his own deed (*cf.*, Düwel 1970, 230; Poole 2012b, 356).

Vask, þars fell til fyllar framm sótti vinr dróttar Ørrabein, enn unnar ítrtungur hǫtt sungu. Ásmóðar gafk Óðni arfa þróttar djarfan; guldum galga valdi Gauts tafn, en ná hrafni. (Finnur Jónsson *Den norsk-islandske skjaldedigtning* I)	I was there, where Ørrabein fell to become food [satisfaction], the friend of the army [warrior] pressed forward and the precious tongues of the warriors [the swords] sung high. I gave/sacrificed (*gefa*) the brave heir of Ásmóðr [Þorgrímr ørrabein], the bold one, to Óðinn; I repayed/gave/sacrificed (*gjalda*) Gautr's [Óðinn's] sacrifice (*tafn*), to the lord of the gallows [Óðinn] and to the raven a corpse. (My translation)[11]

The expressions that have been interpreted also in previous research as references to a sacrifice are Ásmóðar gafk Óðni arfi 'I gave/sacrificed the heir of Ásmóðr to Óðinn' and *guldum galga valdi Gauts tafn* 'I repaid/gave/sacrificed the sacrifice of Óðinn to the lord of the gallows'. The kenning *Gauts tafn* 'Óðinn's sacrifice/prey' is certainly to be interpreted as the slain Þorgrímr. Helgi uses the same motif as in the other cases above, but also puts it in an unmistakable sacrificial context. The slain enemy is mentioned both as Óðinn's sacrificial gift, and as a sacrifice given to Óðinn. We can probably also find a third reference to a sacrifice in the stanza, where Helgi uses the word ON *fylli, fyllr* 'fill (of food)' as an equivalent to ON *tafn* 'sacrifice, prey' when

describing that Þorgrímr fell *til fyllar* 'to become the fill/food (for someone)' (Cleasby & Vigfússon 1874, s.v. *tafn*; Kuhn 1954; de Vries 1977, s.v. *tafn*). In this case it is obviously a word play, where the use of ON *tafn* is meant as both the prey of the raven and the sacrifice of Óðinn, as well as the use of ON *fylli, fyllr* which is meant as both the fill or food for the raven and at the same time the satisfaction for Óðinn. Regarding the poet's skilled use of the language to create double meanings in the expressions, it is also worth being reminded of the possibility that Óðinn could be portrayed here in disguise of the raven. The references to the conception that Óðinn thrives by the killing in battle, to the raven as a scavenger eating the corpses of the slain, to the ravens as an emanation of Óðinn and to Óðinn as the receiver of the sacrifice are interwoven in this stanza.

The killing of Þorgrímr could be interpreted as a sacrifice in a strict sense, done with the intention of being a gift to a divine receiver, or it could be a poetic circumscription of a profane act of violence and of taking revenge. These two intentions do not conflict, a profane restoration of a loss of honour could at the same time be experienced as a religious action, especially if it is preceded by a votive sacrifice.[12] The most important argument to define Helgi's killing as a sacrifice is his own expression and interpretation of it as one.

The ON word *tafn* 'sacrifice' or 'prey' is also used by several other poets, especially in connection with the word ON *valr*, as in ON *valtafn* 'sacrifice/prey of the battle-slain' (Meissner 1921, 202). In these cases, the expression is intentionally dubious as the *valtafn* is said to be offered to the ravens. One example can be found in a *lausavísa* by Gísli Súrsson from the 10th century, stanza 29: *gǫtum vér ... valtafn í mun hrafni* 'we arranged for *valtafn* to be placed in the mouths [beaks] of the raven'. Another is the expression *veitinn valtafn frekum hrafni* 'we will give *valtafn* to ravenous ravens' in a *lausavísa* (20) by Þórmóðr Bersason Kolbrúnarskáld from the middle of the 11th century. One last example is the expression *varð í Veðrarfirði valtafn gefit hrafni* 'in Veðrarfjǫrðr [Waterford] was *valtafn* given/sacrificed to the raven' in *Krákumál*, stanza 16. The anonymous poem *Krákumál* is relatively young, though, dated to the 12th century, even though the poem could still contain older motifs, as the expression is found in a context connected to the cult of Óðinn. This interpretation is strengthened by the use of the word ON *tafn* 'sacrifice' in the poem *Húsdrápa* by Úlfr Uggason, around year 1000 CE. In this example it is the corpse of the god Baldr that is meant by the expression *heilags tafn* 'sacred sacrifice/prey' (Figure 12.1).

The motif of human sacrifices in the skaldic poetry can also be found in a different skaldic context. The newly baptised skald Hallfreðr vandræðaskáld Óttarsson renounces the pagan religion in a *lausavísa* and calls Óðinn *hrafnblóts goði* 'the official of the sacrifice to the raven'. This must be interpreted as an expression that Óðinn is the creator

Figure 12.1. 'Odin's Last Words to Baldr' by W.G. Collingwood. 1908. From, The Elder or Poetic Edda; commonly known as Sæmund's Edda. Edited and translated with introduction and notes by O. Bray. Illustrated by W.G. Collingwood. Image in the public domain.

of strife. If the ravens themselves are not to be interpreted as the receivers of the sacrificial gifts, then Óðinn is also the receiver of the sacrifice offered to the raven, thereby equalising the killing of enemies with a sacrifice to Óðinn.

The expressions of the skalds where the slain is mentioned as a sacrifice to the ravens is a game of words about the conception of the battle and the killing as a sacrificial act, according to the wider semantic field of the Old Norse warrior culture. The poetic metaphors could be a way of constructing something new, to describe something by likening it to what it is not. But they could also be *epitheta significanta* and thereby describing what it really was perceived to be (Wrangel 1912, 128; Clunies Ross *et al.* 2012, lxxxii–lxxxiii). Óðinn could certainly be expected to be present in the battle, and the Old Norse mythology clearly shows the god to be appreciating strife and the killings. When the ravens and other scavengers take part of the slain warriors this could be described as if they are receiving a sacrificial gift, in the Old Norse poetry. I believe this is not only a way of circumscribing the battle with a poetic configuration, it also mirrors a religious conception and experience. When the ravens eat from the fallen bodies they partake of the sacrifice offered to Óðinn, and the god is made present. Within the ritual context, the action (killing of enemies) and the result (the slain) is expressed as a sacrifice to the ravens and to the god at the same time. This parlance mirrors and connects the religious configuration with the religious experience: parallel with the overarching conception that Óðinn partakes in the killing and thrives from it, the god is perceived to be present in the animals that gather among the corpses. Within the analysis we ought to separate these three aspects of the motif in the kennings: one aspect being the overarching configuration that Óðinn

partakes in the killing and the slain, another aspect being the experience of the ravens partaking in the corpses and the third aspect being the poetic conventional parlance with metaphors which may still express and be rooted in ideological and religious conceptions. Together these three aspects form the spectra we must bear in mind when interpreting the Old Norse skaldic poetry.

Conclusion

Within these skaldic stanzas we trace a culturally stipulated interpretation of the killing as a sacrificial act. This interpretation was probably more relevant for some participants of the battle and martial cultural context than for others. The experience of the killing and death on the battlefield could have become meaningful and processed through the conceptualisation of the killing as a sacrifice. For other individuals the poetic expressions were probably only apprehended as poetic circumscriptions and metaphors. Without being necessarily opposing, the depicting of the killing of enemies as a sacrifice in the Old Norse skaldic poetry mediate 1) a convention within the genre; 2) a culturally stipulated interpretation of the act; and probably 3) an individual experience and conceptualisation of the act, relevant for some individuals. The common and recurring patterns in the source material shows us that the idea of human sacrifices was a living conception within the martial cultural context during the Viking Age.

Notes

1 '… establishing a means of communication between the sacred and the profane worlds through the mediation of a victim, that is, of a thing that in the course of ceremony is destroyed' (translation by Halls 1981, see Hubert & Mauss 1981 [1898], 97).

2 The aspect of the gift connects the sacrifice to a wider category of gift-giving (*cf.*, Mauss 1990 [1925]; Pyyhtinen 2014). The criteria of the gift aspect have also been criticised, by for example Richard David Hecht (1976), although I cannot agree with Hecht's arguments.

3 This definition of the analytical tool sacrifice is adapted to the current analysis, although it may not be equally useful in every context. *Cf.* Jensen 1963 [1951], 5–6; Staal 1979; Humphrey & Laidlaw 1994.

4 The number nine could also be of certain significance in this context. Nine seems to be a number strongly related to sacrificial cult and the cult of Óðinn in particular (*e.g.*, Óðinn is hanging nine nights on the tree in *Hávamál*; the sacrificial cult in Uppsala took place each ninth year, lasting nine days, with slaughter of nine victims each night). Some archaeological finds might also support the significance of the number nine – *e.g.*, necklaces with nine amulets and the so-called 'valknútr' motifs seen on various artefacts (three interwoven triangles). See further Hellers 2012.

5 Such as Snorri Sturlusson's *Heimskringla* 42; *Jómsvíkinga saga* 44; Odd monk's *Óláfs saga Tryggvasonar* 18; *Óláfs*

saga Tryggvasonar en mesta 90. In these sources, Hákon jarl sacrifices his son to Þorgerðr Hǫlgabrúðr, not to Óðinn, but this human sacrifice was performed *sem Hákon var vanr* 'as Hákon used to do'. The same episode occurs also in Saxo Grammaticus' *Gesta Danorum* X:4.2 with the minor differences that Hákon here sacrifices several sons to the *diis bellorum* 'gods of war'.

6   Such as Einarr skálaglam's poem *Vellekla*; and Snorri Sturlusson's *Óláfs saga Tryggvasonar* chapter 27 in *Heimskringla* (*cf.*, the version in *Fagrskinna*).

7   *Cf.* an alternative interpretation by Marold 2012, 322.

8   With consideration to translations by Johansson 1991; Finlay 2012.

9   *Cf.* Finnur Jónsson 1912–1915; Poole 2012a.

10 With consideration to translations by Finnur Jónsson 1912–1915; Fulk 2012.

11 With consideration to translations by Finnur Jónsson 1912–1915.

12 The word ON *gjalda* could be a clue to such a conception or act behind the killing of Þorgrímr. ON *gjalda* means both 'giving a gift' and 'recompensing, paying back a debt'. In the latter sense of the word the use of ON *gjalda* could in this context refer to the fulfilment of a votive sacrifice.

References

Primary sources

Einarr skálaglamm Helgason, *Vellekla*. Marold, E. 2012. Einarr skálaglamm Helgason. *Vellekla*. In *Skaldic Poetry of the Scandinavian Middle Ages. Poetry from the Kings' Sagas 1: From Mythical Times to c. 1035*, edited by D. Whaley, 280–329. Turnhout: Brepols.

Finnur Jónsson. 1912–1915. *Den norsk-islandske skjaldedigtning*. Udgiven av Finnur Jónsson. København: Nordisk forlag.

Gísli Súrsson, *Lausavísa*. Finnur Jónsson. 1912–1915. *Den norsk-islandske skjaldedigtning*. Udgiven av Finnur Jónsson. København: Nordisk forlag.

Glumr Geirason, *Gráfeldardrápa*. Finley, A. 2012. Glúmr Geirason, *Gráfeldardrápa*. In *Skaldic Poetry of the Scandinavian Middle Ages. Poetry from the Kings' Sagas 1: From Mythical Times to c. 1035*, edited by D. Whaley, 245–266. Turnhout: Brepols.

Guthormr sindri, *Hákonardrápa*. Poole, R. 2012. Guthormr sindri. *Hákonardrápa*. In *Skaldic Poetry of the Scandinavian Middle Ages. Poetry from the Kings' Sagas 1: From Mythical Times to c. 1035*, edited by D. Whaley, 156–170. Turnhout: Brepols.

Hallfreðr vandræðaskáld Óttarsson, *Lausavísa*. Finnur Jónsson. 1912–1915. *Den norsk-islandske skjaldedigtning*. Udgiven av Finnur Jónsson. København: Nordisk forlag.

Helgi trausti Óláfsson, *Lausavísa*. Finnur Jónsson. 1912–1915. *Den norsk-islandske skjaldedigtning*. Udgiven av Finnur Jónsson. København: Nordisk forlag.

Johansson, K.G. 1991. *Snorre Sturlasson. Nordiska kungasagor I. Från Ynglingasagan till Olav Tryggvassons saga*. Översättning från isländskan av K.G. Johansson. Stockholm: Fabel.

Kock, E.A. 1946. *Den norsk-isländska skaldediktningen*. Reviderad av E.A. Kock. Vol. I. Lund: Gleerups förlag.

Krákumál. Finnur Jónsson. 1912–1915. *Den norsk-islandske skjaldedigtning*. Udgiven av Finnur Jónsson. København: Nordisk forlag.

Tindr Hallkellson, *Hákonardrápa*. Poole, R. 2012. Tindr Hallkellson. *Hákonardrápa*. In *Skaldic Poetry of the Scandinavian Middle Ages. Poetry from the Kings' Sagas 1: From Mythical Times to c. 1035*, edited by D. Whaley, 336–358. Turnhout: Brepols.

Úlfr Uggasson, *Húsdrápa*. Finnur Jónsson. 1912–1915. *Den norsk-islandske skjaldedigtning*. Udgiven av Finnur Jónsson. København: Nordisk forlag.

Þorbjǫrn hornklofi, *Haraldskvæði*. Marold, E. 2012. Þorbjǫrn hornklofi. *Haraldskvæði (Hrafnsmál)*. In *Skaldic Poetry of the Scandinavian Middle Ages. Poetry from the Kings' Sagas 1: From Mythical Times to c. 1035*, edited by D. Whaley, 91–116. Turnhout: Brepols.

Þórleifr jarlskáld Rauðfeldarson, *Hákonardrápa*. Heslop, K. 2012. Þórleifr jarlskáld Rauðfeldarson. *Hákonardrápa*. In *Skaldic Poetry of the Scandinavian Middle Ages. Poetry from the Kings' Sagas 1: From Mythical Times to c. 1035*, edited by D. Whaley, 369–371. Turnhout: Brepols.

Þórmóðr Bersason Kolbrúnarskáld, *Lausavísa*. Fulk, R.D. 2012. Þórmóðr Bersason Kolbrúnarskáld. *Lausavísa*. In *Skaldic Poetry of the Scandinavian Middle Ages. Poetry from the Kings' Sagas 1: From Mythical Times to c. 1035*, edited by D. Whaley, 820–844. Turnhout: Brepols.

Secondary sources

Bell, C.M. 1992. *Ritual Theory, Ritual Practice*. Oxford/New York: Oxford University Press.

Bell, C.M. 2005. Ritual: Further considerations. In *Encyclopedia of Religion*, edited by L. Jones, 7848–7856. Vol. 11. Detroit: Macmillan.

Birgisson, B. 2007. *Inn i skaldens sinn: Kognitive, estetiske og historiske skatter i den norrøne skaldediktingen* (Ph.D. dissertation, University of Bergen).

Bloch, M. 1992. *Prey into Hunter. The Politics of Religious Experience*. Cambridge: Cambridge University Press.

Bronkhorst, J. 2012. Rites without symbols. *Method and Theory in the Study of Religion* 24: 236–266.

Cleasby, R. & Vigfússon, G. 1874. *An Icelandic-English Dictionary*. Oxford: Clarendon Press.

Clunies Ross, M., Gade, K.E., Marold, E. and Nordal, G. 2012. General introduction. In *Skaldic Poetry of the Scandinavian Middle Ages: Poetry from the King's Sagas 1: From Mythical Times to c. 1035*, edited by D. Whaley, xiii–xciii. Turnhout: Brepols.

Düwel, K. 1970. Germanische Opfer und Opferriten im Spiegel altgermanischer Kultworte. In *Vorgeschichtliche Heiligtümer und Opferplätze in Mittel- und Nordeuropa*, edited by H. Jankuhn, 219–239. Göttingen: Göttingen Universität.

Edholm, K.W. af. 2020. *Människooffer i myt och minne: En studie av offerpraktiker i fornnordisk religion utifrån källtexter och arkeologiskt material* (Ph.D. dissertation, Åbo Akademi University).

Edholm, K. af. 2016. Risk, förlust och oviss utgång i vedisk kungaritual. *Chaos: Skandinavisk tidskrift för religionshistoriske studier* 65: 149–72.

Enright, M.J. 1996. *Lady with a Mead Cup: Ritual, Prophecy, and Lordship in the European Warband from la Tène to the Viking Age*. Dublin: Four Courts Press.

Finlay, A. 2012. Glúmr Geirason, Gráfeldardrápa. In *Skaldic Poetry of the Scandinavian Middle Ages: Poetry from the Kings' Sagas 1: From Mythical Times to c. 1035*, edited by D. Whaley, 245–266. Turnhout: Brepols.

Finnur Jónsson. 1912–1915. *Den norsk-islandske skjaldedigtning*. Udgiven av Finnur Jónsson. København: Nordisk forlag.

Fulk, R.D. 2012. Þorbjǫrn hornklofi, Haraldskvæði (Hrafnsmál). In *Skaldic Poetry of the Scandinavian Middle Ages: Poetry from the Kings' Sagas 1: From Mythical Times to c. 1035*, edited by D. Whaley, 91–117. Turnhout: Brepols.

Halsall, G. 1989. Anthropology and the study of pre-Conquest warfare and society: The ritual war in Anglo-Saxon England. In *Weapons and Warfare in Anglo-Saxon England*, edited by S. Chadwick Hawkes, 155–178. Oxford: Oxford University Committee for Archaeology.

Hecht, R.D. 1976. *Sacrifice: Comparative Study and Interpretation* (unpublished Ph.D. dissertation, University of California).

Hellers, T. 2012. *Valknútr: Das Dreiecksymbol der Wikingerzeit*. Wien: Fassaender Verlag.

Herschend, F. 1998. *The Idea of the Good in Late Iron Age Society* (Ph.D. dissertation, Uppsala University).

Heslop, K. 2012. Þórleifr jarlskáld Rauðfeldarson, Hákonardrápa. In *Skaldic Poetry of the Scandinavian Middle Ages: Poetry from the Kings' Sagas 1: From Mythical Times to c. 1035*, edited by D. Whaley, 369–370. Turnhout: Brepols.

Hubert, H. & Mauss, M. 1981 [1898]. *Sacrifice: Its Nature and Functions*. Original title: *Essai sur la Nature et la Function du Sacrifice*. Chicago: University of Chicago Press.

Hultgård, A. 2001. Menschenopfer. In *Reallexikon der germanischen Altertumskunde*, edited by R. Müller, 533–546. Vol. 19. Berlin/New York: Walter de Gruyter.

Hultgård, A. 2017. *Midgård brinner: Ragnarök i religionshistorisk belysning*. Uppsala: Kungl. Gustav Adolfs Akademien för svensk folkkultur.

Humphrey, C. & Laidlaw, J. 1994. *The Archetypal Actions of Ritual: A Theory of Ritual Illustrated by the Jain Rite of Worship*. Oxford: Clarendon Press.

Humphrey, C. & Laidlaw, J. 2007. Sacrifice and ritualization. In *The Archaeology of Ritual*, edited by E. Kyriakidis, 255–276. Los Angeles: Cotsen Institute of Archaeology.

Hüsken, U. (ed.) 2007. *When Rituals Go Wrong: Mistakes, Failure, and the Dynamics of Ritual*. Leiden/Boston: Brill.

Jensen, A.E. 1963 [1951]. *Myth and Cult among Primitive Peoples*. Translated by M. Tax Choldin and W. Weissleder. Original title: *Mythos und Kult bei Naturvölkern. Religionswissenschaftliche Betrachtungen*. Chicago/London: University of Chicago Press.

Kuhn, H. 1954. Gaut. In *Festschrift für Jost Trier zu seinem 60. Geburtstag am 15 Dezember 1954*, edited by B. von Weise and K.H. Borck, 417–433. Meisenheim: Glam.

Landholt, C. 1998. Gefolgschaft. § Sprachlisches. In *Reallexikon der germanischen Altertumskunde*, edited by H. Beck *et al.*, 533–537. Vol. 10. Berlin/New York: Walter de Gruyter.

Liberman, A. 1978. Germanic *Sendan* 'To Make a Sacrifice'. *Journal of English and Germanic Philology* 77(4): 473–488.

Ljungkvist, J. 2006. *En hiar atti rikR. Om elit, struktur och ekonomi kring Uppsala och Mälaren under yngre järnålder* (Ph.D. dissertation, Uppsala University).

Males, M. 2010. *Mytologi i skaldedikt, skaldedikt i prosa. En synkron analys av mytologiska referenser i medeltida norröna handskrifter* (Ph.D. dissertation, University of Oslo).

Males, M. 2017. The last pagan. *Journal of English and Germanic Philology* 116(4): 491–514.

Marold, E. 2012. Einarr skálaglamm Helgason. Vellekla. In *Skaldic Poetry of the Scandinavian Middle Ages: Poetry from the Kings' Sagas 1: From Mythical Times to c. 1035*, edited by D. Whaley, 280–329. Turnhout: Brepols.

Mauss, M. 1990 [1925]. *The Gift: The Form and Reason for Exchange in Archaic Societies*. Translated by W.D. Halls. Original title: *Essai sur le Don. Forme et raison de léchange dans les sociétés archaïques*. New York/London: Norton.

Meissner, R. 1921. *Die Kenningar der Skalden. Ein Beitrag zur skaldischen Poetik*. Bonn/Leipzig: Schroeder.

Neckel, G. 1913. *Walhall. Studien über germanischen Jenseitsglauben*. Dortmund: Ruhfus.

Neff, M.S. 1980. *Germanic Sacrifice: An Analytical Study Using Linguistic, Archaeological and Literary Data* (Ph.D. dissertation, University of Texas at Austin).

Nordberg, A. 2003. *Krigarna i Odens sal. Dödsföreställningar och krigarkult i fornnordisk religion* (Ph.D. dissertation, Stockholm University).

Pongratz-Leisten, B. 2007. Ritual killing and sacrifice in the Ancient Near East. In *Human Sacrifice in Jewish and Christian Tradition,* edited by K. Finsterbuch, A. Lange and K.F.D. Römheld, 3–33. Leiden/Boston: Brill.

Poole, R. 2012a. Guthormr sindri. Hákonardrápa. In *Skaldic Poetry of the Scandinavian Middle Ages: Poetry from the Kings' Sagas 1: From Mythical Times to c. 1035*, edited by D. Whaley, 156–170. Turnhout: Brepols.

Poole, R. 2012b. Tindr Hallkelsson. Hákonardrápa. In *Skaldic Poetry of the Scandinavian Middle Ages: Poetry from the Kings' Sagas 1: From Mythical Times to c. 1035*, edited by D. Whaley, 336–358. Turnhout: Brepols.

Price, N. 2019. *The Viking Way: Magic and Mind in Late Iron Age Scandinavia*. Oxford: Oxbow Books.

Pyyhtinen, O. 2014. *The Gift and its Paradoxes: Beyond Mauss* (Ph.D. dissertation, Åbo University).

Speidel, M. 2004. *Ancient Germanic Warriors: Warrior Styles from Trajan's Column to Icelandic Sagas*. New York: Routledge.

Staal, F. 1979. The meaninglessness of ritual. *Numen* 26: 2–22.

Steuer, H. 1998. Gefolgschaft. § Archäologisches. In *Reallexikon der germanischen Altertumskunde*, edited by H. Beck, H. Steuer and D. Timpe, 546–552. Vol. 10. Berlin/New York: Walter de Gruyter.

Timpe, D. 1998. Gefolgschaft. § Historisches. In *Reallexikon der germanischen Altertumskunde*, edited by H. Beck, H. Steuer and D. Timpe, 537–546. Vol. 10. Berlin/New York: Walter de Gruyter.

Vries, J. de, 1964. *Altnordische Literaturgeschichte*. Vols I–II. Berlin/New York: Walter de Gruyter.

Wrangel, E. 1912. *Dikten och diktaren*. Lund: Gleerup.

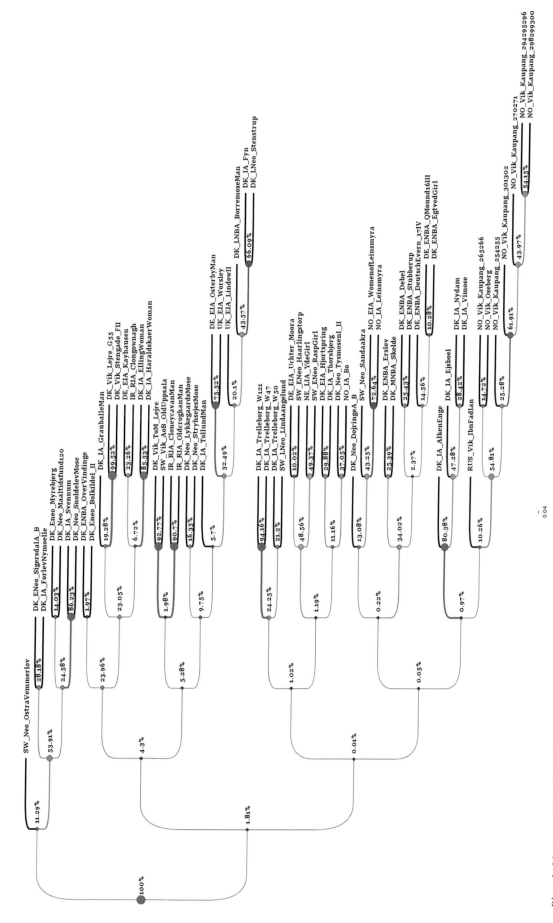

Plate 1. Maximum Clade Credibility Tree (MCCT) generated in FigTree v1.4.4 from Bayesian analysis using BEAST2. Settings: Site Model: Gamma, Category Count: 2, Shape: 1; Clock Model: Relaxed Log; Priors: Coalescent Bayesian Skyline.

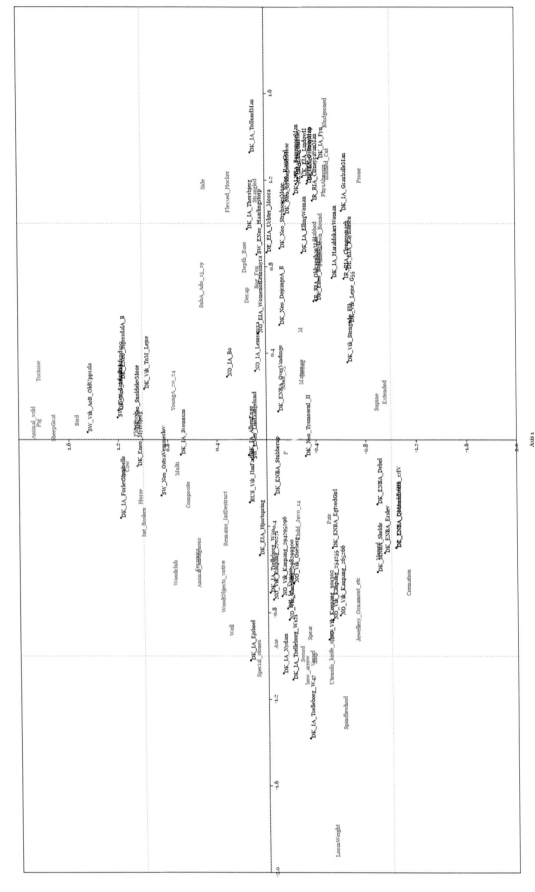

Plate 2. Correspondence analysis scatter plot, showing the cases of possible human sacrificial violence in relation to the associated material culture evidence.

Plate 3. The double burial A137 from Nivå (after Lass Jensen 2016).

Plate 4. Grave 41 from Skateholm containing an
adult male holding a child (after Larsson 1988).

Plate 5. Grave 19 at Henriksholm-Bøgebakken
(after Albrethsen & Brinch Petersen 1977).

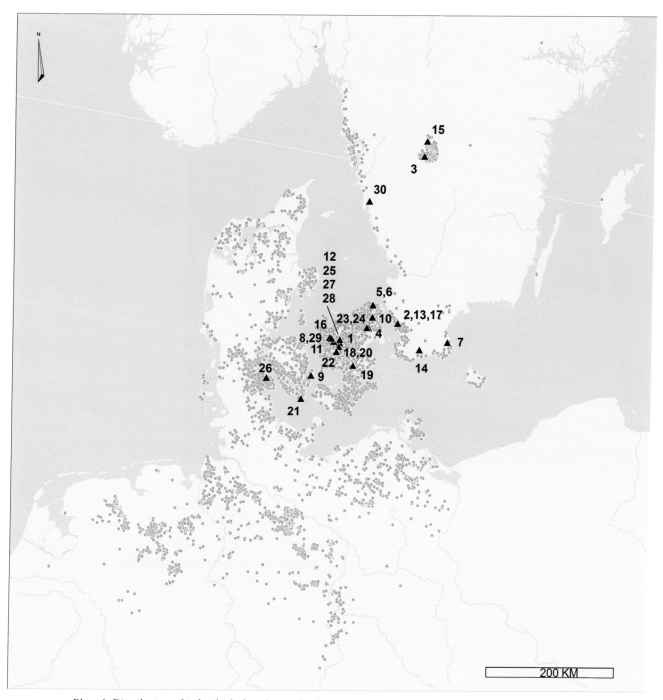

Plate 6. Distribution of individuals found in wetland areas and megalithic monuments in South Scandinavia.

Plate 7. The skull from Porsmose (photo: National Museum of Denmark).

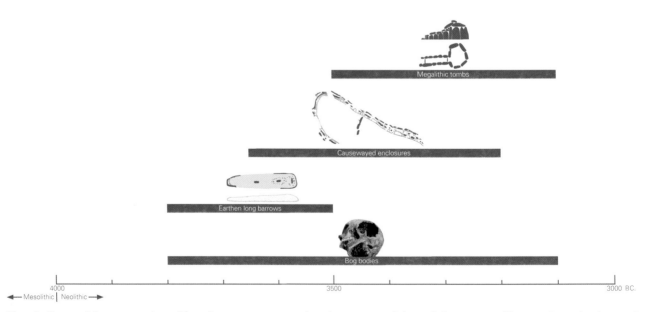

Plate 8. Dates of the construction of long barrows, causewayed enclosures, megaliths and depositions of humans in wetland areas in South Scandinavia (after Sørensen 2020).

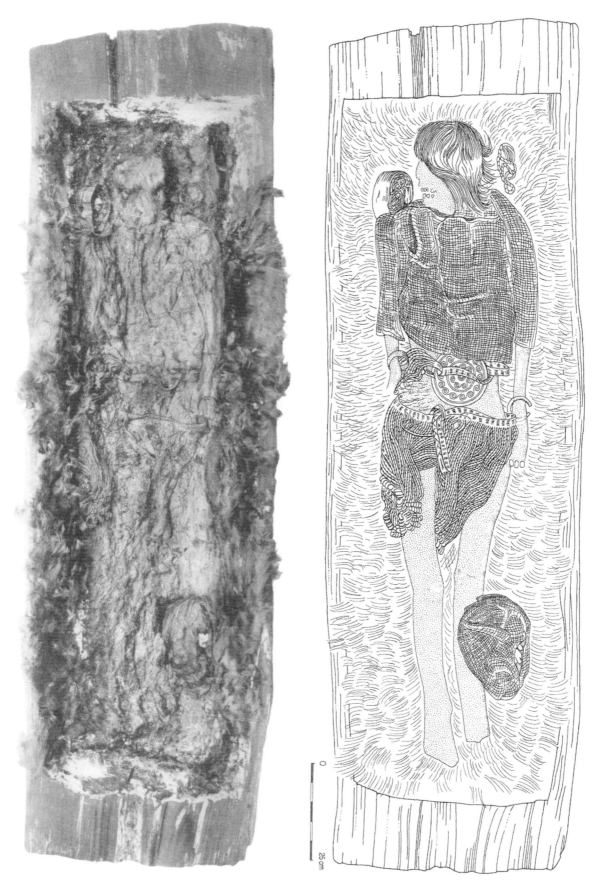

Plate 9. Left: Photograph of the Egtved Girl's coffin (Thomsen 1929); Right: Artist's sketch of the Egtved Girl's burial (after Aner & Kersten 1990, 4).

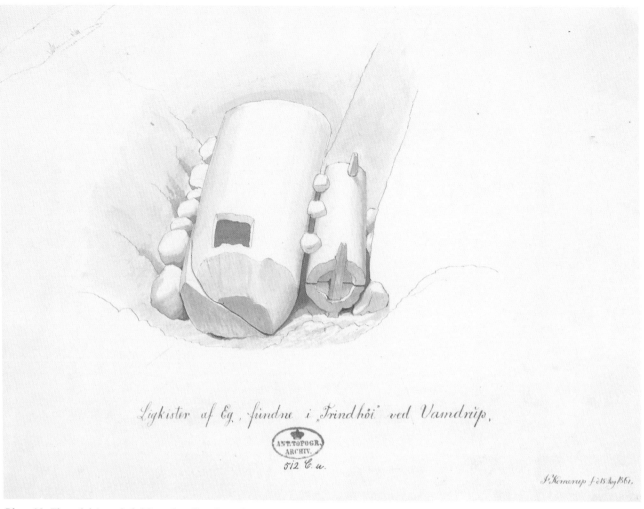

Ligkister af Eg., fundne i „Trindhöi" ved Vamdrip,

ANT.TOPOGR.
ARCHIV.
512 C. u.

J. Kornerup f. 15. Aug 1861.

Plate 10. The adult's and child's oak coffins from the ENBA 'Trindhøj' burial mound (Ribe Amt, Anst Herred, Vamdrup Søgn SB No. 26 (illustration: National Museum of Denmark Archives, J. Kornerup 1861)

Plate 11. The head injury of the Salpetermosen Syd bog body skeleton just after its discovery in 2014 (photo: Museum Nordsjælland).

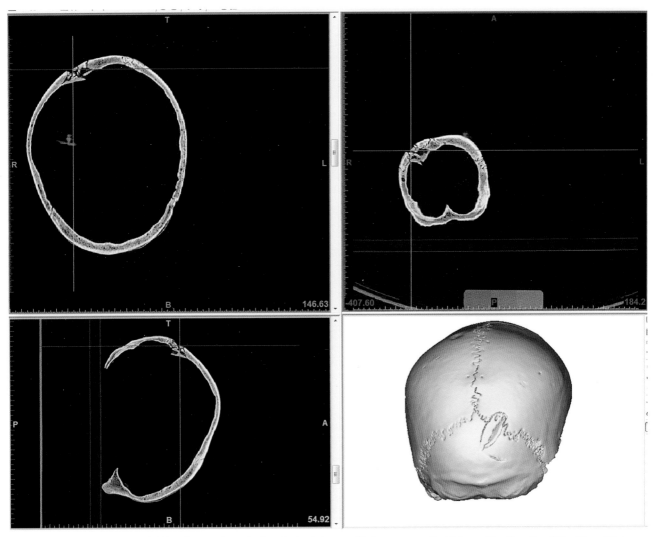

Plate 12. A 3D scan of the lethal head injury from the bog body skeleton of Salpetermosen Syd (photo: The Faculty of Health and Science, Copenhagen University).

Plate 13. The human humerus of 29.5 cm length from MNS50527 Hvidelandsgården (photo: Natural History Museum of Denmark).

Plate 14. The outfit belonging to the Huldremose Woman showing the outer cape, the scarf (Plate 5) and the skirt (photo: Roberto Fortuna, National Museum of Denmark).

Plate 15. The scarf belonging to the Huldremose Woman. The textile was cut in two during the retrieval because they had not noticed the bone pin keeping the textile in place around the neck (photo: Roberto Fortuna, National Museum of Denmark).

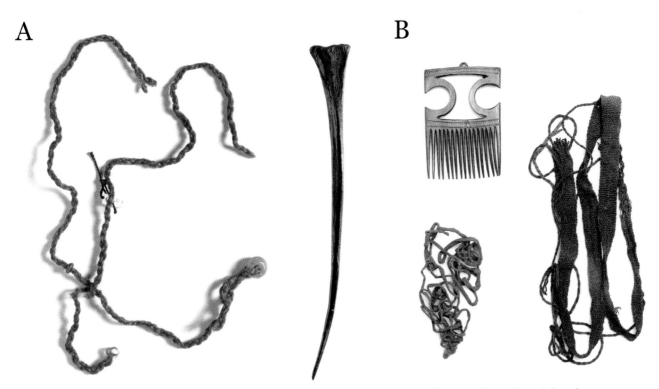

Plate 16. The different objects belonging to the Huldremose Woman. A) The two amber beads on the wool cord that she was wearing around the neck and the 8 cm long bird bone which was used as a dress pin to close the wool scarf that was placed around the neck. B) The horn comb, the blue wool band and the leather cord found inside a patch on the inner cape. The Huldremose did not have access to these objects, as the patch was closed on all four sides (photo: Roberto Fortuna, National Museum of Denmark). Not to scale.

Plate 17. Top: The outer cape belonging to the Huldremose Woman (photo: Roberto Fortuna, National Museum of Denmark). Bottom: The inner cape belonging to the Huldremose Woman with its 22 patches. This clothing item has had a long history of use exemplified by the many differently executed patches (photo: Roberto Fortuna, National Museum of Denmark).

Plate 18. The wrap-around garment found on the Borremose III Woman. The textile was kept in place around the body with a leather cord (photo:Roberto Fortuna, National Museum of Denmark).

Plate 19. The cloak from Skærsø is a single find. The textile has tablet-woven borders on all four sides and is the earliest evidence of this technique being used in Denmark (photo: Roberto Fortuna, National Museum of Denmark).

Plate 20. The wrap-around textiles placed around the lower leg of the Søgård II Man. The two textiles each measuring 33 × 27 cm and 38 × 23 cm are probably coming from one textile which was cut in two halves and hemmed (photo: Roberto Fortuna, National Museum of Denmark).

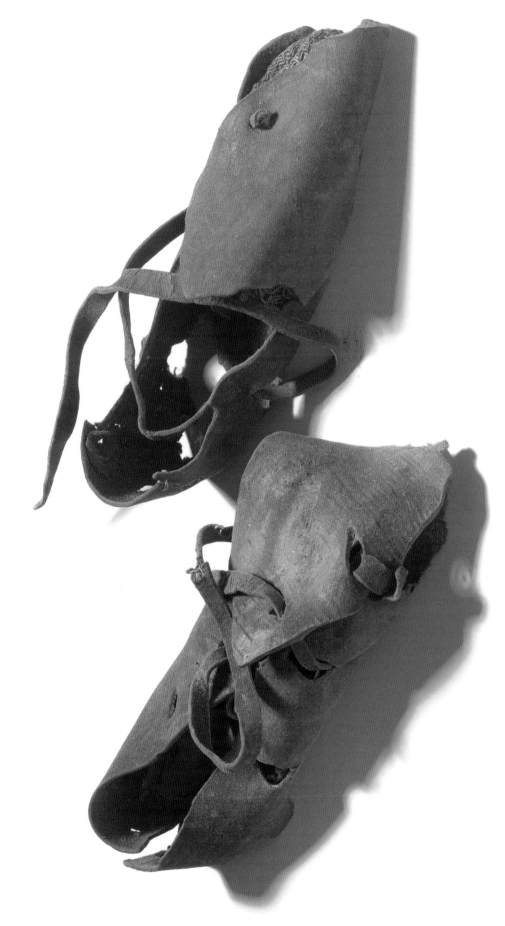

Plate 21. A pair of shoes found together with the Søgård 1 Man (photo: Roberto Fortuna, National Museum of Denmark).

Plate 22. The wrap-around wool textile from Thorup II with its unusual combination of checks and stripes made in naturally pigmented wool. The textile measures 141 × 262 cm and is the largest textile recovered from a Danish bog. It is a single find with no connection to a bog body (photo: Roberto Fortuna, National Museum of Denmark).

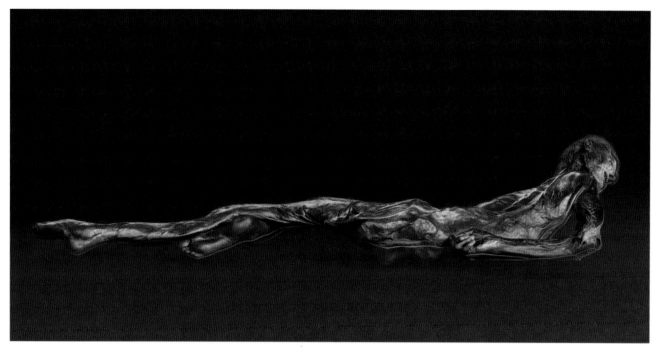

Plate 23. The Grauballe Man as exhibited at Moesgaard Museum, Aarhus, Denmark.

Plate 24. Analysing the CT scanning images of the Grauballe Man, during his examination in 2000.

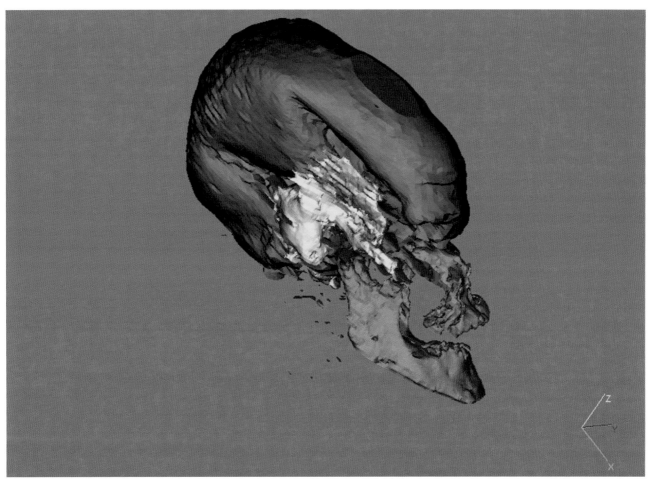

Plate 25. 3D visualisation of the skull of Grauballe Man.

Plate 26. Photo VHM00500_F8230 of Skull VHM00500x77 in situ (© Department of Archaeology, VHM. Used with permission).

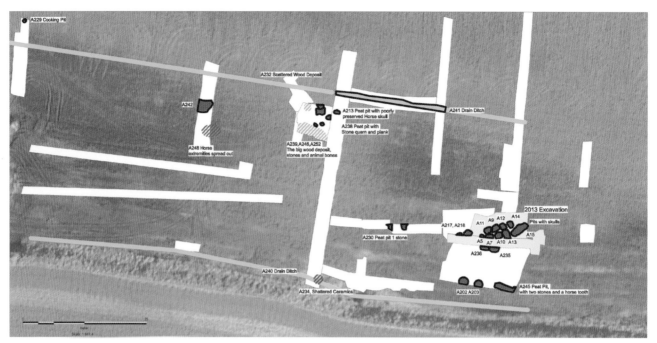

Plate 27. Site plan of Svennum sacrificial bog (VHM00500 in VHM archive, Fund og Fortidsminder (FF) 100106-254 (FF is the National Monument Registry of Denmark) generated in MapInfo. Brown signature: the peat pits. Light blue: the Iron Age drain ditches. Dark blue: ceramic deposit. Green: the wood deposits. Red: cooking pit (S. Wåhlin © Department of Archaeology, VHM).

Plate 28. Svennum seen on the late 19th-century Military Survey Map, and 2015 aerial photography with relief map shadows. Svennum bog is marked as number -254 (Maps © Geodatastyrelsen, Luftfoto; © COWI A/S).

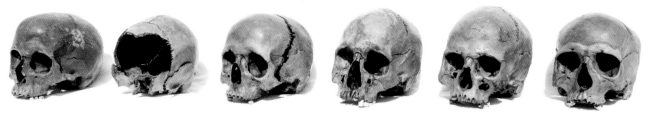

Plate 29. The six skulls from Svennum in order of discovery left to right, VHM00500x1, -x2, -x22, -x73, -x77 and -x81 (photo: VHM Department of Archaeology).

Plate 30. The Haraldskær Woman is one of the first bog bodies that was archaeologically excavated (photo: Vejle Museums).

Plate 31. The leather cloak found after the discovery of the Haraldskær Woman, along with some textiles in the same area (photo: Vejle Museums).

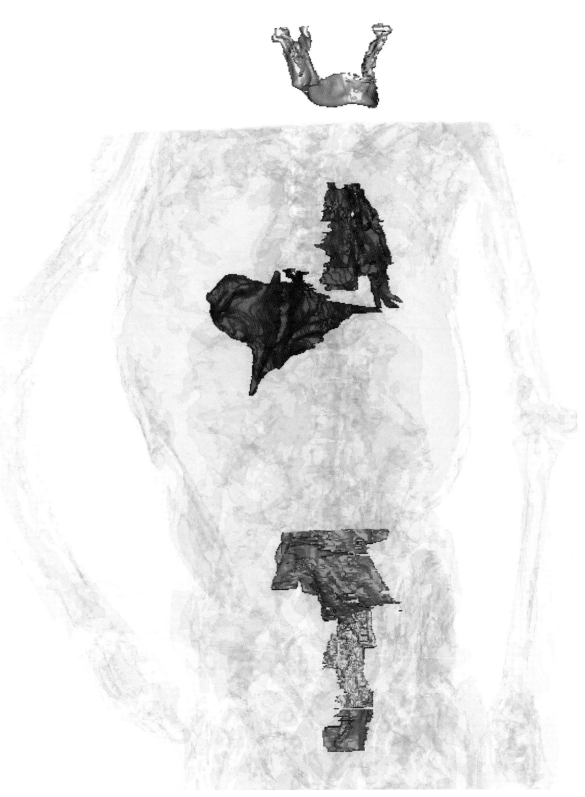

Plate 32. CT scan showing the intestines of the bog body of the Haraldskær Woman (photo: Vejle Museums).

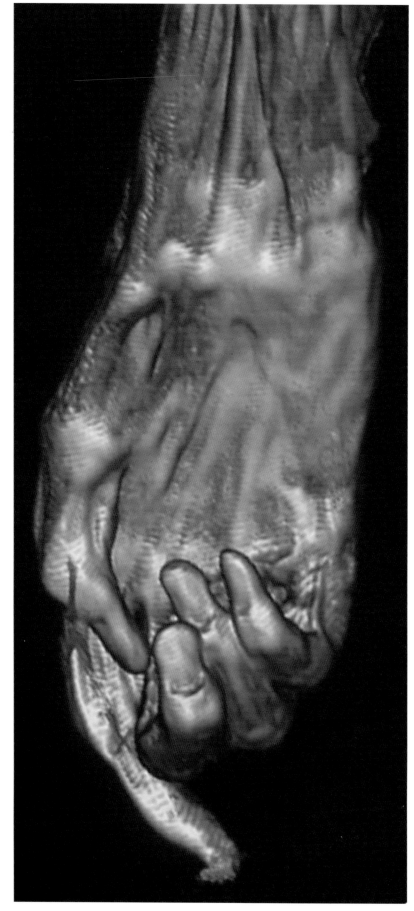

Plate 33. CT scan showing the sinews and muscles in the right hand (photo: Vejle Museums).

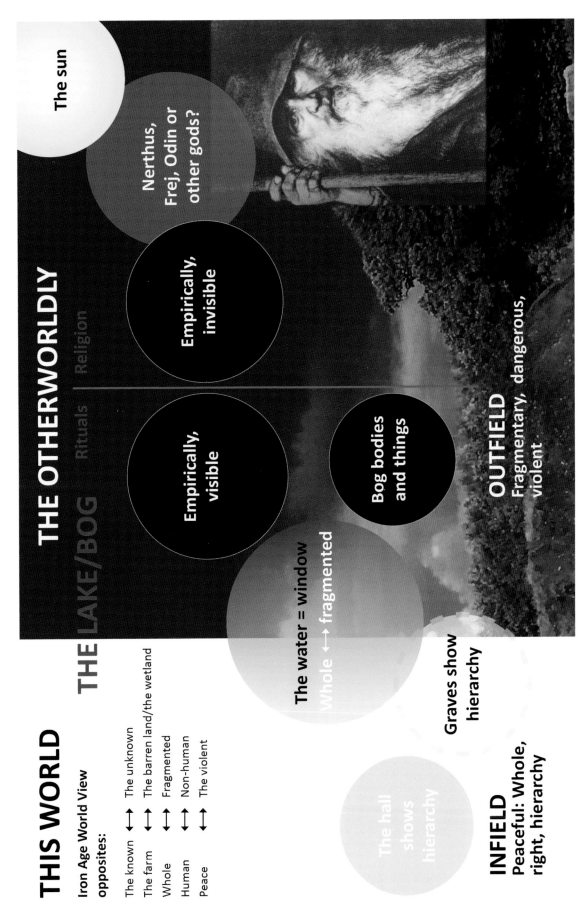

THIS WORLD

Iron Age World View opposites:

The known ⟷ The unknown
The farm ⟷ The barren land/the wetland
Whole ⟷ Fragmented
Human ⟷ Non-human
Peace ⟷ The violent

THE OTHERWORLDLY

Rituals   Religion

THE LAKE/BOG

The sun

Nerthus, Frej, Odin or other gods?

Empirically, invisible

Empirically, visible

Bog bodies and things

The water = window

Whole ⟷ fragmented

OUTFIELD
Fragmentary, dangerous, violent

Graves show hierarchy

The hall shows hierarchy

INFIELD
Peaceful: Whole, right, hierarchy

Plate 34. A model of a possible Iron Age world view. Graphics conceptualised by the author and realised by Vejle Museum's Gitte Jakobsen. Image at right 'Odin, the Wanderer' by George von Rosen, 1886, in the Public Domain.

Plate 35. Top: Scatter of white(ish) stones amongst the bones of domestic animals at Salpetermosen along with a single, larger yellowish stone (photo: Pernille Pantmann). Bottom: White(ish) stones at Salpetermosen concentrated near the end of the remains of tree branches, perhaps used as a bridge or platform (photo: Pernille Pantmann).

Plate 36. White stones submerged in accumulated water during excavation at Salpetermosen. Note that the depth of the water can only be clearly discerned due to the stones, which may have been placed as markers to denote the depth of the wetland fringes (photo: Pernille Pantmann).

Plate 37. Artist's rendition of preparation of an Iron Age sacrificial wetland deposit with white stones (concept: Matthew J. Walsh; illustration: Eric S. Carlson).

Plate 38. *Throwing stones at the gods? Artist's rendition of a hypothetical Iron Age ritual involving the casting of white stones, leading to concentrated scatters of stones among wooden effigies and bundled flax, as e.g., found at Forlev Nymølle (concept: Matthew J. Walsh; illustration: Eric S. Carlson).*

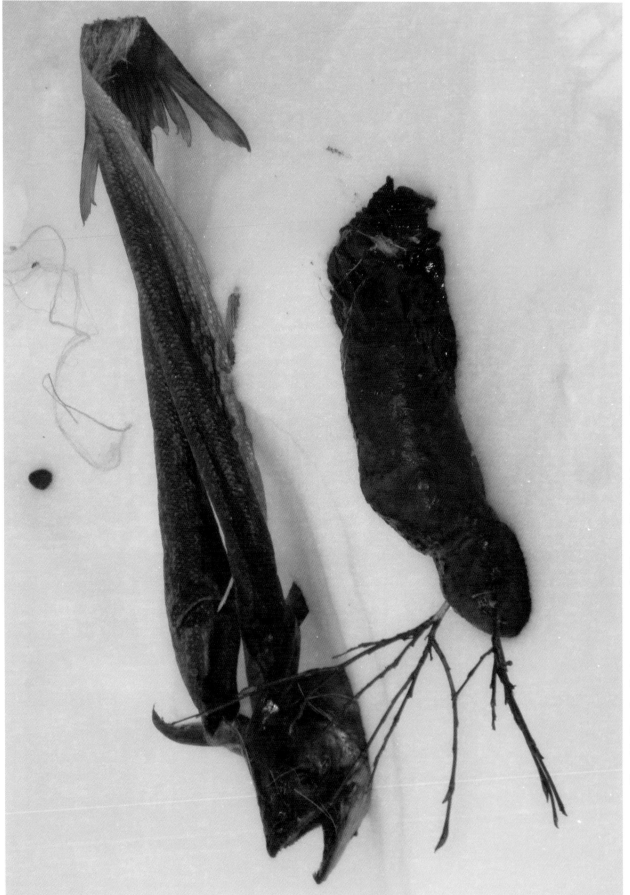

Plate 39. 'Sacrificial' substitutes among the Siberian Chukchi (photo: Rane Willerslev, from Willerslev 2009, 699. Used with permission).

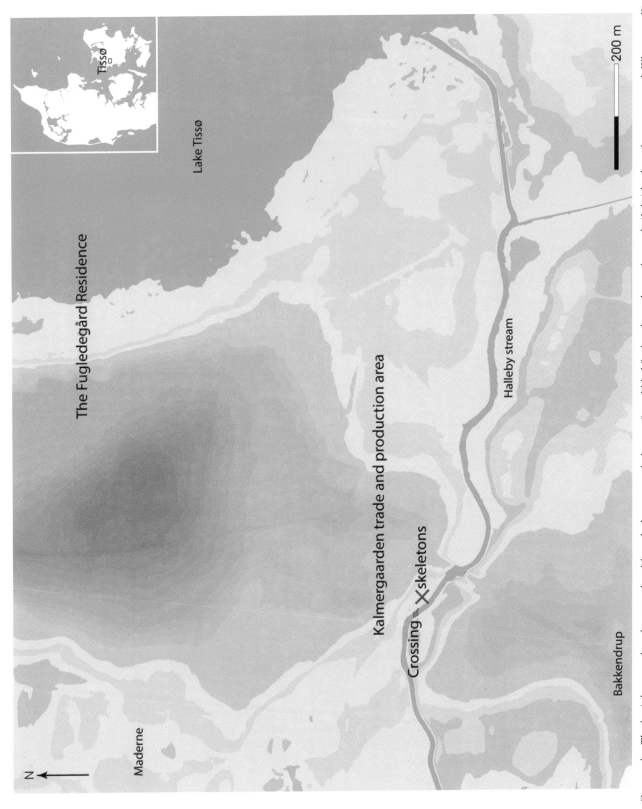

Plate 40. Geography: The burials were placed next to the old road where several phases of a cobbled ford and wooden and stone-built bridge have been excavated. When travelling from the south, this roadway presented the only possible entrance onto the Tissø promontory and further on to the Fugledegaard residence.

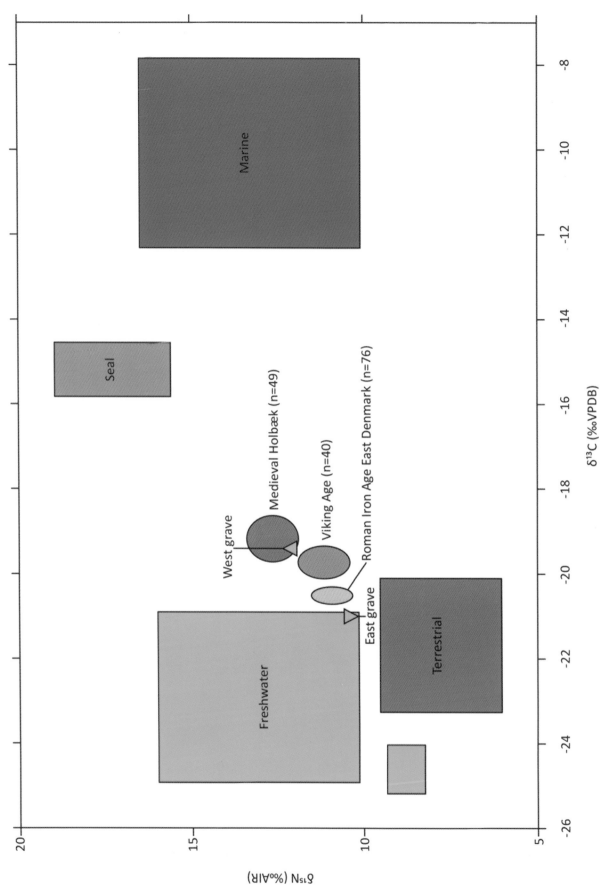

Plate 41. N15 and C13. The Tisso men isotope data compared with other published Danish isotope studies. The food item boxes are from different Mesolithic and Neolithic sites (Fischer et al. 2007). Isotopic values on human bones from the large cemetery Galgedil site on Funen (Kanstrup 2008), several east Danish Roman Iron Age sites (Jørkov 2007) and from a Medieval cemetery in Holbæk on Zealand (Jørkov 2007) are also plotted making comparison to contemporary populace possible. The ellipse axis denotes ±1σ and the centre value is average of all humans for each site respectively (based on Nielsen et al. 2018: Figure 11.1).